1989

Cases and Select Readings in Health Care Marketing

Cases
and Select Readings
in Health Care
Marketing

Robert E. Sweeney
Robert L. Berl
William J. Winston
Editors

The Haworth Press
New York • London

Cases and Select Readings in Health Care Marketing is #2 in the Haworth Series in Marketing and Health Services Administration.

The Haworth Press, Inc., 10 Alice St., Binghamton, NY, 13904-1580
EUROSPAN/Haworth, 3 Henrietta Street, London WC2E 8LU England

Library of Congress Cataloging-in-Publication Data

Cases and select readings in health care marketing / Robert E. Sweeney, Robert L. Berl, William J. Winston, editors.
    p. cm. — (Haworth series in marketing and health services administration, ISSN 1040-7367 ; #2)
  Includes bibliographies and index.
  ISBN 0-86656-429-2
  1. Medical care—Marketing. 2. Medical care—Marketing—Case studies. I. Berl, Robert L. II. Sweeney, Robert E. III. Winston, William J. IV. Series.
  [DNLM: 1. Marketing of Health Services—essays. W 74 C338]
RA410.56.C37 1988
362.1'068'8—dc19
DNLM/DLC
for Library of Congress
                                                    88-16033
                                                       CIP

CONTENTS

About the Editors

Robert E. Sweeney is currently Executive Vice-President of Valley Emergency Physicians Medical Group in Oakland, California. Mr. Sweeney holds his doctorate from Carnegie-Mellon University in American history and also holds three master's degrees, including an MBA in Marketing from Memphis State University. The author of three books and several articles in marketing/management areas, he has taught graduate seminars in health care marketing and is a frequent speaker at health care marketing symposia.

He served for four years as a senior manager in the HMO industry and is currently employed as a national Marketing Manager with a private-sector firm based in San Francisco. He consults in home health care, HMO and alternative systems, and emergency medicine and market planning. He has conducted the national marketing workshop for the American Federation of Home Health Agencies in 1985 and is the editor of the *Journal of Ambulatory Care Marketing* (published by The Haworth Press, Inc.).

Robert L. Berl is an Associate Professor and Chairman of the Marketing Department at Memphis State University, Memphis, Tennessee. He holds his PhD and MBA from Georgia State University and his BBA from the University of Cincinnati, Ohio. Prior to becoming an educator, he had over twenty years of experience in the marketing of both goods and services.

Dr. Berl has consulted with numerous corporations and nonprofit organizations. He has authored articles in various marketing journals and conference proceedings. His publications include "What Is Strategic Market Planning," *Home Health Care Journal* (June 1985) which he coauthored with Robert Sweeney; "New Community Residents' Preferences for Dental Service Information," *The Journal of the American Dental Association* (June 1986); and "An Analysis of Consumer Reliance on Personal and Nonpersonal

Sources of Professional Information," *Journal of Professional Services Marketing* (Winter 1986).

William J. Winston is a Managing Associate of an Albany, California based marketing consulting firm for health and other professional services, Professional Services Marketing Group. Through the years he has developed hundreds of marketing plans for all types of health and human services in his capacity as an educator and consultant. His specialties include board development, strategic planning, marketing planning, market analysis, etc. Formerly, Mr. Winston was the Dean of the School of Health Services Management at Golden Gate University in San Francisco, California. Mr. Winston's instructional areas are in graduate-level economic analysis for health organizations and marketing planning and strategy development for health organizations. In addition, he has been actively involved in developing and lecturing in marketing seminars and workshops for health professionals for most of the last decade. In fact, the graduate course instructed by Mr. Winston in health marketing was one of the first ever offered in the country for practitioners. He presents many marketing and economic papers and speeches for health and medical organizations each year.

Mr. Winston is also the Senior Editor in marketing for The Haworth Press, Inc. He edits four national journals, *Health Marketing Quarterly*, *The Journal of Professional Services Marketing*, *Journal of Hospital Marketing*, and *Journal of Marketing for Mental Health*. Books edited or written by Mr. Winston include *Marketing for the Group Practice*, *Marketing for Mental Health Services*, *Marketing for Long-Term and Senior Care Services*, *Innovations in Hospital Marketing*, *Marketing Ambulatory Care Services*, *Marketing Strategies for Human and Social Service Agencies*, *How to Write a Marketing Plan for Health Organizations*, and *Advertising Handbook for Health Care Services*.

Mr. Winston was also President of Winston & Associates, an economic analysis consulting firm and Principal of Business Economics Development Institute. His graduate education in health administration and planning was completed at the Johns Hopkins University in Baltimore, Maryland and his doctoral dissertation is being completed in Business Administration at Nova University in Florida.

Mr. Winston is a member of the American College of Health Care Marketing and Academy of Health Care Marketing. He was named "Marketing Educator of the Year" for 1986-87 by the Academy of Health Care Marketing. He is also very active in a multitude of different national and international health associations.

Contributors

Thomas J. Coleman is President of Tolman Advertising Associates, a Salt Lake City full-service advertising agency that specializes in advertising, research, and publishing.

Steven W. Demello is Planning Consultant, H.O.M. Group, Inc., in San Francisco, California.

Stanley P. Franklin is Professor of Mathematical Sciences at Memphis State University, Tennessee.

Ellen F. Goldman is Director of Corporate Planning and Marketing Services, South Hills Health System, Pittsburgh, Pennsylvania.

Joan Hammer is President of Hammer & Associates, a Seattle-based medical marketing consulting firm.

Kermit M. Hunter is Executive Director at Memphis Health Center in Memphis, Tennessee.

Nathan Kaufman is Senior Vice-President of Marketing for the Hospital Group, National Medical Enterprises, Santa Monica, California. Mr. Kaufman is the former director of the marketing/consulting group servicing the Hospital Corporation of America.

Nancy Koury is Coordinator of Case Management Services at Breckenridge Village in Willoughby, Ohio.

Edward L. Leven is Assistant Professor of Management and Associate Director of the School of Health Services Management at Golden Gate University, San Francisco, California. He was formerly the Director of Education at the Association of Western Hospitals and a Project Associate with the Health Care Financial Management Association.

Constance W. Mahoney, MA, MPH, is a doctoral candidate at the University of California at San Francisco's Center for Health Policy.

Cosmo P. Morabito is Administrator at Fair Acres Geriatric Center, Diversified Health Services in Lima, Pennsylvania.

Donald W. Nelson is Director of Public Affairs at Scott and White, Temple, Texas. Scott and White consists of a clinic, a 400-bed hospital, and a teaching hospital for Texas A&M University's College of Medicine.

Ira Okun is Executive Director of the Family Service Agency of San Francisco, California.

John Pinto is President of J. Pinto & Associates, San Francisco, California.

Rosanna M. G. Pribilovics, LMFCC, is Associate Executive Director of the Family Service Agency of San Francisco, California. She is also Associate Editor of the *Journal of Marketing for Mental Health*.

David Wolf is a PhD candidate in psychology at Memphis State University, Tennessee.

John A. Yankey, PhD, is a professor at the School of Applied Social Sciences, Case Western Reserve University, Cleveland, Ohio.

Diana Young, MSSA, is Program Manager of the Impaired Driver Program at Alcoholism Services of Cleveland, Inc., in Cleveland, Ohio.

Preface

Marketing managers with any substantial experience realize that the problems and opportunities they encounter seldom fit neatly into classical marketing categories. Particularly in newly emerging professional domains such as the health care industry, the line manager must quickly identify and adapt unclear or partially defined marketing principals in order to survive.

Cases and Select Readings in Health Care Marketing has been prepared specifically for the practicing marketing executive. The text integrates an easy-to-understand explanation of marketing concepts, articles selected for topical timeliness and pragmatic value, and case studies illustrating in depth the detail and complexity of market decisions faced by today's health care and human services marketing professional.

The format for each part is typically a brief but thorough initial presentation of one conceptual area of marketing. The concept is then evaluated, analyzed, or demonstrated in selected articles written by prestigious and successful members of the marketing profession. Finally, a variety of extensive case studies follow which have been gathered to demonstrate further the service marketing profession at work. Many of these excellent cases were prepared especially for this volume and represent path-breaking treatments of such topics as health care marketing auditing, psychographic analysis, pricing in alternative delivery systems, promoting a public health service, and marketing planning for private colleges.

The service professions are going through dramatic change as they become market-driven, competitive, and customer-oriented for the first time. The pressures of the marketplace have compelled these professions — health care, financial institutions, transportation companies, law and accounting, and others — to upgrade their portfolios of management and marketing skills. There is a high demand for proven talent in these areas, and the more progressive, well-financed institutions are turning to private-sector firms for marketing leadership. This is not to say that homegrown managers are incapable of doing the job, just that they will have to change their world view from a focus on institutional control to a focus on customer needs. However, the room for error and time for learning are both significantly compressed. This volume offers a form of career insurance for executives engaged in service institution marketing.

There have been some truly positive developments in the service industries from a marketing perspective, even just in the last year. To begin with, there has been a great increase in the number of hospitals, banks, accounting firms, and so forth acknowledging the properness and value of the marketing discipline. Second, the initial obsession with flashy advertising and PR that preoccupied many institutions first adopting a marketing approach is now giving way to a more lasting, effective, and measurable market planning orientation. Finally, the current consolidation trends in these industries are having two beneficial effects: compelling smaller institutions to become much more knowledgeable and appreciative of their customer base, and introducing a more sophisticated strategic marketing capability.

It is the sincere belief of the authors that this book can substantially increase the knowledge, understanding, and preparedness of service marketing and management executives in this era of unsettling change.

Robert E. Sweeney
Oakland, California

Cases and Select Readings in Health Care Marketing

Part I

Introduction

CHAPTER 1

Basic Health Care Marketing Principles

William J. Winston

INTRODUCTION

Health care marketing has become an important management tool for health administrators during recent years. It has only been an accepted scope of study in research during the last decade. However, marketing has been used in health care for centuries. This is documented in the cases of public health campaigns during the 17th and 18th centuries. It has also been extensively utilized by pharmaceutical firms, hospital supply firms, health maintenance organizations, and public health agencies during the last 40 years.

The recognition and acceptance of marketing in health care during the 1980s is similar to the rise in importance of finance during the 1970s. Finance was considered the "savior" during this decade as budgeting and financial forecasting became popular in health organizations. Budget directors and controllers were promoted to vice-presidency positions. In comparison, marketing has become the name of the game for the 1980s. Directors of public relations are being promoted to vice-presidents of marketing and planning. Unfortunately, marketing is perceived by many administrators and providers as the future savior. As it will be discussed later, no management tool by itself is a savior.

The development of health care marketing is entering its second phase. During the first half of the 1980s, most of the attention was

---

Reprinted from William J. Winston, *How to Write a Marketing Plan for Health Care Organizations*, pp. 1–12, © 1985 by The Haworth Press, Inc.

placed on answering the key questions "what is marketing?" and "why do we need to market?" The second phase during the middle and second half of the 1980s is addressing tools, applications, and sophisticated methodologies for practical use by health administrators and providers. This text describes one of the most important marketing tools: writing a formal marketing plan for the health organization/facility. It is applicable for health managers in all health delivery systems. Before outlining the steps to the marketing planning process in detail, the basic principles of health marketing are surveyed.

WHAT IS HEALTH CARE MARKETING?

Health Marketing is an organized discipline for understanding: (1) how a health marketplace works; (2) the role in which the health organization can render optimum services to the marketplace; (3) mechanisms for adjusting production capabilities for meeting consumer demand; and (4) how the organization can assure patient satisfaction.

COMPONENTS OF HEALTH CARE MARKETING

Marketing includes a variety of functions, such as

1. *Marketing research*, which describes the collection of information about an organization's internal and external environment;
2. *Marketing planning*, which is the framework for identifying, collecting, and capturing select segments in the marketplace;
3. *Marketing strategy development*, which relates to new service development and actions to be taken for taking advantage of opportunities and gaps in the marketplace;
4. *Public relations*, which describes the action of communicating with the publics that interact with the health organization;
5. *Fund Development*, which is the solicitation of resources for the organization or special services;
6. *Community relations*, which acts as a liaison with the publics served;

7. *Patient liaison*, which acts as intermediators between the provision of care and the patient;
8. *Recruitment* for medical providers or staff;
9. *Internal marketing*, which includes staff development in marketing, marketing role expectation, and triage efficiency; and
10. *Contracting* for new modes of delivery, such as preferred provider organizations, IPAs, or HMOs.

MARKETING AS A SUBSYSTEM OF MANAGEMENT

Marketing is one function of management. It is integrated with other management subsystems of *production, finance,* and *human resources*. Marketing determines the needs of the consumer in the marketplace and lays out a plan for satisfying these needs. Production, finance, and human resources follow this lead and initiate the process of satisfying consumer needs through service provision.

TYPES OF HEALTH MARKETING

There are many applications of marketing in health care. Some of these applications include marketing for services, patients, new staff, donors, social causes, creative ideas, goodwill, staff morale, public relations, provider relations, community relations, political and lobbyist activities, new products, fund raising, patient relations, and contracting.

BASIC PREMISES OF HEALTH CARE MARKETING

Before implementing a market program, some basic premises must be established about marketing. These include

1. The patient is a client. There is an exchange process occurring between the consumer and supplier. Even with extensive insurance coverage, every client exchanges time, money, discomfort, and anxiety in obtaining a health service.
2. The best outcome of marketing is a patient or client referral.
3. All providers must continue to assess the effectiveness of their

services and not be satisfied to assume they are good just because people use them.

4. Like a new suit of clothes, services must pass initial examination by clients and continue to hold up after the time of initial purchase by the consumer.
5. Marketing is a management tool. it does not offer all the answers to effectively operating a successful organization. It must be blended among financial management, human resource management, strategic planning, and economic analysis.

TEN KEY QUESTIONS ANSWERED BY MARKETING

Marketing supplies answers to the following basic questions:

1. What business are we in and what is the purpose for the organization's existence?
2. Who is our client?
3. What does our client need?
4. Which markets should the organization be addressing?
5. What are the strengths of the organization?
6. What are the weaknesses of the organization that need to be attended to?
7. Who are our competitors?
8. Which groups (segments/targets) do we want to serve in the community?
9. What are our marketing strategies to communicate to these groups?
10. What strategies should we develop related to pricing, promotion, access, and the types of services offered?

TRADITIONAL VERSUS NEWER MARKETING CONCEPTS

The traditional method for understanding marketing is demonstrated by the following relationship:

PRODUCT + SELLING AND PROMOTION =
PROFITS THROUGH SALES VOLUME

This relationship is based on the traditional "Madison Avenue" aspect of selling being the most important part of marketing. Selling is only one function of marketing, and the real outcome of marketing will be client satisfaction. This is exemplified in the following relationship:

UNDERSTANDING CLIENT NEEDS + INTEGRATED MARKETING = PROFITS THROUGH CLIENT SATISFACTION

Integrated marketing includes researching the environment, developing a marketing plan, and creating communication strategies based on the research and planning.

Marketing programs which have failed are partly due to a lack of preliminary research, analysis, and planning before implementing communication strategies.

The *selling concept* focuses on the services, is solely dependent on public relations, and increases revenues through volume. The *marketing concept* focuses on consumer needs, uses integrated marketing, and increases revenues through consumer satisfaction.

The marketing concept refers to the study or practice of marketing strategies designed to assess consumer preferences about existing or proposed services, implies a direction to delivery services that meet these preferences and needs, and establishes a criterion of effectiveness so that consumers' health needs are satisfied by the services.

PUBLICS, MARKET, EXCHANGE PROCESS

Every organization conducts its business in an environment of both internal and external *publics*. A public is a distinct group of people or organizations that have an actual or potential interest or impact on the health organization. For example, publics for a hospital would be the media, government agencies, other health organizations, the population in the community, medical providers, and its employees.

A health organization functions through the exchange process in a *market*. A market is a process where a minimum of two groups possess resources they want to exchange for some benefit. It is the matching of demand and supply.

Every marketplace has an *exchange*. Exchange involves mutual satisfaction of the groups involved. There must be two parties and each must have something that is valued by the other party. For example, patients exchange time, money, discomfort, anxiety, and inconvenience for the services provided.

THE MARKETING MIX

Just as everyone who has studied economics remembers the basic principles of demand and supply, a marketer always is able to fall back on the foundation of the *marketing mix*. The marketing mix is the mixture or blending of select characteristics of the organization that are utilized to achieve some marketing objective and communicate with a select public.

There are four components of the marketing mix:

1. PRICING: This is becoming an important area of health marketing. It can include the direct cost, indirect costs, opportunity costs, discounting, prepayment plans, contracting, co-payments, credit terms, and deductibles. All organizations must price their services to be able to earn a normal profit which is the amount necessary to keep operations and some capital investment going. Normal profits are a regular part of operating costs. Some factors that must be included in the pricing of a service include demand characteristics for the service, pricing by competitors, consumer expectations for pricing, possible effects on other services provided by the organizational, legal aspects, competitive reaction to changes in prices, profitability, and the psychology of the consumer. Some pricing strategies include *competitive pricing*, which sets the price at the "going rate" in the marketplace; *market penetration*, which sets a below-competition price to capture additional market share; *skimming* which is useful in launching a new service for which the initial price might sustain a high price; and *variable pricing* based on seasonal fluctuations.

2. PRODUCT: Marketing strategies can be developed related to the physical characteristics of the products and services provided. These characteristics include quality of care, atmospherics, style, size, brand name, service, warranties, types of medical providers, quality of staff interactions, level of technology, and research activities. A health organization must have an attractive service that offers some value to the consumer. These values have to satisfy the needs of the consumer. Every new service needs to be researched, have the market screened for potential acceptance, tested for performance levels, and finally, launched into the market selectively. Typically, health organizations offer an array of different services. Therefore, a *product portfolio* needs to be established, which plans out the kind of *product/service mix* most readily acceptable for the market served.

3. PLACE: A key aspect of developing marketing strategies is related to access to the service. The place component of the marketing mix consists of the characteristics of service distribution, modes of delivery, location, transportation, availability, hours and days opened, appointments, parking, waiting time, and other access considerations. Some strategies have included opening a health center on weekends or in the evenings, hiring security guards for evenings, lighting parking lots, possessing excellent triage systems for small amounts of waiting time, locating near public transportation, and changing the mode of delivery to include home services.

4. PROMOTION: The promotional strategies relate to methods for communicating to the publics. Promotion can include advertising, public relations, personal selling, sales promotion, and publicity. A *promotional mix* needs to be established by blending advertising, sales promotion, personal selling, health education, and publicity. The three main ingredients of external communication are the provision of *information* about the service, *persuasion*, and *influence* to use the service if needed. When using promotional strategies, the basic factors to consider are the availability of funds, the stage of the life cycle the service is in, the nature of the service, the nature of the market, and the intensity of the competition.

SERVICE/PRODUCT LIFE CYCLE

Just like the human life cycle, every product or service experiences its own unique life cycle. This life cycle includes phases of introduction, growth, maturity, and decline.

Introduction Phase

In this phase the service is planned for, researched, and developed. It is then introduced into the marketplace for the first time. During this phase, it is usual to experience a considerable amount of technical innovation, research and development, experimentation, initial production and delivery problems, the determination of modes of delivery and channels for distribution, and the development and emergence of the initial marketing mix and promotional strategies. Most strategies relate to informing the publics about the service, educating them about their cost-effectiveness, and instructing them on how to use and obtain the service.

Growth Phase

Expansion occurs and the service becomes accepted by the community. Increased utilization materializes and more resources are inputted into the production process. Typically, new channels for distribution and delivery are created, competitors start to enter the marketplace, attempts are made to entrench the new service in the market by brand loyalty, and emphasis is placed on developing a strong referral network by concentrating on consumer satisfaction.

Maturity Phase

Most health organizations are in the maturity phase. This is usually the longest phase for the organization. The market becomes oversaturated with many similar services and competitors. Utilization and revenues tend to level off. Innovation is attempted by modifying the original service to attract new publics or segments, the development of new services begins, and promotion tends to emphasize the reputation of the organization, its history, quality of service, and reliability and integrity.

Decline

All organizations eventually experience a major decline phase which ends in the attenuation, redefinition or termination of the organization or service. Utilization and revenues usually decline in this phase dramatically, competition becomes aggressive, many new services are attempted for salvation of the organization, and planned obsolescence is a possibility for the original service. Of course, many products and services have indeterminate life cycles while others are very transitory due to trends. No sooner is one service started than another must be in the design stage eventually to replace or complement it.

THE MARKETING PLANNING PROCESS

A key tool in marketing is the development of a formal written *marketing plan*. Unfortunately, most health organizations jump the gun and concentrate on implementing strategies and tactics before a solid foundation is established through planning. Many marketing failures occur due to the omission of the planning process. A marketing plan is a framework that lays out the specific steps to market the health service. Marketing planning allows the organizations to evaluate the marketplace, identify strengths and weaknesses, identify segments to market to, penetrate the market, capture a select market share, and achieve a key positioning/image within the community.

There are four main components of marketing: *organization, research, creativity phase*, and *control*.

The *organizational phase* of the marketing planning process begins by setting up a marketing committee within the organization. This committee should minimally include the director of marketing, executive director, director of patient services, and a representative from the board. It is important to obtain organizational support for the function of marketing. The committee can be helpful in developing relationships and support from providers, board members, and the staff. A marketing philosophy has to be established by the organization for effectiveness. The *marketing mission* should be established. It will answer "What business are we in?", "What is the purpose for our existence?", and "Why are we marketing and what main markets are we addressing?" The mission lays a framework for developing the entire marketing program. Then marketing goals and objectives give us some guidelines for developing the specifics of the program. Marketing goals will outline broad desired results or outcomes we hope to achieve through marketing. The objectives will define the goals by describing specific, measurable outcomes that are to be achieved. For example, a goal could be a broad statement related to increasing utilization. The objective would specify a certain percentage of increased utilization within a time constraint.

The second phase of marketing is the *marketing research or auditing* area. Marketing research provides key internal and external information as background to identify trends in the marketplace and help in creating cost-effective strategies. The audit should include the collection of information related to *demographic factors* (i.e., age, sexual mix of the population, region, county size, population growth, climate, etc.); *economic factors* (i.e., income, occupations, industry trends, etc.); *psychographic factors* (i.e., lifestyle, values, interests, personality traits, etc.); *industrial factors* (i.e., competition, health system trends, legislation, lobbyist activities, new modes of delivery, reimbursement trends, etc.); and *internal factors* (i.e., quantity and quality of staff, training needs, staff knowledge of marketing and their role in marketing the organization, etc.). After the collection of background information is completed, an *opportunity/risk analysis* is done. This activity identifies trends from the audit that possibly relate to potential new services and gaps in the marketplace that our organization could fill. The analysis also examines risks to avoid. The outcome of this phase is the identification of market *targets* that will be marketed to by our programs. First, the audit should allow the administrator to subdivide the marketplace into distinct segments that might merit an individualized marketing program. After the development of this laundry list of segments, a more finite list of primary and secondary targets can be made. It is not feasible to market to every segment. Therefore, the marketing strategies are directed toward select market targets in the marketplace. The primary and secondary targets will consist of those publics in the market which the organization can serve effectively and offer the greatest opportunities.

The three main types of segmentation and targeting are *undifferentiated, differentiated,* and *concentrated.* Undifferentiated targeting relates to mass marketing whereby it is hoped that the right targets will be communicated to by marketing to everyone. Since finances are limited throughout health care, it is important to differentiate your marketing activities. Differentiated targeting identifies a few key targets to address. Concentrated targeting limits the targets to one or two select groups. It has been proven to be cost-effective to approach targeting from a differentiated or concentrated approach rather than from an undifferentiated approach.

The *creative phase* of the planning process includes the development of *strategies and tactics*. Strategies and tactics are the specific actions that will be taken to communicate to select target groups with the satisfaction of specific goals and objectives in mind. The first step for strategy development is to develop *positioning strategies*. Positioning provides an understanding of how people perceive the organization and identifies how the organization is unique in the marketplace. The underlying philosophy of marketing is to position the organization in the minds of the consumers. Positioning can be related to the quality of the staff, the location, pricing of services, access, and other characteristics of the organization that are unique. The marketing strategies and tactics can be developed by itemizing actions that are directed at marketing a select service. An example of a strategy would be the decision to advertise to a select target group. The tactic would then describe the type of ad, location, size, and color. Strategies can be developed according to the four Ps of the marketing mix discussed earlier in this chapter: *price, place, product,* and *promotion*. They can also be developed according to the phase of the life cycle in which the organization fits.

The *control phase* of the marketing process includes developing a *marketing budget, implementation time line, organizational chart for marketing,* and a *control system* to monitor the plan's effectiveness. The budget forecasts all of the direct and indirect expenses for developing, implementing, and controlling the marketing plan. The time line outlines specific dates and times for the planning, strategy implementation, and control phases. The organizational chart describes the lines of authority and reporting requirements for the marketing function. The directors of marketing should definitely have planning, public relations, and fund development reporting to them. Direct access to the executive director and a representative of the board may prevent future implementation problems. The control system outlines when and how the marketing program will be monitored for effectiveness. The control system measures the performance of the marketing program against the expected outcomes, or in this case, the goals and objectives that were established in the first phase of the marketing plan. It provides a guideline for pinpointing any problems or deviations, a mechanism for adjusting the plan if necessary, and it accumulates data for future marketing planning.

Marketing plans are essential for successful marketing programs. However, planning does not assure success, but it does provide a disciplined approach to marketing and can minimize risks. The marketing plan specifies by service who will do what, when, where, and how to accomplish the marketing goals and objectives in the most efficient manner. The plan identifies opportunities, coordinates efforts to attract new clients, stimulates creativity in the organization, supports innovation, and allocates resources more effectively. There is an old saying that a marketer needs to "plan the work and work the plan." This means that a lot of planning is useless unless it is implemented carefully. Implementation is as important as developing a plan. The plan is a guideline. It can be changed and adjusted over a long time frame. This is important because marketing is also a long-term process. Results do not occur overnight. Unrealistic expectations about marketing being a miracle worker is one of the major causes of failure. Marketing can be a major management resource for the health organization if it is understood and applied effectively through the planning process.

SUMMARY:
BASIC PRINCIPLES OF HEALTH
CARE MARKETING

The role of marketing in health care organizations has never been more important. This is reflective of the most competitive health care marketplace in history. Health organizations are examining new and entrepreneurial ways in which to deliver their services in response to this changing marketplace. Despite the fact that marketing has been used for centuries in health care, most health care administrators have not been trained in marketing techniques. This first chapter provides a brief summary, and for some an introduction, of the basic theoretical concepts in marketing. Many of these concepts will be discussed in greater detail and with applications during later chapters.

This first chapter should provide a foundation of (1) what marketing is; (2) its applications; (3) major theoretical concepts utilized in the scope of study; and (4) a brief introduction to the role of the marketing planning function. The next chapter elaborates on the strategic marketing planning process as a continuation of foundation material for the actual steps to use in developing a marketing plan.

Part II

Marketing Planning

CHAPTER 2

Introduction
to Strategic Market Planning

Robert L. Berl

In the ever-increasing competitive environment faced by health care and other social service institutions, it is essential that marketing managers thoroughly understand the circumstances under which they must operate, their customer's needs and wants, and their ability to satisfy these needs and wants. These conditions can be accomplished through the effective use of strategic market planning. Strategic market planning is defined as a method of achieving the institution's objectives by properly allocating resources and managing changing marketing opportunities in a timely way. Figure 2.1 delineates the strategic market planning process.

Strategic market planning has its origins in early twentieth-century efforts to formally analyze and improve the performance of complex organizations. The earliest businesses with a managerial tradition adopted a broad approach known as comprehensive planning. Under the impetus of Herbert Simon and other scholars of organizational psychology and structure, corporations in the 1950s began to adopt a structural approach known as organizational planning. The shift from management-by-profit center to diversification and portfolio management in the early 1960s was accompanied by a shift in planning focus to a functional bias. This period of planning history is known as the financial planning era. The next phase, strategic planning, was a child of the trend toward mergers and conglomerate formation in the late 1960s. Managers tortured themselves with self-questioning as to "What business?" or "What industry?" to be in. Strategic planning yielded center stage to marketing planning in the 1970s. Also a functional approach, market-

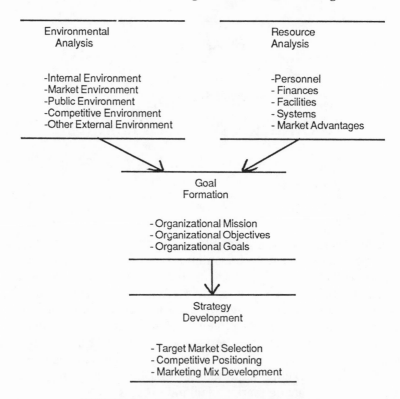

FIGURE 2.1. Strategic Market Planning Process

ing planning reflected the explicit appearance of firms whose primary mission was marketing as opposed to the production and sale of product or services. Strategic marketing planning is the happy marriage of the preceding two phases and represents a shift toward proactive, rather than reactive, evaluation of strategic opportunities.

ENVIRONMENTAL ANALYSIS

Internal Environment

The marketing manager must understand the strengths and weaknesses of the health care or social service organization's internal environment. The internal environment consists of the board of directors, management, medical staff, administrative staff, and volunteers. It is necessary to examine their needs, wants, and interests. For example, an action on the part of management to raise laboratory diagnostic fees might be met with resistance on the part of the medical staff because of the negative reaction on the part of patients.

Market Environment

The market environment encompasses those entities with which the organization must interact to accomplish its primary mission. These entities are the patients or users — also known as clients — and the firm's suppliers. In today's competitive environment the client's needs and wants must be monitored on a continual basis. Client perceptions of the social service organization's personnel, facilities, competency, and the like must also be assessed. If the perceptions are negative, it is imperative that immediate remedial actions be taken. It is immaterial that these negative perceptions may be inaccurate for "reality" is whatever the client perceives it to be.

Dependable sources of supplies are essential. It is necessary for the institution to monitor its suppliers, as well as the clients.

Public Environment

Health care and social service organizations have many publics that are interested in their activities. Some of these publics are the media, regulatory agencies, and the general public. Good relations with the media can facilitate effective public relations efforts. Regulatory agencies can affect the way in which the organization is operated. The general public can influence local, state, and federal legislative actions. The public also act as a source of funding and volunteer personnel.

Competitive Environment

The competitive environment consists of those organizations and individuals that vie for the loyalty of the same clients. A hospital's emergency room services might view other hospitals, emergency care clinics, and doctors as their competitors.

Other External Environment

This category consists of those environmental variables over which the social marketer has little or no control. These would include changes in demographic, technological, economic, political, and social factors. These uncontrollable variables require monitoring so as to keep the firm's strategies focused properly. Part III of this book contains an expanded discussion of environmental analysis.

MARKETING INFORMATION SYSTEM

The adequacy of the firm's marketing information system will determine the organization's ability to assess its environment. Internal records represent one information source available to the health care or social service institution. For example, a hospital has maternity patient records. From these records management can determine the average length of patient stay, the number of normal deliveries, the number of Caesarian deliveries, and other information.

In addition to the firm's internal records, a sophisticated marketing research system is important. Marketing research is the systematic design, collection, analysis, and reporting of data and findings relevant to a specific marketing situation or problem facing an organization. This system can gather information on customer profiles, market profiles, competitive profiles, and information about market behavior. For example, a large hospital is considering expanding its laundry facilities and also wondering if they could sell any excess laundry capacity that might be built. A research project could determine if other hospitals, nursing homes, motels, college dorms, and the like would utilize the facility, what delivery systems would be required, and what price would be necessary to acquire their business. An expanded discussion of marketing information systems appears in Part III of this book.

RESOURCE ANALYSIS

An internal audit of the following areas will determine the health care or social service institution's capabilities and liabilities: personnel, finances, facilities, systems, and market advantages.

Personnel

It is crucially important to assess the strengths and weaknesses of the people working for the organization. Is the organization adequately staffed? How skilled are the personnel? Are they loyal? Enthusiastic? How dedicated are they?

Finances

Are there adequate finances? The dependability of current sources of funding should be determined. Can additional funding be acquired and, if so, to what degree? At what cost?

Facilities

The social marketer should rate the facilities of the agency. Are they adequate? Can they be expanded? Are they properly located?

Systems

The adequacy of the marketing information system should be determined. What is the quality of the organization's planning system? Is there a control system and, if so, what is its quality?

Market Advantages

Does the health care or social service organization have an adequate donor base? If the facility is a hospital, what is the quality of the donor base? What is the general reputation of the associated health care organization?

The resource analysis should assist the management of the institution in determining the firm's specific competencies. Specific competencies are those areas in which the organization is particularly strong. Firms should be especially alert to those competencies which offer a competitive advantage: strengths which the competition does not possess.

GOAL FORMATION

Organizational Mission

The mission is the basic purpose of the institution. For example, Le Bonheur Children's Medical Center, Memphis, Tennessee, is a research hospital dedicated to the cure and treatment of children's diseases. Since, over time, an organization's mission can become unclear, institutions should reexamine their mission periodically.

The mission of an organization denotes a particular type of customer, customer benefits which must be rendered, and the requisite abilities and resources which are required to accomplish the mission. Le Bonheur Children's Medical Center has a customer base of children and their families. Le Bonheur offers technical and advisory benefits differentiated by their quality and complexity; the hospital, therefore, requires sophisticated medical and scientific personnel and facilities to fulfill its mission.

It is recommended that organizations commit the mission statement to writing. This procedure helps in clarifying the role of the institution and serves as a constant reminder of the organization's purpose.

Organizational Objectives

The organization's objectives should stress the major thrust the firm will undertake for the coming period of time. For a health care institution the objectives might be increased regional or national reputation, increased profitability, increased market share, increased private funding, and so on. In more specific terms, a children's medical center might well have as an objective the development of a cure or treatment for a specific childhood ailment. It should be noted that an institution's objectives can and do vary from year to year.

Organizational Goals

Goals are organizational objectives which have been made specific. Effective goal statements should be in writing, have a benchmark from which progress can be measured, and be specific as to magnitude and time. For example, the goal statement for an emergency clinic which desires to increase the number of patients they are treating might well be "to increase the patients treated by 15% over the 1987 patient load by December 31, 1988."

Organizational objectives and goals should be consistent with each other. It would not ordinarily be consistent for a doctor to want to decrease the patient load by 25% and also increase revenues by 15%. Since it is doubtful that the doctor could raise his fees high enough to offset the 25% decrease in patient load, the two goals are mutually exclusive. Nor would a library expect to increase readership by 20% while simultaneously cutting back on its hours of access.

STRATEGY DEVELOPMENT

Target Market Selection

A target market is the set of all people who are the most likely purchasers for a firm's products or services. Few organizations attempt to be all things to all people, at least with any degree of success. Consequently, organizations specialize so as to appeal to a specific segment of the market. Physicians have segmented along the following lines: allergy, anesthesiology, cardiology, dermatology, diabetes, ear-nose-and-throat, endocrinology, family practice, gastroenterology, general practice, gynecology, and so on.

Health care and social service institutions can segment by demographics, geography, consumer benefits (illness treated), and so on. Le Bonheur Children's Medical Center has used demographics (children) to segment their market. Inner city hospitals have established suburban locations to take advantage of demographic and geographic shifts. Consumer benefit segmentation is illustrated by a psychiatric hospital. Part IV of this book provides a fuller discussion of market segmentation and targeting.

Competitive Positioning

Competitive positioning refers to the ability to develop and communicate product/service differences between your institution and those of your competitors. In doing so, the social marketer attempts to capitalize on the competitive advantages identified during the resource analysis. For example, a noted teaching institution such as the Johns Hopkins has a competitive advantage over lesser known medical schools in attracting promising medical students. Competitive positioning identifies and appeals to the major factors used by the target market to evaluate and select among alternatives. The Johns Hopkins would be perceived as having superior personnel and facilities.

Figure 2.2 shows the competitive positioning of three home health care agencies. Agency C was perceived as superior to the other agencies. It had high quality personnel and a convenient service area. Agency A was perceived as having better personnel than agency C, but the service area was considerably less accessible. Agency B, while somewhat convenient, was perceived as having poorer quality personnel than the other agencies. Part V of this book will discuss the positioning of health care services in greater depth.

Marketing Mix Development

At this stage, the institution develops a marketing mix to achieve its corporate goals. The marketing mix is the blend of controllable variables used to achieve the corporate objectives: the product/service, distribution, price, and promotion. For example, an emergency clinic might develop their marketing mix as follows: product/service offering — fast minor emergency service; distribution — multiple suburban locations; price — relatively lower in price than the competition; and promotion — newspaper and radio ads. They are positioned against hospital emergency room service as faster, more convenient, and less expensive. Figure 2.3 depicts the marketing mix as it might apply to health care institutions. Part VI of this book will expand on the development and utilization of the marketing mix.

SUMMARY

Effective strategic planning requires a health care or social service institution to conduct environmental analyses. These analyses cover the internal environment, the market environment, the public environment, the competitive environment and the uncontrollable

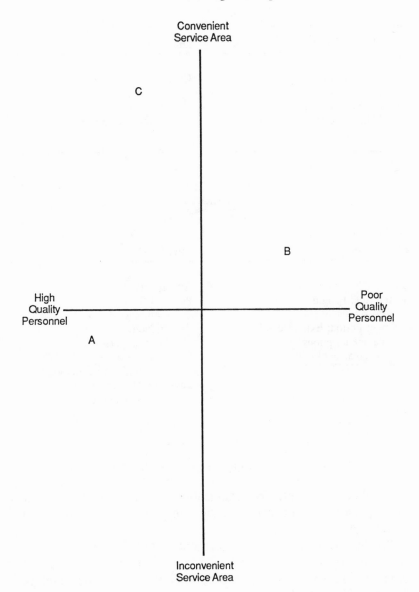

FIGURE 2.2. Perceptual Map of the Competitive Positioning of Three Home Health Care Agencies

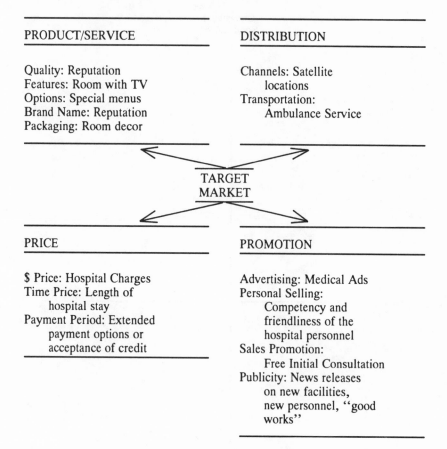

PRODUCT/SERVICE

Quality: Reputation
Features: Room with TV
Options: Special menus
Brand Name: Reputation
Packaging: Room decor

DISTRIBUTION

Channels: Satellite
   locations
Transportation:
   Ambulance Service

TARGET
MARKET

PRICE

$ Price: Hospital Charges
Time Price: Length of
   hospital stay
Payment Period: Extended
   payment options or
   acceptance of credit

PROMOTION

Advertising: Medical Ads
Personal Selling:
   Competency and
   friendliness of the
   hospital personnel
Sales Promotion:
   Free Initial Consultation
Publicity: News releases
   on new facilities,
   new personnel, "good
   works"

FIGURE 2.3 The Marketing Mix for a Health Care Institution

external environment. The organization must also assess the quality of its personnel, finances, facilities, internal systems, and market advantages.

Written corporate mission statements should be developed to ensure the firm's adherence to its purpose for existence. Once the organization is sure of its purpose, objectives should be developed. These objectives should be operationalized with goal statements which are specific as to both time and magnitude.

Once the objectives and goals are established, the organization can select its target market, develop its competitive positioning, and determine its use of the marketing mix variables of product/service, distribution, price, and promotion.

Try to keep this overview of strategic market planning in mind as you read through the following planning articles by William J. Winston. He identifies specific steps which health care or social service organizations can take to install a reliable and lasting marketing planning system. In addition, William Winston provides an actual sample marketing plan for reference. It is applied to urgent care but can be applicable to any health setting.

CHAPTER 3

Introduction to Marketing Planning for Health Care Organizations

William J. Winston

WHAT IS A MARKETING PLAN?

A marketing plan is a framework that lays out the specific steps for marketing the health organization. Marketing plans have become indispensable in health facilities that want to successfully compete in today's marketplace. Before being able to commit marketing resources in the most effective and efficient way, the marketer must establish a systematic approach to marketing needs. This systematic process will be organized in the form of a formal marketing plan. No marketing activities should be initiated without a plan. Unfortunately, the use in health and human services of the formal marketing plan is still relatively rare. In most health organizations marketing tends to be implemented on a piecemeal basis and is concentrated on public relations, advertising, and most recently, contracting. These health organizations rely on separate programs and plans whose coordination is often haphazard rather than synergistic.

The marketing plan specifies by service who will do what, where, when, and how to accomplish the organization's goals in the most efficient method. The plan is a schedule of events and activities of a preplanned marketing effort. It outlines the marketing methods to be used, the resources to be committed, and the policy

Reprinted from William J. Winston, *How to Write a Marketing Plan for Health Care Organizations*, pp. 13–24, © 1985 by The Haworth Press, Inc.

guidelines to be followed in achieving specific marketing goals and objectives.

POSITIVE OUTCOMES
OF THE MARKETING PLANNING PROCESS

A marketing plan allows the health organization to

- Evaluate the facility's existing marketplace
- Evaluate the organization's marketing strengths and weaknesses
- Identify the segments of the marketplace that should be served and marketed to by the organization
- Penetrate a select segment of the marketplace
- Capture a select target
- Maintain a desired market share
- Achieve key positioning/images within the community served
- Lay a framework for new service development of existing service alteration
- Identify specific strategies and tactics for the organization to implement
- Satisfy the patient's needs in the marketplace
- Improve the financial viability of the health organization

The marketing plan assists in identifying marketing opportunities, coordinates and unifies efforts to attract new patients, stimulates creativity within the organization, supports innovation as a planning by-product, encourages participation by all personnel within the organization, reduces costs with increased span of control, and allocates resources more efficiently.

BENEFITS OF MARKETING PLANNING

Planning does not assure performance, but it is a disciplined approach, which can minimize failure. This is very important as most marketing programs in health organizations fail. In other words, they do not satisfy the majority of goals and objectives. Marketing planning is an allocation tool. The major goal of marketing planning is to achieve cost-effectiveness in marketing efforts and resources. This is the main reason why specific tasks are laid out systematically so that performance can be measured against the plan's objectives and goals.

The marketing plan is a communication tool between the health organization and the different groups with whom it serves and interacts. Marketing plans should be well-written documents, so confusion and misunderstanding of functions and activities are eliminated. Effective communication with the organization's personnel and publics served can be obtained with a well thought-out marketing plan. In fact, someone unfamiliar with the organization should be able to read and understand the plan. This can lead to the plan's being effective over a long time frame. marketing planning is an ongoing function that needs to be utilized throughout the existence of the organization. Paying attention to the marketing aspects of the organization can pay large dividends in relation to its marketing resource allocation being cost-effective.

PRELIMINARY STEPS TO WRITING A PLAN

No marketing plan has ever been successful without a dedication and commitment to using marketing within a health organization. Thousands of marketing plans have been thrown into the "circular file" or sat on shelves collecting dust because of a lack of commitment by administration or the medical staff. A marketer must do the homework before ever writing a plan. In other words, they must market the function of marketing to management, staff, medical providers, and boards before developing and implementing marketing activities. Many marketers have wasted an enormous amount of time and energy because of this lack of preparation. Political and economic support for developing a marketing plan must be achieved before implementation. Superficial support, inadequate time to prepare a good plan, and poor implementation can undermine the potential cost-effectiveness of the planning process.

DEVELOPING A MARKETING PLANNING COMMITTEE

One of the most important steps in developing a marketing program is to create a marketing committee within the organization.

This committee can provide excellent input from different perspectives and interests. It can also enhance the potential success and acceptance by all members of the staff, board, and medical staff. The key ingredient to a successful planning committee is the selection of the members of the committee. As an example, let us assume a marketing program is beginning to be discussed by a local community hospital. The minimum areas of the hospital which need to be represented on the committee are the board, executive director, director of patient or clinical care, director of planning, director of finance, chief of the medical staff, and director of marketing.

The committee must start out with the director of marketing's, having the executive director on the committee. It is essential to have the chief executive actively involved in issuing planning policies and giving approvals for action. The executive director should also be involved in developing a marketing subcommittee of the board of directors. Then a key member of the marketing subcommittee can be an active member of the marketing planning committee. Direct access and communication with the board and executive administration is vital for avoiding potential problems in the long run. The director of finance must be part of the committee for financial input and resource allocation decisions. The director of planning can provide coordination between the different planning and new service development activities going on in the organization. The chief of staff provides a key liaison with the medical providers. The director of patient care coordinates activities with the nursing staff and ancillary services. The committee, of course, can be greater in number than seven members. However, these seven members are essential for key representation. Also, a seven-member committee is a good size for accomplishing a considerable amount in terms of decision-making. This first step to developing a marketing plan is necessary. It will be a major contributor to the potential success of the marketing planning process over the long run.

THE MARKETING PLANNING PROCESS

As described in Chapter 1, three are four key sectors to the marketing planning cycle in health organizations. These four sectors include *organization, research, creativity process*, and *control*.

These four phases of the planning process are interrelated throughout the planning cycle.

The key steps which will be described in the following chapters are listed below:

Planning Phase	Marketing Activity
Organization:	Design of marketing function
	Marketing committee activities
	Development of marketing mission
	Establishment of marketing goals and objectives
Marketing Research:	Review historical trends
	Develop an internal audit
	Develop an external audit
	Analyze marketing opportunities and risks
	Identify segments and targets
	Establish positioning statements
Creativity Process:	Specific marketing strategies and tactics
Control and Evaluation:	Create marketing budget and forecast
	Develop control system for performance evaluation
	Time line for implementation and control
	Refine goals/objectives

CONSTANTLY CHANGING ENVIRONMENT

It is quite evident that the health and human service industry will be experiencing significant changes through the next few years. Health policies are constantly being developed to contain costs, expand access, redirect us to preventive services, and alter the economic aspects of the marketplace. Most of the interest in health policy during the last 20 years has been related to allocating health services more equally and, most recently, improving their economic performance. The major emphasis of health policy currently is related to controlling the level of government involvement in health care and stimulating competition and free enterprise in the marketplace.

Within this rapidly changing policy debate over cost-containment and marketplace characteristics, the health care industry has sought out new management tools to help direct it into the future. One of these key tools has been the use of marketing. The most important aspect of developing a marketing program for the health organization is the formulation of a marketing plan. The new emphasis on marketing is typical of industries that have been thrust into heavy competition, are worrying about survival, and are seeking the typical "quick cure" or "savior." Unfortunately, marketing is not a savior. It is only one management technique. The current and future direction of health public policy will enhance the importance of marketing in health organizations. The marketing plan can assist in lowering the incidence and risk of failure.

WHY MOST MARKETING PROGRAMS FAIL IN HEALTH ORGANIZATIONS

It is my estimate that the majority of marketing programs fail in health organizations. I have observed seven major factors that contribute to failures in marketing programs. If attention is paid to these key areas, there is a strong possibility that a reduction of risk in marketing will be achieved. These seven factors are

1. A lack of marketing planning: As mentioned earlier, most health organizations still jump the gun and implement strategies without doing their homework in developing a formal marketing plan.

2. Unsophisticated targeting: Most marketers still use an undifferentiated or mass appeal approach to segmenting and targeting their potential patients or clients. Being more selective in differentiating to whom you are marketing can prove to be cost-beneficial. A select group of strategies needs to be developed for each target group. To increase the sophistication of targeting requires more attention to collecting marketing research information and analyzing the data.

3. Lack of administrative and financial support for marketing: As was mentioned earlier, the formulation of a marketing committee can prevent marketing programs from being sabotaged by boards, medical staff, or administrators who may not really believe in marketing and its benefits. In addition, marketing is not necessarily cheap. Enough financial resources must be allocated over a long time frame.

4. Lack of coordination between directors of marketing, planning, and finance: First of all, the position of marketing should be at a vice-presidency level within most health organizations. The position should have public relations, planning, fund development, and new service development reporting to it. In addition, there need to be excellent communication and working relationships between the director of marketing and directors of planning or finance. The director of marketing should report directly to the executive director of the organization.

5. Marketing directors not possessing enough training in marketing: There are very few directors of marketing in health care with a broad range of knowledge about the wide scope of applications of marketing. Since the formal aspect of marketing has only been accepted within health organizations during the last decade, it is easily understood why so few experienced marketers exist at this time. Most organizations assumed they could promote directors of public relations or planning to this function without exploring if they could adapt to the wider range of applications of marketing.

6. Unrealistic expectations: Marketing will not solve all the organization's problems nor will it be a major success in a short-time frame. Marketing is a management tool and must be adopted and implemented over a long time frame. An administrator must accept marketing as a key management tool, but only one to be integrated with finance, strategic planning, human resources management, economics, and policy analysis.

7. Lack of internal marketing before implementing external strategies: A health organization must develop an internal marketing philosophy and mission. The staff must understand their roles within marketing the organization. Every staff member is a representative of the organization. Everyone markets the organization with every interaction. The organization must educate the board, medical staff, employees, administrators, and clinicians about marketing and direct them to play a role in marketing. The formal people who are affiliated with the organization are its greatest marketing resources.

These seven pitfalls can be avoided by paying attention to the marketing plan that is developed. Each of these reasons for failure can be avoided if the plan is thorough and pays attention to these problem areas.

NATURE OF STRATEGIC MARKETING PLANNING

Major changes are occurring in planning in health care organizations. This is indicated by the various ways in which planning is described, including "business planning," "financial planning," "market planning," "strategic planning," "marketing planning," "strategic marketing planning," and other various combinations. These changes and variations are reflective of the fact that planning is becoming more "strategic" in nature. Planning is becoming more related to marketplace analysis, analyzing opportunities and risks, and laying a framework for new service development. This framework is forming a basis of strategy development as a key ingredient in all types of planning. Planning has shifted from a narrow functional area in an organization to encompass diversified, multiservice health organizations. The concept of the health organization as a collection of service units having various marketing objectives is at the foundation of current approaches to strategic marketing planning. The term "portfolio" is typically used to describe such a group of diversified services within one organization. This metamorphosis in planning is due to the fact that many health organizations are now confronted with limited financial resources because of rising costs of operation and limitations in reimbursement.

A strategic marketing plan is not the same, therefore, as a regular marketing plan. It is a plan of all aspects of an organization's strategies in a marketplace. This means that the financial, human resources, and policy planning aspects of the organization must be coordinated within the strategic marketing plan. This compares to a limited version of marketing planning, which constrains itself to a select service and an individual marketing mix strategy. Effective strategic marketing planning is based on the premise that market opportunities have to be analyzed and the organization's capacity to take advantage of these opportunities requires assessment. The five major components of the foundation of strategic marketing planning are *clients or patients, competitors, environmental trends, market characteristics*, and *internal strengths and weaknesses*.

Strategic marketing planning is a natural outgrowth of the historical comprehensive health planning, financial planning, health systems planning, and more recently, operational strategic planning methodologies. It has evolved during recent times mainly because of the diversification and limited financial constraints, which have materialized during the 1980s. A strategic marketing plan possesses the central theme that market opportunities differ in various markets. This requires every health organization to be strategically alert to take advantage of such opportunities in these diverse marketplaces. Strategic marketing planning has been aided significantly during recent years by computers and other technical processes. However, planning is a creative process which requires an extensive amount of creative strategic thinking by health managers.

The remainder of this book will address strategic marketing planning. It will be directed to developing a marketing plan for interrelating the health organization's future purpose, direction, and services with the organization's marketing missions, goals, and objectives. As mentioned earlier, the efficient allocation of marketing resources for achieving these goals and objectives will be the backbone of the planning process. It should answer (a) where has the organization been?; (b) what is our current business and purpose?; (c) where do we want to be in the future?; and (d) what do we need to do to become what we want our organization to be? By answering these questions, the health organization will be better able to deal with the contrivance of change, rather than just reacting to it. In today's ever-changing marketplace, action rather than reaction has to be the theme of future health management.

SUMMARY FOR CHAPTER 3: INTRODUCTION TO MARKETING PLANNING

One of the major reasons that many marketing programs have failed or have not lived up to expectations has been the lack of the development of a formal written marketing plan. The marketing plan lays the framework from which we can market our services. This chapter has provided some foundations about (1) what strategic planning is; (2) how it differentiates from strategic marketing planning; (3) the role marketing planning plays in the marketing process; (4) benefits of developing a marketing plan; (5) how to prepare for a marketing plan through marketing subcommittees and administrative support; and (6) key pitfalls to be aware of which have caused many marketing programs to end in failure.

CHAPTER 4

Condensed Sample Marketing Plan: Urgent Care Center

William J. Winston

The following marketing plan is based upon a composite of several different marketing plans the author has developed using the systematic framework described in the prior chapters. The sample plan is meant to be a reference and a guideline for any type of health organization or program which is developing a marketing plan. I have referred the reader to select chapters which describe the particular section being discussed. Therefore, it is important for the reader to remember that it is a generic reference and the methodology is applicable to many different types of health and human services. It is an edited version of a formal plan. Most plans can range from about twenty pages to over 100 depending upon the amount of research and analysis. The most common question I receive from health professionals who are preparing a marketing plan is related to the fact that they have never seen an actual plan. It is hoped the plan will alleviate some of these needs but no plan should be exactly duplicated as each organization has unique marketing characteristics and needs. I have selected one of the most exciting areas in health care delivery, that of ambulatory care. The urgent care format of delivery is widespread throughout the country and is multiplying in the form of emergicenters, convenience care centers, express care centers, and same day surgery centers.

Reprinted from William J. Winston, *How to Write a Marketing Plan for Health Care Organizations*, pp. 109–129, © 1985 by The Haworth Press, Inc.

MARKETING PLAN FOR ENTERPRISE HOSPITAL'S URGENT CARE CENTER (CARING CENTER)

Executive Summary and Background

Enterprise Hospital is a general acute hospital located in San Francisco County, California. The hospital is a private not-for-profit health care institution which traces its lineage to 1889. Enterprise Hospital encompasses the 230-bed acute care hospital as well as a full range of ambulatory, ancillary, and rehabilitation programs under its Enterprise Hospital Division. As a teaching hospital, Enterprise also includes a large intern, resident, and fellowship program along with the associated staff faculty members. The majority of the faculty have their private offices in the attached Enterprise Medical Building.

On December 1, 1982 Enterprise Hospital purchased the Sacramento Health Clinic located two blocks from the main hospital, which had been in operation for less than two months. As ambulatory care services have materialized as a progressive new form of health delivery during the past decade, Enterprise decided to convert the clinic into an urgent care center. November 1983 witnessed the opening of the new Urgent Care Center under the name Caring Center. This transition to opening an urgent care center was a response to an overcrowded emergency room and a mechanism for providing same-day appointments for non-emergency care. It was hoped the Caring Center would improve access to care for the hospital's service area, prevent misappropriate usage of the emergency room, provide a new revenue source for the hospital, and lower the cost of health care to the community. In addition, the medical staff developed a keen interest in the urgent care center as a potential source of private referrals to them. The rationale for this interest was that a patient who came to the Caring Center probably would not have a regular physician, might need specialized services, and would theoretically be referred to a participating specialist by the Center.

As with most hospitals in the same geographic area, economic conditions have changed for Enterprise Hospital. Current projected inpatient demand is insufficient; increased competition from local hospitals, HMOs, Group Practices, and Preferred Provider Organizations have materialized; the growth of the local population has stagnated; the hospital's aging medical staff may threaten long-term financial growth; and government changes in reimbursement for Medicare and Medicaid are starting to have some impact on recovering the hospital's cost of care. These trends plus the future outlook for a greater prospective reimbursement emphasis by public and private insurance sources have stimulated the hospital's board of directors and administration to investigate alternative new service development including a consulting division, a same-day surgery center, acquisition of a long-term care center, and a wellness program for contracting with private businesses. Of course, one of their decisions related to this investigation was the opening of Caring Center. At this point in time, the Center has been open for eleven months and is not living up to expectations. Thus, the hospital's board has decided to hire a marketing consultant to develop a marketing plan specifically designed to market the Caring Center for Enterprise Hospital. The following marketing plan is being presented to the Board of Directors of Enterprise Hospital on October 17, 1984 as a potential guideline for the hospital's endeavors in marketing the Caring Center. The plan has been developed over a three-month time frame and can be initially implemented during the next twelve months through the majority of the 1985 calendar year.

Organizational and Marketing Missions

The stated mission of Enterprise Hospital is to (1) provide excellence in medical care within a teaching environment, (2) improve the standards of medical care in the San Francisco area, (3) provide an environment suitable for the training of future physicians and clinical research, and (4) offer a broad range of basic and specialized hospital services on an inpatient and outpatient basis.

The mission of Caring Center is to provide a wide range of ambulatory care services to the population of San Francisco county on a non-emergency basis and to complement the services offered by Enterprise Hospital.

The mission of the marketing plan for Enterprise Hospital's Caring Center is to increase the Center's client base, expand the utilization of Enterprise Hospital's main services, develop an active referral network for the hospital's medical staff, and to let the community become aware of a new alternative mode of care.

Marketing Goals and Objectives

Goal I: To expand the number of clients using the Center.

Objective 1: To increase the Center's utilization by 50% by the end of 1985's calendar year.

Objective 2: To expand the mix of patients to the Center from existing markets and new markets.

Objective 3: To increase the proportion of private-pay patients by 25% by the end of 1985.

Objective 4: To increase the number of business employees using the Center by 100% by the end of 1985.

Objective 5: To attract new target groups to the Center: commuters, local students, and small business owners.

Marketing Audit*

Macroenvironmental Information

Population trends. The population of San Francisco county exceeds 680,000 people. While the U.S. and California have experienced steady growth in population, San Francisco's trend is declining. For example, California's population from 1970 to 1980 has increased over 7%. Meanwhile, San Francisco's population has declined by an average of 1.3% per year from 1970 to 1980. This decline is due to a migration out of the primary San Francisco County into Alameda, Contra Costa, Marin, and Peninsula areas. The greatest migration out of San Francisco has occurred from the southern and central sections of the County. The population projection through 1990 is for a slowing of this population decline to approximately .7%/year.

Ethnic background. San Francisco's racial composition has undergone significant change since 1970. The most dramatic change has been the increase in the Chinese and decrease in the Caucasian

---

*AUTHOR'S NOTE: This audit is only 10% of its original length for editing purposes. Certain categories have been deleted as have the graphs and tables. However, it does provide a good survey of the major systematic approach to an audit for the reader.

population groups. The second biggest increase has been the Spanish-speaking population. These trends appear to be forecasted to continue through 1990.

Age. San Francisco in comparison to the U.S. in 1977 is shown below:

	Less Than 14	15-24	25-44	45-64	+65
U.S.:	16%	18.6%	31.7%	22.4%	11.3%
S.F.:	17.1%	19.1%	25.5%	23.4%	14.9%

The major trend of the population shift has been a steadily increasing senior citizen marketplace.

Sexual breakdown. There are over 340,000 males and 341,000 females in San Francisco County with the median age of 33.2 years for males and 35.3 years for females.

Family unit. S.F. County has 140,490 total families with a total number of households over 300,000. The mean number of people per household is 2.2.

Occupation and Income. The main occupational source in San Francisco is services. The three main occupation groups are retail, finance, and human services. The median adult income in S.F. is over $14,000 per year.

Health status. Heart disease, cancer, stroke, and accidents represent primary causes for death for over 70% of the population in the county. Cancer, heart disease, and accident rates are higher than national or state averages. S.F. also is represented by the highest mortality rates of influenza, pneumonia, cirrhosis, and suicide.

Commute. The majority of workers in S.F. commute from Alameda, Contra Costa, and Marin Counties.

Shopping centers/tourism. There are four major shopping centers near the Care Center. Tourism is S.F.'s largest industry with over 3-1/2 million visitors per year.

Housing/local industry. The average San Francisco home is priced over $130,000 and in excess of 100 of the largest 500 corporations have offices in or near San Francisco.

Access. There is excellent public transportation in S.F. and there is good highway access from the East, North, and South Bay Areas. The Care Center is not near a major freeway but is near excellent bus and BART transportation.

Microenvironmental Information

Clinic utilization during first eleven months. The largest proportion of patients have been between the ages of 18-40 (53%); male (59%); Private Insurance (34%), Medi-Cal (24%), and Private Pay (17%); 60% claimed not having a family physician of which 47% were specifically referred to an Enterprise staff member; heaviest usage occurred between 12-6 pm (57%); 81% of visits were made on Mondays-Wednesdays; 41% were Caucasians; 80% resided in homes; and 75% were employed. In addition, 100% of the clients are derived from S.F. County. Of the local hospital area's population 45% is over the age of 65 but this group counted for only 9.5% of the clinic's activities. The largest proportion of users were in the 18-40 age group; and the largest proportion of clients are walk-ins.

Competitors. There are eight emergency rooms and three other urgent care centers within a two mile radius of the Care Center. The closest one is the Weston Urgent Care Center 1/2 mile on the west side of the city. In terms of access, the Care Center is less than 100 yards from the Enterprise Emergency Room. Competition is fierce for emergency, outpatient, and ambulatory patients. In addition, there are over 12 large group practices and one minor emergency clinic serving the same area as the Care Center. It appears that three other local hospitals are planning new urgent care centers within the next year.

Market share. The local HSA estimates that Enterprise Hospital has a 6% share of the marketplace within S.F. County. This ranks them the sixth largest hospital in terms of serving patients out of thirteen hospitals in the county.

Finances/utilization/staffing. The Care Center currently has a $1,000,000 yearly budget. Break-even has been estimated at 42 patient visits/day. The current utilization rate is 21 patients/day. The Care Center can efficiently handle a maximum of 65 patients/day with current staffing of four physicians, five nurses, and four clerical assistants for a twelve-hour operating day. The Center has a sliding scale fee schedule with the average client paying $34/visit.

Psychographics. There is currently no survey information which has been collected for service, lifestyle, psychological, and behavioristic profiles. From a short survey of 10% of the current patients, a brief profile of the typical client was: satisfied with service; appreciative of the courteous service by the staff and short waiting times; young and quite athletically active; upwardly-mobile; and uses the clinic routinely four times a year due to strong loyalty.

Current marketing activity. Almost no marketing has been done for the Care Center since it opened. Only activity were: brochures sent to 5% of the residents in a five mile radius; and open house for medical staff and; word of mouth referrals that were expected to stimulate growth. the director of public relations at the hospital allocates about two hours per week to the Center.

Demand analysis. Currently 30% of the users are referrals from existing clients. The survey of the general local population indicated that 92% of 3,000 people surveyed in a five mile radius of the Center were unaware of the Center but indicated that they might consider using it after becoming familiar with it. This survey also indicated that 41% did not have a family physician. The survey did indicate that 75% were not satisfied with their current medical services.

Stage of life cycle. Given its current utilization pattern, potential demand in the community, and lack of marketing, the Center is still in the early stages of the Growth Phase.

Physician attitudes. The physician staff from the return of 24% of the surveys sent to the medical staff of Enterprise Hospital indicated the staff had significant desire to see the Center prosper for future referrals, definitely were apprehensive about advertising the Center or using more sophisticated marketing techniques, did not fully understand the role of marketing, and blamed the administration for the Center's not being prosperous. The four physicians assigned to the Center were very enthused and ambitious about the Center and were, of course, most interested that quality medical care be provided. They were a lot more receptive to using other marketing techniques for the Center.

Audit Conclusion

Opportunities. It is apparent that the Care Center has the potential for complementing Enterprise Hospital; may provide new sources of patients for the hospital and the medical staff; can fill a niche in the marketplace for providing ambulatory services to the public; is off to a good start despite the fact that very little marketing has been done; appears to have strong loyalty of those clients who have used the service; has potential in new segments of the S.F. County area plus other counties; possesses a strong financial backing; is well staffed; has good access; is priced reasonably; has the backing of administration and the Board of Directors; has a quality-oriented, long-standing, and competitively strong hospital as a foundation; and needs to explore new service development such as same-day surgery.

Risks. The risks which the Center needs to address include the current and future competition for the same client base; the need to attract more support from the medical staff; a stagnant population growth; attempts to attract clients from other counties in which additional competition is materializing; sensitivity to the medical staff's and board's attitudes about marketing; lack of marketing personnel for implementation; and the need to diversify its referral sources due to a total dependence on S.F. patient origin.

Market Segmentation

Based on the audit information and analysis, the following segments are currently or have the potential to interact with the Care Center:

1. All residents in the county of San Francisco;
2. Residents in other counties in the Bay Area;
3. Hospital's medical staff;
4. Other physicians in the community;
5. Employees of private clinics;
6. Local businesses;
7. The senior care marketplace;
8. Other health agencies and organizations in the community;
9. Commuters and transportation centers;
10. Media;
11. Police/Fire Departments/Ambulance Services;
12. Community associations and groups;
13. Insurance companies;
14. Schools and students;
15. The population group without a physician;
16. The loyal group (30% referrals by existing patients);

17. All current clients;
18. The Hospital staff, administration, and board;
19. Other health institutions in the community;
20. 18-40 year old service workers;
21. Tourists;
22. Religious groups;
23. Industrial injury groups;
24. Workman compensation groups;
25. Downtown white collar workers;
26. New San Francisco residents;
27. Apartment dwellers near Center;
28. Hotels and motels;
29. Rent-a-car centers;
30. Immigration offices;
31. Singles: heterosexual and homosexual groups;
32. Airline agents;
33. S.F. Chamber of Commerce and Information Bureaus;
34. Travel associations such as car clubs;
35. Medical interns and nursing students in local professional schools;
36. Day care centers in the city;
37. Shoppers/department stores/boutiques;
38. Specific ethnic groups: Spanish, Chinese, etc.;
39. Conventions;
40. Local government workers;
41. Construction workers;
42. Local Realtors and bankers;

Market Targeting

Of the segments identified in the prior section, the primary and secondary target groups which deserve the most attention can be prioritized. The primary and secondary targets are being limited initially to ten target groups for the sake of length.

Primary Targets

The primary targets will merit our initial marketing strategies as they concentrate on large segments of the Center's publics which can provide quick returns on the Center's marketing investment. In many cases a formal cost-benefit study comparing the main segments can be very useful in prioritizing these target groups.

1. Commuters and workers in the financial district in service industries;
2. General population in San Francisco;
3. Qun (hospital and care center medical providers and staff);
4. Other health organizations in the County of San Francisco.

Secondary Targets

These target groups will be addressed after the initial strategies are implemented and evaluated for the primary target groups. They can also be utilized as back-up groups in case the primary groups are not as effective as desired.

1. Local residents without a family physician;
2. Local businesses;
3. Other medical providers in the community: i.e., physicians, dentists, therapists, etc.
4. Residents of other counties;
5. Fire Dept./Police Dept./Ambulance services;
6. Tourists;
7. Senior citizens in community.

Market Positioning

In marketing the Center the strategies can be directed to making the Center unique in the minds of the consumers and medical providers. The major perceptions of the Center which are most promising are positioning the Center as:

1. "The" all-purpose ambulatory care Center in San Francisco;
2. A convenient, easily accessible, Center;
3. A Center which will save clients money on not having to stay overnight in the main hospital;
4. The Center which maintains the quality care and mission of the hospital;
5. A way for patients to avoid the emergency room when it is not a serious problem;
6. The family physician for many clients who do not possess one;
7. The Center which has excellently trained and personable physicians, nurses, and staff;
8. Not a competitor to the emergency room but a complement to it and better in terms of time, money, access, convenience, and comfort;
9. Equal if not better qualified to handle non-threatening illnesses and injuries;
10. A Center which is safe and backed by the excellent facilities and services of the hospital;
11. An innovator in providing medical care;
12. Better coordinator with the patient's regular doctor (i.e., medical record sent to primary physician after visit);
13. The Center which provides individual attention and care;
14. "One stop shopping" for minor and intermediate services;
15. An information center for other human resources in the community;
16. Having the positioning statement: "The complete medical service Center where no appointment is needed, the doctor is always available, and the caring never ceases"; or "Caring Center: the emergency room alternative for you and your family";
17. Not just for emergencies but for routine medical care – colds, flu, aches, and pains.

Market Strategies and Tactics

The following sample strategies and tactics are being developed to satisfy *Goal #1* and *Objectives 1 & 2* related to increasing the number of clients utilizing the Care Center and is directed to the main target groups of commuters, local residents, and medical staff of the hospital. Strategy #4 is presented as an array of different tactics to satisfy various goals and target groups. It is important to remember that actual public relations activities are tactics and are interwoven into these tactical examples.

Strategy #1: Promote the Care Center through advertisement, education, public relations, direct mail, and personal selling.

   Tactics: Targeted to Commuter and General Public

   1. Develop an article on emerging trends in urgent care centers with Care Center as the key case study.
   2. Develop an advertisement in the local newspaper which is most widely read by commuters.
   3. Arrange to have some of the Center's doctors on discussion shows in town.
   4. Develop a thorough brochure which can be distributed through the mail for residents of local areas.
   5. Have an open house for the public.
   6. Possibly arrange a supplement to be placed in utility bills or corporate pay checks.
   7. Have a series of personality talks at the Center for the public.
   8. Have give-a-ways such as stickers, brochures, or flyers at the open house or for each client who visits the center.
   9. Check on road signs near the Center.
  10. Take out ads on the morning commute radio stations.
  11. Take out ads on public transportation with tear-out coupons.
  12. Develop an ongoing newsletter to be mailed to residents.

Strategy #2: Communicate with hospital medical staff for reciprocal benefits.

   Tactics: Targeted to Hospital and Center Medical Staff

   1. Meet with family practitioners, pediatricians, and specialists and give a little educational session on marketing and the potential for referrals from the Center and that no significant drop in emergency room visits should occur.

2. Discuss the importance of evening and weekend coverage for their patients.
3. Show examples of quality promotion tools for the Center of which the medical staff would be proud to which they would be associated.
4. Have the medical staff meet and walk with the four main physicians in the Center.
5. Develop a newsletter to keep the medical staff up-to-date on Center activities.

Strategy #3: Develop a referral process from other health organizations.

Tactics: Targeted to Community Health Programs

1. Send personalized letters and brochures to administrators and clinicians in other hospitals, long-term care institutions, human service agencies, etc. Invite them to tour the facility.
2. Have an open house specifically for professionals.
3. Ask for advertising or announcement space in their newsletters or journals which go out to the public or their employees.
4. Make sure every human service organization in the county receives a copy of the newsletter.
5. Make sporadic on-site visits to other human service organizations to communicate in person and show an interest in their programs as well.

Strategy #4: Develop a referral mechanism from many different sources (miscellaneous tactics for the reader's reference).

Tactics: Targeted to Many Different Segments

1. Continually obtain new resident listings and mail brochures.
2. Send letters and brochures or in person discuss Care Center with apartment owners and realtors.
3. Talk with large hotel/motel managers about posting brochures or working out an arrangement for discounts for their guests.
4. Talk with employee benefits directors of local corporations about allowing some information to be directed to employees.

5. Set up booths at conventions or trade shows holding their meetings in San Francisco.
6. Call each patient 24 hours after service is provided.
7. Maintain files for sending out birthday and Christmas cards, etc., to patients or local businesses.
8. Contact department store managers about having posters or brochures about the clinic placed in high-traffic areas.
9. Contact local businesses about referral sources.
10. Provide free bus passes for public transportation for those potential clients who do not have cars.
11. Arrange for parking discounts in local lots.
12. Encourage repeat visits by offering discounts or family packages.
13. Advertise in airline journals and at travel agencies.
14. Get the physicians and staff involved in local social clubs, gatherings, or events.
15. Have some of the staff publish articles in health journals.
16. Arrange for Center physicians to make home visits to those patients who cannot make it to the Center.
17. Contract with a transportation firm for greater access for incapacitated patients.
18. Concentrate on nursing homes and board and care facilities in the vicinity for elderly clients.
19. Hire staff who are bilingual in Chinese or Spanish.
20. Develop a community board consisting of representation of local groups, businesses, and the general population.
21. Develop strong relationships with local and state medical and health associations, lobbyist groups, and consulting firms for referrals.
22. Develop a strong tie to United Way since they make a considerable number of referrals to clinics.
23. Investigate the use of appropriate billboards for advertisement.
24. Advertise in cultural journals such as ACT, Opera, and Symphony programs.
25. Develop a board subcommittee in marketing.
26. Since ancillary services will benefit considerably from the

Center, develop a strong marketing orientation by these staff members for the Center.

27. Contact local Social Security officials for potential referrals.
28. Possibly offer major employers an initial free physical exam for their employees if contracting can be negotiated.
29. Explore preferred provider, HMO, IPA, etc. delivery modes for the Center.
30. Develop good working relations with local Blue Cross and Blue Shield Associations.
31. Patient and public surveys should be initiated to monitor effectiveness and a community lifestyle and values.
32. Make sure a quality yellow pages ad is in place under "health," "clinic," and "emergency care."
33. Contact professional associations before they come to San Francisco for a convention for an inclusion in their program packages about the Center.
34. Advertise in KEY journals which are used in most cities to provide visitors with information about a city.
35. Contact immigration offices and travel agencies for a location to provide immunization shots.
36. Contact local unions about distributing information to their members.
37. Work with workman compensation agencies and insurance plans for potential referrals.
38. Contact local recreation departments and centers.
39. Send out periodical press releases emphasizing the uniqueness of the new service to the press.
40. Visit and distribute materials at mobile home parks in the area.
41. Contract with heavily visited restaurants in the area for shoppers, tourists, and white collar workers' information brochures or posters to be made available.

NOTE: Industrial and occupational medical services are becoming a major boost to urgent care centers. Therefore, marketing to industrial medicine clients is becoming important as companies have seen their health insurance premiums increase by 200-300%. Businesses are definitely observing urgent care centers as a possible way to reduce these costs. In addition, marketing to industry provides urgent care centers with access to large groups of patients, such as members of HMOs or PPOs. For example, several urgent care centers in Seattle have over 400 companies under informal contract and 16,000 employees under formal PPO contracts. A great strategy for this group is to land one of the largest companies, and then others will follow. Credibility by association can be a great strategy for these types of centers. Then if employees are satisfied, a multiplier impact can occur with their families and friends. In addition, it is important not to overlook the hundreds of small businesses that are present in most areas. It is also important for urgent care centers to not assume they know what businesses want in health services. Don't develop brochures before surveying your target markets! Businesses also want quick feedback on employees. For example, they want centers to call and provide a status report within the same day of the visit, and of course, they want their employees to return to work as soon as possible. In addition, having a hospital as a 24-hour backup to the urgent care center is an attraction versus the free-standing center. It is important to decide what the center should really offer; what it is capable of offering; what businesses want you to offer for their employees; and how well the center can meet this demand. Urgent care centers have only recently begun to scratch the surface of this potentially very large segment of the marketplace.

Implementation Schedule

DATE	ACTIVITY
January, 1985	Organize marketing department with a director of marketing and sub-committee or board on marketing.
February, 1985	Begin developing meetings with medical providers and staff of the center and hospital.
March, 1985	Begin developing public relations materials: brochures, flyers, ads, posters, etc.

April, 1985-May, 1985	Initiate open houses for staff, other medical providers, public, and other health organizations.
June, 1985	Initiate visits to local businesses, unions, health organizations, and social groups.
July, 1985	Initiate first phase of advertising in newspapers, radio, newsletters, etc.
August, 1985	***(Initiate cost-benefit study for control system for first six months of plan implementation.)
September, 1985	Begin mailings to local residents, businesses, etc.
October-December, 1985	Begin implementing remaining first phase of strategies and tactics.
January, 1986	***(Initiate second control evaluation for second six months of implementation phase. Lay framework for updating plan for second calendar year and implementing second phase of strategies and tactics.)

Control Systems

Two formal evaluations were to be made in August, 1985, and January, 1986 for measuring cost-effectiveness of marketing strategies and tactics versus expected marketing goals and objectives. In other words, we needed to specifically find out if we were satisfying the objectives of the marketing plan:

1. Have we increased the number of clients by 50%?
2. Have the number of private-pay patients increased by 25%?
3. Have we expanded the number of sources and mix of clients?
4. Have the number of business referrals increased by 100%?

If not, then we needed to revamp different components of the plan, for example:

1. Change targets to secondary groups;
2. Implement different tactics;
3. Re-evaluate the orchestration of the components of the marketing mix;
4. Re-examine the realism of the marketing goals and objectives;
5. Initiate some new surveys to measure psychographics; and
6. Measure which tactics are more effective than others and put more emphasis on them.

Organizational Structure of Marketing the Care Center

1. Hire a full-time director of marketing for the hospital. Initially allocate 10 hours per week of his/her time to the Center for first year.
2. Have the director of public relations and the director of fund development report to the director of marketing; 10 hours per week for first year report to Center.
3. After twelve months hire a 20-hour part-time marketer for the Center who would report to the director of marketing for the hospital; drop hours of director of marketing to five and public relations director to five.
4. The director of marketing will have direct access to the director of the Care Center and its staff.
5. The director of marketing will have direct access to the director of finance, the hospital's board, and legal counsel.
6. Formulate a subcommittee of the hospital board for marketing of which the director of marketing would be a member.
7. Organize a community relations committee for the Center which would be directed by the director of the Center and the director of marketing.

Marketing Budget for Care Center in 1985

Total budget for the center is $1,000,000. An initial request for additional sums for marketing is as follows:

Labor: Implementation and Control of Plan

10 hours/week of Dir. of Mkt.	$12,000
10 hours/week of Dir. of Public Rel.	$8,000
Administrative/secretarial support . . . P/T	$5,000
	Total $25,000

Materials

Typeset, Printing, xeroxing of Brochures, Flyers, Posters . . .	$7,000
Advertising development fees, ad agency, placement fees, rental space . . .	$15,000
	Total $22,000

Implementation Costs

Mailing Lists Purchase . . .	$1,000
Mail Order House for Stuffing, Posting of Mailings . . .	$5,000
Postage . . .	$10,000
	Total $16,000

Misc. Expenses

Travel (mileage, car rental, air fare, parking, etc., ...)	$3,000

Estimated rough budget for first year of implementation of marketing plan . . .	Total $66,000

The first year of marketing can be the most important. Therefore, the budget presented is a little more than 6% of the Care Cen-

ter's total budget. This can be a very common investment during the first year if long-term results are expected. A range for any center of this type should be a minimum of 2-3% to a maximum of 7-8%. A guideline can be 3-4% of the Center's total budget after year 1.

CHAPTER 5

Marketing Planning
for Mid-Town Health Center

Kermit M. Hunter

INTRODUCTION

The Mid-Town Health Center* is a federally funded organization for delivering primary health care in Memphis and surrounding Shelby County, Tennessee. The plan presented here represents a systematic approach to implementing a marketing concept throughout the entire organization. Before the Center embarks on a concerted effort to market externally its portfolio of services, an intensive internal marketing effort must be undertaken. The logical point to begin is with the board, the executive director, and the staff.

Furthermore, a marketing committee needs to be organized and actively involved in formulating goals and objectives. The committee should consist of board members and key staff.

If implemented properly, a marketing approach will convert the organization's reactive position to a proactive posture, with direct implications for increasing utilization and revenue. Although specific goals and objective explicit in most marketing plans are not evident here, a more general yet crucial goal of this plan is the permeation of the marketing concept throughout the Center. The goal is a model for implementing a strategic marketing management plan based on the marketing approach to planning.

---

*A pseudonym.

BACKGROUND

The Mid-Town Health Center (MHC) was formed as a private nonprofit corporation in 1970. Members of the Cotton City Medical Society* and various community constitutents organized and formed the Center. The same year, a federal Office of Economic Planning Grant was awarded to the Center to develop a health maintenance organization. During the feasibility study for this project, attention was directed to creation of a community health center project.

In 1973, all federal responsibility for neighborhood health centers was transferred to the Department of Health, Education and Welfare (DHEW) under the auspices of the Public Health Service. This reshuffling was accompanied by a commitment that these programs, renamed community health centers, would become a continuing component of the health delivery system. In 1983, MHC was still receiving funds from the Department of Health and Human Services (DHHS—DHEW's successor) under a program known as the Urban Health Intitiative. The urban Health Initiative attempts to develop integrated systems of care within a referral-driven network system. Emphasis is given to communities with the greatest need for primary care services.

MHC offices opened in a storefront in 1970 in the Downtown Shopping Plaza* with services initially consisting of dental and preventive health care delivery. In 1974, MHC obtained three trailers to be used as temporary medical and dental facilities. In the first five months of operation in the trailers, an average of 50 patients per day were seen. By 1975, the Center moved to permanent facilities.

MHC submits an annual continuation application as part of section 330 funding under the Urban Health Initiative. The regulating federal office, located in Rockville, Maryland, is the Bureau of Health Care Delivery and Assistance (formerly the Bureau of Community Health Services). This agency is a component of the Public Health Service—the Health Resources and Services Administration (HRSA). The regional office is located in Atlanta, Georgia, and is one of ten regional subdivisions of the HRSA.

---

*Pseudonyms.

The federal strategy called "positive programming" identifies priority underserved areas for the development of primary care systems. These areas must be characterized as

- medically underserved
- health manpower shortage areas
- high infant mortality areas
- high impact of migrant or seasoned workers

MHC is governed by a 21-member board representing technical, provider, and consumer members from a mixed background in the city and surrounding county. The Center has been providing primary health services for over ten years.

According to DHHS regulations, the board of directors should consist of people from community organizations, e.g., hospitals, local health departments, menthal health agencies, health planning groups, and actual consumers of the offered services.

in 1980, 58% of the people served nationally by this federal program had annual incomes of less than $6,000; 23% of the people served has no family member employed; 69% were dependent on primary care centers as their usual source of care; 89% belonged to racial or ethnic minority groups; and 40% served were under 18 years of age.

There are three sites for service within the Center's system: (1) the main center located in the southwestern part of the city (2) a satellite located in the northwestern part of the city, and (3) a satellite located in the north central portion of the city. In 1983, MHC began operating on Saturdays and evenings.

MHC's fiscal year runs from July 1 to June 30 the following year. Services, activities, and functions to be provided in Financial Year 1984—1985 included medicine, adolescent health, family planning, optometry, laboratory services, radiology, health promotion and disease prevention, medical records, social services, personnel services, fiscal services and data processing, and occupational and environmental health services. Limited family health services were to be provided at the two satellites. These two sites began delivering services in the second quarter of 1984.

SERVICE AREA DEFINITION

The service area consists of 31 census tracts in the southwest area of the city. The area is approximately 11.4 square miles in size. It is bounded by a major river and an artery of a major railroad line on the west. A major thoroughfare runs south to north on the east connecting with an interstate system at each end. The two satellite centers were located so as to help rationalize the geographic service area where the need was greatest.

Since the Center is designed for low-income residents and consumers, there is a very strict policy on registering for treatment. Procedures requiring validation of income status through proof of check stubs if employed, utility bills, personal income tax returns, and so forth are enforced. Patients are recertified as to their payment status every six months through the Center's Department of Consumer Services.

The approximate number of Medicaid recipients for the County as of December 1, 1981, was 82,000, or approximately ten percent of the county population. The MHC consumer breakdown is shown in Table 5.1.

TABLE 5.1 MHC Consumer Breakdown

Third-Part Coverage	Service Area	Patients
Medicare	Data not Available	5%
Medicaid	by Census Tracts	34%
Medicaid/Medicare	"	8%
Medicaid/SSI	"	11%
No insurance	"	42%

% of Poverty Level Income	Service Area	Patients
Over 200%	Data not Available	13%
150% – 199%	by Census Tracts	1%
100% – 149%	"	11%
Below 100%	"	75%

According to 1970 U.S. census data, less than 20% of the county population was reported as being below the poverty level. Approximately 39.04% of the 1970 population in the MHC service area was below the poverty level, ranging from a high by census tract of 84% to a low of 11%.

ECONOMIC FACTORS

The November 1981 unemployment rate for the county was 9.2%. Eighty-four percent of all users of the Center are black, and the unemployment rate among this group is about three times higher than average. Several manufacturing plants have laid workers off or shut down completely. These conditions and the overall cutback in federal financial support for domestic programs have increased utilization of MHC by the near and new poor.

AREA HEALTH RESOURCES

The Center is located in an urban community of some 800,000 residents. In addition to primary care providers, there are major medical centers contiguous to the Center's service area. There is a major teaching hospital center for the health sciences with a broad range of secondary levels of care available in the area. There are four major hospitals in Memphis, as well as a speciality children's hospital.

A breakdown of primary care physicians in the MHC service area is as follows:

Specialty	Number of Physicians
Family Practice	3
General Practice	7
Internal Medicine	59
Ob-Gyn	13
Pediatrics	2
	Total 84

PRIMARY CARE DEMAND

The Center had 54,000 total encounters in 1981, or about 17% of all primary care encounters in the service area. Utilization of the Center averages approximately 2.6 visits per patient per year.

The 1983 MHC staffing for full-time equivalent (FTE) providers was 10.01, including 4.29 primary care physicians; 0.05 surgical specialists; and 5.67 mid-level practitioners. These providers accounted for approximately 43,000 encounters during the fiscal year.

EPIDEMIOLOGICAL ANALYSIS

The infant mortality rate for Shelby County overall has remained relatively constant since 1980; the infant mortality rate for nonwhites is 20 deaths per 1000 live births. The infant mortality rate for the Center's service area is 20.9 (53 infant deaths ÷ 2,533 live births × 1000).

PLANNING MARKETING RESEARCH (PMR) OBJECTIVES FOR 1984

Formal objectives for 1984 are

1. to provide administrators and supervisors with the necessary statistical data, reports, and results of evaluation activities in order to make accurate and quick decisions
2. to update marketing and health promotion activities
3. to incorporate within the formal marketing plan a choice of services and prices for consumers
4. to conduct evaluation studies by using consumer survey data, results of Center employee surveys, and secondary data
5. to develop videotape presentations for marketing to staff and external organizations.

A long-range planning committee has been established; goals and objectives for planning purposes were to be finalized by June 30, 1984.

Promotional activities have been conducted in conjunction with a health promotion and disease prevention program. Transit buses and billboards have been used for displays. Radio public service announcements have also been developed. A slide presentation about the Center was developed in conjunction with the health promotion and disease prevention staff. These program elements were being marketed to community groups, external organizations, and key staff in 1984.

CONSUMER SERVICES

During the first half of FY 1984, 6,400 new patients were registered. Goals for consumer services in 1984 were to

1. establish new linkages with other health service agencies in the area
2. set up protocol and provide registered patients with information on emergency physician coverage during nonoperating hours
3. improve the efficiency of the switchboard system (call-sequencing equipment)
4. develop procedures for handling the transportation of physical therapy patients to and from the Center
5. increase revenue collections via better management and a patient promissory note system developed for credits in the pharmacy.

INTERNAL MARKETING

Goals were developed by the board and management for internal marketing to MHC staff. The 1984 goals were to

1. maintain a smooth and cooperative relationship among all members of the Center staff
2. minimize employee turnover; personnel has a particularly acute problem in the area of physician recruitment and retention
3. continue training and job motivation programs for employees
4. review the current manual of "Personnel Policies and Procedures" for any revisions and propose changes accordingly.

Recruitment was intensified in 1984, both nationally and locally through professional associations, professional journals, and national newspapers. The American Public Health Association and the Tennessee Association of Primary Health Care Centers have been used in this capacity.

Retention has become a problem with respect to medical personnel and other technically skilled personnel. The Center's competitive position is at a decided disadvantage because MHC cannot compete with other providers on a salary basis. Employee motivation is a related problem. To help combat this, a full-time personnel coordinator was hired in 1983 to identify and forestall personnel problems and issues. In-service programs and motivational seminars were subsequently developed. A new handbook for employees was being prepared in 1984. Personnel policies and procedures have been reviewed and updated.

To operate the extended-hours clinic, a grant was received from the Public Health Service under the Emergency Expenditure Needs Act of 1983. All unemployed residents in the service area were mailed brochures and flyers. Since its inception, the clinic has increased client utilization by ten percent per month. Other segments of the population that have increased utilization are "near poor" working patients, who cannot afford to lose a day's work, elderly patients who depend on their working relatives to bring them to the clinic, and pediatric patients with working parents.

Services Portfolio

MHC offers the following services:

- general adult medical services
- adolescent medical services
- family planning services
- physical therapy services
- patient education
- medical social services
- optometry
- obstetrics and gynecology
- laboratory services
- radiology

- pharmacy services
- dental services

The Center's formal Promotion and Disease Prevention Program goal is to "increase the community's awareness of preventive actions that assist in the control of hypertension, diabetes, and related risk factors, e.g., obesity, smoking and so forth." A proposed service extension in this area would be a new Occupational and Environmental Health Program. The goal would be to develop and implement a comprehensive range of services for employee groups and employees.

FINANCIAL HISTORY

For more than ten years, MHC has been serving Memphis, beginning as a small preventive health care organization serving only a few thousand residents of south Memphis. By 1983, the agency was delivering 43,000 comprehensive ambulatory health care visits to over 4,000 individuals all over Memphis and Shelby County. Moreover, for the 65 practicing black physicians in Memphis, 24 started out with MHC.

1979–1980

The board was reorganized with consumers, providers, and community affairs leaders. The new board sought to clarify its role as a policymaking entity. Between 1975 and 1980, federal revenue shifted from a proportion of 90% funding to the current 55% of MHC. Patient encounters increased from 42,182 in FY 1979 to 49,206 in FY 1980. In 1977, a Family Planning Program was added; in 1978, a Physical Therapy Department. The year 1979 brought on line the first computer system in use at an ambulatory health care facility in the country. Additionally, in 1977, the first adolescent health program was added.

From 12,123 registered patients in 1975, the Center's first year of on-site operation, the number has grown to approximately 43,000 in 1980. Of these, approximately 17,000 are active patients (used the Center at least once in the past 18 months). The number of encounters grew from 20,089 in 1975 to almost double that number, 42,000, in 1979.

By 1977, it was necessary to expand the physical plant by 2,100 square feet.

Revenue sources changed drastically between 1975 and 1976 (see Table 5.2).

TABLE 5.2. Sources of Revenue in 1975 and 1976.

Net Revenue	$FY '75	$FY '80
Self-pay patients	$2,592	$104,101
Medicare	$23,261	$130,127
Medicaid	$83,988	$499,563
Commercial insurance	$0	$92,292
Subtotal	$109,841	$826,083
Federal grant	$738,507	$1,074,561
Total	**$848,348**	**$1,900,644**

1980–1981

In FY 1981, MHC produced a surplus in revenue for the first time in five years. Through adherence to a carefully planned financial goal, MHC eliminated a previous deficit and generated a surplus of revenue over expenditures. This achievement enabled MHC to invest these revenues in facility renovation. During the year MHC expanded its space capacity by approximately 40%, or 5,394 additional square feet. Renovations created greater waiting-room space for comfort and added aesthetics.

1983

The board chairman specified the MHC mission as providing affordable health care to the medically underserved and indigent in Memphis. Revenues for FY ending June 1983 were $3,318,000 compared to the previous fiscal year total of $2,638,000. In 1984, revenues were expected to exceed $3,913,000.

MHC was requesting federal financial support in the amount of

$3,258,000 for FY 1985, a ten percent increase from the previous year. This budget reflects the expansion of the Center in the northern portion of the city. MHC projects generating $2,335,600 from other sources for a total budge of $5,593,600.

MARKETING BUDGET AND STAFF

With an annual budget approaching $6 million, management would like to insert a line item in the budget of at least one percent or $60,000 for marketing. However, the Center relies heavily upon the federal government for financial support. Because marketing is not a high priority function with the Public Health Service, previous requests by the Center for a marketing budget have been disapproved.

The Center has a director of marketing, planning, and research. However, this individual serves more as an assistant administrator. Marketing should be a specialist position, and the responsibilities of planning and research should be separate. The employee filling the marketing position has no formal training in marketing.

Market plans for the organization are brief and lack a systematic approach. Appendix A is the text of a brochure encompassing the MHC marketing approach.

Board members and staff are not involved in implementing the marketing concept. Marketing objectives are not tied to a marketing plna. There is no strategic marketing management. MHC attempts to promote the entire organization instead of specific projects.

The organization's image among local providers is not well understood. The health educator and health coordinator alternate in plan development. A marketing audit has never been performed at the Center. Service area residents have never been segmented based on benefits sought or categorical beliefs.

Promotional material is prepared without surveying the target market to determine exactly where their interests lie. The material included in the quarterly newsletter is technical and generally not appropriate for a low-income market.

The board chairman characterizes the organization as very complex with many disjointed goals and objectives. High staff turnover and morale are emphasized as management problems. Employee titudes toward patients are often negative, and general apathy was believed to permeate the organization.

RECOMMENDATIONS

Before attempting external marketing, the organization should embark on an intensive internal marketing project. The natural starting point is with the board. A weekend retreat should be held and an outside marketing consultant brought in to orient the members to the marketing concept. A marketing committee with exclusive functions should be created by the board. This committee should include a cross section of board members and staff and perhaps an outside consultant for professional guidance.

The board must be apprised of marketing planning and accept marketing philosophically as part of a comprehensive business system. Further they must understand how this system will contribute to organizational growth and income. Also, marketing must be placed in proper perspective. Education is needed to change the image of "gimmickry" associated with marketing.

The committee should meet at least quarterly to monitor progress toward marketing goals. Goals and objectives should be "up-down" and planning should be "down-up." The executive director arbitrates this process. The committee should be key in plan approval. Long-range planning should come first, and the annual implementation should be a detailed version of the first year of the long-range plan.

Regular in-service training for staff is needed to familiarize staff to the new approach. Sessions held quarterly are adequate. Steps to foster a marketing-oriented organization should include

- top management support
- effective organizational design
- better employee hiring practices
- rewarding marketing-oriented employees
- a plan for system improvement

Organizational objectives should be negotiated so that agency personnel not only feel part of the project but also are enthusiastic about carrying out their own individual portions of the task.

Marketing Plan Development

When the system for internal marketing is in effect attention may then focus on a strategic marketing management plan with the overall goal to increase utilization and revenues. Additionally, the organization must practice the marketing planning process versus the traditional health planning process (see Figure 5.1). The marketing planning process must begin with the consumer; strategies are developed for market segments, not the entire market.

There are three steps in formulating a marketing plan:

1. *Market Audit*. The audit is the first step involved in developing a marketing plan. It is systematic, comprehensive, independent, and periodic. The market audit assesses current marketing activities and the marketing environment (see Appendix B for a sample market audit structure applied to MHC).

2. *Marketing Research*. Survey instruments are developed to determine the level of satisfaction among current users. Former users are surveyed to determine reason(s) for discontinuing use, and finally a sample of nonusers is surveyed to determine why they never use the Center. This research is vital in identifying potential target market(s).

3. *Market Segmentation*. The target market is grouped into homogeneous segments of patients/consumers with similar wants and needs. Programs and services are designed based on the benefits sought or held by the segmented groups which the Center wants to pursue.

The marketing plan developed from this process must be written, reviewed, and approved by the board and updated annually. The plan should also specify a marketing budge, a schedule of tactical implementation, staff-responsibilities, and criteria for evaluation.

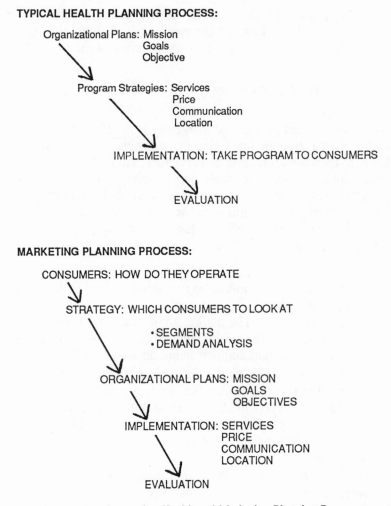

FIGURE 5.1. Comparing Health and Marketing Planning Processes

Implementing the Marketing Plan

At MHC, five potential markets have been targeted. Customers in these markets should be described along two axes: demographic and psychographic. Psychographic profiles reveal what patients want from a health facility and facilitate the design of more effective marketing strategies. This analysis should lead to a ranked table of market segments sharing demographic and/or psychographic traits across the superficial target group boundaries previously identified. Since determinants of health care quality and outcome are highly subjective, consumer satisfaction is never attributable to medical excellence alone. The burden on ambulatory care manages to understand and to meet consumer behavior expectation is particularly heavy. Segmentation provides insurance against improper categorization of customers, e.g., "everybody of 65," "black women," etc.

Because the market usually consists of multiple consumers with differing needs and because the service delivery requirement is mandated and regulated, the problem of developing and implementing a marketing plan becomes even more challenging.

Another output of the implementation phase is promotional tactics and materials based on segmentation findings. Brochures, pamphlets, newsletters, and logo/motto are common but crucial. Channels of distribution will also be determined by findings from market research. A market intelligence system should also be in place. This monitoring system should make administration more proactive to the market.

Implementing the diversified programs and services called for in the marketing plan will involve the "marketing mix." The four "Ps" of the marketing mix include price (consideration), place (channels of distribution), promotion, and product (service).

The four Ps are fairly controllable factors employed by the marketer in setting strategy and following marketing objectives. Price includes both the financial price of service and all financial activities, plus the "psychic" price experienced by users; place involves the delivery of the services and includes referral arrangements, transportation, access, and the organization's physical plant; promotion is persuasive communication by the organization to those who use or would use its services or facilities; product or service incorporates the range of services and people who use it.

The objectives of the marketing plan require monitoring so that any necessary corrective action can be taken in the second year of the plan. Monitoring progress includes monitoring target responsiveness to product/service diversification and the promotional

strategies of the plan. Progress reports must be developed and reviewed quarterly by the MHC marketing committee. These reports
will indicate the progress of the marketing plan. Each department
head should fill out a quarterly report describing marketing effects
in his/her area.

The purpose of monitoring/control is to maximize the profitability that the organization will achieve via its short-run and long-run
objectives in the marketplace. The control systems are an intrinsic
part of the marketing plan and ensures that the organization is
achieving the marketing objectives established during the planning
process. The marketing director and committee diagnose any serious deviations in performance and choose corrective actions to
close the gap. The monitoring of the marketing plan will be built
into the MHC management information system to be developed.
This integration into the management information system comes by
way of a report-generating system that highlights variances from
"acceptable range" performance.

Each marketing strategy employed is continually evaluated, and
adjustments to the marketing plan are made when necessary. A self-
appraisal approach to evaluating and controlling the marketing
plan's effectiveness is well suited to MHC. Consequently self-ap-
praisal forms should be developed for staff with responsibilities in
(1) marketing and its effect on the Center, (2) the marketing planning system, and (3) the promotion and support systems.

Once self-evaluation input is evaluated by the marketing director,
he/she must make immediate changes or prepare an implementation
schedule for changes.

Appendix A to Chapter 5:
Mid-Town Health Center, Inc.:
Our Goals and Our Commitments

Goal #1: To provide comprehensive high quality mix of health
services for the City of Memphis and particularly the residents of
South Memphis.

As a comprehensive community health center, Mid-Town Health
Center offers its patients the broadest possible range of health services available in an out-patient, or ambulatory, setting. These ser-

vices include general medical care, pediatrics, prenatal care and gynecology, optometry, dental care, health education, x-ray services, laboratory services, physical therapy, and pharmacy services.

In addition, special programs aimed at particular patient populations are offered, such as the Family Planning Program, Adolescent Health Services, and the Home Health Program.

Beyond the convenience and cost-efficiency of comprehensive services being provided at one location, Mid-Town Health Center patients also benefit from the quality of services offered. That quality is demonstrated by both the training and credentials of the Center's staff and by the state-of-the-art technology of the equipment available in all departments.

All of the Center's full-time physicians are board certified or board eligible. Nurse practitioners, who follow medical protocols and work under physicians' supervision, all have years of training and experience in their specific fields.

The management of the Mid-Town Health Center exhibits this same high degree of expertise, experience, and education. All directors of the health center hold advanced degrees, and combined, the center's administration has over 73 years of experience working in a hospital, ambulatory health care, and/or academic settings, yet neither the staff nor the organization is content with current levels of expertise. Recognizing the ever-changing nature of medicine and health care, the agency is committed to continuing education for all levels of the staff.

New equipment and procedures in the laboratory, radiology, physical therapy, and data departments also exemplify Mid-Town Health Center's commitment to the provision of high quality, efficient services. In our laboratory department, for example, recently acquired computerized equipment increases the accuracy of test results, greatly reduces turnaround time in the laboratory, and increases patient flow. During this fiscal year, the radiology department has expanded its capabilities to include several new diagnostic and treatment procedures. These include the air-contrast upper GI (gastrointestinal) series and air barium enemas. Patients suffering from neck pain now have access to the Intermittent Cervical Traction Unit recently acquired by the Center's physical therapy department.

The installation of an on-line computer system has enhanced the efficiency, accuracy, and quality of services in virtually all departments of the health center. It has made both our appointment and billing systems more accurate, and it has increased the efficiency of record-keeping and data gathering for reports submitted by our Planning Department. With automated systems, the pharmacy department is able to maintain a complete drug profile on each patient and to keep an inventory of all supplies. The medical records department uses this system to gather the medical audit data necessary to implement the Center's quality assurance program.

Goal #2: To maximize the utilization of available resources by determining which services may be offered effectively and efficiently and arranging for the provision of certain services outside the Center through the development and implementation of linkages and referral arrangements with existing providers of health delivery in the community at large.

In order to assure high quality services at a reasonable cost, the Mid-Town Health Center is constantly evaluating its services on an ongoing basis. This evaluation is designed to reflect the attitude of patients toward services received and the cost of providing these services. Special arrangements have been made for the provision of certain services to our patients. Obstetrical-gynecological services are provided at the Mid-Town Health Center through arrangements with Board Certified OB-GYNs in private practice and with the University Center for the Health Sciences. On-site eye care is available to our patients through an arrangement with the Shelby College of Optometry. Mental health services are available through linkages with the Southwest Menthal Health Center and the MHC Department of Social Services.

Hospital care is available through the City Hospital, and with other hospitals upon patient admission by one of our physician providers.

Goal #3: To insure the availability of health services by maintaining clinic hours that allow working persons to receive health care without having to miss work and forego the earnings associated with that work.

One aspect of accessible health care is to make services available to patients at a convenient time and convenient place. Patients can schedule appointments for most services after their work hours or early in the morning prior to going to work. In addition, the Center's physicians are on call after hours to handle emergency situations at one of the local hospitals.

Goal #4: To insure the availability of health services by maintaining clinic outreach services that could either deliver some type of care in the home and/or provide transportation.

Home health care is available through the Mid-Town Health Center to provide skilled nursing care and other routine services for Mid-Town Health Center patients requiring care in the home.

Transportation services are available for elderly patients, the handicapped, disabled, or for those families on AFDC (Aid to Families with Dependent Children) who are without any other means of transportation to and from the Mid-Town Health Center.

Goal #5: To maximize the acceptance and recognition of the Center in the community through the establishment of referral networks and arrangements, linkages with existing modes of health delivery, positive public relations, information dissemination, and establishment of an overall marketing approach.

Regardless of the quality and comprehensiveness of services and staff of Mid-Town Health Center, unless the public is aware of us and what we do, the health center cannot function at its maximum level. We must be known to our patients, potential patients, and other health care providers and agencies. such awareness, especially among other health care providers/agencies, fosters a higher quality of patient care. Recognizing this need, Mid-Town Health Center has established referral networks and entered into linkage relationships with various agencies. These agencies include Southwest Mental Health Center; Children's Hospital; City Hospital' Women's Hospital and the University Department of Obstetrics and Gynecology; Shelby College of Optometry; Comprehensive Home

Health Care; University Center for the Health Sciences, School of Physical Therapy; and Disabled Children's Hospital. To further co-ordinate health services available to Memphis residents, the health center participates in several coalitions and consortiums, such as the High Blood Pressure Coalition, the Patient Education Committee, and the Wellness Task Force of the Medical Center Council.

Goal #6: To provide proper management controls through the design, implementation, and revision of the necessary policies, procedures, and control systems.

The key element in the success of an organization is the effectiveness of its management. Attaining effective management requires the use of proper management controls which assure the effective and efficient use of available resources in day-to-day operations. The Center is constantly reviewing its policies, procedures, and methods and, as necessary, revising them in order that the management control system will bring about the desired goals.

Goal #7: To maximize the recapture of revenues generated as a result of service delivery in the Center.

The financial well-being of the Center is essential to its continued existence. A major goal of the Center is to maximize the collection of money for services rendered from commercial insurance companies, Medicaid, Medicare, other third-party payors, and the patients themselves.

The process begins with the registration or re-registration of patients. It is axiomatic that accurate registration data is the foundation for achieving the best collection results. Any misinformation, intentional or not, any withholding of data, any oversight, or any recording errors will, in addition to causing a great deal of wasted time, effort, and money, result in lowered collections. The process continues through the rendering of services and the accurate recording and compiling of data regarding those services. At the Center, this and the subsequent parts of the process are enhanced by an on-line computer system. The on-line computer system allows data concerning services to be entered into the computer files immediately after the services are rendered. The final phase of the process is the development of the billing documents and their subsequent handling. Bills that are delivered to the payor promptly, that are accurate and complete, are paid without delay. It is the Center's task to ensure that the latter happens and to follow up immediately when it does not.

Successful achievement of the collection goal is measured by the dollars collected and the size and age of the accounts receivable.

Goal #8: To establish an ongoing rapport with the medical community in order to insure the availability of physician services for the Center in the future.

The Center has an ongoing program to maintain close ties with various health organizations in the community. Members of the Cotton City Medical Society and the Health Professionals Association serve on our board of directors. Members of the provider and administrative staff are members of the local and national professional organizations. Ties are maintained with the University Center for the Health Sciences which promote our mutual interests. These and actual contractual working relationships with providers all act to enhance the Center's image as a desirable place to practice the medical and dental arts.

Goal #9: To provide the community with health education and patient education programs required to foster positive health behavior.

At Mid-Town Health Center, health education is perceived as a vital, integral part of ongoing patient care services. Thus, individual one-to-one counseling occurs, as well as large group educational sessions, in conjunction with several specific patient care programs. These include the Dental Hygiene Programs held bi-monthly, a monthly series of classes for young expectant parents, and Natural Family Planning courses for couples choosing this method of birth control. Additionally, staff at Mid-Town Health Center are actively involved with a number of professional and community-based groups interested in providing patient and community education.

One of the major obstacles of the health education program has been the lack of adequate space. This problem has been overcome, however, with the completion of the renovation project at the Downtown Shopping Plaza site. This facility will have ample space for classroom activities and for storage and distribution of educational materials. In fact, with the anticipated growth of the Center's Health Education Department, this services will come to be seen as a resource for the entire community.

Goal #10: To assure accessibility to quality health services for the children and youth of Memphis.

Mid-Town Health Center recognizes that the only long-term hope for a healthy community lies in raising healthy children and youth. We are committed to working toward not only the physical health of our young people but also striving for their emotional, educational, and social well-being. To this end, the health center participates in the Early Periodic Screening, Detection, and Treatment (EPSDT) Program for children. This program is designed to detect, treat, or refer for developmental problems and chronic diseases. The pediatricians and nurse practitioners at the health center also conduct school physical exams, give immunizations, and provide adolescent health care services. Our dentists and dental hygienists offer a full range of preventive dentistry services aimed specifically at patients under 18 years of age.

Provider, support, and administrative staff at the health center have been very involved with area schools. This involvement ranges from doing outreach, telling parents, groups, and students about services at the Center; speaking to students on various health topics; participating in workshops with health teachers; speaking at award programs and registering families with preschool children; and participating in career days at several high school and junior high schools. Through such programs and activities, we have increased the accessibility of health services for the young of our community; we have also served as role models for their future.

Goal #11: To provide some employment opportunities for residents of Memphis.

In addition to providing a comprehensive range and mix of quality health services, the Mid-Town Health Center provides employment opportunities for residents of its target area. Over 75% of the employees of the Mid-Town Health Center currently reside in the Center's target area.

The Center has been a training center for medical students, nurse clinicians, optometry students, social work students, CETA workers, medical assistants, nurse assistants, laboratory assistants, health administration students, and selected high school students.

The Center's location, its employment practices, and much of its purchasing of various goods and services help to keep income within the inner City of Memphis.

Appendix B to Chapter 5:
A Simplified Marketing Audit for
Health Care Organizations:
Who Speaks for Your Center

PART I. THE MARKETING ENVIRONMENT REVIEW

A. MARKETS

    1. Who are the Center's major markets and publics?

        A. The medically underserved and indigent population

        B. Housing projects

        C. Employer groups

        D. Churches

        E. Schools (Primary, secondary, and day care)

        F. _____

        G. Plans -- for senior citizens groups, county government

        H. _____

    2. What are the major market segments in each market?

        A. Geographic by census tract

        B. Age and sex for service development and delivery

        C. Income

        D. Education -- above high school and below

        E. Family Life Education

        F. Family planning

        G. Adolescent

        H. _____

3. What are the present and expected future size and the
    characteristics of each market or market segment?

    A. Using 1970 and 1980 census data, it appears that all age

    B. segments except the 25-44 year age groups have remained

    C. constant, however, in the aforementioned group there was a

    D. 10 percent increase.

    E. _____

    F. _____

    G. _____

    H. _____

B. CONSUMERS

    1. How do the consumers make their decisions to use your
        services?

        A. Research required

        B. _____

        C. _____

        D. _____

        E. _____

        F. _____

        G. _____

        H. _____

    2. How do the consumers feel toward, and see, the center? How do
        you know?

        A. Survey to be conducted

        _____

        B. _____

        _____

        C. _____

        _____

        D. _____

        _____

        E. _____

        _____

F. _____

_____

G. _____

_____

H. _____

_____

3. What is the present and expected future state of client needs
    and satisfaction?

A. Client needs will continue to increase _____

B. _____

C. _____

D. _____

E. _____

F. _____

G. _____

H. _____

C. COMPETITORS

1. Who are the center's major competitors?

A. Physicians in the service area: 3 family practice: 7 _____

B. general practice: 59 internal medicine: 13 OB-GYN: and 2 _

C. pediatricians. Minor competitors are University Center _____

D. for the Health Sciences, Lutheran Hospital Central, _____

E. Southern Hospital, Children's Hospital, St. Peter's _____

F. Hospital, and the Regional Medical Center. _____

2. What trends can be foreseen in competitions?

A. PPOs; Physician group practices _____

_____

B. Emergency medical -- Ambulatory surgical center _____

_____

C. Hospital outpatient department/free standing _____

_____

D. Hospital home health systems _____

_____

E. _____

_____

D.   MACROENVIRONMENT

   1.   What are the main relevant developments with respect to
        demography, economy, technology, government, and culture that
        will affect the center's situation?

        A. Population shift with downtown development toward _____

           _____ upper income bracket _____

        B. Shift in the aged population service _____

           _____

        C. Cultural value systems are in need of revamping, e.g., ___

           ___ free health care _____

        D. Local government may reimburse the center for indigent ___

           ___ care _____

        E. Strategy to develop satellite centers within the higher __

           ___ income area _____

        F. 3rd party reimbursement mechanism at the state level -- __

           ___ under the controller's office _____

        G. House Bill 1843 _____

           _____

        H. _____

           _____

PART II. THE MARKETING SYSTEM REVIEW

A.   OBJECTIVES

   1.   What are the center's long-run and short-run overall
        objectives and marketing objectives?

        A. To provide a comprehensive high quality mix of health ____

           ___ services for the city and particularly the southern part

        B. To insure the availability of health services by maintain-

           ___ ing accessible clinic hours for all classes of residents

        C. To provide proper management controls through the design, _

           ___ implementation, and revision of the necessary policies _

D. <u>To maximize the recoupment of revenues generated as a</u>

   <u>result of service delivery to the center</u>

E. <u>To provide the community with health education programs</u>

   <u>required to foster positive health behavior . . .</u>

Marketing goals and objectives are fragmented.

2. Are the objectives stated in a clear hierarchical order and in a form that permits planning and measurement of achievement?

       ____ Yes   _X_ No

3. Are the marketing objectives reasonable for the center given its competitive position, resources, and opportunities?

       ____ Yes   ____ No

Comments:

   <u>Marketing objectives are not centrally located. Some are</u>

   <u>found under the organization's long range planning goals</u>

   <u>and objectives.</u>

   <u>Further, these goals are not time phased and measurable.</u>

   _____

   _____

   _____

   _____

   _____

   _____

   _____

   _____

   _____

   _____

   _____

   _____

B. PROGRAM

1. What is the center's core strategy for achieving its objectives, and is it likely to succeed?

   <u>There are many core strategies; the problem is fitting</u>

   <u>together all the pieces.</u>

   _____

2. Has the center allocated enough resources to accomplish the marketing tasks?

   It appears that the manpower, finances, and facilities are

   sufficient.

3. Are the marketing resources allocated optimally to the various markets, territories, and services of the center?

   A. Optimally allocated are the resources for developing

      additional market segments through development of the

   B. satellite facilities.

   C. _____

   D. _____

   E. _____

4. Are the marketing resources allocated optimally to the major elements of the center's marketing mix?

   A. This point is debatable. On the surface it appears so,

      however, after reviewing carefully the resources and the

   B. marketing mix, there are some inequalities of match.

   C. _____

   D. _____

C. IMPLEMENTATION

   1. Does the center develop an annual marketing plan? Is the planning procedure effective?

      _____ Yes   __X__ No

   2. Does the center implement control procedures (monthly, quarterly, et cetera) to insure that its annual plan objectives are being achieved?

      _____ Yes   __X__ No

D. ORGANIZATION

1. Does the center have some type of marketer to analyze, plan, and implement the marketing work of the organization?

   __X__ Yes   _____ No

2. Are the other persons in the center aware of, and involved in some way, in the marketing activities of the center? Is there a need for more training in marketing?

   _____ Yes   _____ No

   Other people are involved in the marketing activities but more training is needed.

3. Do the center's personnel understand and practice the marketing concept?

   _____ Yes   __X__ No

PART III. DETAILED MARKETING ACTIVITY REVIEW

A. PRODUCTS (SERVICES)

1. What are the main products (services) of the center?

   A. Adult Health Care

   B. Dental Care

   C. Family Planning

   D. General Medical Care

   E. Health Education and Counseling

   F. Home Health Services

   G. Immunizations

   H. Laboratory Services

   I. Obstetrics and Gynecology

   J. Optometry

   K. Pediatrics

   L. Pharmacy Services

   M. Radiology

   N. Physical Therapy

   O. Social Services

   P. Referral Services

2. Should any services be phased out?   No

   A. None

   B.

   C.

   D.

3.   Should any services be added?   Yes

A. There are no care services in need of addition, only

B. peripheral services on features such as a computerized EKG

C. machine.

D. _____

4.   What is the general state of "health" of each service--and
     the service mix--as a whole?

     Transportation

     Social Services

     Family Planning

     Marketing

     Financial Planning

     _____

     _____

     _____

     _____

     _____

     _____

     _____

     _____

     _____

     _____

B.   PRICE (BUDGET)

1.   What budget cuts have occurred which affect your service
     offering?

     A. None as of yet.

     B. _____

     C. _____

     D. _____

     E. _____

     F. _____

     G. _____

     H. _____

     I. _____

     J. _____

2. What additional budget allocations have allowed your service offerings to be increased?

A. Expansion funds for satellite development _____

B. New market development _____

C. Services have been differentiated with the breadth and ___

D. depth of delivery patterns. _____

E. _____

F. _____

G. _____

H. _____

I. _____

J. _____

3. How have any decreases/increases in services affected your clients (patients)?

A. Services have not been increased/decreased _____

B. Home Health is expanded _____

C. _____

D. _____

E. _____

F. _____

G. _____

H. _____

I. _____

J. _____

4. What would the likely response of demand be to increased or decreased services by your center?

A. Decreasing services would be viewed in a negative way. _____

_____

B. _____

_____

C. _____

_____

D. _____

_____

E. _____

_____

5. What can your center do to maintain or increase budget allocations?

A. Comply with the financial and clinical indicators to marketing

B. Patient indicators - all the indicators

C. Political and community support -- public officials

D. Meet the required indicators of 4200 encounters per FTE

E. Physician: Keep administrative cost below 16%; maintain cost per encounter at $18 - 26; Collectables at 90% of billings and charges to cost at 80%

C.   PROMOTION (HEALTH EDUCATION, PUBLIC RELATIONS)

1. Does your center advertise at all?

    __X__ Yes   _____ No

2. Is your center associated or aligned with any other organization which does advertise?

    _____ Yes   __X__ No

3. Does your center have a carefully formulated program of publicity/public relations?

    _____ Yes   __X__ No

4. Does your center run public service messages for the community?

    __X__ Yes   _____ No

5. Does your center distribute public service announcements and posters to public buildings?

    __X__ Yes   _____ No

6. Does your center offer any type of promotional material to inform and remind the public of its offerings?

    __X__ Yes   _____ No

7. Are members of your center staff involved with public relations/community activities?

    __X__ Yes   _____ No

NOTE: Go back through 1-7 above and examine each. Is the "promotional" or the "marketing" concept used in each?

Comments: _____

_____

_____

D.   PLACE (LOCATION)

1. Is your center conveniently located within the service radius it was originally designed for?

      __X__ Yes   _____ No

    Each center site is located in the proper place.

    _____

    _____

    _____

    _____

2. Does your center make _frequent_ visits to schools and other institutions to provide site services?

    Yes_____

    Health educators_____

    School health educators_____

    Dental_____

    _____

    _____

3. Are there methods by which your center could improve on-the-site service?

    Patient flow_____

    Employee attitudes and accountability_____

    Waiting time_____

    Aesthetics at waiting time_____

    _____

    _____

4. What are the population shifts for your service area? Will
    this affect the service you are able to provide in the
    future?

    No, any population shifts have been more than compensated for

    through the development of the two satellite facilities.

    _____

    _____

    _____

    _____

DETERMINATION OF A MARKET POSITION (NICHE)

1. DETERMINE, THROUGH A SITUATION ANALYSIS, YOUR CURRENT POSITION:

    A. What business are we currently in?

        Providing life enhancement to service area residents

        _____

        _____

        _____

        _____

    B. How do our "clients" currently view us?

        Research required

        _____

        _____

        _____

        _____

2. ESTABLISH YOUR MARKET POSITION OPTIONS:

    A. What does the market need and want?

        1) From an epidemiological perspective:

        2)   a.   reduction in the infant mortality rate

        3)   b.   reduction in hypertension, obesity, diabetes . . .

        4) Research is needed to determine felt need.

        5) _____

        6) _____

B. How do you know? (List your informational sources, etc.)

    1) Health System. Agency's five year plan.

    2) Needs Demand Assessment

    3) _____

    4) _____

    5) _____

    6) _____

C. What are the key factors required for success?

    1) Education

    _____

    2) Monitoring

    _____

    3) Evaluation and more education from a health standpoint

    _____

    4) _____

    _____

    5) _____

    _____

    6) _____

    _____

D. How can we make our services distinctive and develop a
    competitive advantage (find our "niche")?

    1) Delivery patterns

    _____

    2) Community responsiveness

    _____

    3) Employee attitude toward patients

    _____

    4) Innovative repositioning such as with the medical
       community

    5) _____

    _____

    6) _____

    _____

3.   WHAT MARKET POSITION DO WE WANT?

    A.   What business do we want to be in?

        1) Wholeness health care delivery _____

        2) _____

        3) _____

        4) _____

        5) _____

    B.   How big can we afford to be?

        As big as we are, the strategy presently is share maintenance
        and growth in new markets where satellite centers are
        operating.

        There is an uncontrollable factor and that is the funding
        level of the public health service.

    C.   Do we have the resources to achieve our desired position?

        For the most part, Yes.

D. Do we have the resources to maintain the position we already hold?

Yes _____

_____

_____

_____

_____

_____

_____

_____

_____

_____

_____

E. How many market positions ("niches") should we hold? Why?

Two -- 1. We presently serve the indigent. _____

_____ 2. We must develop a strategy to increase full pay

_____ patients through market development. _____

_____

_____

_____

_____

_____

_____

_____

_____

_____

_____

_____

_____

_____

_____

_____

4.   WHAT STRATEGY SHOULD WE FOLLOW TO ACHIEVE OUR CHOSEN POSITION?

    A.   How should we place, in order of importance, the target markets we have chosen?

       1) Each market is equally important. _____

       2) _____

       3) _____

       4) _____

       5) _____

       6) _____

       7) _____

       8) _____

       9) _____

      10) _____

      11) _____

    B.   How can we best set up our service-mix in order to provide the best system effort for our client?

       1) Prenatal -- Education, especially nutritional counseling

       2) Family Planning -- Education training programs

       3) Adult Health monitoring technique and training

       4) Geriatric -- maintenance -- social environment

       5) Adolescent -- family life education, social activities

       6) _____

       7) _____

       8) _____

       9) _____

      10) _____

      11) _____

HEALTH SERVICE MIX - A PLAN

1.   DEVELOP A SERVICES' INVENTORY FOR:

    A.   Our Center:

       1) _____

           _____

       2) _____

           _____

3) _____

_____

4) _____

_____

5) _____

_____

6) _____

_____

7) _____

_____

8) _____

_____

9) _____

_____

10) _____

_____

11) _____

_____

B. Our Competition:

1) _____

_____

2) _____

_____

3) _____

_____

4) _____

_____

5) _____

_____

6) _____

_____

7) _____

_____

8) _____
_____

9) _____
_____

10) _____
_____

11) _____
_____

2. DETERMINE THE MARKET AND THE MARKET SIZE FOR OUR SERVICES AND OUR
    COMPETITORS:

    A. Our Market:

        __Indigent_____
        __Industrial_____
        __School_____
        __Churches_____
        _____
        _____
        _____
        _____
        _____
        _____
        _____

        Our Competitors' Markets:

        __Indigent_____
        __Middle Class_____
        __Upper Class_____
        __Industrial_____
        _____
        _____
        _____
        _____
        _____
        _____

B.   Our Market Size:

   Approximately 80,000

   Our Competitors' Market Sizes:

   Approximately 100,000 +

3.   DETERMINE THE FUTURE FOR EACH OF OUR SERVICES:

   A.   To Increase Growth:

      1) _Section A, B, and C to be completed after consultation_

         with K. Hunter

      2) _____

      3) _____

4) _____

_____

5) _____

_____

B. To Maintain Status Quo:

1) _____

_____

2) _____

_____

3) _____

_____

4) _____

_____

5) _____

_____

C. To Demarket:

1) _____

_____

2) _____

_____

3) _____

_____

4) _____

_____

5) _____

_____

4. DEVELOP CENTER'S PRODUCT (SERVICE) MIX:

	What Services	To What Market
1)	Occupational Service	Industrial
2)	Adolescent Services	School Age
3)	Family Planning	Male and Female 15-44 Age

4) <u>Geriatric Service</u>   <u>Over 64 Age Group</u>

5) <u>Adult Health</u>   <u>18-64 Age Group</u>

6) <u>Prenatal Services</u>   <u>Expectant Females</u>

5. DEVELOP MARKETING OBJECTIVES FOR EACH APPROPRIATE SERVICE:

	Service	Objective
1)	To be completed after external research.	
2)		
3)		
4)		
5)		
6)		

Part III

Market Auditing and Research

CHAPTER 6

Introduction to Environmental Analysis

Robert L. Berl

This chapter deals with analysis of the total environment in which the health care or social service institution must operate. This can be defined as follows:

> A company's environment consists of the firm's strengths and weaknesses, suppliers, marketing intermediaries, customers, competition, other publics, and uncontrollable external forces that affect marketing management's ability to successfully serve its target market.

This environment can be assessed through the use of a marketing audit combined with an effective marketing information system. In addition, it is necessary for the service organization to determine the level of demand that exists for the firm's services. This can be accomplished through the utilization of demand forecasting procedures. Figure 6.1 depicts this environment.

THE MARKETING AUDIT

The marketing audit is "a comprehensive, systematic, independent, and periodic examination of a company's . . . marketing environment, objectives, strategies, and activities with a view to determining problem areas and opportunities and recommending a plan of action to improve the company's marketing performance" (Kotler, 1984, p. 765). Based on this definition the components of the marketing audit are as follows:

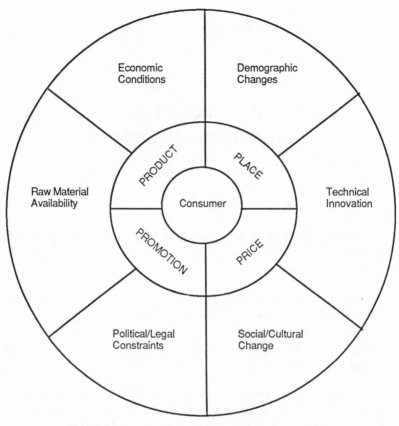

FIGURE 6.1. The Marketing Manager's Environment

Source. From *Basic Marketing: A Managerial Approach* (8th ed.) (p. 59) by E. Jerome McCarthy and William D. Perrault. Homewood, IL: Richard D. Irwin, Inc. Copyright 1984. Adapted by permission.

Marketing environment. This phase of the audit should examine such uncontrollable factors as the company's markets, customers, competitors, distributors, suppliers, and facilitators. It should take into account the uncontrollable variables such as demographic changes, economic conditions, raw material availability, technological innovations, political/legal constraints, social and cultural changes, and the like.

Marketing strategy environment. Company objectives and marketing strategies should be evaluated to determine if they are consistent with the current and forecasted marketing environment.

Marketing organization environment. This portion of the audit requires the company to assess the capability of the marketing organization to implement the necessary strategy for the forecasted environment.

Marketing systems environment. The quality of the firm's system for analysis, planning, and control should be evaluated.

Marketing productivity environment. This phase of the audit deals with determining the profitability of the company's marketing activities and the cost-effectiveness of marketing expenditures.

Marketing function environment. The marketing variables of products, price, distribution, sales force, advertising, sales promotion, publicity, and the like should be critically evaluated.

Figure 6.2 links the marketing audit to the corporate/marketing strategy process. As an example, the shift of population from the northeastern sector of the United States to the southeast and southwest would suggest the expansion of hospital facilities in rapidly growing areas such as Florida.

THE MARKETING INFORMATION SYSTEM

A marketing information system is "an organized way of continually gathering and analyzing data to help marketing managers make decisions" (McCarthy & Perrault, 1984, p. 161). This system has two major components: internal information and external information.

Internal Information

The internal accounting system has a wealth of information. This system has a record of orders received, sales, inventory levels, receivables, payables, returns, and the like. While the information is abundant, it usually is not in a form that is readily usable by the marketing manager. The data is used for accounting purposes and normally requires a restructuring to make it useful to the marketing manager.

When the internal portion of the marketing information system is

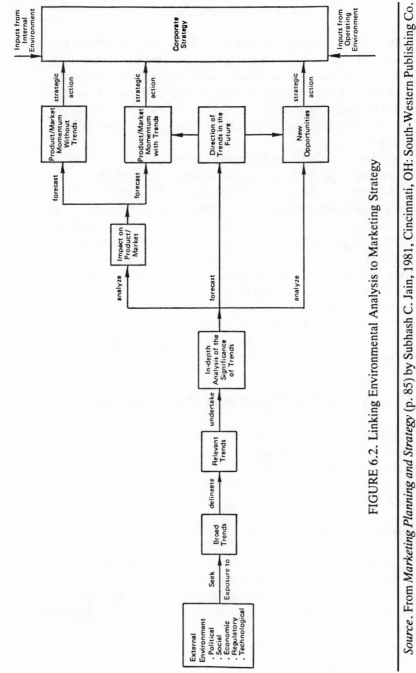

FIGURE 6.2. Linking Environmental Analysis to Marketing Strategy

Source. From *Marketing Planning and Strategy* (p. 85) by Subhash C. Jain, 1981, Cincinnati, OH: South-Western Publishing Co. Copyright 1981. Adapted by permission.

110

designed, it is important to provide only the information that is *really* needed. The system design should take into consideration what managers think they need, what marketing managers really need, and the amount of information which is economically feasible to provide. It is extremely easy to provide too much information. This overwhelms the manager and many times makes the system highly ineffective and inefficient. While the information provided should be current, if it is too current, managers may overreact to short-term sales fluctuations.

External Information

Marketing Information Needs

An organization's management require a multitude of information. In general terms, it has been determined that firms seek information about marketing problems and opportunities, acquisition leads, technical data, broad issues, and other material. Table 6.1 provides a list of the general information needs required by companies. Often marketing research is required to gather the required information.

TABLE 6.1. External Information Needs

Category	Type	General Concept
Marketing problems & opportunities	Market potential	Supply and demand consideration for market area of current or potential interest: e.g., capacity, consumption, imports, exports.
	Structural change	Mergers, acquisitions, and joint ventures involving competitors, new entries into the industry.
	Competitors & industry	General information about a competitor, industry policy, concerted actions in the industry, and so forth.
	Pricing	Effective and proposed prices for products of current and potential interest.

TABLE 6.1 (continued)

	Sales negotations	Information relating to a specific current or potential sale or contract for the firm.
	Customers	General information about current or near-potential customers, their markets, their problems.
Acquisition leads	Leads for mergers, joint ventures, or acquisitions	Information concerning possibilities for the manager's own company.
Technical data	New products, processes, & technology	Technical information relatively new and unknown to the company.
	Product problems	Problems involving existing products.
Technical data	Costs	Costs for processing, operations, and so forth for current and potential competitors, suppliers, and customers, and for proposed company activities.
	Licensing & patents	Product and processes.
Broad issues	General conditions	Events of a general nature: political, demographic, national, and so forth.
	Government actions & policies	Government decisions affecting the industry.
Other material	Suppliers & raw material	Purchasing considerations for products of current or potential interest.
	Resources available	Persons, land, and other resources possibly available for the company.
	Miscellaneous	Items not elsewhere classified.

Source. From *Marketing Planning and Strategy* (pp. 72-73). By Subhash, C. Jain. Cincinnati, OH: South-Western Publishing Co. Copyright 1981.

Suppliers of Marketing Research

Companies have many available sources which can provide marketing research. Many large firms have in-house marketing research departments. Since health care providers have "discovered marketing" only recently, many health care institutions will probably not have an in-house department. Several other options are available. Companies can ask college professors from a local college or university to design and implement a research project. Outside marketing research firms are also available. These may be classified as syndicated-service research firms and custom-design marketing research firms. Syndicated-service research firms gather periodic market information which they sell to clients. A. C. Nielsen Company is the largest of these firms and sells their clients television audience information. Custom-design firms design and implement specific research projects. The report, when completed, becomes the property of the client.

The Marketing Research Process

Marketing research is the gathering and analysis of information to help marketing managers make better decisions (McCarthy & Perrault, 1984, p. 815). Effective marketing research involves five steps: (1) defining the problem and research objectives, (2) developing the research plan, (3) collecting the information, (4) analyzing the information, and (5) presenting the findings. Figure 6.3 outlines the marketing research process.

Defining the Problem and Research Objectives: This is the *most important step* in the research process. If the problem is not correctly identified, the resulting information will not provide marketing managers with the information which is needed to make an effective marketing decision. Considering the costs associated with conducting a research study, the resulting data might well be referred to as "expensive garbage." For example, if a hospital clinic is experiencing declining revenues, it would be easy to suggest that the problem is declining sales. However, the sales decline is a symptom of some underlying problem, much as a fever is a symptom of some other malady.

FIGURE 6.3. The Marketing Research Process

Care should also be taken not to define the problem too broadly or too narrowly. If a hospital administrator told a marketing researcher to find out everything he can about patients' reactions to hospitals, the administrator would receive much more information than is needed. On the other hand, if the problem is too narrowly defined, not enough information is gathered.

Developing the Research Plan: This phase of the research process includes developing the necessary information sources, determining the research approach which is appropriate, designing the questionnaire, deciding on the proper sampling plan, and deciding on which contact method will produce the best results.

Information Sources: The second step in the research process involves the use of secondary data and, potentially, primary data. Secondary data is information that already exists and that has been collected for some other purpose. One source of secondary data is internal information. Internal information was discussed earlier in this chapter.

External secondary data is also available and would include such materials as government publications, periodicals, books, and commercial services. Normally, secondary data acts as a starting point for the research project. Seldom is secondary data found that is directly relevant to the specific project or sufficiently current that it could be relied on for decision-making purposes. However, secondary data can assist the researcher in a better understanding of the problem at hand and developing a more effective design than might otherwise be utilized. This form of data can be found relatively quickly and at a lower cost than the collection of primary data.

Primary data involves the collection of information specifically for the research project. Compared to secondary data, it is much more expensive and time-consuming. The remainder of this discussion of the marketing research process will concentrate on the collection of primary data.

Research Approaches: Primary data can be gathered using three approaches: observation, surveys, and experiments. In general, observation is used for exploratory research, surveys for descriptive research, and experiments for causal research. Observational research might entail observing patients in a doctor's waiting room to hear how they talk about the doctor and his personnel. Surveys are used to learn about the target market's knowledge, beliefs, preferences, satisfaction, and the like.

Experimental research attempts to develop causal relationships. It requires selecting matched groups of subjects, giving them different treatments, controlling for outside influences, and determining if the outcomes are significantly different. As an example, a dental clinic, with multiple locations, wants to determine if the acceptance of credit cards would increase its business. Two locations are selected which have the same characteristics (similar patient demographically, similar volume of business, and so on). For a 90-day period, credit cards are accepted at one of the locations, and patients are informed by information posters and the clinic's personnel. During this same period, credit cards are not accepted at the other location. The results are compared to see if the clinic accepting credit cards had a significantly higher volume of business than the clinic which did not permit the use of credit.

Questionnaires: Questionnaires are the most common form of re-search instruments. The careful construction of a questionnaire is essential. Responses can be influenced by the questions asked, the form of the question, the wording of the questions, and the sequencing of the questions. Some common types of questions are:

Dichotomous Questions:	Have you used an emergency health care clinic in the past?
	Yes_____ No_____
Multiple-Choice Questions:	How often in the past have you used an emergency health care clinic?
	5 or more times _____
	3 or 4 times _____
	1 or 2 times _____
	Never _____
Open-End Questions:	What is your general opinion of emergency health care clinics?

Attitude and opinion measures can also be assessed as demonstrated in Figure 6.4. Since questionnaire design is extremely difficult, the practitioner should refer to other sources which discuss this topic in greater detail.*

Sampling Plan. The first decision that must be made by the researcher is "Who is to be surveyed?" This is often not easy to ascertain. For example, if a hospital wants to gather information regarding gift shop patrons, who should be questioned? Should patrons under age 21 be questioned? How about both husbands and wives?

---

*For more information on questionnaire design, see Gilbert A. Churchill, Jr., *Marketing Research: Methodological Foundations* (3rd ed.), New York: The Dryden Press, 1983, pp. 211-240 or Paul E. Green and Donald S. Tull, *Research for Marketing Decisions* (4th ed.), Englewood Cliffs, NJ: Prentice-Hall, 1978, pp. 101-131.

(A) Please check your level of agreement with each of the following statements.

	Strongly agree	Agree	Uncertain	Disagree	Strongly disagree
(1) In general, I prefer health care emergency clinics to hospital emergency facilities.	_____	_____	_____	_____	_____
(2) Health care emergency clnics are more expensive hospital emergency facilities.	_____	_____	_____	_____	_____

(B) Please rate how important each of the following is to you in selecting a health care emergency clinic:

	Not at all Important				Very Important
(1) Price per visit	_____	_____	_____	_____	_____
(2) Waiting-room time	_____	_____	_____	_____	_____

(C) Please check the rating which best describes your feelings about the last time you used a health care emergency clinic:

	Poor	Fair	Good	Excellent
(1) Price per visit	_____	_____	_____	_____
(2) Waiting-room time	_____	_____	_____	_____

FIGURE 6.4. Questioning Methods to Measure Attitudes and Opinions

The sample size is also important. In general, larger samples give more reliable results than do smaller samples. Sample sizes can be determined mathematically. For more information regarding sample size, other marketing research books should be consulted.*

Another decision involves how respondents should be selected. Probability sampling ensures that the sample is representative and permits the researcher to infer the results to a population of interest. For example, a probability sample of 300 dental clinic patients permits the researcher to infer the results to the entire population (1,000 patients) of the clinic. If 80% of the sample indicated that they were unhappy about the attitude of the receptionist, it could be said that 80% of the clinic's patients felt that way.

Nonprobability sampling is quicker, easier, and less expensive to conduct than probability sampling. However, the use of nonprobability sampling does not provide the researcher with the ability to infer the results to the population of interest. Using the previous example, it could only be stated that 80% of the 300 person sample felt unhappy regarding the receptionist. Table 6.2 provides a list of probability and nonprobability techniques.

Contact Methods. After the sample has been selected, the next step is to determine how the sample is to be reached. Three methods are available: personal interviews, telephone interviews, and mail questionnaires. Personal interviews are much more flexible than the other two methods since they permit the interviewer to show the respondent pictures, advertising copy, and so on. It is the most expensive and time-consuming of the contact methods. Telephone interviews get a higher response rate than mail questionnaires and can be conducted very quickly. However, telephone interviewing is limited to oral communications; thus, visual aids cannot be used. The mail questionnaire is used when the respondents are spread over a wide geographic area. While mail questionnaires are the least

---

*For more information on sample size, see Danny N. Bellenger and Bellenger and Barnett A. Greenberg, *Marketing Research: A Management Information Approach*, Homewood, IL: Richard D. Irwin, 1978, pp. 153-158 or Gilbert A. Churchill, Jr., *Marketing Research: Methodological Foundations* (3rd ed.), New York: The Dryden Press, 1983, pp. 340-398 or William G. Cochran, *Sampling Techniques* (3rd ed.), New York: John Wiley, 1977.

TABLE 6.2. Types of Probability and Nonprobability Samples

(A) Probability Samples

Simple Random Sample	Every Member of the population has a known and equal chance of selection.
Stratified Random Sample	The population is divided into mutually exclusive groups (such as sex groups), and random samples are drawn from each group.
Systematic Sample	The selection process starts by picking some random point in the list. Then every nth element is selected until the desired number is secured.

(B) Nonprobability Samples

Convenience Sample	The researcher selects the easiest population members from which to obtain the information.
Judgment Sample	The researcher uses his or her judgment to select population members who are good prospects for accurate information.
Quota Sample	The researcher locates and interviews a set number of people in each category.

---

expensive, they have the lowest response rate as compared to the other methods. Table 6.3 compares the three contact methods.

Collecting the Information. Researchers must take care to minimize the degree of error which can be introduced during the data collection period. Four sources of potential error exist when one conducts a survey: (1) not-at-home respondents that must be recontacted, (2) respondents who refuse to cooperate, (3) respondents who provide

TABLE 6.3. Comparison of the Three Basic Survey Methods

Criteria	In-person	Telephone	Mail
Versatility to adapt to special needs of respondent	High due to face-to-face contact	Moderate	None
Cost	High (average $30 per interview); travel time drives it up	Quite low (average $6 per interview); no travel time	Low (average $4 per completed interview), but can be much higher given poor return rate
Time	Moderately fast, depending on sample size	Very fast	Potentially quite slow, depending on interviewees' speed in returning questionnaire
Sample control (who answers the question)	High	High if there is a good list of numbers to select from	Poor
Quantity of data one can collect	Very large amounts	Moderate amount	Quite large amounts
Bias	Most biased response for sensitive questions	Moderately effective on sensitive questions	Best on sensitive questions
	Confusing questions can be clarified	Clarification possible	Clarification not possible
	Interviewer cheating possible	Close supervision of interviewees possible	———

Source. From *Principles of Marketing* by Thomas C. Kinnear and Kenneth L. Bernhardt (p. 200). Copyright 1983 by Scott, Foresman and Co. Reprinted with permission.

biased or incorrect answers, and (4) the likelihood of interview bias or dishonesty.

Analyzing the Information. After the data is collected, the researcher analyzes the data to uncover pertinent findings. Various statistical techniques are used in this process.

Presenting the Findings. This is the final step in the research process. The researcher must take care not to overwhelm management with a host of numbers, fancy statistical techniques, and technical research jargon. It is imperative that the researcher communicate with management in terms that are readily understandable and provide management with the key information which will facilitate better decision making.

After the firm has conducted a comprehensive marketing audit to understand its strengths and weaknesses and developed a marketing information system to determine the client's needs and wants, it is necessary for the service organization to assess the level of demand for its services. Potential sale volume is determined through the use of various sales forecasting techniques.

MARKET DEMAND

Market demand for a product is "the total volume that would be bought by a defined customer group in a defined geographical area in a defined time period in a defined marketing environment under a defined marketing program" (Kotler, 1984, p. 228). This represents the total market demand for a product for an industry. In turn, company demand is an estimate of company sales at various levels of company marketing effort. When management has selected the appropriate level of marketing effort, the resulting level of sales is referred to as the company sales forecast. The sales forecasting process can be thought of as a funnel. At the top of the funnel is the development of a national economic forecast. Unless a company is quite large and has in-house economists, this information is acquired by purchasing economic forecasts from some forecasting service. Marketing management must next develop an industry sales forecast. In other words, based on the outlook for the national economy, what does this mean for my industry? At the bottom of the funnel, is the creation of the company sales forecast by product.

The sales forecast is an extremely important decision-making document. Its influence is felt far beyond the marketing department. Production uses the sales forecast to plan its production schedules. All affected departments use the sales forecast to determine their staffing needs. Staffing levels must be committed in advance of the actual need so the personnel department can hire and train new employees. Finance use the document to anticipate the acquisition of new plant and equipment, the resulting capital requirements, the effect of the firm's cash flow, and the balance sheet and income statement implications.

Sales Forecasting Techniques

The most frequently used sales forecasting techniques can be classified as judgmental techniques and trend extension techniques.

Judgmental Techniques

Sales force composite, jury of executive opinion, and survey of buyer's intentions are the most frequently used judgmental sales forecasting methods.

Salesforce composite. With this method, marketing management asks the sales force to estimate what they will sell for the forthcoming period. On the plus side, the sales representatives are the closest to the marketplace and should be able to estimate the future. However, there are several drawbacks to this technique. The sales representatives are fully aware that they must live with their estimate and are likely to provide the lowest possible volume that will be acceptable to management. This makes living with next year's sales quota much easier. In addition, the territory sales representative is not as aware of the national and regional economy and its effect on next year's sales volume.

Jury of executive opinion. A group of marketing managers develops the sales forecast. While this can be considered a "swag" (simple wild ass guess), depending on the aggregate level of experience and the uniqueness of the current environment, the resulting forecasts can be quite accurate.

Survey of buyer's intentions. With this technique, the firm asks its customers their intentions of buying in the coming period. This method tends to be used in the industrial marketing area because industrial marketers have a limited number of customers to contact. Consumer marketing firms, with millions of customers, would not use this technique.

Trend Extension Techniques

Trend extension methods can be classified as time series methods or causal methods. Figure 6.5 depicts the basic nature of trend extension techniques. Since it is based on historical data, their accuracy is dependent on the future resembling the past. If the future

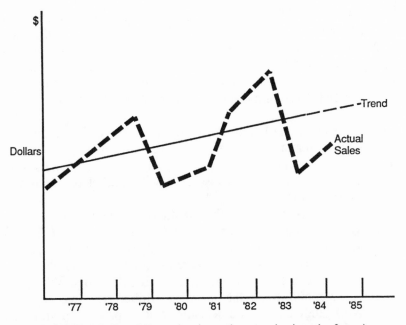

FIGURE 6.5. Trend Extension (extends past sales into the future)

environment is materially different from what has transpired in the past, the techniques will tend to be unreliable. Time series analysis, regression, and correlation analysis are trend extension techniques. A technical discussion of these methods is beyond the scope of this book.*

SUMMARY

Environmental analysis deals with a firm scanning its entire environment to assess the company's ability to satisfy the target market. The company starts by evaluating its own internal strengths and

---

*For more information on trend extension techniques, see Gilbert A. Churchill, Jr., Neil M. Ford, and Orville C. Walker, Jr., *Sales Force Management: Planning, Implementation and Control*, Homewood, IL: Richard D. Irwin, 1981, pp. 139–147 or Rolph E. Anderson and Joseph F. Hair, Jr., *Sales Management: Text with Cases*, New York: Random House, 1983, pp. 307–319.

weaknesses. In addition, the firm's suppliers, marketing intermediaries, customers, competition, and other publics are rated. Such uncontrollable factors as demographic changes, economic conditions, technological advances, political and legal constraints and social and cultural changes are taken into consideration. This process requires the use of a critical and comprehensive marketing audit.

A sophisticated marketing information system will facilitate the environmental scanning process. Often the information needed for the appropriate decision to be made requires the use of marketing research. The company must also assess its market potential and develop a sales forecast.

Part III focuses on the marketing audit and how it is used by service organizations. The two case studies in this section (Chapter 8 and 9) examine the auditing process in two different types of organizations serving the senior citizen markets. John A. Yankey, Nancy Koury, and Diana Young present Breckenridge Village, a retirement community in the midwest. Robert E. Sweeney and David Wolf guide us into the decision-making process of an urban home health care agency in the midsouth.

REFERENCES

Kotler, Philip. *Marketing Management: Analysis, Planning and Control*. 5th ed. (Englewood Cliffs, NJ: Prentice-Hall, Inc., 1984).

McCarthy, E. Jerome and Perrault, William D. Jr. *Basic Marketing: A Managerial Approach*. 8th ed. (Homewood, IL: Richard D. Irwin, Inc., 1984).

CHAPTER 7

The Marketing Audit —
A Strategic Necessity:
Marketing Management
for the Mature Non-Profit

Robert E. Sweeney

A frequently cited definition of a marketing audit describes it as "a systematic, critical and impartial review and appraisal of the total marketing operation . . . "[1] The same source identifies five purposes for a marketing audit:

- Appraisal of the overall marketing operation.
- Evaluation of objectives and policies, and their underlying assumptions.
- Evaluation of prospects as well as current status.
- Search for market opportunities and identification of weaknesses.
- Prevention and/or cure of marketing problems.

One can hardly quarrel with this conceptual structure, especially as it applies to the market position of small service organizations in initial development or start-up. As presented by most commentators in the health care or human services field, the marketing audit is tied closely to the early research, market definition and targeting that go hand-in-hand with the creation of the organization's market-

Reprinted from William J. Winston, ed., *Professional Practice in Health Care Marketing*, pp. 93–97, © 1985 by The Haworth Press, Inc.

ing department. At best, a long-term or recurrent role for auditing receives lip service. Moreover, unless a compelling reason can be given for doing so, mature service organizations are usually unwilling to invest more than once in the substantial time and staff resources which a full-fledged marketing audit requires. The collection of marketing and management information to support the audit may by itself require from one to two man-weeks unless the data has been compiled regularly and in an easily intelligible format. For the typical operating non-profit, state-of-the-art information is seldom readily available.

A strong case can be made in theory for an ongoing marketing audit in the non-profit sector because these organizations:

- Are less attuned to changes in the competitive environment.
- Generally have scant financial resources or are at the mercy of the political system for funding.
- Have less sophisticated management than the private sector.

Therefore, non-profits need current and accurate information. A volatile regulatory environment, the unexpected entry of for-profit competitors, sudden changes in the politics of funding or the appearance of generic competition can all generate a sudden atmosphere of jeopardy where the threatened traditional service organization must take stock of its strategic position and develop immediate and effective responses. An established auditing process could facilitate preparation or defense of the proper market strategy. Recent examples of "industries" caught unaware by these types of major forces include

- Hospitals (volatile regulatory environment: e.g., DRGs)
- Home health agencies (entry of for-profit chains and hospitals seeking vertical integration)
- Mental health centers (loss of Federal funding)
- General practitioners (generic competition: chiropractors, aerobics classes, jogging)

Auditing would be adopted more frequently and enthusiastically by mature non-profits if

- The time and manpower costs of information collection could be distributed throughout the planning cycle, as opposed to being concentrated at one point in time.
- The information retrieved and decisions arrived at had ongoing value in terms of day-to-day decision making.

The marketing audit should be introduced and structured in mature non-profits as a recurring series of decision points based upon the collection, evaluation and use of information for tactical and strategic planning. The short-term or tactical framework will involve weekly, monthly and quarterly reports; the longer-term or strategic framework has an annual cycle.

There are two points worth noting in this respect:

- The proposed audit system is broader than and encompasses the marketing information system (MIS) concept because the audit process includes *decisions*; certainly, an effective MIS would be a most valuable component of the ongoing audit system, but few non-profits have installed any reliable market data gathering system.
- The proposed audit system is cumulative; that is, information collected and decisions made at the tactical intervals accumulate in the organization's "recorded history"; this formal recording greatly reduces the time and manpower costs associated with the annual strategic audit, thereby reducing or eliminating a common source of resistance to its use.

The schema in Table 7.1 illustrates the timing, reporting relationships and focus of the proposed audit system for established non-profit organizations. All reporting documents are formal written submissions to the designated organizational level.

Obviously, this structure is illustrative and not exhaustive. Required reports from financial management are not shown, although, since they would affect the availabilities of marketing resources, in reality such information would be part of the auditing system structure. Also, for space considerations, the input from operations is shown only at the Weekly and Monthly intervals. One could also envision periodic required reports from legal, accounting and the purely medical or delivery sectors.

TABLE 7.1

TIMING	REPORT PREPARED BY	REPORT SUBMITTED TO	FOCUS	TYPICAL CONTENT	DISCUSSION/ DECISION FORUM
WEEKLY	MARKETING EXEC OR SENIOR EMPLOYEE WITH MARKETING RESPONSIBILITY	EXECUTIVE DIRECTOR	TACTICAL	• REVENUE BY "PRODUCT LINE" • ADVERTISING/ PROMOTIONAL ACTIVITY	WEEKLY EXECUTIVE STAFF MEETING
WEEKLY	OPERATIONS DIRECTOR OR EQUIVALENT	EXECUTIVE DIRECTOR	TACTICAL	• UTILIZATION: E.G., VISITS PATIENTS, BEDS USED, VACANCIES, HOURS BILLED	WEEKLY EXECUTIVE STAFF MEETING
MONTHLY	MARKETING EXEC	EXECUTIVE DIRECTOR	TACTICAL	• REVENUE: ACTUAL VS. PLAN • NEXT MONTH'S PLAN • MEDIA PLAN AND BUDGET NEXT MONTH	MONTHLY MEETING OF BOARD OF DIRECTORS
MONTHLY	OPERATIONS DIRECTOR	EXECUTIVE DIRECTOR	TACTICAL	• UTILIZATION: ACTUAL VS. PLAN • STAFFING PATTERNS • NEXT MONTH'S PLAN	MONTHLY MEETING OF BOARD OF DIRECTORS
QUARTERLY	MARKETING EXEC	MARKETING COMMITTEE OF THE BOARD	TACTICAL	• PERFORMANCE TO PLAN PAST QUARTER • REVIEW OF NEXT QUARTER'S PLAN • COMPETITION • MARKETING BUDGET • STAFFING	QUARTERLY PLANNING MEETING OF THE BOARD OF DIRECTORS
ANNUAL	EXECUTIVE DIRECTOR AND OTHER SENIOR MANAGEMENT	BOARD OF DIRECTORS	STRATEGIC	• LONG RANGE PLAN • MARKET OPPORTUNITIES AND THREATS • COST CONTROLS • MARKETING MIX • STAFFING REQUIREMENTS • EXPANSION/ CONTRACTION • ANNUAL BUDGET AND FINANCIAL STATEMENT • COMPETITION	ANNUAL MEETING OF THE BOARD OF DIRECTORS

CHAPTER 8

Utilizing a Marketing Audit in Developing a New Service: Case Example: Breckenridge Village

John A. Yankey
Nancy Koury
Diana Young

Experts generally agree that auditing is the foundation to successful market planning. According to Kotler (1981), the market audit is "a comprehensive systematic, independent, and periodic examination of an organization's marketing environment, objectives, strategies and activities with a view of determining problem areas and opportunities and recommending a plan of action to improve the organization's marketing performance." In brief, Bell (1972) writes that "a marketing audit is a systematic and thorough examination of a company's marketing position."

The purpose of the market audit is to collect and analyze data toward the following objectives:

Reprinted from William J. Winston, ed., *Marketing Strategies for Human and Social Service Agencies*, pp. 37–50, © 1985 by The Haworth Press, Inc.

• To identify problem areas to be corrected.
• To evaluate the overall marketing performance.
• To identify strengths and opportunities to be maximized.
• To understand and anticipate key factors and trends in the marketplace.

Clearly, there is no single "best" market audit method or tool. An audit may take several forms depending on an organization's needs. Different types of non-profit agencies emphasize different areas of investigation. The market audit illustrated in this article contains four components: consumer analysis, internal audit, environmental analysis, and competition analysis. Through the use of a case example, this article will demonstrate how the market audit can be applied as part of the planning process in the development of a new service.

CASE EXAMPLE

Breckenridge Village is a full-service retirement community located in Lake County, Ohio. It is one of seven such retirement communities in the statewide organization of Ohio Presbyterian Homes. Established in 1922, Ohio Presbyterian Homes' mission is

> . . . in response to the Lordship of Jesus Christ and consistent with His ministry, is to provide full-service, non-profit retirement communities and life enrichment outreach programs. Our communities are dedicated to the enhancement of spiritual, physical and mental well-being, independence, security, and the fullest possible potential for a high quality of life with an environment which promotes human dignity, purpose and self-esteem.

Opened in 1979, Breckenridge Village is the newest facility in the Ohio Presbyterian Homes network. The organization offers a range of care to its residents, including independent living ranch homes, two high-rise assisted living apartments, and a skilled nursing facility. Further, the agency planned to expand its residential base and offer case management and ten other outreach services, e.g., friendly visitors, transportation, and meals-on-wheels, to the elderly in the surrounding communities.

An extensive market audit was conducted by Breckenridge Village, specifically focusing on the developing of a case management program. This service was singled out because it posed the greatest financial risk to the organization in that it would require a significant financial commitment.

Case management is a service which provides assessment, linkage, and coordination of services to the frail elder and his/her caregiver. The goals of the service are as follows:

1. To enhance the ability of the older person to remain in the community.
2. To provide support and guidance to the older person and concerned family members.

The market audit was conducted to determine the feasibility, opportunities, and constraints the organization would face in providing case management. The results of the audit were used as a basis for requesting start up funds for community outreach services, including case management, in a proposal to the Robert Wood Johnson Foundation.

CONSUMER ANALYSIS

In a marketing approach, the consumer is the focal point of the planning process. Thus, the market audit begins with an examination of the organization's target consumers—current and potential. The organization seeks to identify its consumers in terms of number, location, demographics, as well as behavior patterns, attitudes, and lifestyles.

In short, data should provide the agency with answers to the following questions:

• Is there a market for this service?
• Is the market substantial and reachable?
• What are the demographics and characteristics of the target group?

- What are service utilization and buying patterns of the target group?
- Are there areas where primary market research is required?

The case management program planners defined the market as individuals 65 years and older living in the western half of the country. The geographic boundaries of this market were selected based on the location of the program facility and the anticipated resources to adequately service this area. Of those 65 years and older, the service specifically targeted the frail — those with physical, mental, and/or social impairments which limit their ability to live independently. This group of elders is traditionally targeted for case management services since they often require multiple health and social services in order to remain in the community.

As shown in Table 8.1, information from the consumer analysis was the basis for numerous marketing activities of the case management program. For example, based on census data and the planning organization's report, it was determined that a market for case management existed. Further, this market could be segmented into substantial and reachable sub-groups. Also, these sources, along with journal articles and the Agency on Aging's needs assessment, provided descriptive information about the characteristics and needs of the target market. These data were useful in developing the program's design and promotional plan. Finally, an unpublished study and the annual reports from local social services agencies offered insight as to service utilization and patterns of the target area's elderly. Uses for this information included further identification of consumer needs, data for the competition analysis, and development of a promotional plan.

The consumer analysis for the case management project also included an investigation of the services decision-making unit. Kotler (1981) has defined five roles in the decision-making unit for any product or service:

Initiator: The initiator is the person who first suggests or thinks of buying the particular product or service.
Influencer: An influencer is the person whose advice and views carry some influence on the final decision.
Decider: The decider is the person who ultimately determines any

TABLE 8.1. Consumer Analysis

Source of Information	Type of Information	Uses of Information
Census	. Population 65+ . Demographics (income, age, distribution) . Population projections	. Market identification . Pricing strategy . Market substantiation
Planning Organization Report	. Number of frail persons . Degree of frailty	. Market segmentation . Placement strategy . Market definition
Local Area Agency On Aging Needs Assessment	. Social resources of elderly . Living arrangements of elderly . Health status . Mental health ratings . Unmet needs of elderly . Hospital utilization	. Market segmentation . Demand verification . Promotional strategy . Service design . Decision-making unit analysis
Professional Journals	. Cohort characteristics of elderly . Service utilization patterns . Service needs of elderly . Family caregiving activities	. Service design . Promotional strategy . Decision-making unit analysis . Market segmentation
Unpublished Study of Service Utilization	. Types of services used by frail elders . Levels of frailty	. Service design . Decision-making unit . Market segmentation
Local Human Service Agencies' Annual Reports	. Target group service utilization . Types of services provided	. Market share analysis . Competition analysis . Competitive positioning

part or the whole of the buying decision: whether to buy, what to buy, how to buy, when to buy, or where to buy.

Buyer: The buyer is the person who makes the actual purchase.

User: The user is the person who consumes or uses the product or service.

Analysis of the case management decision-making unit included investigation into the following questions:

- How would the older person learn about, gain acceptance of, and make the decision to use this service?
- Who are the significant others in the elder's life who play a part in the decision-making process?
- What are the buying patterns of this market?

Table 8.2 illustrates the decision-making unit analysis for the case management program—based upon information collected in the preceding section of the consumer analysis. An important finding resulting from this analysis was that older persons are frequently reluctant to initiate services for themselves. Data from several sources reported that many elderly are "too proud" to accept help from outsiders; too, some elders fear that calling the attention of professionals to their situation may result in institutionalization. Additionally, much has been written about how the frail older person, due to physical impairments and/or social isolation, is often not even aware of existing services.

Because of these factors, the case management planners sought to determine who, besides the elder himself, could act as the initia-

TABLE 8.2. The Decision-Making Unit

	Initiator	Influencer	Decider	Buyer	User
Neighbor	X	X			
Clergy	X	X			
Social Service Workers	X	X			
Hospital Discharge Planners	X	X			
Physicians/Health Professionals	X	X	X		
Employee Assistance Programs	X	X		X	
Relative	X	X	X	X	
Daughter/Son	X	X	X	X	X
Spouse	X	X	X	X	X
Guardian	X	X	X	X	
Elder	X	X	X	X	X

tor of case management services. Research, interviews, and agency care records revealed that the family of the elder, along with physicians, clergy, friends, human services workers, and other significant persons would typically initiate or suggest a service to the elder. Indeed, these individuals also may be involved as influencers, deciders, and buyers as the decision-making roles are not mutually exclusive. Also, the family of the older person may be a secondary consumer of the service.

Results of the decision-making unit analysis were implemented in several marketing activities. First, service buying behaviors and other characteristics of the elderly were incorporated into staff training. Second, because of identified family involvement, an educational component for families was added to the service's design. Third, both target selection and the design of promotional activities were greatly influenced by the decision-making unit analysis of the case management service.

INTERNAL AUDIT

Once the consumer analysis has been conducted, the organization assesses its own capabilities and constraints in meeting the determined needs of the target consumers. Objectives of an internal analysis may include

- To assess the organization's management capabilities.
- To identify organizational strengths that can be maximized.
- To identify current problems to be corrected.
- To prevent possible future problems.
- To evaluate the organization's abilities in providing services and reaching consumers.

The internal audit is best conducted by a person(s) who is independent and objective. To assure this, an outside consultant may be hired. In some cases, however, a staff member may be assigned to conduct the audit if he/she is sufficiently removed from the consequences of an honest assessment. A consultant often will work with a group of staff members in a team approach to the internal audit.

The internal analysis for Breckenridge Village was first conducted by an outside consultant one year prior to and in preparation for the development of community outreach services, including case management. The analysis was updated and revised by staff members and the chief executive officer a year later as part of the program and market planning process.

The result of the revised internal audit is summarized in Table 8.3. The audit identified several problem areas of the organization, many of which were remedied since the time of the audit. For ex-

TABLE 8.3. The Internal Analysis

AREA	STRENGTHS	WEAKNESSES
Facility	. Beautiful facility . Central location in target area	. Expensive to maintian
Public Perception	. Excellent reputation . Strong community support	. Not known for community services
Staff	. Administration has demonstrated ability for program development and management . Dedicated, hard working staff	. Relatively inexperienced with outreach services
Volunteers	. Excellent track record in volunteer management	. Program recently hurt by lack of coordinator
Fundraising	. Highly successful fundraising	. Facility departments compete for resources . Need to expand relationships
Advisory Council	. Influential and talented members . Active and effective fund-raisers	. Not well informed about plans for outreach services
Marketing	. Technical assistance in marketing offered by local university	. Market orchestration problems
Current Consumers	. Highly satisfied with organization . Active in fundraising and volunteering . Important link to community	. Not well informed about outreach service plans

ample, orientation to the plans for case management and outreach services was presented to the organization's council and residents. In addition, monies were allocated for staff to receive special training to compensate for its lack of experience in outreach service provision. Also, administrative and development staff became more aware of how fundraising would become increasingly difficult as numerous agency needs and programs would compete against each other for limited funds.

Likewise, staff became more aware of how competition for marketing space and attention among organizational departments would also increase. Additionally, the public's perception of the agency as a residential facility would need to be carefully expanded to include community outreach services. The organization responded, in part, to these difficulties by creating a marketing/public relations committee consisting of staff members from various departments.

As problem areas of the organization were identified, so were strengths and capabilities. An excellent track record in fundraising, a top reputation in the community, effective volunteer management, and highly satisfied residents demonstrated strong support from the organization's various constituents. The organization was offered (and accepted) technical assistance in marketing from nearby Case Western Reserve University. Further, foundation interest in case management, coupled with strong staff and management, favored the inclusion of the case management program in the proposal.

ENVIRONMENTAL ANALYSIS

No organization exists in a vacuum. Each is continuously affected by its external environment. The external environment is the context in which an organization provides, promotes and distributes its services. In most cases, an organization has limited or no control over environmental factors, yet must be alerted to the threats and opportunities they pose. According to Rubright and MacDonald (1981), "If any organization has any weaknesses, it would be a tendency to overlook the opportunities or obstacles in its marketplace, the external environment." Thus, an important component of the market audit is the analysis of the threats, opportunities and trends in the agency's environment.

Kotler (1981) identifies six components of the "macro environment" which impact an organization's marketing activities. In his model, an examination of political, demographic, economic, ecological, technological, and cultural factors should be incorporated in the market audit. Again, individual organizations may design and structure the environmental analysis with variations based on the needs of the particular agency.

Like the internal audit, the environmental analysis may be conducted by an outside consultant or staff person(s). Board members may be involved in information gathering and should be perceived as sources of information about the community. Other sources of data include the census, local and national newspapers and magazines, professional journals, and interviews with experts.

As seen in Table 8.4, the external analysis for the case management program covered legal/political, social, demographic, economic, technical and professional trends and issues. These areas were investigated and assessed as to their impact on the development of the case management program.

Several opportunities for the development of case management were found in the external environment. For example, demographics and population trends pointed to a growing target market. Further, DRG legislation and the improvements in medical technology would likely result in more frail older persons living in the community. Social trends indicated a need to relieve and support growing numbers of family care-takers who, because of jobs, age, children and/or geographic distance, cannot provide all the necessary care themselves. Finally, the increase in the number of case management projects reflect a national trend toward this method of service delivery.

While the environment offered many opportunities, several threats to the case management service also existed. These threats were identified in the political and economic fields. For instance, social workers, the primary staff of case management, were not licensed in the state and would not receive third-party reimbursement for service. Consequently, the fees for the service would be paid directly by the user(s). However, a trend toward user fees is

TABLE 8.4. Environmental Analysis

Field	Key Factors	Opportunities	Threats
Political/ Legal	. Local government strongly supports organization . Diagnostic related groupings regulations . Social workers not licensed in state	. Community support for organization . Increased numbers of frail elders in community	. No 3rd party reimbursement . Less credibility
Economic	. Skyrocketing costs of institutional care . Large proportion of middle to upper income elders in target area . Unemployment 12%	. Alternatives to institutionalization sought . Service may be affordable to many	. Cost of service may be prohibitive to some
Technical	. Medical advances have enabled people to survive longer	. Increased need to serve this frail population	. Medical advances may not improve quality of life
Demographic	. County projects 47.5% increase in 65+ age group by 1990 . 95% of elderly living in community	. Increase in target market . Opportunity to maintain elders in their home	. Competition to serve this group likely to grow
Social	. Families provide 80% of care to aging relatives	. Opportunity to support family and relieve some of caregiving stresses	. Families may act as informal "case managers"
Professional	. Trend to community based care . Growing numbers of case management programs nationwide	. Case management program follows 2 national trends in services to elderly	. Competition likely to grow

developing as human services agencies seek non-governmental sources of revenue. Beyond this trend, the demographics of the target market indicated a potentially large proportion of middle to upper income consumers.

Importantly, other agencies may also recognize the environmental opportunities for case management and develop similar programs that would compete with the case management service at Breckenridge Village.

COMPETITION ANALYSIS

While many human service agencies deny that competition exists, the non-profit sector does have its share of rivalry. Organizations compete for funding, clients, referral sources, qualified staff, community endorsement, and market attention. Indeed, almost all market planning activities are affected to some extent by what competitors do.

Thus, an important step in market planning is conducting a competition analysis. This part of the market audit examines the organization's current and potential competitors. Questions to be answered in the competition analysis may include:

• Who are our current competitors?
• What are their competitive positions?
• What market share does the competition claim?
• Which market segments do our competitors target?
• What are the fee scales, locations, hours, staff qualifications, and funding sources of our competitors?
• Who are our likely future competitors?

Information about the competition may be obtained by several means. Data can be sought through direct requests to agencies for annual reports, promotional materials, and fee scales. Staff and board members of competing organizations may be interviewed. Articles, conferences, and public hearings also provide relevant information. Finally, if data are difficult to obtain by these means, the agency may assign staff or volunteers to call other organizations as potential service users to learn more about the competition.

Table 8.5 summarizes the competition analysis conducted by the staff of Breckenridge Village in planning for case management program. For purposes of illustration, six variables were selected from the analysis to demonstrate its use in market planning. The six variables selected were location, fees, related services, market share, market segments, and staff qualifications. At the time of the audit, no other formal case management service existed in the county. Therefore, the competition analysis included all organizations in the aging "industry" focusing on those who may become future competitors.

Results of this analysis aided in refinement and decision-making in several marketing activities, including the selection of a competitive position. For example, the agency's unique location in the west end of the county, its plans to hire a Master's level staff, and the fee-for-service basis all contributed to the formation of a competitive position. Based on these factors, the agency was able to identify its niche in the market as a professional, for-pay service designed particularly for those older persons in the west end of the county. Further, based on a comparison of market shares, the Breckenridge Village case management program chose to aim for a small market share and further position itself as a service where caseloads are low, staff is accessible, and individualized service is possible. Finally, since other organizations provided certain components of case management or offered the service on an informal basis, Breckenridge Village would also claim a unique market position as having the only formal, comprehensive case management program in the county.

CONCLUSION

The market audit is an effective and necessary marketing activity, especially in the planning and development of a new service. As illustrated in the example of the case management program, results from this audit may be utilized in developing the market mix and competitive position for the service and organization. Importantly, in order for an organization to remain competitive and current, this audit must be updated and revised periodically. Indeed, the organization, the environment, the competition, and the market-

TABLE 8.5. Competition Analysis

	PRIMARY RELATED SERVICE	STAFF	LOCATION	FEES	MARKET SHARE	MARKET SEGMENT
Agency A	Counseling elders and their families	Masters	East	Sliding scales	1%	County elders and families
Agency B	Protective Services	Bachelors	East	No	5%	Abused, neglected, dependent elderly in county
Agency C	Outreach Services	Non-degree	East	No	10%	Persons 60 and over in county
Agency D	Home Health	Nurses and Nurses Aides	East	Yes, supplemented by Medicare	4%	Health impaired elderly
Agency E	Mental Health Services	Bachelors	Border	Sliding scales	2%	Mentally impaired, emotionally disturbed elderly in county
Breckenridge Village	Case Management	Masters	West	Yes, fee for Service	0% Goal: 5%	Frail elderly in western portion of county

place are likely to undergo frequent and significant changes. A periodic and systematic market audit will help assure that the organization maximizes the opportunities and minimizes the threats these changes bring.

REFERENCES

Bell, M.L. *Marketing Concepts and Strategies*. Boston: Houghton Mifflin Co., 1972.

Kotler, P. *Marketing for Nonprofit Organizations*. Englewood Cliffs: Prentice Hall, Inc., 1981.

Rubright, R. and D. MacDonald. *Marketing Health and Human Services*. Rockville: Aspen Publications, 1981.

CHAPTER 9

Southern Home Health Care: A Case Study

Robert E. Sweeney
David Wolf

PART I: THE MARKET AUDIT

In late 1982, Bob Sweeney, marketing consultant, wrote the following letter to his client:

December 20, 1982

Ms. Claudia Bernal
Southern Home Health Care
283 Main Street
Midsouth City, TN 38000

Dear Claudia:

I have read over the summary report on your promotional efforts which you submitted to me. In order to have a concise basis for developing a feasible marketing plan for Southern, I should like to have you or your staff provide me with the following information, some part of which is already embedded in your report.

My objective is both to gather data and to encourage gradually a marketing

---

Robert E. Sweeney wrote Part I of this case study; David Wolf wrote Part II of the case study. The agency's real name and the names of real people have been camouflaged.

prospective at your agency. It may take us some time and effort to elicit this material, but it's really crucial. Would it be possible to pull it together by no later than January 14? This exercise will give you, me and Southern an overview of where you stand, what you don't know, and what needs to be in your marketing plan.

Cordially,

Robert E. Sweeney
Marketing Consultant

A. Corporate Structure

1. What is Southern's corporate status? Who owns or controls the organization? Who are the board members and what are their affiliations? Who are the managerial personnel and what are their responsibilities?
2. Please provide an organizational chart.
3. Provide a brief history of Southern emphasizing main events.
4. What regulatory agencies influence Southern? How?

B. Personnel

1. How many employees do you have and what are their responsibilities?
2. Please provide a resumé for each senior manager. How long has each been in this role?
3. Who is explicitly responsible for marketing? What are his/her full range of duties?
4. What precise marketing activities does he/she engage in?
5. How many employees have resigned or been terminated in the last two years?
6. How are employees recruited? By whom?

C. Corporate Goals

1. Provide a behavioral statement of your mission.
2. What are your top two or three five-year goals?

3. What are your short-term objectives (6 to 24 months)?
4. Provide a balance sheet and Changes of Financial Position statement for the last three years.
5. Provide a copy of this year's budget.
6. Does Southern plan any major capital expenditures for the next year?
7. What are your strengths and weaknesses in:
   a. medical facilities
   b. medical/technical staff
   c. managerial assets
   d. equipment
   e. market reputation

D. Market Audit

1. Market service area and segments
   a. What is your geographic service area? How was this determined?
   b. Who are your customer segments? Write a sentence describing each. Why does each buy your services?
   c. Are there other attractive segments who do not buy your services now? Why?
   d. How is your market distributed? Dispersed, urban, rural, bedridden? Describe in detail.
   e. Do your consumers use third-party payment? Which sources?
   f. For each consumer segment, provide data on age, income, sex composition, marital or family status if known.
   g. What is your image in the marketplace? Why?
2. Competition
   a. Who are your major competitors? Who controls or owns each?
   b. Has the number increased or decreased in the last five years? By how much?
   c. On what basis do you and they compete? Price? Service? Other? Explain for each competitor.

      d. What is your market position — size, strength, linkages — relative to the competition?

      e. What is the market share for you and each major competitor? Has the pattern changed significantly in the last five years?

3. Products and services

      a. List your current and any proposed products or services.

      b. Describe the salient features of each.

      c. How is each superior or inferior to competitor offerings?

      d. Do competitors offer any important products or services that you do not offer?

      e. What is the total unit cost per product or service?

      f. Is any product or service over/underutilized?

      g. Do users of each product or service have distinct characteristics?

      h. How does Southern decide upon the number and type of services? How are additions/deletions to service decided?

      i. In the last five years, what products or services have been added or dropped? Why?

      j. Has demand for each product or service risen or fallen in the last five years?

      k. For each service, how many complaints have been registered in the last two years?

      l. How are complaints resolved? What is your grievance procedure?

      m. How could your service mix be changed to improve your market position?

4. Price

      a. What is your pricing strategy?
- cost-plus
- return on investment (ROI)
- meet the competition
- demand analysis
- other

      b. What is the current unit price of each service?

      c. How often are prices reviewed?

      d. How often are prices changed?

e. How has the price of each service changed in the last three years?

f. What is the price charged for each service by your competitors?

g. Are your pricing policies constrained by any external influences?

5. Promotion

 a. List and briefly describe each major type of promotional activity conducted by Southern.

 b. For each, how often?

 c. What is the explicit objective of each type of activity? Why?

 d. Does Southern do any advertising? If so, provide details.

 e. Provide a copy of your budget for promotional activities.

 f. What media are used?

 g. Provide samples of all PSAs (public service announcements), press releases, brochures, and other promotional materials employed in the last year. Who designed each? At what cost for each?

 h. Do you have a public relations function? Why or why not? If so, who handles PR and how?

 i. In what specific ways has your promotional effort been effective or ineffective?

6. Place

 a. How is each of your products or services distributed?

 b. By whom?

 c. Where?

 d. How was your current location of facilities decided upon?

 e. What suppliers or distributors do you work with, sell to, or buy from?

 f. How would you evaluate the current location and distribution of your services?

PART II:
ANATOMY OF A HOME HEALTH
CARE AGENCY

In 1983, David Wolf reviewed the market audit prepared by Bob Sweeney and Claudia Bernal. As he finished his evaluation, Wolf thought back over what he had learned.

Southern Home Health Care was reorganized, after an absence of thirty years, in 1953 under the auspices of the Junior League of Midsouth City and the Community Chest (now the United Way). At the time, the city was without an independent home nursing care agency. Metropolitan Insurance Company had closed its home nursing care operation about a year earlier. Home medical care was the exclusive province of the joint City/County Health Department plus those private physicians who continued to make house calls. The reentry of Southern was a welcome addition to the medical community, and with its philanthropic backing, it served the community's need to provide home medical care to those lacking the ability to pay the full cost of receiving such care.

Southern and the health department had the home health market in Midsouth City virtually to themselves until 1971. Home health care became eligible for Medicare reimbursement in 1966, and demand for the service gradually increased until the mid-1970s; thereafter, skyrocketing demand, both nationally and locally, resulted in the more rapid entry of competing organizations to provide health care services in patients' homes. In 1969 Medicare provided reimbursement for 8.5 million home health visits at a cost of $78.1 million. By 1978, the Medicare tab for the nation's 17.1 million home health care visits had risen to $426.9 million, a better than fivefold increase.

The response of Southern to the entrance of new competitors was one of accommodation and, to some extent, relief that others were now available in the community to provide home health services to an ever-increasing number of clients. During this same period, referrals to Southern declined precipitously. Figure 9.1, reproduced from Bernal's 1982 paper, traces this drop and reveals that 1981 referrals to the agency were less than half of those received in 1969.

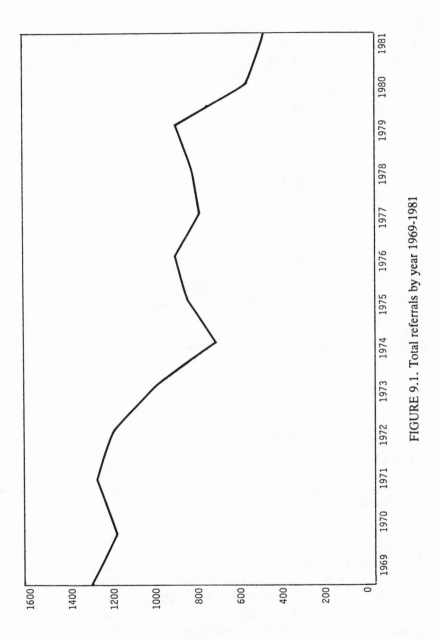

FIGURE 9.1. Total referrals by year 1969-1981

Based on figures compiled by the Midsouth City Medical Center Council, Southern ranked fifth in revenues among the area's home health agencies, garnering 8% of the $4.75 million market during fiscal year 1980–1981 (see Table 9.1). The Council monitors revenue from five sources. The source breakdown for Southern during this period was as follows:

Revenue Source	Percent of Total Agency Revenue
Medicaid (State)	5.2
Medicare (Federal)	69.2
Private Insurance	0.0
Private Pay	0.5
Donations (United Way)	25.1

The amount of charity revenue reported by Southern represented 98.7% of this type of revenue reported by all of the Council's reporting home health providers during the period covered.

TABLE 9.1. Revenue Shares of Largest Midsouth City Home Health Agencies, FY 1980–1981

Agency	Share	Cumulative Share
Mid-South Home Health Express	42.4%	42.4%
Home Health Unlimited	14.9%	57.3%
Elite Health Care Services	14.7%	72.0%
Upward Bound Medical Care	12.6%	84.6%
Southern Home Health Care	8.0%	92.6%
Elder Citizens Services	4.0%	99.6%

Since these figures were gathered, the number of home health agencies in Midsouth City has risen to a current total of eighteen. A list of the agencies providing home heath care is presented in Table 9.2. Not only has the number of home health providers increased, but many are for-profit organizations lacking Southern's philanthropic funding base and concomitant commitment to provide indigent care. The environment for home health care services took on a more competitive nature to which the agency failed to respond adequately.

TABLE 9.2. Midsouth City Home Health Care Providers

Older Care, Inc.
Upward Bound Medical Care
Home Health Unlimited
Hospice of Midsouth City
Mid-South Home Health Express
Quality Care Nursing Services
Staff Builders Health Care Services
Elite Health Care Services
Southern Home Health Care
American Nursing Resources
Kelly Health Care
Heart & Home Ministries
Licensed Pracitical Nurse and Attendant Registry
Elder Citizens Services
Helping Hands Nursing Care
Home Patient Care

Certain of the problems facing Southern were recognized by their senior personnel. Wilbur Boggs and the agency's Board of Directors' planning committee reviewed progress made on recommendations contained in the agency's "1974 Long Range Plan" and discussed the status of each. Of particular interest was the first short-term recommendation made in the 1974 plan:

> That a more aggressive promotion program be developed to acquaint the Midsouth City community with the excellence and desirability of the Southern Home Health Care program. This program of promotion should be designed to stimulate medical referrals with the endorsement of the local medical societies and the Midsouth City Medical Center Council.

The committee concluded that such activities needed to be performed on a continuing basis. Constraining such efforts, however, was their concern with medicare regulations. These rules permit reimbursement for activities and materials attempting to educate the general public or the medical community but not for those construed as soliciting increased patient utilization. Bernal's 1982 internal study reviewed the agency's promotional program and showed that Medicare reimbursement guidelines seemed to play a dominant role in the selection of promotional activities undertaken in the past by Southern. Naturally, actions requiring minimal financial outlay were chosen. Despite the caution exercised in promotional activities, Figure 9.1 shows that referrals to Southern recovered somewhat in 1974–75 from the low levels experienced in 1973. Whether or not the recovery was due to the limited promotional efforts of the agency is not known. Referrals from 1976 to 1979 remained relatively flat. In 1980 referrals fell by about a third, and even further declines were recorded in 1981.

An interesting point in the committee's report on the 1974 recommendations was the lack of reference to the erratic history of the agency in gaining additional referrals. Other information in the 1980 plan reveals that between 1975 and 1980 the number of annual patient visits increased by about 25% with only about a 15% rise in number of patients served by the agency. The average number of visits per patient during this period remained about the same, varying between fourteen and fifteen visits. The implication of this data is that Southern, as might be expected, has been serving an increasing proportion of chronically ill patients with an extended need for services.

The agency's "1980 Long Range Plan" also outlined areas considered to be important to the agency over the next five years. Besides pointing out the need for an improved management information system (MIS) to meet the increasing demand for information supportive of third-party billings, the recommendations tended to focus on expanded program offerings in areas the planning committee saw potentially rewarding: (1) expanded hours of operation; (2) hospice care; (3) child health; and (4) adult health promotion. The plan also revealed the intention of the board to monitor the development of health maintenance organizations in the area and investigate potential linkages between such organizations and Southern.

The final paragraph of the 1980 plan reads as follows:

It is the goal of Southern Home Health Care to pursue a course of slow, steady, manageable growth of both size and scope of programs, which is responsive to the needs of the community.

Entering 1981, then, Southern maintained its commitment to provide home health care to the entire community and, due to its philanthropic backing and humanitarian philosophy, to do so without regard to the ability of the individual to pay for the service. The agency also maintained its policy on promotional activities.

In March of 1981, Claudia Bernal was appointed Executive Director of Southern. Bernal was quick to recognize the agency's weakening position in the market and the lack of response of the agency to its declining position in the changing environment.

Bernal soon recognized a number of obstacles to overcome. To begin with, many of the agency staff were unable to adapt to the changing marketplace and to Bernal's more aggressive leadership. As a result, by the end of 1982, the agency had experienced a turnover of two-thirds of its employees. Also, Southern had participated in blocking an attempt by the community's second largest regional hospital system, Lutheran Hospital, to obtain licensure for their own home health agency. The hospital thereupon acquired a management contract with the area's second leading home health care provider, Home Health Unlimited (see Table 9.1). Ironically, the hospital had previously been Southern's largest source of referrals. Finally, in 1982, Southern was threatened with the loss of its license to operate in the state of Mississippi due to low levels of utilization. Southern was, of course, also licensed to operate in Tennessee and was unique among local home health care providers in that it had Certificate of Need authorization to operate and provide services in nearby Crittendon County, Arkansas. This permit became crucial in subsequently negotiating an affiliation with the area's largest regional hospital system, Southern Memorial Hospital System (SMH). The relationship was accomplished in 1983 through the placement of responsibility for naming eleven of Southern's twenty-one member board members with the hospital.

Operationally, Southern is a relatively small organization (see Figure 9.2 for an organizational chart). Of the agency's staff of 43, 32 are direct service providers. Of this latter group, six are contract

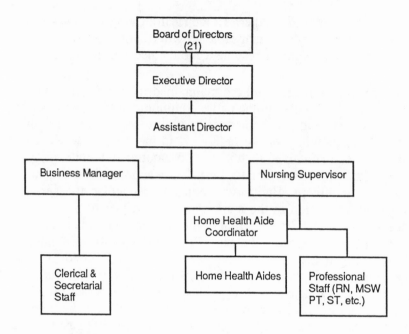

Note: Recently appointed was a Hospital Liaison to coordinate
    activities with SMH. Staff position probably accountable to
    Executive Director.

FIGURE 9.2. Organization Chart: Southern Home Health Care

employees who provide services on an as-needed rather than on a
salaried basis. Most of these employees provide specialized rehabilitation services (for example, physical therapy and speech therapy).
Two registered nurses (RNs) also work for the agency on this basis.

Direct service providers, primarily registered nurses and home
health aides, are expected to provide five home care visits per day.
Each day begins with a work planning session at the agency office.
There, needed supplies are picked up, cases assigned or reallocated
to staff, phone calls made, and other administrative matters taken
care of. Each patient is assigned to an RN who serves as the patient's case manager and is responsible for coordinating other
needed services — rehabilitative or home health aid — and scheduling them for the patient. The case manager also acts as a contact

person with the physician who has authorized home health services. Each RN handles a caseload varying from 15 to 35, depending on a variety of factors, e.g., type and frequency of treatments needed, nurse skills, and locale. Cases, when possible, are allocated on a geographical basis to minimize travel between visits. Exceptions are made to this scheme when necessary to balance cases against staff availability (see Appendixes A and B to this chapter for a description of agency services and case mix information).

Such then was the situation facing Southern and Claudia Bernal in 1983. Moreover, new federal government prospective payment plans based on Diagnostic Related Groups (DRG) were scheduled for implementation at SMH in the fall. Exactly how the change would affect referrals to the agency was unknown.

For the first time since taking the position of executive director of Southern, Bernal was not facing a crisis situation. The agency's staff was intact and comfortable with the more aggressive posture and leadership of the agency; the affiliation with the SMH hospital system was in place and expected to replace some of the referrals lost when Lutheran acquired the home health agency contract; and the agency had retained its authority to provide services in Mississippi. Perhaps, for the first time, Bernal could devote her efforts to defining problems the agency was likely to face and outlining the areas of opportunity for Southern to reverse the eroding market share experienced by the agency in recent years.

Case Analysis of Southern Home Health Care

Environmental Analysis

The environment in which home health care providers operate is regulated along several key dimensions. Entry into a geographical market is controlled by the designated agency in each state charged with licensure and/or issuing Certificates of Need to health care providers. In addition state agencies may impose requirements which an organization must meet in order to continue operating in a given territory. Such a problem may be viewed as a recurrent, if not continuing, threat to Southern's operations in north Mississippi. Such has not yet been the case in either Arkansas or Tennessee.

Agencies receiving Medicare reimbursement are subject to U.S.

Department of Health and Human Services regulations governing covered services. These regulations affect most, if not all, aspects of a provider's operation. The Department's Region IV office in Atlanta interprets regulations and monitors compliance in the territory in which Southern operates. Blue Cross/Blue Shield of Tennessee-Chattanooga provides fiscal intermediary service for the Department and approves or denies claims covered by Medicare. *Reimbursement is on the basis of the lower of cost or charge.* Routine audits and agency cost reports assist the intermediary in determining the agency's allowable cost levels and in setting reimbursement rates. The appointment of the Chattanooga BC/BS office as fiscal intermediary is a recent development. Previously, BC/BS-Memphis handled claims for the region. Southern was one of the area's first home health agencies shifted to the Chattanooga office, and after experiencing some initial difficulties with claims denials, Southern worked out these problems and has a minimal denial rate. As other home health agencies are required to shift their fiscal intermediary relationships to the Chattanooga office, they too might be expected to experience a higher than normal level of claims denial. However, these problems are not likely to result in curtailment of their participation in the market area.

Each state, of course, has its own set of Medicaid standards with which provider agencies are required to comply. As with Medicare regulations, state standards affect most of an agency's operating procedures.

In Southern's case, however, state agencies in Arkansas and Mississippi accept compliance certification by the Tennessee Department of Public Health's Division of Medicaid. It is not known whether or not this reciprocity would continue if market penetration in these states by a Tennessee agency increased significantly, causing Arkansas- or Mississippi-based operators to pressure their respective state departments for closer scrutiny.

In summary, the various regulatory agencies by which Southern and other home health agencies are scrutinized influence most phases of their operations. Particularly stringent are documentation requirements for supporting claims for benefits. Documented cost information is also crucial since both Medicare and Medicaid reimbursement rates are based on allowable costs incurred in providing covered services to eligible recipients. (Note: If a provider submits 97.5% or better acceptable claims, regulations permit reimbursement for the questionable 2.5%. A higher rejection rate subjects the provider to retroactive denial of the questionable claims and requires that the monies be returned.)

Other sources of third-party payments play a negligible role in providing home health revenues and, by implication, in placing additional quasi-regulatory requirements on the agencies to receive reimbursement. At present few insurers provide home health benefits. Given the trend toward cost containment in the health care field, however, this condition might be expected to change in the future. Figures reported by BC/BS of Maryland indicate a savings of $1.3 million in 1981 by covering home health care visits. This benefit resulted in covered persons foregoing 13,700 inpatient hospital days, or an average of 11.4 days per person and $1,123 per case (Brumfield, 1983). Expanded offering of this benefit in Southern's service area represents a potential growth opportunity. It is unlikely that much additional administrative effort or paperwork would be required on the part of the agency and its staff to tap into an expanded private insurance benefit covering their services.

The following figures show the percentage of revenues collected by source for all home health care agencies operating in Midsouth City during the 1980–1981 fiscal year.

Revenue Source	Percent of Total Revenue
Medicaid	9.2
Medicare	86.8
Private Insurance	0.9
Private Pay	1.0
Other Sources	2.0

These figures suggest the importance of federal and state programs to the ongoing success of home health care providers. At the same time, these programs may be candidates for cutbacks as governments at all levels look for ways to reduce spending. One advantage of United Way funding for Southern is that it provides a source of revenue not available to other agencies and can serve as a cushion in the event of government cutbacks in health care expenditures. In no way, however, should the presence of this funding source be taken for granted, or should it slow agency efforts in attempting to increase revenues from government reimbursement programs.

A further regulatory constraint for some sectors of the health care industry is the federal government's prospective payment plan. Under this plan hospitals are paid a predetermined amount for treating a person falling into one of the designated Diagnostic Related Groups. Costs incurred under/over this predetermined amount represent the hospital's profit/loss on any given patient. While this program is due to be phased in over a four-year period, it is likely that average length of stay for many injuries and/or illnesses will decrease as this phase-in occurs and more and more care will be given in the patient's home. The opportunity exists, then, for both hospitals and home health agencies to review each of the DRGs (product lines, if you like) and associated care requirements and to anticipate the sort of home health care services likely to be required in the diagnostic categories where hospitals seem most at risk of incurring costs in excess of payment.

General medical treatments and procedures as well as specialized care modalities are likely to experience rising demand. An agency might well begin preparing for this eventuality by making sure their staff includes persons with skills necessary to deliver home treatment to patients afflicted with what might be termed "growth DRG" maladies. Public discussion of home health reimbursement changes accompanying introduction of the prospective payment system has been limited, but some changes might certainly be expected if utilization increases faster than anticipated. Agencies, such as Southern, with hospital affiliations, may be in a prime position to exploit these expanding opportunities.

A final government regulatory pressure not usually associated with nonprofits is the Internal Revenue Service. Diversification by many nonprofits into for-profit operations has come under closer IRS scrutiny mainly at the behest of small businessmen providing similar services. Although Congress and the courts have not generally agreed that such activities by nonprofits represent unfair subsidized competition in the private sector, the IRS has ruled that the activity of the for-profit operation of the nonprofit organization must be related to the agency's primary reason for existence (*Business Week*, 1983, pp. 191–192).

The growth of home health care participation in Medicare reimbursements has already been mentioned. Also mentioned was the proliferation of organizations providing home care services and competing for the same dollars in the West Tennessee area (Table 9.2). The state's licensing division has been receiving requests for home health licenses at the rate of one per month. In Midsouth City at least four new agencies opened their doors in 1982–1983 alone.

Other trends in the increasingly competitive home health care environment may prove more threatening to Southern than the number of competitors. Many of the newer marketing-oriented home health agencies are parts of larger organizations which provide other services, such as temporary staff nurses, private duty nursing care, live-in companions, and the like — all of which complement home health care, at least in the eves of primary referral sources, and provide a built-in referral pipeline for home health care services. Many of these competitors provide services on a 24-hour basis seven days a week in comparison to Southern's eight-hour Monday through Friday schedule. Southern does, however, provide emergency and essential care during the same hours on weekends. Furthermore, many of Southern's competitors, due either to their for-profit status or having higher costs, came into an undersupplied market and followed a skimming strategy or some other segmentation scheme to achieve their initial success. Southern did not recognize nor respond to these competitor actions to protect market share and has, as a result, lost its predominant market position.

Midsouth City, site of a major teaching hospital and medical school, has higher than average medical care costs and somewhat of an excess of specialist physicians — two variables critical for the emergence of organizations providing alternative delivery systems (ADS) for medical care. A health maintenance organization (HMO) owned and managed by the Prucare division of the Prudential Insurance Company has been in operation for a number of years and has close to 15,000 subscribers; Blue Cross/Blue Shield sponsors an individual practice association (IPA) plan; and several preferred provider organizations (PPOs) are under consideration by some of the large metropolitan employers, e.g., County Government, Lutheran Hospital, Southern Memorial Hospital, City Hospital, and many others. The area has seen the growth and proliferation of free-standing urgent care centers, extended office hours among selected medical groups, and the advent of outpatient surgery centers at area hospitals. As yet, there are not any free-standing surgical centers in the area, but efforts to establish them are underway. Smaller hospitals specializing in offering limited services are also on the drawing board. Each of these ADS has developed in an attempt to slow the rise in the cost of health care. While many start-ups have been successful, it has been at the expense of other health care providers, most often the full-service hospital.

Southern is already, it seems, a fairly low cost provider. Budget projections for the coming year indicate that the agency is making further cost-cutting efforts. As yet, however, the agency has done little to investigate potential relationships with emerging ADS in the area. The recent affiliation with the SMH system may provide the opportunity to do so for the following reasons:

1. SMH is the hospital used by the Prucare HMO
2. an outpatient surgical unit is located at the SMH satellite hospital in suburban Midsouth City
3. the hospital system wants to establish a PPO.

The existence of this hospital affiliation, though, dictates that Southern be cautious in approaching free-standing clinics until all aspects of such affiliations are thoroughly investigated by the board of directors, including the likelihood of future conflicts of interest. In any case, the overall growth of competition in the local health care market suggests several alternatives for exploration.

Participation in the Arkansas and Mississippi markets must be maintained and is likely to benefit from the continued expansion of the SMH system. Less is known about the competition in these areas.

Home health agencies are not really in competition with intermediate care facilities (i.e., nursing homes), except to the extent that ICFs are entering the home health field. Instead, the two groups are actually complements to one another. Nursing homes and home health agencies are alternative treatment modes based on the level of care a particular patient requires. Patients leaving the nursing home mode are probably doing so in response to changing health, family, or economic circumstances rather than whether or not a home health option is available. Potential cross-referral arrangements between the two types of agencies were among the possibilities under evaluation by Southern. The role of the home health agency in deferring a patient's entry into a nursing home was also a possibility to explore. Depending on the relative rate of cost increases in the two sectors, the day might come when 24-hour coverage by home health personnel would be more cost-effective than care in an ICF. More likely, some combination of home health services less intensive than round-the-clock coverage could be used by families desiring to keep older relatives out of nursing homes except as a last resort.

Life care centers for wealthier individuals were also emerging in the local area. These centers, while playing a minor role in the overall health care market, could be expected to siphon off the upper end of the consumer market. Their appeal would be to individuals able to afford increased luxury and amenities in their waning years when they might have occasional need for a more monitored environment. Few opportunities would seem to exist for home health agency participation in this type of setting.

The final environmental factor was population trends. The elderly are the largest segment consuming health care services. The Medical Center Council had projected a rise in Shelby County's over-65 population to 9.8% by 1987, up from the 1983 estimate of 9.2%. The Council also reported that 82.3% of patients served by home health agencies are in this age group. From these figures, it was clear that this group would continue to demand growing health care services in the Midsouth City area. This group, however, is not homogeneous, and opportunities exist for segmentation of persons over 65 in terms of health care needs. These same figures also pointed to the need to investigate potentially attractive home health opportunities in the remaining 90% of the population. (Characteristics of Southern's 1981 patient mix by age, race and sex are found in Table 9.3.)

TABLE 9.3. 1981 Utilization Statistics

Female Visits per Month	
Black	375/871
Caucasian	243/671
Oriental	11
TOTAL	629/1542

Environmental considerations represent the greatest challenge all health care administrators will have to deal with over the next few years. That the situation is especially critical for home health agencies in the Midsouth City area is suggested by the following set of circumstances:

1. The nursing shortage in Midsouth City has been much less acute than was in the past. Current estimates of the shortage fell in the 2–3% range.
2. Utilization of agency nurses at a number of local hospitals was decreasing.
3. Employee layoffs, including professional nursing staff, had been experienced at some local hospitals.
4. Increases in local nursing education facilities were planned.
5. Help-wanted ads were shrinking for RNs in local newspapers.

Assuming that currently licensed RNs remained in the labor pool, home health could be a growth area with many RNs searching for positions in this sector. Failure of existing agencies to absorb them might lead to a still further proliferation of groups providing home health care and still more fragmentation of the market. Furthermore, it was conceivable that hospital and nursing home affiliated agencies would become more aggressive since they have larger capital investments to protect and support through cross-referrals. This scenario was plausible when one considers that all provider types, while not in direct competition in the usual sense, were pursuing the same Medicaid and Medicare dollars. The federal government had already taken measures to stem the flow of Medicare dollars to hospitals. One had to wonder in what sort of sequence other providers might have to deal with constraints similar to DRG-related payment.

History and Personnel

"Southern leads with pride . . . professional pride." This slogan represents the attitude of many RNs employed by the agency. Local home health care organizations were established in the U.S. in the mid-1880s and numbered 205 by 1912. A predecessor of Southern operated in Midsouth City under that name from 1910 to 1923. The current organization goes back to 1953.

The history and tradition of Southern appeals to nurses who take particular pride in their profession and desire independence from traditional hospital supervision and roles, as well as the desire to plan and perform patient care independently — opportunities which employment with Southern can provide. In addition many of the RNs appreciate the fact that home health care was started by nurses and believe that nurses should maintain control of the industry and use it to foster professional goals and standards for both themselves and their agency.

In the past, this desire for professional recognition coupled with a public service orientation attracted nurses to work for Southern at salaries typically below those prevailing in the community. These nurses tended to remain with the agency for many years, and turnover was low. Salaries, today, still lag behind community levels. Staff turnover since the arrival of Ms. Bernal has been dramatic as employees who had been with the agency for 15 to 20 years were unable to accept the new direction of Southern in response to the competitive situation in the market. The agency had several staff nurse vacancies in 1983. The reason was not known; nor was the difficulty that Southern encountered in filling staff nurse positions readily understood. Whether or not the intangibles operative in the past to offset lower salaries continue to operate today is probably open to question.

Given that the supply of nurses may, over the next few years, come to exceed demand for their services and that the majority of nurses are female and just as likely as not to be part of a low-income household bearing a high tax burden, the role of salary may take on a lesser importance in the agency's compensation package in favor of other benefits providing tax advantage. These might include an expanded retirement plan, deferred income schemes, increased insurance benefits, and the like. Given the likelihood of increased turnover and the expectation of higher utilization requiring more staff, the organization would need to review its hiring and other personnel policies and procedures, much of which is now performed by administrative and supervisory personnel. At some point, the agency would probably have to consider adding a person to their staff to devote a majority of time to personnel matters.

Strategic Perspective

Appendixes A and B to this chapter contain a brief statement of the philosophy and purpose of Southern as well as a description of the services provided by the agency and a draft revision of the agency's philosophy. It is not surprising that the focus of these documents is primarily on providing medical treatment and educational services for patients and their families. Of note, too, is Southern's continuing emphasis on services relevant to meeting community needs as well as providing for community education with regard to health promotion and disease prevention.

The orientation prevalent in these documents is probably the result of traditionally being controlled by nursing professionals. Close community ties have developed as a result of caring, nurturant attitudes, and motivations present in many of the agency's original personnel; its close relationship with the public health department during its formative years; and its dependence on United Way contributions for part of its funding, specifically to provide health care to the indigent. The board of directors seemed to believe that providing care for the sick is Southern's primary focus and that education, health promotion, and disease prevention programs are secondary. Questions which the agency must face with regard to these secondary activities include the following:

1. What, if any, benefits are derived from such activities in excess of their costs?
2. What is the role of such activities in the agency's overall promotional program?

3. Should the agency continue to devote resources to activities ancillary to its primary purpose; are such activities more properly the domain of the public health department in the community?

The user of home health care, of course, is the acutely or chronically ill individual who, for whatever reason, is unable to meet appointments outside the home except at great inconvenience and/ or expense, e.g., ambulance transportation. In most instances, however, the purchaser of such services is the third-party payer, usually Medicare and Medicaid. The decisionmaker determining the use of such services is the physician. The decision to make use of a particular home health agency rests with various configurations of influencers including the patient, the patient's family, the physician, and the hospital discharge planner. Sources of information considered in the selection of a particular agency include peers, past experience, and the agencies themselves. The relative role of each influencer category and information source has not been precisely determined.

Referrals to Southern are split about evenly between hospitals and physicians. Assuming that this is also the case for competing agencies, several potential challenges for home health agencies were on the horizon. Southern had already affiliated with the SMH system, the city's largest with about 30% of the available bedspace. Lutheran, the city's second largest system, controls an agency through a management contract. Assuming this trend continued, many agencies would be left without hospital affiliations. Half of the market, then, might be unavailable to other agencies if hospitals referred only to their affiliates. With DRG-related payment for Medicare patients becoming a reality, demand for home health care for hospital discharges was expected to increase. As demand increased, home health provider resources of the affiliates might become strained and expansion necessary. One avenue for this expansion could be absorption of unaffiliated agencies by the affiliates.

In the case of the SMH-Southern relationship, the hospital, according to SMH Vice President Abe Royal, would reap no direct financial benefits. Rather, majority board representation was the hospital's way of ensuring continued quality. The affiliation, then, theoretically had the effect of enhancing the position of Southern with the discharge planners of the system. The hospital gained a mechanism with which to afford itself additional protection in the event a patient should require additional care after being discharged from the hospital earlier than what he might have been in the past.

As the market for hospital referrals tightens, home health agencies could be forced to rely more on private physicians for their patient base. As pointed out earlier, physicians in the community were coming into oversupply and ADSs beginning to emerge. So far, few, if any, agencies seem to have made contractual arrangements with any ADS. The private physician market, then, might shrink or remain static as more primary care becomes centralized. Specialists at secondary and tertiary care levels might be lured into multidisciplinary group practices or PPOs, most of which have contractual agreements with hospitals and, possibly, their affiliated home health agencies. This type of agreement, however, might be separate from the hospital's contract and might be based on competitive bidding, with or without the hospital being able to influence the decision.

The product of a home health agency includes medically related equipment and treatments or procedures delivered to a patient's home under prescriptive authorization from a physician. In addition, other supportive, nonprofessional services are provided. Southern, like other home health agencies, defines its products under traditional categories. An expanded concept was implied in the agency's definition of its purpose (Appendixes B and C). However, Southern never explicitly included this in defining their product.

Service Benefits

The following partial list identifies benefits which might be provided to the patient and the patient's family by home health visits:

- Recovery of function
- Hope of recovery
- Social interaction
- Advocacy with physician
- Dollar savings
- Diagnostics

- Family involvement in care of the patient and guilt aversion that may result from placing a relative in a nursing home
- Health education
- Security of being at home
- Convenience
- Health monitoring
- Professional attention
- Future care planning

The perceived value of home health services varies with the type of service required in the treatment of a given patient. Value may also vary with the source of payment for the required services. Perceived value in health care, as with other services, is difficult to measure. Consumers often view "more" as "better" and "more expensive" as better still when it come to health care. This sort of attitude may reflect the nature of medical care which is often arbitrary (in the sense that treatment may consist of one of a number of alternative strategies, each associated with a probabilistic rather than certain outcome), and often beyond the ability of the consumer to understand without extended, time-consuming explanation. These difficulties, of course, do not preclude the need to measure consumer assessment of home health care services relative to other modes of care. The value of home health care to referral sources, usually a hospital or physician, is intangible and included in the patient's evaluation of the total care received under the source's sponsorship, so to speak.

In terms of product lines, Southern's medical care offerings were somewhat limited. What the agency did offer was competitive in price with offerings of other providers. However, Southern did not provide hospice care, psychiatric services, respiratory therapy, and private duty nursing. Nonskilled service offerings also failed to measure up to those of competing agencies whose offerings included live-in companions, aides, and homemakers. Each of these areas were under review by Southern's board and administration as possible additions to present service offerings.

One service which seemed to be generating a lot of attention at Southern was that of hospice care. A full outpatient hospice program includes a comprehensive package of medical and related services aimed at assisting terminally ill persons to continue life with minimal disruption of daily activities while remaining at home. Inpatient hospice care is provided when the patient's symptoms must be more closely monitored or controlled than is possible at home, or to provide family caretakers a period of relief from tending for the terminally ill patient (respite care). Recent changes in Medicare regulations provided reimbursement under a hospice benefit in lieu of standard Medicare coverage. The hospice benefit was scheduled to end on September 30, 1986, unless extended by Congress.

The hospice benefit is usually time-limited due to Medicare regulations and available only once to an individual. Should the patient outlive the benefit period, the hospice care provider is required to continue providing care without Medicare reimbursement unless the patient asks for such care to be discontinued. This benefit is, therefore, not without risks to the provider of care. Specifically, the probability of the patient living beyond the period of time for which reimbursement is allowed under the regulations obviously places the provider at some slight risk for a potentially open-ended financial drain. Diversifying into such an area of care might pose an even greater than average exposure to potentially large losses due to Southern's commitment under United Way funding rules to provide indigent care. While the financial risks could be limited through corporate restructure, the moral questions would remain in the mind of the community and, perhaps, the United Way directors: Is it equitable for hospice care to be available only to those who are eligible for government assistance or able to afford such care out of personal resources, or should it be available to all in the community? If so, how should it be provided and by whom?

Other services into which Southern might wish to expand do not carry the potential for losses of the magnitude possible with even a single hospice care patient.

Competition and Affiliation

In relation to competitors, Southern held certain advantages with which to capitalize in the future. The benefits of its affiliation with the Southern Memorial system not only precluded direct entry by SMH into the home health market but also gave Southern an inside track on referrals from the largest hospital system in the area. The hospital's relationship to the Prucare HMO might also lead to additional utilization in the future.

The most distinct advantage Southern held over its local competitors was holding a Certificate of Need to provide care in Arkansas, a point which played a large role in negotiating for the hospital affiliation. The state of Arkansas was a battleground among major hospital systems in the area for community hospital buyouts and other patient referral sources. The agency, therefore, kept a close eye on Arkansas regulators and legislators to protect itself from actions or laws which could adversely affect the agency's operation in that state, such as almost happened in Mississippi.

Southern held a reputation with SMH for providing quality care as well and had excellent relationships with the medical community in general. United Way funding provided a relatively stable revenue base which subsidized service provision to indigent patients in the agency's three-state service area. Due both to external regulations and management efforts, Southern was a fairly low cost provider of quality home health services in a limited number of categories. Should the opportunity present itself, this combination of agency traits could make Southern highly competitive with other providers in attempting to negotiate service provision for other organizations, or in contract bidding to provide the necessary services.

Personnel

Management of Southern changed in the recent past. The agency was traditionally staffed almost totally by nursing professionals in service-delivery, supervisory, and administrative positions. While still true for the most part, Claudia Bernal (an RN), the executive director, had been trained in administration and had taken courses in business administration. The agency has recently hired an assistant director (January 1983) who had a business degree and was not only the first non-nurse but also the first male to hold an administrative position with the agency. The administrative staff, then, was not only new to the agency, but in the case of Bernal and the assistant director, new to the area.

Personnel turnover since Bernal taking her position had been high. Many of those who left the agency did so in reaction to the more aggressive, goal-oriented, marketing-centered orientation and leadership. By mid-1983, these types of personnel problems were seemingly behind Southern and efforts were being focused in other directions: developing professional management systems and techniques within the agency, reversing the trend toward declining market share, and planning for expanded participation in the highly competitive home health care market.

Market Recognition

Southern's lack of promotional activity was not uncommon for older agencies. Agency administration had an idea of how the agency was perceived in the local marketplace and by various publics but had little hard data to support these ideas. It was believed that Southern was viewed as a small, struggling, public service welfare-type agency responsible for providing home medical care to those who could not afford to pay for it. While this was a somewhat negative image, it might not be widely held. The agency maintained a relatively low profile in the community and was probably not known to vast numbers of people. Home health care itself was only correctly identified by a minority of general public respondents in a 1983 telephone survey. Those who had heard of home health care or Southern by name were not very familiar with its operations or reputation unless members of their own families had been treated. This information suggests that any promotional activity undertaken by the agency directed at consumers should be more informative than persuasive. Persuasive efforts are better directed at influencers and decisionmakers than the users of agency services.

Pricing

Fee-based service providers traditionally set prices with the objective of full-cost recovery. Prices are set, then, on the basis of a costing system designed to measure all relevant incurred expenses. Medicare reimbursement is based on the lower of cost or price charged, as is Medicaid. Prices then are always set, if possible, to exceed cost and still remain competitive with those of other agencies offering comparable services. Some services for which Medicare does not reimburse the agency are allowable in the sense that they may be included in calculating agency overhead, which must then be allocated to service units. Cost and price data from Southern's 1981 cost report are shown below.

Type of Service	Price	Unit Cost
Nursing	$42.00	$47.14
Physical Therapy	$40.00	$21.41
Speech Therapy	$40.00	$21.49
Social Worker	$25.00	$44.59
Home Health Aide	$25.00	$15.04

The above figures reveal a serious situation. Nursing visits, the primary agency service, traditionally were, and in 1983 still were, priced below cost. Based on a salary plus fringes estimate of $20,000 and a charge of $42.00 per visit, the break-even point on nursing personnel costs should occur with 477 visits. At the expected rate of five visits per day, this should require somewhere in the neighborhood of 100 working days, or four and a half months, to recover costs for a full-time staffer from Medicare reimbursement levels alone. Even ignoring incidental visit costs (travel, supplies, etc.) a heavy overhead burden is carried by nursing services, more than half the annual working days.

Social worker visits, also priced below cost, represent a minor portion of agency revenue. Expenses in this area could be expected to generate revenue in other departments of the agency, however, because the social worker arranges for other modes of service and aids the patient and the family in completing applications for other forms of entitlement assistance.

The situation with regard to the cost of providing nursing visits deserves further study. In light of the cost-price relationship holding in the nursing area relative to other service categories, the overhead allocation must be reviewed. While regulatory restrictions may inhibit more realistic or creative allocation schemes, any possibility to

shift some of the costs allocated to nursing services must be investigated. Favorable cost-price relations in the home health aid category make shifts to this category a particularly attractive possibility
since this is a highly used service as well.

The agency might also wish to review other pricing objectives
and strategies with regard to the overall operation as well as in
regard to each of its services in attempting to bring the cost of providing nursing visits more in line with other cost-price relationships
of the agency. It is obvious that the long run effects of providing
one's leading product at a price 12% below unit cost, given regulatory limitations, can lead to undesirable consequences. While such
a situation, by itself, might not threaten the survival of the agency,
it might restrict future development in other areas Southern might
wish to pursue.

Service Delivery

Most services were provided in the patient's home during regular
business hours. Since most patients are essentially homebound, few
opportunities were available for providing services at alternative
locations, at least with the current patient mix. Primary segments
served by Southern included elderly persons covered by Medicare
or Medicaid, eligible for such coverage, or indigent with care subsidized by United Way funds.

A prime variable in Southern's delivery strategy was service
hours. Many competing agencies regularly offered services 24
hours, seven days a week. Southern's 1980 annual plan reviewed
advantages and disadvantages of expanding service hours but de-
layed making a decision. Although recognizing the trend to expanded service hours, especially for home health aides, the board
stated that requests for service during other than routine hours were
few to the agency. It was not known whether or not this was due to
the agency's reputation as somewhat traditional and inflexible, or
because other agencies were already meeting the demand for after-
hours and weekend services.

One problem with expanding the agency hours was cited by the
1980 plan:

There are problems inherent in this program; there are certain areas of the community where it is not safe after dark. Therefore, this program could not be implemented without the use of escorts. Escorts, of course, would increase the cost of the program. (p. 8)

This statement represented a possibly myopic view of the agency's service area. It was true that many patients, then as now, lived in some of the less desirable areas of Midsouth City. However, action or inaction based on such a consideration would seem to indicate board acceptance of Southern's image as an agency providing care solely to the indigent. Accepting this role might ignore other possibilities in outlying suburbs containing more affluent individuals with the ability to pay full price for their care.

Southern has a single office located in the central part of Midsouth City. It has not established satellite offices in other areas of the city or in the surrounding states in which it provides home care. The possibility of setting up an office in Mississippi was discussed in 1982. The likelihood of establishing satellite locations has probably increased due to the affiliation with SMH and its market presence in areas not currently heavily served by Southern. The agency could also undertake expansion in counties where the hospital system already serves the area.

Southern's active consumer segments were described in Appendix A to this chapter. The exhibit also lists potentially attractive segments. The agency was beginning to gather additional information on these groups to further define market segments along relevant dimensions. It might be expected that the agency's recent affiliation would enable them to gain at least partial access to the SMH data base, thereby allowing for further specification of attractive market segments.

Financial Position

Audited financial statements for 1981–1983 are found in Appendixes C, D, and E to this chapter. During the past three years, Southern's revenues and expenses had more than doubled while their fund balance increased by approximately 65%. The agency's balance sheet was currently strong. Fixed assets increased by 54% since 1979 but accounted for only 19% of total agency assets. Such a situation would be expected in this type of service operation. Net accounts receivable represented the agency's largest single asset category—83% of total assets on December 31, 1982. These monies were due primarily from Medicare and Medicaid reimbursing agents and should be collected in full since Southern submitted few questionable claims. Any delays experienced in collecting these amounts would present the agency with temporary cash flow problems since sufficient liquid funds were not maintained in agency accounts to cover current obligations. Such an occurrence, however, would not impair the long-term financial health of the agency.

A portion of the agency's current funds were maintained in both restricted and unrestricted accounts. The agency's Memorial Fund was a restricted account that provided monies to purchase items and services for indigent patients who would otherwise have to go without certain necessities, e.g., medication, bedroom slippers, sickroom supplies, and the like. Other restricted accounts were used to pay for board-approved special projects or activities. Unrestricted fund balances provided a cushion against yearly revenue fluctuations. Interest earned on these account balances was channelled back into agency operating accounts.

Personnel costs, as would be expected, represented Southern's largest expense, 57.2% of total expenses in 1982. General and administrative expenditures had decreased to 25% of total expenses in 1982 from 28.9% in 1980. The extent to which G & A expenses could be further reduced is open to question. As professional management techniques take stronger hold, the downward trend might be expected to continue down to some minimum. On the other hand, growth of the agency would, no doubt, require the creation of positions not currently found on the agency's organization chart, e.g., SMH liaison, personnel administrator, satellite office staff, and the like.

The agency was in decent financial health. The financial implications and demands of the recent affiliation with the SMH system were yet to be fully explored. The presence of professional managers was expected to result in closer attention being paid to maintaining and improving the agency's operating results and financial position. Resources available to the agency seemed sufficient to fund further growth of current service utilization and to pursue attractive diversification opportunities in either service offerings or in geographic territory served. The direction of Southern's future to a large extent would be indicated by the response of the agency's board of directors to the challenges facing the organization and whether or not they wished the agency to remain a limited or full-service home health agency.

Two factors were likely to influence board decisions. The first of these was anticipated levels of United Way funding in future years. Until now United Way contributions to the agency had been sufficient to cover the care provided indigent patients. Whether or not this would continue to be the case was not known. A second factor likely to influence the direction of the agency would be the preference of referral sources and consumers to deal with a single provider of all existing and potential home health services as opposed to several providers of only limited services.

Critical Issues

Southern Home Health Care, like all health care providers, faced an unsure future in what was becoming an increasingly hazardous environment characterized by a number of factors with which the agency was unfamiliar:

1. increased competition from both profit making and nonprofit organizations
2. increased regulatory efforts to contain health care costs and slow the rate of increase prevalent in recent years
3. increased incidence of persons without sufficient resources to pay for health care
4. increased awareness of and participation by consumers in health care issues and decisions
5. the emergence of new forms of health care delivery systems (ADSs).

In brief, much of what was occurring in the health care industry had already occurred in other deregulated business sectors, most notably in transportation. Agencies such as Southern were faced with economic and competitive pressures threatening their very survival. Evidence pointed to instances where changes were occurring in the environment yet the agency had failed to respond appropriately. One result was that Southern had seen its market share fall from close to 100% to 8% in the last decade. What issues, then, were critical for Southern to address in order to maintain its market viability?

The past focus on increasing internal efficiency coupled with the exigencies of high staff turnover negotiations with SMH and the possible loss of Mississippi licensure had deferred emphasis from delineating a strategic direction for board consideration. Many of the necessary staff and tools for strategy definition and development were in place but had yet to be put to effective use. The agency had passed the stage in development where it must feel compelled to meet most or all of the health care needs of the entire community. The first critical issue facing the agency, then, was that of planning the future direction the agency would take.

A second concern closely associated with strategic and organizational development was that of the agency's image and reputation in the community. Southern's history and tradition was that of providing community (in the sense of public health) care to all in need of it regardless of ability to pay. This fact, and the agency's past connection and close association with the public health department, resulted in the agency having developed a reputation and image in the community of medical providers as well as the general public. While not a completely accurate description, provider of last resort might not be too wide of the mark in describing the role occupied by Southern in the minds of many. Further contributing to this problem was agency reliance for part of its funding on United Way contributions, clearly a two-edged sword. On the one hand, United Way participation provided Southern with a stable revenue source, but it also helped to perpetuate its image as a primary provider of health care to those with diminished ability to pay for services. The agency was committed to maintaining its association with the United Way. The agency had not, however, attempted to capitalize on this association to foster its own reputation.

While a complete list of issues facing Southern would include many more than the two just mentioned, these two—organizational development/strategic planning and image/reputation management—were the most crucial facing the agency in 1983 and deserving of the application of additional resources to address.

Appendix A to Chapter 9:
Southern Home Health Care
Customer Information

CONSUMER SEGMENTS

1. *Elderly:* those over 65, unstable condition, usually home-bound; referred by physician or post-hospitalization; do not make their own choice.
2. *Indigent and Working Poor:* usually under 65, not eligible for Medicare or Medicaid; limited resources and high medical bills.
3. *Poor:* no choice but to use Southern as provider of last resort.
4. *Rehabilitation:* age range from 35 to over 65; need services due to accidents or physical occurrence (MI, CVA, etc.); also dependent on physicians and rehab units.
5. *Infants and Children:* birth defects, abuse victims, neonatal care, and parent education.
6. *Elderly:* minimal, nonprofessional care needs; heavy United Way support; primary revenue source for home health; usually limited income; referred by discharge planners.

   Each of the above segments has a chronic and acute (unstable) subsegment.

7. *Medicaid:* all age groups; heavy utilization with 60 visit/year limit.
8. *Private Pay:* minimal or limited insurance and income; use Southern due to sliding scale fees; needs beyond skilled services.

ATTRACTIVE POTENTIAL MARKETS

1. Suburban locations
2. Younger and middle-aged physicians
3. Other hospitals
4. Worker's compensation
5. Clinics for businesses and industrial firms
6. Private duty services

Appendix B to Chapter 9:
Goals of
Southern Home Health Care

PHILOSOPHY OF THE AGENCY

Southern Home Health Care was founded to provide part-time, intermittent health care in the home, by a staff of multidisciplinary health professionals and supportive personnel. Care is provided under medical supervision to the sick and disabled in the community who need such care, regardless of race, color, creed, or ability to pay.

PURPOSE OF THE AGENCY

1. Instruction and guidance in care and rehabilitation for the sick and disabled and their families.
2. Provision of necessary and feasible services such as nursing, physical, speech and occupational therapy, medical social service, home health aide service, and medical supplies and equipment. When needed services are not available, Southern Home Health Care will help the family secure these services from other community agencies whenever possible.
3. Participate in the education of appropriate health professionals in the field of community health.
4. Provide the individual and his family with information for the promotion of health and the prevention of disease.

5. Provide the community with information for the promotion of health and the prevention of disease.

SERVICES OF THE AGENCY

Professional Nursing Service

General Nursing Service

The professional nurse gives care to the sick and disabled under medical direction and demonstrates, teaches, and supervises care given by families and ancillary personnel. She is responsible for the management of patient care, coordinating the services of other disciplines, within and out of the agency. Care is family centered and consideration is given to the total needs of the patient and family, for nutritional guidance, health promotion, and disease prevention as well as the rehabilitation of the patient.

Home Health Aide Service

The Home Health Aide in the agency is an unlicensed nonprofessional worker. Under the direction of the professional nurse, she gives personal care to patients and helps maintain the patient's immediate environment in a manner which is conducive to good health.

Male Attendant Service

The male attendant is an unlicensed worker who has received special training in the area of the male genitourinary system. Under the direction of the professional nurse, he changes catheters of selected male patients.

Physical, Speech, and Occupational Therapy Services

Physical, speech, and occupational therapy are provided by appropriate licensed therapists who give specific treatments under specific medical prescriptions and evaluate patients through the use of specific tests. They instruct and supervise others such as patients,

families, home health aides, and nurses in carrying out specific procedures. Advisory assistance is given to nurses who participate in
the rehabilitation care of patients.

Medical Social Services

Medical social service is provided by a master's-prepared social
worker who prepares social histories, provides social case work,
makes referral to social agencies, and provides advisory assistance
to other professional staff.

Program Objectives and Activities: Care of the Sick

Objectives	*Activities*
1. Fifteen hundred of the area's residents who are essentially home bound and ill and who are referred for service will have their nursing needs assessed and identified.	1. Referrals are screened by nursing administration to determine what services appear to be indicated and whether these services are within the scope of the agency's program and services.
When the needs are within the agency's admission policies, the patient will be admitted for continued service.	Referrals which are deemed appropriate are assigned to a staff nurse for determination as to whether further service will be provided.
2. Each patient admitted for continued service will receive skilled nursing care to meet those needs which fall within the scope of service.	2. Based on the assessment of the skilled needs of the patient and in accord with the physician's plan of care, the nurse formulates a written nursing care plan outlining planned nursing care intervention and mutually established goals.

The nurse provides the skilled nursing intervention as well as the teaching and supervision of the patient and others involved in his care as outlined in the plan.

The nurse supports the patient, his family and others involved in his care in relation to the effects of the disease process.

The nurse reevaluates the plan of care in line with the expected outcome of the nursing intervention and modifies the plan when indicated.

3. Patients will be aware of existing community resources when appropriate and will be assisted in their utilization.

3. The nurse acquaints the patient and family with other resources to meet identified needs.

The medical social worker will provide consultation and direct case service when indicated.

4. Patients referred for physical, speech, or occupational therapy will have these needs assessed and identified.

4. Each referral is screened by nursing administration to determine what therapy services are within the scope of the agency.

All referrals which are deemed appropriate are routed to the appropriate therapist(s) for assessment and possible admission to that service.

5. Patients whose therapy needs are appropriate will be provided service.

5. Based on the therapist's assessment of the patients' needs and in accord with the written physician's plan of care, the therapist formulates a written care plan outlining the planned therapy intervention and mutual goals.

The therapist provides skilled therapy as well as consultation, teaching and supervision of the patient and others involved in his care as outlined in the therapist's care plan.

The therapist offers emotional support to the patient, his family, and others involved in his care in relation to the effects of the disease process and their acceptance or nonacceptance of it.

6. Patients will be made aware of other community resources when appropriate and will be assisted in their utilization.

6. The therapist will acquaint patients and families with other community resources to meet any needs identified by the family or therapist which are not appropriate to the agency.

Appendix C to Chapter 9:
Statement of Philosophy

Southern Home Health Care meets a need in the community for delivering health services to patients and families. Southern is a nonprofit organization which serves all age groups in the provision of services. While these services are provided primarily in the client's home, services are also provided in other settings. Southern recognizes that the changes in the health care delivery system have a direct impact on the nature of service we must provide to serve clients effectively. Therefore, we must ensure that the services are relevant to the community's needs and provided in a cost-effective manner. The board of directors and the agency staff are committed and responsive to this belief.

The services provided by agency staff meets standards of care which are consistent with those established for the health care professions generally. The service provided is comprehensive and co-ordinated and available to defined segments of the community. The quality of service is monitored by staff and through internal and external review. The scope of service is a reflection of community needs.

While the agency recognizes that the majority of its services is covered by third-party reimbursement, we reserve the right to refuse requests to provide service when either the safety of staff is in jeopardy or when referrals for service exceed the availability of staff in adequate number to provide safe quality care.

The agency is also committed to provide services when no reimbursement from any source is available except from United Way funds. Established priorities guide the staff in the determination of clients to be served within the limits of United Way allocations.

The agency has responsibility to the staff and the community to provide quality services relevant to the community. The agency assures relevancy through its long-term planning committee, medical professional advisory committee, and periodic needs assessment involving the board of directors. We assure relevancy to the staff through involvement and representation on agency committees to review services and establish standards of care.

The purposes of Southern Home Health Care are to:

- Restore maximum health and well-being through therapeutic rehabilitative care for all age groups.
- Promote individual, family and community health.
- Promote adaptation and optimal functioning of the individual and family within limitation of their health status.

- Maximize the ability of individuals and families to cope with health problems.
- Assist individuals and families to make informed and self-directed decisions about their health and health care.
- Assist individuals to identify and utilize appropriate health services and community resources.
- Promote coordination of health-related services with those of other agencies or organizations.
- Bring to the attention of planning bodies identified areas of unmet need within the community and to participate as appropriate in planning to meet these needs.
- Provide educational experiences for health professionals and students.

SOUTHERN HOME HEALTH CARE BALANCE SHEET

| | December 31, 1982 | | | | | December 31, 1981 |
| | Current Funds | | | | | |
	Unre-stricted	Re-stricted	Plant Fund	Memorial Fund	Total All Funds	Total All Funds
ASSETS						
Current Assets						
Cash	$ 2,648	$	$	$ 604	$ 3,252	$ 6,073
Savings Accounts	286	28,814		4,925	34,025	71,053
Accounts Receivable-Net	242,272				242,272	118,390
Inventories	7,696				7,696	6,008
Prepaid Insurance	1,812				1,812	1,524
TOTAL CURRENT ASSETS	254,714	28,814		5,529	289,057	203,048
LAND BUILDING AND EQUIPMENT			97,461		97,461	90,218
Less Accumulated Depreciation			(30,462)		(30,462)	(33,101)
			66,999		66,999	57,117
	$254,714	$ 28,814	$ 66,999	$ 5,529	$356,056	$260,165
LIABILITIES AND FUND BALANCES						
Current Liabilities						
Accounts Payable	$ 63,944	$	$	$	$ 63,944	$ 3,257
Current Portion						
Long-Term Debt	4,584				4,584	7,646
TOTAL CURRENT LIABILITIES	68,528				68,528	10,903
Long-Term Obligations						
Less Current Portion	853				853	4,148
Fund Balance	185,333	28,814	66,999	5,529	286,675	245,114
	$254,714	$ 28,814	$ 66,999	$ 5,529	$ 356,056	$260,165

187

SOUTHERN HOME HEALTH CARE
STATEMENT OF REVENUE AND EXPENSES AND CHANGES IN FUND BALANCES

| | Current Funds | | | | | December 31,1981 |
	Unrestricted	Restricted	Plant Fund	Memorial Fund	Total All Funds	Total All Funds
	December 31, 1982					
REVENUE						
Contributions	$	$	$	$ 598	$ 598	$ 224
United Way	122,203				122,203	99,262
Program Services Fees-Net	734,126				734,126	489,237
Interest	1,935	4,363		252	6,550	3,327
Patient Medical Supplies and Equipment-Net	295				229	4,340
Maintenance Level Care	4,241				4,241	469
TOTAL REVENUE	862,804	4,363		850	868,017	596,859
EXPENSE						
Nursing	346,352		5,025		351,377	207,133
Home Health Aide	167,521		1,898		169,419	92,141
Senior Citizen	876		23		899	459
Physical Therapy	58,944		773		59,717	39,852
Speech Therapy	12,882		34		12,916	1,742
Medical Social Worker	25,247		375		25,622	18,024
Gen. & Administrative	203,266		3,240		206,506	127,410
TOTAL EXPENSES	815,088		11,368		826,456	486,761
EXCESS REVENUE (EXPENSE)	47,716	4,363	(11,368)	850	41,561	110,098
OTHER CHANGES IN FUND BALANCES						
Equipment Acquisitions from unrestricted funds	(21,250)		21,250			
Transfer of Memorial Funds	499			(499)		
Transfer of Unrestricted Funds	13,482	(13,482)				
FUND BALANCE - Beginning	144,886	37,933	57,117	5,178	245,114	135,016
FUND BALANCE - Ending	$185,333	$ 28,814	$66,999	$ 5,529	$286,675	$ 245,114

188

Appendix D to Chapter 9

SOUTHERN HOME HEALTH CARE BALANCE SHEET

	December 31, 1981					December 31,1980
	Current Funds		Plant Fund	Memorial Fund	Total All Funds	Total All Funds
	Unrestricted	Restricted				
ASSETS						
Current Assets						
Cash	$ 5,568		$	$ 505	$ 6,073	$ 2,774
Savings Accounts	28,477	37,933		4,673	71,053	12,925
Accounts Receivable-Net	118,390				118,390	78,287
Inventories	6,008				6,008	5,800
Prepaid Insurance	1,524				1,524	1,531
TOTAL CURRENT ASSETS	159,937	37,933		5,178	203,048	101,317
LAND BUILDING AND EQUIPMENT			90,218		90,218	74,831
Less Accumulated Depreciation			(33,101)		(33,101)	(26,271)
			57,117		57,117	48,560
	$159,937	$ 37,933	$57,117	$ 5,178	$ 260,165	$149,877
LIABILITIES AND FUND BALANCES						
Current Liabilities						
Accounts Payable	3,257				3,257	7,352
Current Portion Long-Term Debt	7,646				7,646	2,843
TOTAL CURRENT LIABILITIES	10,903				10,903	10,195
Long-Term Obligations Less Current Portion	4,148				4,148	4,666
Fund Balance	144,886	37,933	57,117	5,178	245,114	135,016
	$159,937	$ 37,933	$57,117	$ 5,178	$260,165	$149,877

189

SOUTHERN HOME HEALTH CARE

STATEMENT OF REVENUE AND EXPENSES AND CHANGES IN FUND BALANCES

| | December 31, 1981 | | | | | December 31, 1980 |
| | Current Funds | | Plant Fund | Memorial Fund | Total All Funds | Total All Funds |
	Unrestricted	Restricted				
REVENUE						
Contributions	$	$	$	$ 224	$ 224	$ 234
United Way	99,262				99,262	95,829
Program Services Fees-Net	489,237				489,237	286,228
Interest	1,871	1,217		239	3,327	1,857
Patient Medical Supplies and Equipment-Net	4,340				4,340	(3,989)
Maintenance Level Care	469				469	
TOTAL REVENUE	595,179	1,217		463	596,859	380,159
EXPENSE						
Nursing	204,049		3,084		207,133	185,945
Home Health Aide	90,976		1,165		92,141	70,132
Senior Citizen	445		14		459	
Physical Therapy	39,377		475		39,852	28,697
Speech Therapy	1,721		21		1,742	276
Medical Social Worker	17,794		230		18,024	12,659
Gen. & Administrative	125,421		1,989		127,410	121,250
TOTAL EXPENSES	479,783		6,978		486,761	418,959
EXCESS REVENUE (EXPENSE)	115,396	1,217	(6,978)	463	110,098	(38,800)
OTHER CHANGES IN FUND BALANCES						
Equipment Acquisitions from unrestricted funds	(15,535)		15,535			
Transfer of Memorial Funds	425			(425)		
Transfer of Unrestricted Funds	(30,480)	30,480				
FUND BALANCE - Beginning	75,080	6,236	48,560	5,140	135,016	173,816
FUND BALANCE - Ending	$ 144,886	$37,933	$57,117	$ 5,178	$245,114	$ 135,016

190

Appendix E to Chapter 9

SOUTHERN HOME HEALTH CARE BALANCE SHEET

| | December 31, 1980 | | | | | December 31, 1979 |
| | Current Funds | | Plant Fund | Memorial Fund | Total All Funds | Total All Funds |
	Unrestricted	Restricted				
ASSETS						
Current Assets						
Cash	$ 2,068	$	$	$ 706	$ 2,774	$ 4,969
Savings Accounts	2,255	6,236		4,434	12,925	26,069
Accounts Receivable-Net	78,287				78,287	92,608
Inventories	5,800				5,800	7,586
Prepaid Insurance	1,531				1,531	4,483
TOTAL CURRENT ASSETS	89,941	6,236		5,140	101,317	135,715
LAND BUILDING AND EQUIPMENT			74,831		74,831	65,126
Less Accumulated Depreciation			(26,271)		(26,271)	(21,542)
			48,560		48,560	43,584
	$ 89,941	$ 6,236	$48,560	$ 5,140	$ 149,877	$179,299
LIABILITIES AND FUND BALANCES						
Current Liabilities						
Accounts Payable	7,352				7,352	5,483
Current Portion Long-Term Debt	2,843				2,843	
TOTAL CURRENT LIABILITIES	10,195				10,195	5,483
Long-Term Obligations Less Current Portion	4,666				4,666	
Fund Balance	75,080	6,236	48,560	5,140	135,016	173,816
	$ 89,941	$ 6,236	$48,560	$ 5,140	$ 149,877	$179,299

SOUTHERN HOME HEALTH CARE
STATEMENT OF REVENUE AND EXPENSES AND CHANGES IN FUND BALANCES

	December 31, 1980					December 31,1979
	Current Funds Unrestricted	Restricted	Plant Fund	Memorial Fund	Total All Funds	Total All Funds
REVENUE						
Contributions				$ 234	$ 234	$ 353
United Way	$ 95,829				95,829	90,843
Program Services Fees-Net	286,228				286,228	312,426
Interest	1,064	652		141	1,857	677
Patient Medical Supplies and Equipment-Net						
Maintenance Level Care	(3,989)				(3,989)	(4,032)
TOTAL REVENUE	379,132	652		375	380,159	400,267
EXPENSE						
Nursing	183,846		2,099		185,945	188,845
Home Health Aide	69,342		790		70,132	62,864
Senior Citizen	28,373		324		28,697	37,084
Physical Therapy	268		8		276	1,588
Speech Therapy	12,501		158		12,659	7,878
Medical Social Worker						
Gen. & Administrative	119,901		1,349		121,250	97,408
TOTAL EXPENSES	414,231		4,728		418,959	395,667
EXCESS REVENUE (EXPENSE)	(35,099)	652	(4,728)	375	(38,800)	4,600
OTHER CHANGES IN FUND BALANCES						
Equipment Acquisitions from unrestricted funds	(9,704)		9,704			
Transfer of Memorial Funds	413			(413)		
Transfer of Unrestricted Funds						
FUND BALANCE – Beginning	119,470	5,584	43,584	5,178	173,816	169,216
FUND BALANCE – Ending	$75,080	$ 6,236	$48,560	$ 5,140	$135,016	$173,816

192

Part IV

Segmentation and Targeting

CHAPTER 10

Introduction to Market Segmentation and Targeting

Robert L. Berl

WHAT IS A MARKET?

In theory, a market is an easy concept to understand. A market is a group of people who need a particular product or service, have the ability to purchase the product, are willing to use their purchasing power, and have the authority to buy. All four criteria must be present. In a complex society, such as ours, there are many markets. It is up to management to determine which markets are best suited to the company. In practice, the selection of a market is a difficult and crucial decision.

TARGET MARKETING

Target marketing is the process of examining the total market, the market's various segments, selecting one of more of the segments, and developing products/services tailored to the market. For example, there is a market for footwear which has various segments such as boots, rubber wear, men's shoes, women's shoes, and so on. A footwear manufacturer might decide to concentrate on men's boots or to provide a complete range of men's footwear or market both men's and women's boots.

The target marketing process has three steps:

1. *Market Segmentation*. Market segmentation entails dividing a market into distinct segments of buyers who could require different products/services and different marketing mixes.
2. *Market Selection*. The various distinct market segments are analyzed and evaluated to determine which segment or segments to enter.
3. *Product Positioning*. This is the process of determining how to position the product in the consumer's mind and developing the appropriate marketing mix to reach the target market.

MARKET SEGMENTATION

Markets are made up of people, but people vary in many respects. They may want different products, have different resources on which to draw, are located in different geographical areas, and the like. The segmentation process attempts to take a heterogeneous mass market and locate distinct groups of consumers who are homogeneous. This homogeneity permits the marketer to develop a marketing mix to reach and appeal to this segment. Markets can be segmented according to geographic, demographic, psychographic, and behavioral patterns.

Bases for Market Segmentation

Geographic Segmentation. Geographic segmentation involves dividing the market on a geographic basis: by regions, by states, by counties, and the like. In a large metropolitan area, a centrally located hospital may choose to develop satellite locations to take advantage of the movement of population to the suburbs. For example, Methodist Hospital in Memphis, Tennessee, not only has a central city location but also has hospital facilities located in the northern and southern areas of the city.

Many times consumers vary in different geographical areas. People in the deep south (e.g., Mississippi) tend to be more conservative than people in the far west (e.g., northern California). In general, people living in large urban areas tend to better educated and more cosmopolitan than individuals living in a rural atmosphere.

Demographic Segmentation. Under demographic segmentation, the market is divided by such variables as age, sex, income, education, religion, and so on. Since demographic variables are easy to measure, this is a very common means of market segmentation.

An examination of the Yellow Pages of a telephone book indicates that many physicians segment their market based on demographics: pediatrics (infant and child care), gynecology (women's reproductive system), gerontology (care of the aged), and the like. In addition, virtually all urban areas have hospitals which specialize in the treatment of children.

The examples which have been cited represent demographic segmentation based on a single socioeconomic variable. Often demographic segmentation is accomplished using multiple socioeconomic variables. For example, a home for blind people who need residential care, psychological counseling, or vocational training has encountered budget problems. Due to limited facilities and resources management must determine what segment of the market the home is best suited to serve. Twenty segments were examined by using four segmentation variables: number of handicaps, degree of blindness, when handicaps occurred, and the age of the patients. Figure 10.1 shows the segmentation of the blind market using multivariable segmentation (Clarke, 1977).

Psychographic Segmentation. Psychographic segmentation consists of dividing the market into groups based on people's activities, interests, and opinions. Warner's Slimwear, a subsidiary of Warnaco, Inc., used psychographic segmentation to identify five lifestyle categories of bra buyers: (1) conservative, (2) fashionable, (3) brand conscious, (4) outgoing, and (5) price oriented. This information assisted the firm in developing products, advertising, and sales promotions designed to reach these specific segments (Richards & Sturman, 1977). Activities cover such dimensions as work, hobbies, shopping and so on. An individual's family, home, and job are the type of variables in the interest category. Social issues, political views, and economic positions are examples of the opinion dimension.

Behavioral Segmentation. Under behavioral segmentation buyers are divided based on the benefits they seek from a product/service,

		Single Handicapped		Multiple Handicapped	
		Partially sighted	Totally blind	Partially sighted	Totally blind
Congenital	Elderly				
	Working-age adult				
	Child				
Adventitious	Elderly				
	Working-age adult				
	Child				

FIGURE 10.1. Segmentation of the Blind Market

Source. From *Marketing for Nonprofit Organizations* (2nd ed.) (p. 222) by Philip Kotler. Englewood Cliffs, NJ: John Wiley. Copyright 1982. Reprinted with permission.

user status, usage rate, and the like. Many marketers segment their market based on the benefits the consumer receives. In Memphis, Tennessee, there are hospitals which concentrate on alcohol and drug abuse treatment, eye and ear treatment, and psychiatric treatment. Dentists also use benefit segmentation with specialties in facial surgery, orthodontics, periodontics, and prosthodontics.

User status refers to categories such as former users, regular users, first-time users, and so on. "Social marketing agencies pay close attention to user status. Drug rehabilitation agencies sponsor rehabilitation programs to help regular users quit the habit. They sponsor talks by ex-users to discourage young people from trying drugs" (Kotler, 1984).

Usage rate such as light, medium, and heavy usage patterns are used to segment the market. Marketers strive to gain information on the heavy user to improve their promotional messages. Social cause campaigns against smoking, for birth control, and against drinking and driving are normally directed at heavy users.

Pricing and Segmentation

Various market segments have different demand elasticities.* This recognition permits a marketer to price at different levels to each market segment. A washing machine manufacturer produces three models: deluxe, standard, and economy. The demand curve for the deluxe model would be relatively inelastic which would permit the marketer to charge a higher price. At the other extreme, the demand curve for the economy model would be quite price sensitive (elastic) and would suggest a low price. The standard model would have a mid-range elasticity and would be priced between the deluxe model and the economy model. Using a multiple pricing policy the resulting profit would be greater than offering one product at a single price. Airlines, theaters, and sporting events use a multiple pricing segmentation strategy.

Segmentation Criteria

When evaluating segments to decide if they offer marketing opportunities, three criteria must be present: (1) segment must be measurable particularly as to its size and purchasing power; (2) the segment must be accessible (i.e., the company must be effectively able to reach and serve the segment); and (3) the profits generated from the segment must be substantial enough to justify the firm's marketing investment.

Benefits of Segmentation

In addition to the ability to tap different demand elasticities, segmentation analysis assists the marketing manager

1. to design product lines that are consistent with the demands of the market and that do not ignore important segments
2. to spot the first signs of major trends in rapidly changing markets

---

*Elasticity refers to the price sensitivity of a product. For example, a product which is very price sensitive is said to have an elastic demand.

3. to direct the appropriate promotional attention and funds to the most profitable market segments
4. to determine the appeals that will be most effective with each market segment
5. to select the advertising media that best match the communication patterns of each market segment
6. to modify the timing of advertising and other promotional efforts so that they coincide with the periods of greatest market response (Yankelovich, 1964).

MARKET SELECTION

Three market coverage options are available for a firm: mass marketing or undifferentiated marketing, differentiated marketing, and concentrated marketing. Figure 10.2 illustrates each of these options (Kotler, 1982).

Market Selection Strategies

Mass (Undifferentiated) Marketing

A company that adopts a mass marketing strategy goes after the market as a whole. It develops a single product which will appeal to the broadest number of buyers. The firm depends on mass distribution and mass advertising.

The rationale behind this approach is cost savings. By producing a single product with mass appeal, a company has economies of scales in production and distribution expenses. There are lower advertising costs and marketing research expenses. Examples of a mass marketing strategy would be (1) a doctor prescribing the same blood pressure medication for all patients or (2) a family-planning organization that promotes the identical birth control method for everyone.

Differentiated Marketing

A firm using a differentiated marketing strategy goes after several market segments. Different products would be developed for

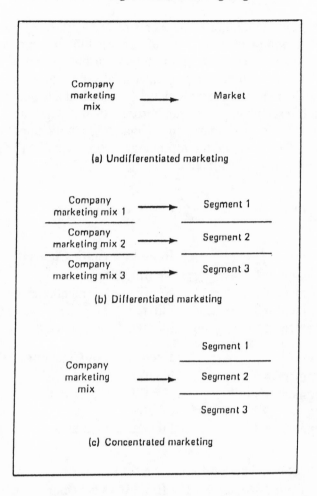

FIGURE 10.2. Marketing Coverage Strategies

Source. From *Marketing Management: Analysis, Planning, and Control* (p. 268) by Philip Kotler. Englewood Cliffs, NJ: Prentice-Hall, Inc. Copyright 1984. Reprinted with permission.

each segment. The other components of the marketing mix (price, promotion, and distribution) would be varied to take into consideration the differences between the buyers in the various segments. While this approach generates greater total sales than mass marketing, it also creates higher cost levels. Product management costs, marketing research expenses, and promotional expenditures will be higher than with mass marketing. Cigarette manufacturers use this approach. They produce the following products which are designed for different market segments:

Segment	Cigarette Type
	Regular Length Cigarettes
Segment #1	Nonfiltered
Segment #2	Nonfiltered & mentholated
Segment #3	Filtered
Segment #4	Filtered & mentholated
	Extra-Length Cigarettes
Segment #5	Nonfiltered
Segment #6	Nonfiltered & mentholated
Segment #7	Filtered
Segment #8	Filtered & mentholated

Care should be taken not to oversegment.

Concentrated Marketing. If a firm uses a concentrated marketing strategy, the company concentrates on one or a few marketing segments. A children's hospital and a doctor that specializes in brain surgery are examples of concentrated marketing in a health care setting.

Concentrated marketing offers an advantage because the company can develop a loyal following of customers within the market segment. However, the company is putting all its "eggs in one basket." Should major problems occur with the product or market segment, it can be extremely harmful to the firm.

Factors to Consider

Before the selection of one of the three market coverage strategies, a number of factors should be evaluated. How substantial are the firm's resources? A company must have considerable resources to use a differentiated coverage approach. How unique is the product? Unique products are ideal for differentiated marketing, while homogeneous products lend themselves to a mass marketing strategy. What is the product's stage in the product life cycle? In the early stages of the product life cycle, a single product makes sense. Later in the cycle, the firm may introduce other versions of the product and engage in differentiated marketing.

How homogeneous is the market? If buyers tend to have the same tastes, buy in similar quantities, and the like, a mass marketing strategy would probably be appropriate. What marketing strategies are being employed by the competition? If the competition is using a differentiated marketing approach, it forces a company to follow suit. However, if the competition is using mass marketing, a differentiated marketing strategy might give the company a competitive edge.

SUMMARY

The process of target marketing requires a company to examine all possible market segments. A market can be divided based on geographics, demographics, psychographics, and buyer behavior. After the segments have been evaluated, the company selects one or more market segments to enter. Three market coverage strategies are possible: mass marketing, differentiated marketing, and concentrated marketing.

The two chapters that follow illustrate two different aspects of segmentation and targeting. Stephen W. DeMello (Chapter 12) describes the practical adaptation of segmentation techniques to a mental health agency's planning cycle. William J. Winston (Chapter 11), on the other hand, provides an in-depth explanation of the most recent and least understood segmentation factor – psychographics and lifestyle segmenting.

REFERENCES

Clarke, Roberta N. "The Richardson Center for the Blind," pp. 61-72. In *Cases in Public and Nonprofit Marketing.* Christopher H. Lovelock and Charles B. Weinberg, Eds. (Palo Alto, CA: Scientific Press, 1977).

Kotler, Philip. *Marketing Management: Analysis, Planning and Control.* 5th Ed. (Englewood Cliffs, NJ: Prentice-Hall, Inc., 1984), p. 261.

Kotler, Philip. *Marketing for Nonprofit Organizations.* (Englewood Cliffs, NJ: Prentice-Hall, Inc., 1982), p. 222.

Richards, Elizabeth A. and Sturman, Stephen S. "Life Style Segmentation in Apparel Marketing," *Journal of Marketing* (October 1977), 89-91.

Yankelovich, Daniel. "New Criteria for Market Segmentation," *Harvard Business Review* (March-April 1964), 83-84.

CHAPTER 11

Psychographic/Lifestyle Aspects for Market Targeting

William J. Winston

SEGMENTING A MARKETPLACE

Through my experiences as a consultant and educator I have found marketing activities in health and human service organizations implemented randomly and haphazardly. It has only been during recent years that health marketers have started to pinpoint their potential clients with any form of marketing sophistication. The subdividing of a human service market into distinct sections is known as 'segmenting.' The action of evaluating and concentrating on those segments of the marketplace which appear to be the most cost-beneficial is called 'targeting.' This article attempts to demonstrate the importance of 'segmenting' and 'targeting' the health service organization's current and potential clients. In this way the organization can provide the optimum services to the population.

TRADITIONAL FORMS OF SEGMENTATION

Segmenting a marketplace is similar to cutting a pie into many different pieces. Each piece becomes a segment which can be addressed by the health care organization. Whether we are dealing, for example, with a psychiatric facility, outpatient service, counseling agency, private mental health practice or alternative forms of

Reprinted from William J. Winston, ed., *Marketing for Mental Health Services,* pp. 19–26, © 1984 by The Haworth Press, Inc.

mental health delivery systems, it has become vitally important to direct our marketing endeavors to the most cost-beneficial individuals or groups.

Traditionally, segmenting a market was directed towards 'mass appeal'. Health care attempted to be 'all things to all people'. Unfortunately, resource constraints prevented us from being able to serve all the health needs of society. This has led administrators to be more selective in allocating their precious resources. As the health industry grew competition expanded. This stimulated health organizations to 'differentiate' their services within the community. Human services began to identify their uniquenesses in comparison to other forms of human services in the same geographic area. This 'differentiation' was accomplished by physical features of the facilities, quality of care, types of care and service provided, types of providers involved and even the image or 'positioning' of the organization within their marketplaces.

Segmenting a marketplace has typically limited itself to the variables of

- geographic location: regionalization, city, size, density
- demographic factors: age, sex, family size, educational level
- economic factors: occupation, income, wealth
- social factors: religion, nationality, social class

All segmentation variables are important in dividing up a consumer and provider marketplace. Once these segmentation processes are completed, the 'targeting' or segment prioritizing begins. Targeting attempts to pick out primary and secondary individuals or groups within the marketplace which the health organization needs to communicate with through marketing. Targeting has usually been divided into three main approaches:

1. *Undifferentiated targeting:* attempts to market services to a 'mass' audience and to as many potential clients as possible;
2. *Differentiated targeting:* narrowed the approach to several market segments with a common denominator of characteristics; and
3. *Concentrated targeting:* emphasized marketing to a select segment(s).

Typically segments selected are divided into primary ones which have the greatest cost-benefit ratio and potential return. Secondary segments are also grouped for long-term marketing attention.

WHAT ARE PSYCHOGRAPHIC/LIFESTYLE AND BEHAVIORISTIC ASPECTS

Marketers have long used demographic characteristics for estimating the client's propensity to consume or utilize a health service. Most of these analyses are based on 'who' and 'what' characteristics rather than 'why' clients use services. Psychographics and lifestyle variables attempt to complement demographic, economic and social variables in selecting the promising target groups. Psychographics may be viewed as the practical application of the behavioral and social sciences to marketing research. Psychographics seeks to describe human behavior characteristics of clients/patients on their lifestyle, attitudes toward health services, interests and opinions, and personality traits and perceptions of the services/products' attributes. These characteristics definitely cross the socio-economic boundaries to develop a *client profile* of consumer belief and attitude towards select services. This analysis is especially useful in the initial stage of marketing planning. By identifying practical outcomes of psychographics an insight into consumer response to marketing stimuli can materialize.

Psychographic/lifestyle analysis can be divided into four specific categories:

1. *Psychological attributes:* These answer basic questions related to (a) what kind of individual a client is?; (b) how does a client perceive themselves?; (c) why do clients do the things they do? Most of the attributes include PERSONALITY traits. These traits are related to populations being: aggressive, gregarious, ambitious, creative, risk-taking, passive, depressed, abused, disciplined, competitive, resistant to change and others. For example, the stereotypic comments such as, 'Clinics are to be used only by those of lower social classes' and 'Only seriously mentally ill people go to psychologists' are derived from people's psychographic attributes.

2. *Lifestyle variables:* Lifestyle attributes of a client population

involve an examination of people's allocation of time and resources for themselves and their families. The various activities that an individual participate or not participates in become the framework for developing a lifestyle profile. Some lifestyle variables that become important are: sexual preferences, dress, athletic activities, political-involvement, work habits, daily routines, eating/drinking characteristics, travel, community involvement, hobbies and cultural endeavors. These attributes formulate a lifestyle sketch or portrait of individuals or groups in their interests, opinions and attitudes.

3. *Behavioristic or purchasing variables:* These variables evaluate a person's purchasing habits. A person can obtain a health service based on their (1) regularity of purchase; (2) user status; (3) loyalty strength; (4) level of need for service; (5) benefits of service perceived; and (6) motivation for utilization. Clients develop characteristics utilization patterns for different reasons. These purchasing variables can mean the difference, for example, of a client returning or making a referral.

4. *Service attributes and perceptions:* Last, but not least, are the perceptions people develop towards select physical or psychological characteristics of a service. For example, price and value aspects are the foundation for the question of 'Are these trips to the therapist worth it?'; taste factors are depicted in the comment that, 'This cough medicine tastes like cherry.'; quality is the basis for the comment, 'Only the best physicians are associated with this mental health center?'; benefits derived from the service are important in the statement, 'I feel so much better after my therapy session.'; and trust is the underlying factor in the statement, 'I need to rest daily as my doctor prescribed.'

STRENGTHS OF
PSYCHOGRAPHIC/LIFESTYLE TARGETING

By psychographic/lifestyle marketing the health administrator can construct an operating model of its attitudes and activity processes that the organization's marketing and technical capabilities can serve. This approach can provide an orientation to the health service's market that no statistical description of its demographics can provide. This gives the health administrator a chance to not just *know* their markets, but to virtually *become* part of the market by understanding its humanistic characteristics.

The results of using this type of targeting are to

1. restimulate existing services which are being utilized below their capabilities;
2. be better able to identify and develop new client needs, and thus, new services; and
3. strengthen the financial viability of the health organization and serve their clients/patients cost-effectively.

Psychographic/lifestyle marketing is rooted in market needs. Since these characteristics are built up over a period of years, they can be researched, modeled, planned for and marketed to over a period of time. Understanding emerging lifestyles and forecasting their impact on developing market segments is becoming a major concern of health marketers. There is too much time spent analyzing demographic data. In fact, even the technical sampling and interviewing techniques of gathering data are becoming suspect. For example, door-to-door interviewing is becoming prohibitively expensive and respondent cooperation more resistant. As a result, telephone and mail interviewing are becoming the only cost-effective techniques in marketing research.

One manifestation of a psychographic/lifestyle change is the emergence of smaller segments within the health marketplace. Health marketers are gradually learning that they need to measure the performance of new services whose only differences may be positioning. Gradually, there will be fewer really new breakthrough health services. New services are likely to be in existing categories with only minor benefits differentiating themselves in the eyes of the consumer. Positioning, target identification, and media effectiveness will dictate service success. As health service positioning becomes more precise, target identification will become very important. The main question will be 'Who is the real user of our services and have we communicated to them and motivated them positively?' The answer to this key question will require the use of 'understanding' and 'relating' to our consumer through psychographic/lifestyling.

EXAMPLES OF PSYCHOGRAPHIC/LIFESTYLING
IN NEW SERVICE DEVELOPMENT

The process that was described is the first step in a new service development phase that attempts to meet the needs of its clientele. By identifying the population target by socio-demographic characteristics first; life-styling the group based on the four categories of psychographic profiling; and discerning what service opportunities can be generated to fill health gaps, new service development is initiated. These new services can supplement, complement, or replace existing services. When psychographic/life-styling has been identified, it is divided into distinct life-style roles. These outcomes are the net result of life-styling marketing. Thus, these roles become the select target groups which the health organization must address. Each target group is then prioritized and ranked according to its apparent potential and organizational constraints. By targeting in this fashion the health organization is able to 'reposition' itself in the marketplace. Repositioning allows the organization to be perceived in a fresh, new light by their clients/patients. Repositioning could, for example, make the organization the leader in a specific new service. Some examples of health services which have developed according to psychographic/lifestyle characteristics include

- Sport-care programs targeted at the athletic client—(i.e., jogger, physical fitness advocate);
- Alcohol rehabilitation centers—(i.e., lifestyle of alcohol consumption);
- Meals on wheels programs for the elderly—(i.e., non-mobile senior citizens/lack of income/fear of crime);
- Child abuse 'talk lines'—(i.e., physical and mental abuse);
- Wellness programs—mental health employee assistance programs—(i.e., health advocacy/productivity and cost-containment attitudes);
- Stress management programs—(i.e., workaholic attitudes/ pressure);
- Medical information phone centers—(i.e., self-administered health treatment or diagnosis);

- Single parent communication groups — (i.e., divorce, single parent, attitudes towards seeking assistance);
- Weight-loss centers — (i.e., appearance, vanity, job role, health awareness);
- Ambulatory care centers — (i.e., cost conscious, lack of time);
- Herpes resource center — (i.e., sexual activity, attitude towards acknowledgment of potential problem and seeking of assistance);
- Biofeedback programs — (i.e., stress activities, time allocation); and
- Pain management programs — (i.e., new awareness of treatment, acceptance of alternative forms of care).

These examples are services that were designed in relation to psychographic/lifestyle/behavioristic attributes of the populations served.

Another key example of using psychographics is the marketing and advertising campaigns aimed at medical providers. This is especially important when taking into account the psychographics of physicians in target specialties. Research has demonstrated that psychographic data indicates a major difference between the general practitioner and the internist in terms of personality and attitudinal preferences. The personalities of certain specialties are unique and do affect the way in which doctors interact with their peers, patients, and even their own families. For example, in key studies in Chicago, psychiatrists were found to be free-thinking, open-minded, and quite comfortable with the ambiguities of their professional and personal lives. In contrast, obstetricians were characterized by their patients as patronizing and hard to communicate with. These types of studies have key applications, for example, in developing advertising campaigns. Obstetricians/Gynecologists apparently do not spend as much time dealing with their patient's emotions as they do treating the medical conditions. Therefore, a step-by-step, direct, matter-of-fact campaign might be more effective. The key point is that psychographics/lifestyle information would be very helpful in recruiting select medical personnel to the health organization.

CONCLUSION

Lifestyles have changed and are continuing to change through the 1980s. The new independence of lifestyle; dual income earners in households; increased crime; higher energy expenses and new energy sources; acceptance towards more preventive care services; self-diagnosis procedures and equipment; computers coming into the home; intensive new medical technology; movement towards continuing education for working professionals; improved child care centers; telecommunication breakthroughs; video equipment and technology impacting leisure activities; nuclear warfare threats; more competitive employment opportunities; less affordable single-family housing; alternative family units; acceptance of alternative sexual relations; extremes of increasing fast-food and gourmet cooking; renovation and maintenance of historical sites; modern architectural designs and cooperative work/living space conversions are examples of many changes in our living environment. These pressures for change create major impacts on people's attitudes, perceptions and lifestyles.

Psychographic/lifestyle information can complement each other. The demographic information can describe the physical attributes while psychographic/lifestyle data can analyze the psychological and emotional aspects of the health consumer. Each marketing strategy can be organized to meet the needs indicated in our psychographic/lifestyle profile. In other words, the marketing mix components of price, product, place and promotion can be specifically designed to meet the psychographic/lifestyle needs of the consumer. Psychographic/lifestyle targeting is an essential ingredient for a successful marketing program. This is especially true in today's environment of scarce financial resources for health care. As health marketers become more adept in analytically selecting marketing targets, the use of psychographic targeting will increase. Based on these advanced statistical tools it will be constantly possible to determine market information about the relationship between the consumer's lifestyle and health service utilization.

REFERENCES

Fuchs, Victor. *How We Live*, Harvard Press, 1983.

Hanan, Mack. *Life-Styled Marketing*, Amer. Mgt. Assoc., 1980.

Luck, David. *Marketing Strategies and Planning*, Prentice-Hall, 1979.

Jain, Subhash. *Marketing Planning & Strategy*, South-Western, 1981.

Kotler, Philip. *Marketing for Non-Profit Organizations*, 2nd Edition, Prentice-Hall, 1982.

Lambert, Zarrel. "Product Perception: An Important Variable in Price Strategy", *Journal of Marketing*, 1970, pp. 68-71.

Mossman, Frank. *Financial Dimensions of Marketing Management*, John Wiley & Sons, 1978.

Reynolds, Fred. *Psychographics: A Conceptual Orientation*, University of Georgia, College of Business Administration, Division of Research, 1973.

Simon, Julian. *Basic Research in Methods in Social Science: The Art of Empirical Research*. New York, Random House, 1978.

Smith, James. *Analyzing Future Business Environments*, Stanford Research Institute, 1976.

Weinrauch, Donald. *Applied Marketing Principles*, Prentice-Hall, 1975.

Wells, William. "Psychographics: A Critical Review", *Journal of Marketing Research*, May, 1975, pp. 196-213.

Wells, William. *Lifestyles and Psychographics*, American Marketing Association, 1974.

Wind, Yoram. *New-Product Forecasting*, Lexington Books, 1978.

CHAPTER 12

Market Planning for Mental Health: A "Target Group" Based Approach

Steven W. De Mello

The concept and potential uses of marketing have captured the attention of mental health and other health care managers in recent years. The professional literature has demonstrated the theoretical applications of strategic marketing management in an increasingly competitive environment; it has also illustrated a number of tactical successes accomplished through the introduction of marketing techniques and practices.

One aspect of marketing which has received less attention, but is of critical importance, is its fundamental *interdependence* with other management practices. The ultimate success of marketing activities will depend in large part on their ability to integrate with and shape other management processes. This is particularly relevant to health care institutions, where marketing is being introduced into an environment rife with existing practices and long-standing assumptions about the nature of the market and the behavior of the patient/ client. Any or all of these assumptions and biases may limit the use and potential effectiveness of marketing management in the mental health setting.

An early and key relationship is between marketing and corporate planning. The basic premise of this paper is that the successful marketing management in mental health will depend on early integration with corporate planning work. The chief impact of this integra-

Reprinted from William J. Winston, ed., *Marketing for Mental Health Services*, pp. 13–17, © 1984 by The Haworth Press, Inc.

tion is to broaden management thinking about the range of basic market strategies available to help shape its future environment.

This paper proposes a specific market planning process to achieve that integration, based on two major elements:

1. The identification and selection of a limited number of key "Target Groups" of people to be served by the organization, who will receive the majority of corporate attention and resources.
2. The development of specific "Programs" composed of multiple projects and tactics, aimed at meeting the broadly defined mental health needs and demands of key group members.

The first key concept is that of the Target Group. A *Target Group* is a segment of the population that shares unique health care needs or preferences, and can be defined either demographically or medically. The concept can be readily applied to the market for mental health services.

"Mental Health", broadly defined, covers a wide range of services and problems. Those needs and demands are not homogeneous, however; they are composed of the specific needs of many smaller groups, such as:

- The *elderly*, who are at specific risk for disorders such as Alzheimer's Disease, and who have specific functional limitations in seeking and obtaining care.
- *Local business*, for whom the impact of substance abuse and other medical/social problems represents an increasingly critical cost.
- *Families*, whose need for counseling and other services follows patterns dictated by major events such as divorce, death, children leaving the home, and others.

Each of these population segments, as well as many others, are potential Target Groups. The two elements which determine their usefulness for market planning are the ability to define and isolate specific characteristics of the group, and the ability to relate specific mental health needs and demands to group members.

Target groups represent a departure from most health planning, which can be described as developing "inside out." The provider selects services to be offered, then decides internally how to introduce them; if they are used, they are "justified" and reimbursed. The results of such an approach are plans which are technology and service intensive, but with little provision made for the process and logistics: payment mechanisms, hours and locations of service, relationship to other area services and providers.

Target Group based planning works from the "outside in": key groups of people are chosen, whose characteristics and needs drive all other planning decisions. In contrast with provider-driven plans, Target Group based plans more often concentrate on improving how care is delivered and market ties created, as well as new clinical services to be performed.

There are two major advantages to a Target Group based market planning approach over more traditional forms. The first is that Target Groups bring a tangible focus to planning work. It is often difficult to achieve clarity on abstract concepts such as "market areas" and "community mental health." On the other hand, medical and lay persons alike can more easily grasp the needs of the elderly, teens, families with a recent death, or the substance abuser—they know them, work with them, and can bring personal knowledge and experience to bear immediately.

Using Target Groups as the starting point for market planning makes the process tangible and practical, rather than a technical exercise that few gain from or are interested in. This in turn improves participation, and leads to a better plan.

A second rationale for a focus on target groups fits with a key suggested future market strategy: serve limited groups of people intensively over a long period of time. Mental health providers are faced with increased competition from a wide variety of sources, both traditional and new. In addition funding restrictions are becoming more severe, particularly in the public sector, with politically sensitive agencies in a substantially more vulnerable position for future funding.

Faced with these conditions, a given provider could take one of two general strategies:

1. An unfocused, venture-oriented approach of developing a wide range of new services which would appeal to many different publics: offer and deliver what sells, regardless of market.
2. A focused approach of aligning the organization with a limited number of groups, for whom it becomes the "provider of choice" – the first contact for a wide range of services over time.

The crux of the second approach is the belief that long-term security depends on creating a loyal market, rather than a high success rate for new ventures. It also requires commitment to a central corporate mission, which can get lost in a flurry of unfocused activity.

The use of Target Groups as a logical organizing base for program development leads to a second phase of planning and marketing activity. This phase involves assembling all organizational elements which support a given Target Group into a single planning activity – the "Program Plan." All interventions – services, management activities, payment methods, media and promotion – are incorporated into a single development plan covering one to five years for a given Target Group.

The logic of the concept can be seen by looking at the "patient path" – the type and sequence of services commonly used by a given Target Group. Program planning looks at these services as a whole, regardless of existing organization structure, and attempts to plan for them as a unit. If done successfully, all people and services within the organization who regularly work with the Target Group will be aware of, and can anticipate and coordinate their work, around the Target Group.

The development of Target Group driven plans will require a great deal of input from many different elements of the organization. This can be accomplished primarily through a series of interviews with key leaders – physicians, nurses, managers, patients and community leaders. These interviews can be used to both elicit information and test ideas for new services and the like, and represent an excellent opportunity to increase management visibility and lines of communication across the organization.

The process for identifying, selecting, and conducting specific market planning around key Target Groups can be accomplished in four steps:

1. *Identify all major target groups for planning and service development.* A core management group can begin the process by brainstorming a list of potential target groups. The purpose of the listing is not to make final decisions; rather it is to identify those groups which should be studied further.
2. *Set criteria for selection and prioritization of key target groups.* The basis for selecting key Target Groups for planning emphasis should be their compliance with established criteria related to characteristics of groups which the organization considers to be most important or desirable. The criteria can cover a wide range of concerns: medical need, historical commitment, financial feasibility, potential for long-term growth, and the like. The intent is to select a limited number of parameters for the Target Group studies, specifically looking at their relation to the criteria rather than producing general market research.
3. *Analyze target groups, select and prioritize key groups.* An in-depth study of each Target Group on the final list, aimed at measuring how they relate to the final set of criteria, should be performed. The result should be a formal report and recommendation of key Target Groups to be identified as the major focus for marketing activities in the future.
4. *Develop specific program plans for each key target group.* The conclusion of the process will be development of specific program plans for each key target group. The process should include data analysis, staff and community interviews, and conclude with a five-year plan incorporating all tactics and services aimed at a particular target group.

The market planning process outlined above can be instituted over a short or long period of time, depending on the degree to which the organization wishes to involve internal staff. The process of completing the first three tasks, leading to definition of key Target Groups, will require approximately one to three months, depending primarily on staff availability and interest.

The production of Program Plans is likely to require one to two months development time per Program. Two alternative work plans can constitute a complete planning cycle. The first would call for the development of a lower intensity, basic plan for each Target Group, which emphasized the current status of the group and projects to be undertaken immediately. As an alternative, the organization could schedule a limited number of Target Groups each year for intensive study, ensuring that each major group received detailed consideration on a rolling two to three year cycle.

The ultimate success of marketing management in mental health will depend in large part on two elements: the organization's ability to think broadly and aggressively about its approach to the market, and the ability to instill that approach in other management processes. A Target Group based market plan is a strong initial step toward both elements.

CHAPTER 13

Designing a Promotional Tool: Practical Application of Market Targeting and Research: Case Example: Alcoholism Services of Cleveland, Inc.

John A. Yankey
Diana Young
Nancy Koury

As social services agencies face a decrease in funding, many aggressively seek new sources of revenues, including an increase in the number of paying clients. To accomplish this, they often turn to marketing. Although marketing is not a "cure-all" for their problems, it does offer benefits to the non-profit sector.

The focus of a good marketing program is the consumer. This is congruent with social services' long-term declaration of being client-centered. With a marketing approach, all aspects of the program package (price, promotion, placement, and product) should be an agency's response to client needs and wants. In this way the consumer becomes the focal point for key decisions in marketing the agency's services.

Two important marketing concepts play an integral part in mak-

Reprinted from William J. Winston, ed., *Marketing Strategies for Human and Social Service Agencies*, pp. 59–71, © 1985 by The Haworth Press, Inc.

ing the client/consumer the focus of an agency's decision-making: targeting and market research. Rubright and MacDonald (1981) define a marketing target as "any organization or individual that can affect the outcome of the marketing project objective for better or for worse . . . " Market targets for social services often include more than just the user of the service. Older consumers include funders, referral sources, supporters (e.g., citizen groups), and or legislators.

The other major marketing concept discussed in this article is marketing research. Marketing research can be defined as the organizational activity of systematic gathering, recording, and analyzing the information needed to make planning and implementation decisions relevant to any marketing problem or issue (Flexner & Gerkowitz, 1979; Kotler, 1974; Lovelock, 1984; Rubright & MacDonald, 1981). Data resulting from marketing research do not provide "magic" answers for marketing agency services; rather, such data serve as the guidelines for agencies to make better decisions about the program package. Marketing research identifies client needs and preferences on which to base these key decisions instead of management merely guessing what the client needs.

Through the use of a case example, this article will illustrate how one agency program utilized these marketing concepts in developing a promotional tool, the redesign of a program brochure. A brief discussion of the background of the program is followed by the steps undertaken to develop this promotional tool.

AGENCY AND PROGRAM BACKGROUND

Alcoholism Services of Cleveland, Inc. (ASC) is a private, non-profit United Way member agency. The agency serves Greater Cleveland, Ohio (Cuyahoga County) and the surrounding area. The Board of Trustees decided to address the area of drunk driving in conjunction with a new state law, which mandated 72 consecutive hours in jail or 72 hours in a DWI (Driving While Intoxicated) school in lieu of jail for all first-time offenders. However, the new state law also provided for "municipal option," i.e., it allowed for each municipality to enforce its own DWI code. In ASC's target area, there are 13 municipal courts and 17 mayor's courts, representing a total of 52 judges. The result is a wide range of sentencing of DWI offenders throughout the county and even among the different judges within the same municipal court. With no uniformity of jail sentences, a number of existing DWI schools (varying in length and quality) are utilized in lieu of jail time. This creates a highly competitive environment for the several DWI schools in the county.

ASC's Impaired Driver Program (IDP) offers a 72-hour residential and a 40-hour non-residential DWI program. Both require the participation of a family member or close friend for 16 hours of the program, a unique feature of the IDP. Other DWI programs which require less time involvement for the DWI offender and charge a lower price, present competition for the IDP. It was imperative for ASC's program to implement a marketing plan, including effective promotional tools.

STATEMENT OF MARKET RESEARCH PROBLEM AND OBJECTIVES

After a year of operation, the Impaired Driver Program (IDP) identified the need to redesign its "temporary" brochure to incorporate two aspects: (1) a more professional appearance in the brochure; and (2) update the information with changes made during that year.

As the promotional tool must be consumer-focused, one preliminary step is the identification of the program's market targets. Results of the initial marketing audit, conducted in the product development phase, revealed a decision-making unit made up of several different "influences" and "decision-makers" (depending on which court or judge was involved). These "influencers" and "decision-makers" are judges, probation officers, bailiffs, lawyers, and the offenders themselves (see Figure 13.1). Thus, written communication, including the brochure, should be targeted at each of these segments (Kotler & Levy, 1969; Rubright & MacDonald, 1981).

Two decisions concerning the development of the brochure rested with management. As part of maintaining a uniform agency

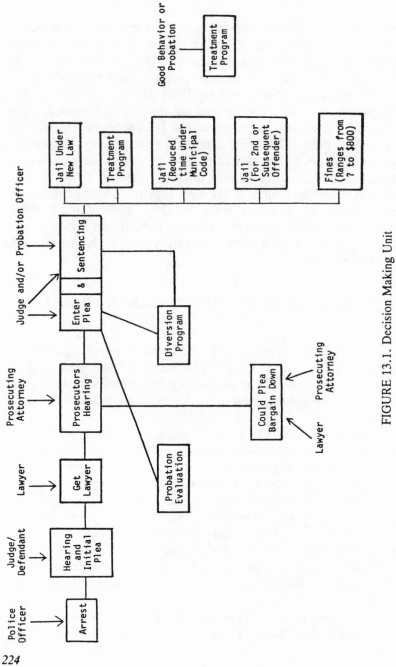

FIGURE 13.1. Decision Making Unit

image, top management required that several parts of all agency program brochures remain consistent (e.g., agency logo, general agency information, statements required by law and funding bodies, etc.). Middle management (program manager and her supervisor) determined what basic information must be included as a minimum in the brochure (e.g., what, when, price, telephone contact number, etc.). With these as "givens" the question became: What should be the exact nature of the content for the brochure(s) which would target all the various market segments?

This, therefore, became the market research purpose: To develop the most effective brochure, targeted at the various segments of the decision-making unit, in order to increase the Impaired Driver Program's share of the market. In refining this to specific market research objectives, clarification was needed on the following:

1. What information is misunderstood or missing in the present brochure?

2. What facts are important to the decision-making process? $\left\{ \begin{array}{l} \text{judges} \\ \text{lawyers} \\ \text{probation officers} \\ \text{offenders} \end{array} \right\}$ in their

3. What attributes of the IDP appeal to each segment?
4. What "exchanges"/"benefits" exist for each target segment?
5. Can these different factors be represented in one brochure or are several brochures needed?

SELECTION OF RESEARCH TECHNIQUES AND PROCEDURES

The program manager and her supervisor determined it was feasible to obtain answers to these questions and further, that both primary research (process by which data must be generated) as well as secondary research (data already exist and are available to the program) would be utilized. The following techniques were selected to answer the research objectives:

Objective	Technique	Primary or Secondary
• Information to be clarified	• Key informant interviews with staff members	• Primary
	• Other DWI School brochures	• Secondary
• Important factors in decision-making for	• Program Reports	• Secondary
• Judges	• Key Informant Interviews	• Primary
• Lawyers	• Key Informant Interviews	• Primary
• Probation Officers	• Focus Groups	• Primary
• Offenders	• Client Satisfaction forms	• Secondary
	• Telephone inquiries	• Primary
	• Utilization reports	• Secondary
• Attributes which appeal to various segments	• Same as preceding	• Same as preceding
• Exchange or benefits for each segment	• Same as preceding	• Same as preceding
• One brochure or several	• Analytical step in market research	
	• Management decision	

IMPLEMENTATION OF RESEARCH METHODS

Staff developed an outline of activities required to complete the research and a corresponding task time table. It was decided the program manager of the IDP would have the major role in coordinating and conducting the research activities. Although this raises some question concerning staff bias, operating in a highly competitive environment offered strong incentive for the program manager to remain honest and open in order to formulate the most responsive brochure. Furthermore, two other procedures helped to counter the possibility of staff bias. First, in the latter stage of the development, a draft brochure would be "field-tested," i.e., other agency staff would have input. Second, a consultant team would provide scrutiny over the research procedure. A marketing project team from Case Western Reserve University offered technical assistance through three major tasks: monitored the process to insure validity of activities; provided a "sounding board" for analyzing the data; and brainstormed with staff to develop recommendations.

Staff: The process began with "in-house" key informant interviews. Key staff of ASC were interviewed; namely, those who registered offenders for the program or received initial requests about the program. These staff (professional paid staff, volunteers, and clerical—totaling 5) were asked for their input regarding the brochure. These interviews lasted an average of 15 minutes. Questions covered such areas as:

- Content misunderstood or confusing in the present brochure
- Information currently missing
- Most frequent question(s) asked by service inquirers or registrants
- Attributes of IDP as noted by inquirers

Judges: The next set of key informant interviews was conducted with judges. Program reports were reviewed to ascertain which judges were most actively referring to the program. The program manager attempted to contact 4-5 judges who actively referred to the program and 4-5 who had not yet referred. The key interviews were easily executed by the program manager since her duties as court liaison provided continual contact with the judicial system. Although most judges were available for a personal interview, when necessary interviews were conducted by phone. The sessions lasted between 30-60 minutes and included questions centered around such areas as:

- Typical sentence for a DWI offender
- Conditions appropriate for referral to a DWI program
- Reason for referring/expected outcomes for referral
- Barriers in referring offenders

Attorneys: Attorneys can be significant "influencers" in the decision as to which DWI program an offender attends; therefore, attorneys become a second important target segment. Key informant interviews with attorneys were somewhat more difficult to execute. Several attorneys from the agency's Board of Trustees were interviewed, as well as two attorneys who called for their clients to request information about the program. Typically, attorneys would not afford as much time as the judges. Interviews lasted 15–30 minutes and included such questions as:

- How did you hear about the program?
- What is the most important factor(s) in selecting a DWI program for your client?
- What aspects of the program do you feel are most appealing to your client?

Probation officers: A third target segment for research activities was the probation officers. A focus group offered the opportunity for input by 6 probation officers from different municipal courts. Eight probation departments (varying in size and representing demographically different municipalities) were initially contacted by phone, followed by a formal written request to those who responded favorably. A skilled volunteer (Master's level student intern) served as the group facilitator, rather than the program manager, to enhance the probation officers responding candidly. Some questions were similar to those asked the judges and lawyers, but additional ones were added concentrating particularly on referral procedures (as probation officers are often the court's channel for completing assignment forms with offenders). The focus group lasted approximately 90 minutes, following which those participating were provided lunch.

Users of the Service: Input from the actual user of the service (DWI offender and his/her family member) was gained in several ways. At each month's session, the participants (offenders) and the co-participants (family members) complete evaluation forms on the final day of the program. The evaluations consist of rating general areas of the program and responding to open-ended questions. Monthly summaries of these evaluations reflect the group's ratings as well as all written comments. In reviewing the summaries, recurring comments provided insight as to what attributes of the program seemed especially appealing to the participants and co-participants; what areas of the program warranted further explanations; what areas created negative feelings; and clues as to misconceptions formed prior to attending the IDP.

Secondly, for a two-week period, those receiving initial requests were asked to make note of reoccurring questions from the offender and/or the family member. Thirdly, utilization reports were reviewed to determine what reasons potential users offered for not completing registration. Those aspects identified as least appealing to offenders could then either be minimized in the brochure, turned into a positive attribute of the program in the reader's eyes, or more fully explained to provide a satisfactory rationale for the program's methods.

ANALYSIS OF DATA

The next step was to analyze the information gained through these research activities. Analyzing was primarily the task of the program manager, her supervisor, and the development officer (whose graphic skills and creativity were to aid in the brochure design and wording, and who also offered an objective perspective). As previously mentioned, the marketing project team from Case Western Reserve University also offered an objective review of the data.

The authors will not attempt to reflect all the information gained through the analysis techniques. However, examples will be presented to illustrate how these activities answered the market research objectives. Most evident in the feedback were those items commonly misunderstood or missing in the temporary brochure:

- Program's status as to state certification
- Session content
- Eligibility requirements
- Requirements of co-participants
- Hours for attendance (residential vs. non-residential vs. family)
- Location

Commonalities noted among the factors employed by the "decision-makers" included the need to meet 72 hours (in some courts); what courts are utilizing the school; and cost. The analysis led to important findings regarding the perceived program benefits/exchanges for each target group:

Judges:	• Concerned with over-crowding jails • Reduction in recidivism • Need to answer to community voice (e.g., MADD)
Lawyers	• Need state-certified school • Least costly and restrictive
Probation Officers:	• Easy method of referral • Thorough assessment of probationer's drinking
Participant:	• Comfortable facility, privacy • Non-threatening experience • Caring staff, who "treat you like human beings"

APPLICATION OF FINDINGS

Based on the findings from the market research activities, a draft brochure was designed and "field tested" with agency staff and the marketing consultants, as well as members of the general public. The brochure integrated data regarding currently missing or misunderstood information with the necessary and factual information needed by all those seeking to learn about the program. The feedback on readability and accuracy resulted in few changes.

As a result of the field testing, it was noted that the initial draft did not expound on the various benefits or desirable attributes for the different market segments; rather, it made general statements which did not adequately cover these specific points. Through further discussion with staff and the technical assistance team, three inserts were designed for the brochure. One insert was designed to target members of the judicial system (judges, bailiffs, probation officers, lawyers) which allowed for each segment to be targeted separately on this insert (see example in Figure 13.2). A second insert was targeted at the individual participant. It serves as an informal discussion with the offender to inform him/her in more detail what happens there and to create a caring, accepting tone (see excerpt from insert in Figure 13.2).

A third insert was designed to target family members. This attempts to recognize the feelings a co-participant holds in being required to attend the session; and, further helps him/her to understand what is expected of a co-participant during the session. Because this component is the most misunderstood, the desired outcome is to lessen co-participants' anxieties and initial hostilities. (See Figure 13.2 for excerpt from this insert.)

MONITORING AND EVALUATION

No market strategy is complete without a plan for monitoring and evaluation. Semi-annually, the IDP's statistics are reviewed by its program staff and management of ASC. This promotional tool will be reviewed as part of that process. Additionally, feedback from the target segments will be solicited on an on-going basis as staff receive service inquiries from offenders and their attorneys. The IDP staff meet quarterly to review program issues. An item for discussion will be any feedback received on the brochure, particularly if staff have observed an attitude change by the family on the initial day of the program. Finally, on an annual basis, evaluation forms containing questions concerning the brochure are mailed to judges and probation officers for their feedback.

CONCLUSION

Many agencies do not fully embrace the practice of marketing, especially marketing research. The reasons cited for this are usually lack of skilled staff, inadequate time available and/or no monies allocated for such activities. It is true that some marketing activities may require seeking outside marketing expertise. However, as Lovelock (1984) notes in his reference to market research, "The goal of marketing research is to reduce uncertainty to tolerable lev-

TO MEMBERS OF THE JUDICIAL SYSTEM:

Judges - By sentencing the DWI offender to the Impaired Driver Program you can:

> . provide an alternative to overcrowded jails.

> . reduce recidivism

> . provide viable answers to your community's questions about drunk drivers and their treatment in the court system.

Attorneys - By referring your client to the Impaired Driver Program you will offer them:

> . a state-certified program recognized by the courts of Cuyahoga County

> . an educational experience which can be long-term positive benefits

Probation/Parole Officers - Referral to and involvement with the Impaired Driver Program offers many benefits:

> . you secure an easy method of referral

> . you receive an assessment regarding your probationers/parolee's drinking

> . you have access to three-way conferences and useful follow-up information which can save you time and effort in your casework

TO THE PARTICIPANTS:

It is a shock to be convicted for a DWI offense. If this is your first time through an IDP you must be wondering what's in store for you ...

The setting is comfortable and safe. The food is good and the surroundings combine the atmosphere of a hotel setting and an educational workshop ... There will be films, lectures, group discussions and private sessions with caring and skilled professionals.

TO THE FAMILY:

"Why do I have to come to this program? I wasn't the one caught drinking and driving!"

Most family members involved in the Impaired Driver Program ask this question, usually with a bit of anger and upset feelings ...

You will see films, hear lectures and have many chances to ask questions. You will meet others who have to face the same problems and worries and learn how others cope.

FIGURE 13.2. Excerpts from the Inserts of Impaired Driver Brochure

els at a reasonable cost.'' In other words, expending dollars in the present can keep the agency from spending unnecessary dollars on activities which do not effectively address the problem. Without the implementation of targeting and marketing research in the case example, an ineffective brochure would have been developed which ignored the essence of the marketing principle — the exchange value for its market targets.

Furthermore, this case example illustrates that marketing research does not always have to be complicated and time-consuming. Most research activities fit into the daily tasks of the program manager; therefore, limited additional time expenditure is required on the part of the staff. All activities with the target segments served as additional visibility for the program. With very little money expended, the agency was able to avoid wasting money on an inadequate promotional tool. Instead, two marketing concepts — targeting and market research — were invaluable in the development of an effective IDP brochure.

REFERENCES

Flexner, W. A. & Berkowitz, E. N. Marketing Research in health services planning: a model. *Public Health Reports*, November-December, 1979, *94*(6), pp. 503-513.

Kotler, P. *Marketing for non-profit organizations*. Englewood Cliffs, New Jersey: Prentice-Hall, Inc. 1975.

Kotler, P. & Levy, S. Broadening the concept of marketing. *Journal of Marketing*, January, 1969, *33*, pp. 10-15.

Lovelock, C. *Services Marketing*. Englewood Cliffs, New Jersey: Prentice-Hall, Inc., 1984.

Rubright, R. & MacDonald, D. *Marketing Health and Human Services*. Rockville, Maryland: Aspen Systems Corporation, 1981.

Part V

Positioning
the Health Service

CHAPTER 14

Introduction to Positioning the Health Service

Robert L. Berl

Positioning is the "act of designing the company's product and marketing mix to fit a given place in the consumer's mind" (Kotler, 1984, p. 272). An example can be seen in Seven-Up's use of the "Uncola" theme to position itself as a distinct alternative to cola beverages.

POSITIONING STRATEGY DEVELOPMENT

Positioning stems from a company having conducted market analysis, competitive analysis, and a corporate analysis. The company uses the marketing mix variables (product, distribution, promotion, and price) so that the company's product/service stands apart from the competitor's offering. The following procedure can be used to determine a firm's positioning strategy:

- analyze the product attributes which are important to consumers
- examine these attributes in different market segments
- determine the optimal position for the product in regard to each attribute, taking into consideration the positions occupied by competition
- determine the overall match between the product attributes and their distribution among the segments and against the positions of existing brands
- select an overall position for the product (Jain, 1981, p. 257-8).

TYPES OF POSITIONING

The following alternative types of positioning strategies are available to the health care marketer of health care or social services.

Product/Service Attributes. Eastwood Hospital of Memphis, Tennessee, advertises that its emergency room will see a patient within one minute. This attribute of speed implies a benefit of quick relief.

Product/Service Benefits or Needs. Some health care providers stress the problem solution or need fulfillment. Sports Medicine Clinic of Memphis positions itself as specializing in the rehabilitation and prevention of all sports related injuries.

Product/Service Specific Usage Occasions. All medical emergency clinics position themselves as providing emergency care quicker, less expensively, and with less red tape than the hospitals.

Product/Service User Category. Every major metropolitan area has hospitals which are positioned to provide medical services for such users as children, drug addicts, alcoholics, and the like.

Product/Service Positioning Against Competition. There are many marketers who advertise that their product is superior to their competition's. Anacin argues that it has more "pain killer" than does Bayer Aspirin. Because of many years with strict codes of ethics regarding advertising and a concern for professionalism, health care marketers tend not to position themselves overtly against the competition. The Eastwood ad, previously referred to, implies that they are faster than other emergency care providers, but the competition is never specifically named.

Product/Service Class Dissociation. This type of positioning calls for the marketer to put himself in a product class other than the one expected. An examination of the Yellow Pages for a large city, for example, disclosed a clinic located in a shopping center advertising itself as a hospital.

REPOSITIONING

Under certain conditions, a company may want to reposition a product/service. If consumer preferences have changed (moved away from a traditional product offering), a firm would want to reposition the product accordingly. Another reason for repositioning a product would be the discovery of new market segments which might offer more promising profit opportunities. If a competitor introduces a product which has cut into a firm's market share, repositioning is a viable strategy. In addition, repositioning is imperative if the original positioning strategy was incorrect.

Existing customers. The aim of repositioning among current users is to revitalize the sales of a product and extend the life cycle of the brand. For example, Levi's is attempting to reposition its jeans line by producing them in fabrics other than denim.

New users. Repositioning a product to attract new users requires presenting the product offering in a new light. However, caution should be taken so as to not lose existing customers. As an example, when it became apparent that many American consumers were increasingly concerned with health and weight control, Jell-O was advertised using a fashion-oriented, weight-control appeal.

New uses. Products can be repositioned by developing new uses for which the product was never originally intended. If successful, this strategy will revitalize sales and extend the product's life cycle. Arm & Hammer baking soda is an example of repositioning through new uses. In addition to its original purpose, it is used widely today as a refrigerator deodorant.

SUMMARY

Positioning is the process of developing a product and marketing mix to fit a given place in the consumer's mind. Positioning is accomplished by analyzing the market, the competition, and the company and selecting market segments in which the company believes it has product offerings with a competitive advantage. Product/services can be positioned based on product features, consumer benefits derived, usage and type of user, and strength of competition.

Often it is necessary to reposition a product. This can be accomplished by getting existing customers to use more of the product, attracting new users, and developing new uses for the product.

The following chapter by William J. Winston illustrates a strategic approach to positioning health care services for senior citizens. The case studies for this section demonstrate how positioning opportunities are addressed in a small denominational college (Dewana Alexander).

REFERENCES

Jain, Subhash C. *Marketing Planning and Strategy*. (Cincinnati, OH: South-Western Publishing Co., 1981.)

Kotler, Philip. *Marketing Management: Analysis, Planning and Control*. 5th ed. (Englewood Cliffs, NJ: Prentice-Hall, Inc., 1984.)

CHAPTER 15

Positioning the Health Organization into the Minds of the Health Consumers and Providers

William J. Winston

POSITIONING STATEMENTS

One of the most important aspects of marketing planning for a health care service is the use of market positioning. Before you begin to develop specific marketing strategies and tactics for select segments and targets, the health organization must consider the positioning or market niches it desires to obtain. *Market Positioning* is an attempt to distinguish the health care organization from its competitors along real dimensions in order to be the preferred service to select segments of the marketplace. Positioning aims to educate the medical provider and consumer along real differences between alternative services. This differentiation assists providers and consumers in matching themselves to the service that can be of most value. The tool of positioning is (1) image-making, (2) perception-oriented, and (3) personality-directed. The organization develops an image, perception, and a personality in the minds of the consumer.

Positioning is not necessarily a new tool in marketing. Historically, the concept of positioning was mainly concerned with what marketers did to the service or product being marketed. Today, it

Reprinted from William J. Winston, *How to Write a Marketing Plan for Health Care Organizations*, pp. 65–76, © 1985 by The Haworth Press, Inc.

usually relates to what the health administrator or marketer does for the service in the minds of the provider or consumer. The original aspect of positioning was derived from "product positioning" which utilized the product's physical appearance, size, form, and price compared to its competitors. Today, it is important to market the organization's image, but it is vital to create a position in the provider's or consumer's mind. The following questions need to be answered to lay the framework for the development of a positioning strategy for the health care service:

1. How is my service currently perceived by the marketplace?
2. What do I want my providers/consumers to think of my service?
3. What are the weaknesses and strengths of my services?
4. Have I emphasized the service's strengths and can I improve the weaknesses?
5. What are the strengths and weaknesses of my competitors?
6. What is the "positioning gap" that is apparent in my competitors' services and how can I fill the gap?
7. How can I influence the prospective or existing provider/consumer to perceive my services related to the market position you desire?

All of these questions lay the framework for the development of a *positioning strategy*. The positioning strategy describes what your service stands for, how you would like providers/consumers to think of your services, and how you will communicate the positioning perception of the service to your providers/consumers in the community. Today's health care marketplace is no longer responsive to the strategies that worked in the past. There are just too many products, services, programs, and facilities. In this overcommunicated marketplace there is a strong need to be selective and concentrate on specific target groups and communicate to these groups using narrowly defined strategies. One of these key strategies – is the *Positioning* of your programs or services into the mind of the medical provider or health consumer.

APPLICATION OF POSITIONING
TO LONG-TERM CARE SERVICES

The proliferation of new services and increased demand for their services has required long-term and senior care administrators to "position" their services in the minds of consumers. Marketers in all sectors of the health industry will be trying to communicate to the senior sector of the population during the next decade.

The maturing of the American population has brought about a more highly educated and discriminating consumer for senior care services. it has also created a tremendous current and future demand for these services. "Smart positioning" will have to replace "hard positioning" in marketing to the mature population and their families. It will become very difficult to con the senior marketplace as the educational levels of this group become higher and higher. Proven services with quality dimensions and positions in the marketplace will be the successful ones since this expanding group is quality-oriented. Products/services have to be marketed using more detailed information about the services. Proven services and word of mouth recommendations will be selected. Peer group pressure to try something new just because it is new or innovative will not be as effective.

The maturity market comprises at least 44 million individuals and one-third of all households. This group is quality-oriented and demands long-lasting effects from services. It will be a major mistake to market to the senior marketplace the same as the youth market. It demands a different positioning strategy. These strategies must relate to the senior marketplace in terms of quality, proven worthiness, and long-lasting qualities of the products or service.

One of the basic methods for developing positioning strategies is to apply them to the components of the marketing mix. In other words, positioning strategies can be developed according to the marketing mix components of pricing, place, product, and promotion.

The following are some examples of specific market positioning strategies, as applied to long-term or senior care services:

Pricing the long-term care service can be a powerful positioning strategy in order to attract an adequate market share without also attracting a devastating competitive reaction. For example, some pricing strategies could be related to developing perceptions within the community:

1. Are the prices of the services to be perceived as "high-priced and high-quality" or as "low-priced and quantity-oriented" for easier access to care?
2. Depending upon the local reimbursement levels, are the services to be priced at a level related to Medicare coverage or will there be a higher co-payment?

The medical provider who refers clients to your services or the consumer who directly seeks care will develop an image or perception within their minds about how your services are priced. In other words, think how you would like the community to perceive your services' costs and fees.

The characteristics of the service are a way to differentiate one's services by positioning the service to be general or specialized; available to all mature adults or to select segments of the marketplace, provided in a personal or factory-line mode of delivery, or by a courteous or disrespectful staff. The product component of the marketing mix relates to the physical aspects of the service or the way in which it is delivered. The following are some other examples of positioning questions:

1. Do medical providers and discharge planners perceive the senior service as highly professional and easy to work with or as difficult and unprofessional?
2. Does my staff perceive our organization as possessing a good physical environment in which to work?

All quality of care, staff relations, procedures, cleanliness, and service are involved in positioning the service through the use of the product component of the marketing mix.

The way in which services are delivered is important in relationship to the services being perceived as highly accessible or limited in accessibility, flexible in hours, possessing adequate parking and public transportation, operating in a safe location, or requiring a short waiting period before service is rendered.

The place component is a very important one as it relates to location, mode of delivery, and access to care. These three characteristics can be very important to the senior care client.

How one promotes their services positions the service as being hard sell, soft sell, educational, or good will-oriented; serving the community or just the financial needs of the organization; or being widely or little known within the community.

Other examples would be the questions:

1. Is the organization perceived as being secretive or readily available to distribute needed information about the services or treatment procedures?
2. Does the community perceive our service as being professional if we advertise on the radio or in the newspaper?

All of these positioning strategies relate to the amounts, quality, and direction of the information communicated to the population. Since advertising is becoming much more common in health care it is important to be selective of the media channel. Populations perceive an organization's position according to which media channel is utilized.

BEING FIRST INTO THE MARKETPLACE

In an overcommunicated marketplace positioning becomes an organized system for entering the consumer's mind. The easiest way in which to make a mental impression is to be first into the marketplace. The organization can build loyalty for the services by getting there first and providing no reason for the health consumer to ever switch. History demonstrates that the first product or service into the consumer's mind gets twice the long-term market share as that of the nearest competitor. The major reason that market leaders lose market share is change.

An example of being first for a positioning strategy is the new expansion of Life Care Services. Life Care is still a relatively new concept integrating the traditional services of a retirement community with the long-term health care found in a nursing home. There are some 600 Life Care Communities throughout the United States.

The services for residents include: medical care, transportation, living quarters, personal assistance, emergency service, funeral expenses, recreational activities, counseling, and continuing education centers. With the population maturing at such a fast pace, these initial Life Care Communities may have positioned themselves successfully for the long-term.

REPOSITIONING IN A HIGHLY COMPETITIVE ENVIRONMENT

The majority of the time most services cannot be the first into a marketplace. Most health services, especially senior services, are in the maturity phase of their existence and have many competitors. The traditional positioning strategy is to reposition the organization in the minds of the consumer. It is necessary to move the positioning of the competitors out of the minds of the consumer. This can be accomplished by positioning the services as being better or providing a key service which the competition does not. Comparative positioning is not illegal in most cases. Performed honestly, comparative repositioning can be positive for the marketplace. It keeps the providers alert and responsive to the needs of the community. Health care organizations have used repositioning extensively as related to offering services in a unique fashion or emphasizing better quality of care than its competitors.

COMPETING DIRECTLY WITH YOUR COMPETITORS

Most organizations do not attempt to take on the strongest competitor in the marketplace. You can go around, under, or over, but never directly against the dominant provider. The position required in this case is to take advantage of weaknesses or gaps in the marketplace. A great example of this positioning strategy is the HMO marketplace in Northern California were Kaiser's HMO is the dominant force. Yet over twelve HMOs have been developed during the last decade. These new HMOs market themselves related to services not available through Kaiser, better fees, etc. The new HMOs identified a niche in the marketplace and went after it. These new HMOs are trying to position themselves as being differentiated from Kaiser in terms of weaknesses in the Kaiser system or gaps in service delivery within the marketplace.

POSITIONING WITH A GOOD NAME

Goodwill and brand loyalty are vitally important concepts in marketing health care organizations. People want to be "attached" to a particular health care organization or service for security and trust factors. One of the most important aspects of brand loyalty is developing a quality and memorable name for the organization. Health care organizations have traditionally been delinquent in deciding on marketing-related names for their services.

Developing a name for a service can be approached from various perspectives. First of all, a strong positioning name is one in which the consumer relates to the type of service provided. For example, the Meals on Wheels program reflects a uniqueness and explains the basic service which is provided. A second approach is to keep the name simple yet find a unique marketing niche for the name. For example, a local crisis telephone line having the name Talk Line with the actual phone number related to the letters in the name is well-positioned. A third perspective is to be creative and develop a catchy name with a historical perspective, such as On Lok Senior Health Services. Other senior services with well-positioned names include: Gray Panthers, Senior Escort, Retirement Jobs, Inc., Golden Gate Senior Service, and YMCA Christmas Camp for Seniors. Sometimes a full name is not necessary as abbreviations become the positioning strategy. Think about the recognition and positioning of names such as: HHS, L-T-C, HUD, IBM, CARE, WHO, UN, AMA, and AHA. These are powerful positioning statements and highly recognizable.

POSITIONING SLOGANS AND LOGOS

An increasing concept in thinking about positioning the service is the use of slogans which represent these services. A slogan usually represents (1) a feeling we want to express about our services and (2) a key characteristic of the service. Slogans can be very creative and stylish. Who can forget "Where's the Beef?," "I Ate the

Whole Thing," "It Takes Two Hands to Handle a Whopper!," "Ring Around the Collar!," "Reach Out and Touch Someone," or "We Try Harder!"? These products were successfully positioned in the minds of the consumer by these slogans. Some examples in health care include a dental service named Smile America and its slogan "Smile America is here to keep you smiling." The slogan reflects the purpose of the preventive cleaning service and is also memorable. Another example would be a wellness program with its slogan "Let's Work Together for Life." A third example would be St. Luke's Hospital of Kansas City's "100 – A Century of Service/ A Heritage of Excellence."

An alternative to a slogan can be a well-developed logo for the organization. There are successful organizations which just specialize in developing the most appropriate and potentially effective logo for a specific organization. A well-developed logo can position the service in the minds of the consumer. One of the most successful logos and symbols in health care is the picture of the palms of two hands with a rainbow underneath representing United Way. Another successful one has been the Family Service Agency's symbol of two adults and two children with an oval parameter. Others include Blue Shield's medical insignia involving the staff of Aesculapius; Blue Cross' cross with an artist's sketch of a person in the middle with a circle around him; The Blood Center for Southwest Louisiana's two hearts on top of each other with one heart filled with blood dripping into the bottom of the heart; Adventist Health System-West's map of the United States marked off with the western states for territory they serve; and many different wellness programs with their derivative of a rising sun logo.

SUMMARY OF POSITIONING

Positioning can be one of the most powerful and long-lasting marketing tools. It is an integral part of any strategic marketing plan. The positioning section of the plan should include a laundry list and qualitative discussion of the specific positions which the organization desires to imprint into the minds of its consumers and providers. Positioning services requires some creativity, risk-taking, vision for the future, adaptability to change, subtleness, patients, and a willingness to use marketing as a key tool. Before any marketing strategies are developed in our next steps, positioning statements and thoughts must be analyzed and agreed upon by the marketing committee. These images and perceptions direct us to develop specifically applied strategies which will inform us how to position these services in the minds of the consumer.

SUMMARY:
POSITIONING THE HEALTH ORGANIZATION
INTO THE MINDS OF THE
CONSUMERS AND PROVIDERS

Before creating marketing strategies and tactics, it is important to examine what perceptions our target groups already have about the organization and to decide on specific perceptions we desire to have these groups possess. There are many ways to examine the use of positioning. The reader should have developed an understanding of: (1) the basic concepts of market positioning; (2) applications of positioning to the components of pricing, product, place, and promotion; being first into the marketplace; establishing positioning oriented names and slogans, etc.; and (3) how positioning lays the framework along with the marketing missions, goals, objectives, auditing, and targeting for developing marketing strategies and tactics.

Market positioning is a form of market strategy development. All of the actions we select to market the services to the target groups must be directed toward achieving select market positions.

This chapter lays the framework for the next one which thoroughly examines the creative phase of marketing—the development of strategies and tactics.

CASE EXAMPLE:
MARKET POSITIONING OF A PREVENTIVE
DENTAL CARE CENTER

INTRODUCTION

This short case is presented to demonstrate the applicability of the positioning techniques discussed in the prior chapter. The emphasis is a need to differentiate the health and human service from its competitors in the minds of the consumer. In this case, the reader is shown the positioning niches in the marketplace for a preventive dental service. The dental service is attempting to distinguish itself from other similar or identical dental practices according to unique characteristics of the practice.

BACKGROUND

A private dental group practice owned by Dr. Smith Johnson opened up PreventCare in the downtown financial district of the San Diego, CA metropolitan area. Dr. Johnson was in partnership with three other practicing dentists. The dentists also maintain two conventional dental practices in the same geographic area. Dr. Johnson and his partners had been in general dentistry in the San Diego area for approximately ten years. As more and more local dental graduates started practices or were attracted from other locales to this desirable region of the country, the level of competition began to increase significantly. They began to experience a stagnation of demand for their services from new patients. This situation stimulated them to investigate new market opportunities. Dr. Johnson commissioned a marketing consultant to evaluate the dental market in the San Diego area. The results of the market analysis indicated a large gap in traditional dental services in the downtown area of the City. Dr. Johnson then contracted with the same marketing consultant to explore the need for preventive-type dental services. The consultant surveyed a sample of employee benefit directors in local corporations, small business owners, random street interviews, and hotel/restaurants within a two mile radius of the center of the downtown financial district. The questionnaire attempted to inquire as to their use of preventive dental services, and if used, to question the need for such a new service in the area. The survey identified a demand for such services but some confusion as to what preventive dental services were and how busy while collar workers would be able to obtain them during working hours. The consultant then identified that there was not only no such type of service in this area, but no dental practices in the country which totally dedicated themselves to preventive services for this group of workers. Dr. Johnson discussed these findings with his partners and financial planner. Dr. Johnson and his partners began to firmly believe there was a market for a preventive dentistry-type services. They decided to open a small store front preventive dental service in a busy section in the middle of the downtown financial district of San Diego. The name they decided upon was PreventCare. (It should be noted that three major positioning decisions have already been made by the dentists: type of service, location, and name. First of all, there is no similar service in the area; only preventive services will be provided; and the name of PreventCare is simple to remember and reflects the purpose for their existence and the service rendered.)

PREVENTCARE SERVICES

PreventCare offers cleaning, brushing, polishing, and preventive check-ups with x-rays on a walk-in or appointment basis. It is open five days per week from 7 am to 6 pm. A licensed dentist is available at all times with a dental hygienist and a receptionist. It is attractively decorated with hanging plants, comfortable sofas and chairs, and a snack tray and wine. All prices are approximately 20% lower than the average private dental practice.

TARGET GROUPS

From the marketing analysis the consultant identified the following groups as the most promising primary and secondary marketing targets to pursue:

1. Young, upwardly-mobile white collar workers in the downtown area; these workers were limited to ages 18-45, working within a five-block radius of the practice;
2. Since San Diego is a major tourist attraction, tourists became a possible walk-in target group;
3. Conventioneers from the nearby convention center and many local hotels;
4. Shoppers from the five main downtown shopping malls;
5. Students from three nearby colleges;
6. Restauranteurs from the local 130 restaurants; and

7. Construction workers from the ten high rise projects being completed in the downtown area.

POSITIONING PREVENTCARE

As part of the marketing strategies for PreventCare, the positioning aspects became important in order to make a strong mental impression upon the potential target groups and to develop service loyalty. The unique characteristics which will cause these target groups to potentially use PreventCare reflect the organization's position in the marketplace and in the minds of the consumers.

Positioning Statement or Slogan

The positioning statement became "Come to PreventCare and leave with a better smile within twenty minutes!" This statement related to the characteristics of the service (cleaning), walk-in availability (no appointments), quick service (20 minutes or less), and physical improvement (improved smile). These basic ingredients comprised the framework for the positioning strategies.

Positioning Characteristics of the Service

The most important aspects of positioning is to have all aspects of the service reflect the image of the positioning statement. The unique characteristics, or positions, of PreventCare were developed to create client perceptions according to the following:

- Quick service—i.e., come in during your lunch hour, before work, after work, or by appointment;
- Convenience with no appointments necessary—i.e., walk-in service at any time;
- Geared toward self-gratification and appearance of upwardly mobile and ambitious people;
- Pleasant environment—i.e., plants, wine, comfortable furniture, boutique-oriented, modern pictures on walls, classical music, up-to-date modern literature on tables, glass partitions, handsomely dressed and very pleasant receptionist, etc.;

- Reasonable costs – i.e., large display and brochures listing exact prices for services;
- Back-up of full dentistry office – i.e., two offices within walking distance if needed;
- Emphasis on prevention – i.e., cleaning prevents future problems;
- Creative and modern quality service – i.e., relating to young upwardly-mobile people;
- Personal decision – i.e., emphasis on placing the responsibility of these young adults to decide when, and if, their teeth need cleaning rather than the dentist telling them so;
- Quality service with professionally trained and experienced dentists and hygienists to serve you.

All of the brochures, flyers, advertisements, and other information pieces constantly projected the positioning perceptions of these characteristics in the minds of the target groups selected in the marketing plan. The next step for the dental practice is to develop specific marketing actions (strategies and tactics) which will reflect these positioning characteristics and will be used to attract new patients. It is important to remember that all of the positioning characteristics can be transformed into strategies and tactics.

Part VI

Marketing Mix

CHAPTER 16

Introduction to
the Marketing Mix

Robert L. Berl

The firm's marketing management endeavors to satisfy the needs and wants of their target market. To achieve this objective, the manager uses four basic variables. These variables, known as the marketing mix, are product, distribution (place), promotion, and price. Product includes such attributes as features, accessories, service, branding, and packaging. Distribution, sometimes called "place," refers to the channel of distribution, types and location of branches, and so on. Promotion covers the ways in which the firm communicates with its various publics; such as advertising, personal selling, sales promotion, and public relations. Price includes pricing objectives, strategies, and the like. The remainder of this chapter will cover the marketing mix variables in more detail.

PRODUCT CONSIDERATIONS

A product is a "set of tangible and intangible attributes which provide want-satisfying benefits to a buyer in an exchange. . . . A 'product' may be a physical good, a service, an idea, a place, an organization, or even a person" (Stanton, 1984, p. 673). There are three levels of a product: core, tangible, and augmented. Figure 16.1 illustrates the three levels of a product.

The core product is the minimum expectation that the target market has of the product offering. It is what the target market is really seeking. In the case of a hospital, it would be medical treatment

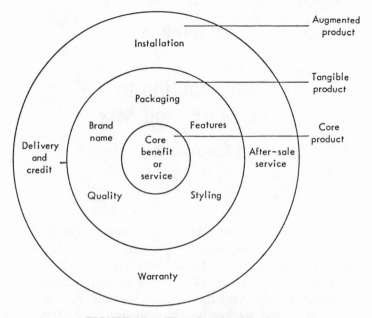

FIGURE 16.1. Three Levels of Product

Source. From *Marketing for Nonprofit Organizations* (2nd ed.) (p. 292) by Philip Kotler. Englewood Cliffs, NJ: Prentice-Hall, Inc. Copyright 1982. Reprinted with permission.

which provides the patient with the hope of a recovery from an illness, pain and suffering, or an accident. The core benefit is made available to the target market in a tangible way.

The tangible product is comprised of five characteristics: features, styling, quality, brand name, and packaging. As applied to a hospital, the characteristics would be as follows:

Features: Extended visiting hours, gourmet food
Styling: Professionally decorated rooms, stylish nurses' uniforms
Quality: Professionally qualified personnel, efficient administration
Brand Name: Well-known reputation, a name which the public can identify with
Packaging: The architecture and landscaping of the hospital facility

The offer of additional benefits, going beyond the tangible product, is the essence of the augmented product. For example, a hospital that offers an extended payment plan has augmented its tangible product.

Product Mix

Most firms have one or more product lines. A product line is a group of products that are related in some way. A hospital might have a diagnostic and cure product line. It would be made up of inpatient care, an outpatient clinic, emergency room services, laboratories, x-ray facilities, and so on. A product mix is all of the product lines the firm offers. In addition to the diagnostic and cure product line, the hospital might also offer a health education program and a research program. These three product lines would be the hospital's product mix.

Not all of the products are of equal importance. Some products constitute the firm's primary reason for existence, while other products are ancillary in nature. The diagnostic and cure program is the primary product for the hospital, while the health education program is an ancillary product.

Product Life Cycle

"Products are like living organisms. They are born, they live, and they die. A new product is introduced into the market place. It grows, and, when it loses appeal, it is terminated" (Pride & Ferrell, 1980, p. 190). This process is known as the product life cycle.

The product life cycle has four distinct phases: (1) introduction stage, (2) growth stage, (3) maturity stage, and (4) decline stage. Figure 16.2 shows the product life cycle.

When a product is first introduced, it is in the introductory stage. Due to heavy promotional and distribution expenditures, profits are normally nonexistent. Promotional efforts are designed to make the customers aware of the product's features, benefits, and uses. There are a limited number of competitors.

During the growth stage, both sales and profits increase rapidly. Profits peak toward the end of the growth stage. More competitors

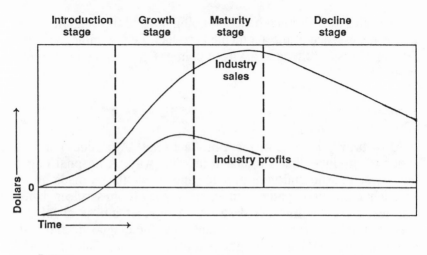

FIGURE 16.2

enter the marketplace. These new entrants usually try to win market share by offering a low price. This makes it necessary for the original competitor to cut the price of its product. Advertising in the growth phase is competitive in nature, stressing the advantages of the firm's product offering.

Sales peak and profits decline in the maturity stage. During this stage, there are many competitors. As profits continue to decline, weak competitors leave the market.

The decline stage is characterized by rapidly falling sales and the continued erosion of profits. All unnecessary costs are eliminated. Eventually the product is eliminated. For example, health maintenance organizations (HMOs) or emergency health clinics are at the early stages of the product life cycle, while regular health care insurers and hospital emergency room services are in the maturity stage of the product life cycle.

There is no set time frame associated with the product life cycle.

It is essential for a firm to take advantage of new marketing opportunities to expand existing product lines and introduce new product offerings. This ensures that some of the firm's products will always be in the growth stage of the product life cycle.

DISTRIBUTION CONSIDERATIONS

It is important for a company to make its product available to the target market, at the right time, and at the right place. Health care services use many distribution channels.

Historically, health care was delivered through the private physician and the hospital. While these channels of distribution still exist, many new innovations have been developed. Most physicians have formed group practices which permit them to provide the patient with a greater level of expertise and permits the doctor to better manage his or her work hours. Many hospitals have opened satellite locations in shopping areas which, for a fee, treat minor ailments and direct more seriously ill patients to the hospital. Health clinics have been established in poorer neighborhoods to provide "no-charge" service to the needy. Health maintenance organizations (HMO) have been created. After joining the HMO, the customer pays a monthly fee which permits them to see a staff doctor. Hospital costs are also covered. In addition, freestanding minor emergency and minor surgery clinics have been developed.

Distribution Decisions

Companies must decide the level and quality of customer service they wish to render. Ideally, they would first want to optimize customer service and minimize distribution costs. In most cases, the maximization of customer service results in excessive distribution costs. It is necessary to strike some balance between customer service and distribution costs. This dilemma is sometimes known as the "logistics trade off" problem. For example, doctors have found that while house calls maximize customer service, they materially increase health care delivery costs and reduce the quality of medical care that can be provided.

Many health care and social service organizations must decide on the number and location of branches. While the most economical decision is a single location, multiple locations will attract more clients. As branches are built, the firm must decide on design of the facilities. The appearance of the facilities affect customers' attitudes, opinions, and behavior.

Consider how the "atmosphere" of a hospital can affect patients. Many older hospitals have an institutional look, with long narrow corridors, drab wall colors, and badly worn furniture, all contributing a depressed feeling to patients who are already depressed about their own condition. Newer hospitals are designed with colors, textures, furnishings, and layouts that reinforce positive patient feelings. They have circular or rectangular layouts with the nursing station in the center, permitting nurses to monitor patients better. Single-care units are replacing the traditional semiprivate rooms, based on the overwhelming preference for single-care units by both patients and physicians. (Kotler, 1982, pp. 324-325)

Many times a company must decide on whether it is appropriate to use intermediaries. For example, a small hospital with limited resources might find it preferable to contract for ambulance services rather than maintaining its own vehicles and personnel. If a firm decides to use intermediaries, it must determine which middlemen are the best from those that are available. In addition, the middlemen used must be evaluated on a periodic basis.

PROMOTIONAL CONSIDERATIONS

Communication Process

The communication process consists of a source, message, receiver, and a feedback link. Figure 16.3 depicts the communication process. When a source, such as a physician, delivers a message, he or she must decide on what words, gestures, and the like will be used in the process. This is known as encoding. In turn, the receiver, such as a patient, must interpret or decode the message. If the doctor uses technical jargon to inform a patient of his medical

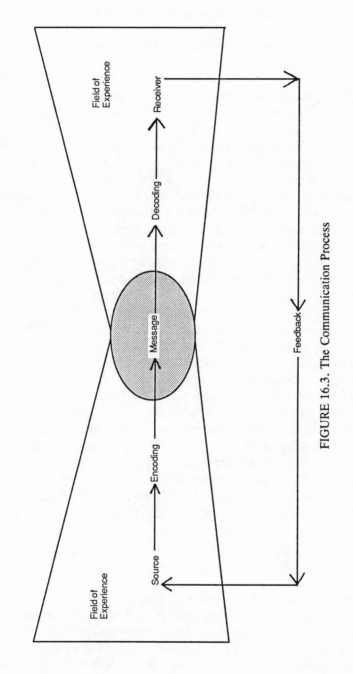

FIGURE 16.3. The Communication Process

condition, he or she might well receive feedback by the perplexed look on the patient's face.

A number of problems make the communication process difficult. First, many words have multiple meanings. Words have primary meanings and, in some cases, secondary meanings. For example, "grass" is the "green stuff you mow" on the weekends and a "dog" is a "furry animal pet." To some people "grass" is something you "smoke" and a "dog" is the "person you went out with" last weekend.

In addition, there are many other distractions. People are exposed to over fifteen hundred commercial messages a day. This doesn't take into consideration all of the other things which compete for a person's attention. We may not receive the message which was sent because we may not notice the message among the clutter (selective attention). People tend to distort the message so as to hear what they want to hear (selective distortion). We can retain only a small portion of the messages we are exposed to (selective recall).

Each person has a frame of reference which acts as his or her field of experience. It is only when the source's field of experience overlaps with the receiver's field of experience that communication takes place. For example, if an aborigine were transported to New York City, he would be bombarded with a host of messages. However, little communication would take place because of the vast difference in the sender's and receiver's fields of reference.

The following steps are part of the marketing communication process: (1) identify the target market, (2) establish communication objectives, (3) design the message, (4) determine which communication channels are to be used, (5) establish the promotional budget, (6) decide on the promotion mix, and (7) evaluate the promotion's effectiveness.

Promotion Mix

The promotional mix consists of four tools: (1) advertising, (2) sales promotion, (3) personal selling, and (4) public relations. A company must determine how much money and other resources to allocate to the elements in the promotion mix. For example, industrial companies concentrate the majority of their promotional budget on personal selling. On the other hand, consumer product companies place an emphasis on advertising and sales promotion. Consult other sources for more detailed information on managing the promotion mix (see also Engel, Warshaw & Kinnear, 1979).

Advertising

Advertising is a "paid form of nonpersonal communication about an organization and/or its products that is transmitted to a target audience through a mass medium" (Pride & Ferrell, 1980, p. 411). Some mass media used to transmit advertising messages are television, radio, newspaper, magazine, direct mail, and outdoor advertising. Table 16.1 compares the relative size, costs, advantages, and disadvantages of the major media.

Advertising budgets are established by the following manner: percentage-of-sales method, competitive-parity method, what the firm can afford method, and objective-and-task method. Many companies use forecasted sales or the previous year's sales to establish their advertising budget. For example, a company sets its advertising budget by allocating 10% of forecasted sales of $2,000,000 for a budget of $200,000. Under this method, when times are good, more is spent on advertising, and, when times are bad, less is spent on advertising. Ironically, during the bad times the firm needs more promotional efforts and not less.

If a company matches its competitor's advertising expenditures, the competitive-parity method is being used. In reality, many small firms with limited resources allocate what they can afford.

The preferred way to establish the advertising budget is the objective-and-task method. Using this method, the company establishes specific advertising objectives. The tasks are determined which must be accomplished to achieve these objectives. Cost estimations are determined for each of the tasks. The total of these costs is the amount of the advertising budget.

Many nonprofit health care and social service organizations rely heavily on public service announcements (PSA). PSAs are ads which the radio and television stations run for free. Other than the cost of production, which often is also donated, the nonprofit firm has no cash outlay. However, PSAs are run in those time slots

TABLE 16.1. Relative Size and Cost, and Advantages and Disadvantages of the Major Media

Kinds of Media	Sales volume—1982 (billions)	Typical costs—1983	Advantages	Disadvantages
Newspaper	$17.7	$15,000 for one page weekday, Cleveland (ADI Network)	Flexible Timely Local market Credible source	May be expensive Short life No "pass-along"
Television	$14.3	$2,800 for a 30-second spot, prime time, Cleveland	Offers sight, sound, and motion Good attention Wide reach	Expensive in total "Clutter" Short exposure Less selective audience
Direct mail	$10.3	$25/1,000 for listing of 103,000 engineers	Selected audience Flexible Can personalize	Relatively expensive per contact "Junk mail"—hard to retain attention
Radio	$4.7	$150 for one minute drive time, Cleveland	Wide reach Segmented audiences Inexpensive	Offers audio only Weak attention Many different rates Short exposure
Magazine	$3.7	$45,915 for one page, 4-color in *U.S. News & World Report*	Very segmented audiences Credible source Good reproduction Long life Good "pass-along"	Inflexible Long lead times
Outdoor	$0.7	$4,159 (painted) for prime billboard, 30–60-day showings, Cleveland	Flexible Repeat exposure Inexpensive	"Mass market" Very short exposure

Source. Reprinted with permission from the May 30, 1983, issue of *Advertising Age.* Copyright 1983 by Crain Communications, Inc. Source: Robert J. Coen. McCann-Erickson, Inc.

which the media select. This is often in the middle of the night when the ad has a limited exposure.

Figure 16.4 provides an overview of the advertising decision-making process. Due to the complexity of this topic, it is beyond the scope of this book to cover this area in detail. For more information, other sources should be consulted (see Wright, Winter & Zeigler, 1982).

Sales Promotion

Sales promotion consists of activities which coordinate and supplement personal selling and advertising. They are short-term incentives to encourage the sale of the product. The following are examples of the type of sales promotion activities:

Consumer Promotions	Dealer Promotions	Sales Force Promotions
Samples	Free goods	Bonuses
Coupons	Merchandise allowances	Sales contests
Refunds	Cooperative advertising	Meeting
Contests	Sales contests	Sales aids
Calendars		Training materials

The following are examples of sales promotions which have been used by health care and social service organizations:

> Some hospitals have sponsored filet mignon candlelight dinners for new mothers; televised bingo games for patients; and provided country club memberships for new doctors joining their staff. And family planners in many parts of the world have offered incentives — transistor radios, cookware, costume jewelry, free bank accounts and so on — to potential adopters of birth control measures. (Kotler, 1982, p. 372)

See other sources for more detailed discussions of sales promotion (see Schultz & Robinson, 1982a; 1982b).

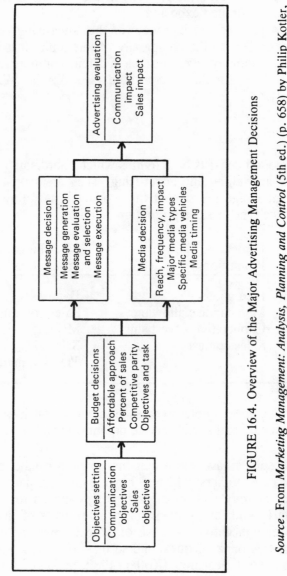

FIGURE 16.4. Overview of the Major Advertising Management Decisions

Source. From *Marketing Management: Analysis, Planning and Control* (5th ed.) (p. 658) by Philip Kotler, Englewood Cliffs, NJ: Prentice-Hall, Inc. Copyright 1984.

Personal Selling

Personal selling is the most effective communication tool available to the firm. It is the most potent because it is a face-to-face meeting with a client. It enables contact personnel to cultivate relations, provide detailed explanations, and elicit immediate responses. However, it is also the most costly of the communication tools.

Contact personnel consist of salespeople (those hired specifically to sell clients) and service personnel (those who provide the organization's services to the client). For example, a hospital's sales personnel would consist of the administrator and executive staff members who through contact with the community are constantly selling the hospital. Many nonprofit hospitals also have professional fund raisers on their staff. A hospital's many service personnel consist of doctors, nurses, orderlies, and so on. While these service personnel do not think of themselves as salespeople, it is important that they be client-oriented. A smile is contagious. When clients are treated with friendliness and warmth, it induces customer satisfaction and loyalty. The opposite is also true. Rude and cold service personnel many times drive clients away.

It is beyond the scope of this book to provide a detailed discussion of the sales and sales management function of the firm. Consult other references for this type of material (see Stanton & Buskirk, 1983; Churchill, Ford & Walker, 1981).

Public Relations

Public relations consists of promotional activities designed to create and maintain favorable relations between the organization and its publics such as clients, employees, stockholders, government and regulatory officials, and the community. There are many types of public relations vehicles. Such items as the annual report and company newsletters are designed to promote good relations with stockholders and employees. Press releases, speeches by corporate executives, and film and slide presentations are aimed at the public at-large. Many companies sponsor special events such as art exhibits, auctions, bingo games, dances, walkathons, and the like. Some health care organizations have established information telephone lines which feature messages about specific symptoms and diseases.

Publicity is used to provide news of marketing developments, changes in company policies, information of general interest, reports on current developments, personalities, and so on. Table 16.2 shows the possible issues for which public relations efforts might be required.

TABLE 16.2. Possible Public Relations Issues

Marketing developments
New products
New uses for old products
Research developments
Appointments and changes of marketing personnel
Large orders received
Successful bids
Awards of contracts
Special events

Company policies
New guarantees
Changes in credit terms
Changes in distribution policies
Changes in service policies
Changes in prices and pricing policies

News of general interest
Annual election of officers
Meetings of the board of directors
Anniversaries of the organization
Anniversaries of an invention of the company
Anniversaries of the senior officers of the organization
State or national holidays that can be tied into the organization's activities
Annual banquets, luncheons, parties, and picnics
Local pageants in which the organization participates
Local sports events in which teams for the organization compete
Special weeks, such as Candy Week, Clean-up Week, and so on
Festive occasions, such as Valentine's Day, Mother's Day, Father's Day, and so
    on
Founders' Day
Foundation meetings
Conferences and special meetings
Welfare activities
Open house to members of the community

Athletic events
Successful bids
Awards of contracts
Golf tournaments
Awards of merit to employees
Laying of cornerstone
Opening of an exhibion

Reports on current developments
Reports of work on new experiments
Reports on conditions of the industry
Progress reports on the company

Reports on current developments
Employment, production, sales, and other statistics showing trends
Reports on new discoveries, inventions, and safety devices
Tax reports
Speeches by principals
Predictions and analyses of economic conditions
Employment gains
Financial statements
Organization appointments
Opening of new markets, both foreign and domestic

Personalities — names are news
Visits by famous personages, including well-known customers, noted educators,
   local, state, and federal government officials
Personal accomplishments of individuals
Winners of company contests
Employees' and officers' advancements
Interviews with company officials
Company employees serving as judges for various contests
Interviews with employees

Slogans, symbols, endorsements
The company's slogan — its history, development, aim, and fulfillment
A tie-in of company activities with local slogans
Creation of a slogan for a particular purpose or occasion
The company's trademark
The company's name plate
The company's trade character
Endorsements of the company's policy, products, or methods by prominent
   people

Source. From *Marketing Handbook*, (2nd ed.) (p. 19) edited by Albert Wesley
Frey, New York: Ronald Press. Copyright 1965.

PRICING CONSIDERATIONS

Price is the value which people place on a product. In addition to monetary considerations, price also includes the time, effort, and psychic costs associated with engaging in some activity. For example, a middle-aged female patient is reluctant to take a breast examination. Her reluctance may stem from fear (psychic cost) of hearing bad news about her health, unwillingness to travel to the test center (effort costs), impatience over waiting in the office for the tests to commence (time costs), or concern over the financial obligation of $50 (monetary cost) to take the test. It is in the best interest of the health care organization to consider all of these cost factors in setting prices.

Pricing Objectives

The first step in the pricing process is to establish pricing objectives. Some possible pricing objectives might be to maximize either long-run or short-run profits, to increase market share, or to make the product highly "visible." Table 16.3 provides a list of possible pricing objectives.

TABLE 16.3. Potential Pricing Objectives

---

1. Maximum long-run profits.
2. Maximum short-run profits.
3. Growth.
4. Stabilize market.
5. Desensitize customers to price.
6. Maintain price-leadership arrangement.
7. Discourage entrants.
8. Speed exit of marginal firms.
9. Avoid government investigation and control.
10. Maintain loyalty of middlemen and get their sales support.
11. Avoid demands for "more" from suppliers – labor in particular.
12. Enhance image of firm and its offerings.
13. Be regarded as "fair" by customers (ultimate).
14. Create interest and excitement about the item.
15. Be considered trustworthy and reliable by rivals.
16. Help in the sale of weak items in the line.
17. Discourage others from cutting prices.

18. Make a product "visible."
19. "Spoil market" to obtain high prices for sale of business.
20. Build traffic.

Source. Reprinted from the *Journal of Marketing*, published by the American Marketing Association. In "A Decision-Making Structure for Price Decisions," by Alfred R. Oxenfeldt, *Journal of Marketing*, January 1973, p. 50.

Pricing Strategies

Once the pricing objectives have been established, the next step is to decide on the appropriate pricing strategy. Pricing strategies tend to be based on cost factors, demand considerations, and competitive concerns.

Cost-oriented pricing refers to the firm's setting its prices so as to cover its costs plus earning some reasonable margin of profit. For example, hospital gift shops use mark up pricing. This is similar to any retail operation. On the other hand, some companies use cost-plus pricing. If a charitable foundation asked a research hospital to develop a piece of diagnostic equipment for a specific illness, the research hospital might well ask that all of its costs be covered, as well as, some reasonable profit margin, such as ten percent. Of course, this revenue might be recorded in some account other than profit, e.g., "financial reserves." But the financial meaning is equivalent.

Demand-pricing concentrates on the level of consumer demand rather than on cost considerations. For example, noted medical facilities such as the Johns Hopkins and Menninger Clinic can charge far higher prices than lesser-known hospitals.

Competitive-oriented pricing looks at what the competition is charging as a basis for establishing price. A company can select to charge above the competition, the same as the competition, or below the competition. If the firm cannot materially differentiate itself from its competition, it must either meet the competitor's price or price below the competition. For example, emergency health care clinics have positioned themselves as a lower-price alternative to hospital emergency facilities. If a firm can differentiate itself from its competition, it has more flexibility as to its pricing.

Changing the Price

Prices are not etched in stone. Over time, firms find it expedient to change prices. If the demand for a product has significantly increased, the firm has the ability to increase its price. Firms will also consider price increases if their costs have materially increased. Many companies reduce price as a way of stimulating demand.

The concept of the elasticity of demand for a product underlies the firm's response to price change. If a product is demand elastic, it is price sensitive. A relatively small reduction in price will result in a significant increase in the quantity sold, such that total revenues will increase. Figure 16.5 (A) depicts the elastic demand relationships. If the product has an inelastic demand curve, it is not price sensitive. A change in price will result in a relatively small change in the volume sold. Figure 16.5 (B) shows the relationships associated with an inelastic demand schedule.

Elasticity assumes that the consumer makes his or her decisions on a rational basis. Often decisions are arrived at in an emotional manner. Price decreases and increases are often perceived by the consumer as symbolic of some problem or special feature within the firm. Price decreases might be interpreted as symbolic of poor service, financial troubles, or the belief that price may come down even further so it may be advisable to wait. Price increases might mean that service is improving or that the service is exceptionally good. If a firm can develop a prestige image, a higher price might stimulate demand. If an organization is perceived as problem-ridden and providing poor service, even at a lower price demand will fall off.

Often a firm will change its price for promotional reasons. For example, a department store will reduce its prices several times a year for special sale events. Some time in the past, a chiropractor in Memphis, Tennessee, offered a "Christmas Special" with the first visit for new patients costing only $15.00 during the month of December. While the above example may invite criticisms in terms of professional codes of ethics, it clearly demonstrates promotional pricing.

Other sources should be consulted for more information on pricing considerations (see Monroe, 1979).

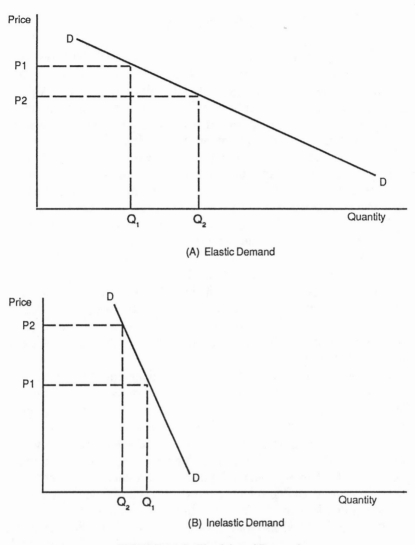

(A) Elastic Demand

(B) Inelastic Demand

FIGURE 16.5. Elasticity of Demand

SUMMARY

Marketing managers use four major variables to satisfy consumer needs and wants: (1) product, (2) distribution, (3) promotion, and (4) price. Marketers use an expanded definition of product. A product includes not only its core benefit but also its tangible elements of style, features, quality, brand name and packaging, as well as such augmented considerations as credit, delivery, and after-sale service. Products go through an aging process known as the product life cycle. It is important that a firm be aware of which of the product life cycle stages (introduction, growth, maturity, and decline) its various products are in.

Distribution considerations involve the firm's desire to optimize customer service and, at the same time, minimize distribution costs. Firms must decide on the number and location of branches and the design of their health care delivery facilities.

Companies communicate with their various publics using four promotional mix variables: (1) advertising, (2) sales promotion, (3) personal selling, and (4) public relations. They must decide on how resources are to be allocated among these variables and which of these tools they will emphasize.

Pricing considerations include the establishment of pricing objectives and determining the appropriate strategy to achieve these objectives. Firms must also remember that there are psychological ramifications associated with pricing the product.

The following chapters for Part VI are selected with an eye for illustrating the variety of issues encompassed by "marketing mix" decisions. Nathan Kaufman addresses the product component from the perspective of "product integrity." Then, Connie Mahoney demonstrates how a "service product" is developed in her case study of the Prenatal Program for the Shelby County Public Health Department. Edward Leven introduces some pricing fundamentals for health care and human services marketers in his chapters on price; Bob Sweeney illustrates in detail the development of a pricing structure in his HMO case study. The concept of place is dealt with in (To Be Determined); the practical side of access (or "place") marketing is revealed in Ellen Goldman and Cosmo Morabito's case study of a community-based residential facility for the elderly. Finally, Joan Hammer offers guidelines for promotion, as illustrated by the marketing of new and existing clinics; Gregory Nelson and Mary Beth Barboro develop the promotional aspects of concept marketing in their case study of consumer attitudes toward mental health care.

REFERENCES

Churchill, Gilbert A., Jr., Ford, Neil M. and Walker, Orville C., Jr. *Sales Force Management: Planning, Implementation and Control.* (Homewood, IL: Richard D. Irwin, Inc., 1981).

Engel, James F., Warshaw, Martin R. and Kinnear, Thomas C. *Promotional Strategies: Managing the Marketing Communications Process.* 4th ed. (Homewood, IL: Richard D. Irwin, Inc., 1979).

Kotler, Philip. *Marketing for Nonprofit Organizations.* 2nd ed. (Englewood Cliffs, NJ: Prentice-Hall, Inc., 1982).

Monroe, Kent B. *Pricing: Making Profitable Decisions* (New York: McGraw-Hill Book Company, 1979).

Pride, William M. and Ferrell, O. C. *Marketing: Basic Concepts and Decisions.* 2nd ed. (Boston, MA: Houghton Mifflin Co., 1980).

Schultz, Don E. and Robinson, William A. *Sales Promotion Essentials.* (Chicago, IL: Crain Books, 1982).

Schultz, Don E. and Robinson, William A. *Sales Promotion Management.* (Chicago, IL: Crain Books, 1982).

Stanton, William J. *Fundamentals of Marketing.* 7th ed. (New York: McGraw-Hill Book Company, 1984).

Stanton, William J. and Buskirk, Richard H. *Management of the Sales Force.* 6th ed. (Homewood, IL: Richard D. Irwin, Inc., 1983).

Wright, John S., Winter, Willis L., Jr. and Zeigler, Sherilyn K. *Advertising.* 5th ed. (New York: McGraw-Hill Book Company, 1982).

CHAPTER 17

Product Integrity:
The Missing Link in a Hospital's
Marketing Process

Nathan Kaufman

A necessary component of any marketing process is to monitor the product for deficiencies which may be inhibiting the sales or utilization of that product. Or more simply put, "if you're going to sell food, it better taste good." This concept of insuring that a product meets the needs and demands of its consumer is what I refer to as *product integrity*. A marketing process which does not include an assessment of the integrity of the product will have minimal chance for success. In the hospital industry today, we typically ask the question, "How can I increase utilization of my existing products?" In my judgement, a more critical question is, "Is there something inherently wrong with my existing product which is inhibiting utilization?"

The marketing process which I use involves three basic steps:

1. assessment of customer need and product integrity;
2. improving product integrity;
3. communicating and promoting the product.

Reprinted from William J. Winston, ed., *Innovations in Hospital Marketing*, pp. 29–32, © 1984 by The Haworth Press, Inc.

ASSESSMENT OF CUSTOMER NEED
AND PRODUCT INTEGRITY

The first step in the marketing process involves objectively assessing the needs and demands of key customers as well as their perceptions of your product. Through a series of survey research, focus groups, interviews, and literature reviews, a hospital should be able to identify the critical factors associated with consumer choice. These factors must be identified by a direct assessment of consumer attitudes, i.e., an "outside-in" approach. In many cases, hospital managers think they know their customer's needs and the perception of their products and skip the empirical assessment step. The down-side risk of this approach is great for misreading the consumer's needs or their perception of the product and could result in the development of products which are inappropriate for the marketplace. At best, research should provide a confirmation for the direction the hospital management is planning to follow.

COMMUNICATIONS/PROMOTIONS

Communications/promotions is the current panacea for health care managers. More and more it is believed that promoting a product in the community will increase its utilization over the long term. Thus, hospital marketers are viewed as "census developers," who can increase utilization by simply sending out flyers, advertising in the newspapers and so forth. Experience in other industries has shown that marketing a product which does not have integrity may increase utilization on the short term, but will have a devastating impact on the product's success over the long term. Using catsup as an example, through television advertising, coupons, and sales promotions, it is possible to increase the sales of our catsup product; however, if that product does not taste good, we are exposing the consumer to a poor product and future purchases of this product, or any product with the brand name, will be in jeopardy. In summary, prior to communicating/promoting a product, a manager must be certain that that product is of acceptable quality to the consumer.

It is common to find hospitals using a marketing process involving only needs assessment and communications/promotion. This process has a minimal chance of success over the long term. A hospital marketing program will only be effective if management is first willing to modify its existing product such that it meets the local standards for integrity. Only then will promotional efforts be effective.

PRODUCT INTEGRITY

Product integrity can be defined as the extent to which your product meets both real and perceived needs and demands of the consumer. The concept is made more difficult by the fact that hospitals have multiple consumers with different needs and demands. In the case of an urgent care center for example, the patient's primary concern is rapid, high quality medical attention, while the private practicing physician's primary concern is the extent to which the urgent care center will compete with his/her existing practice and/or provide referrals.

The process for determining product integrity is simple and straightforward. During the assessment phase of the marketing process, product integrity should be determined for each major service within the hospital. The analysis is accomplished by first identifying the critical purchasing criteria for a given service. And then determining the extent to which your hospital meets those criteria. Again, it is imperative that this assessment exercise be conducted for every major customer of the hospital (at minimum, a product integrity analysis should be conducted for the patient and physician customer). The basic framework for product integrity analysis is a simple matrix (see Table 17.1) with each customer's needs/demands listed in priority order. From the data collected, a hospital manager should have sufficient information to determine the extent to which the hospital is addressing the priority decisions criteria of each of its major customers. Significant deviations between customer needs (both real and perceived) and hospital product should either be addressed, or a hospital must recognize that utilization of that product has little chance of increasing over time.

TABLE 17.1. Product Integrity Analysis for the Emergency Service at X Hospital

Priority	Selection Criteria	Hospital Rating	Selection Criteria	Hospital Rating
1	Quality of MD coverage	2.8	Close to home	3.5
2	Source of referrals	3.7	Community image	2.9
3	Facilities and equipment	3.4	Quality of MD coverage	2.0
4	ER nursing	3.0	length of wait	3.0
5	Community image	3.0	Facilities and equipment	3.5
	Private Physician		Patient	

Note: Scale 1 = Poor 4 = excellent
    Priority determined from needs assessment

The following is an example of how product integrity can influence a hospital's management decision:

A hospital expressed the desire to increase utilization in the emergency room. During the assessment phase, it was determined that a patient's needs and demands include confidence in the physician, short waiting times, and proximity to home. While proximity and waiting time were not major problems, the local residents reported that they lacked confidence in one of the physicians practicing at the hospital E.R., and would call in to the hospital to find out if that physicians was on duty prior to utilizing the Emergency Room. This product integrity analysis isolated the key issue associated with the sub-optimal utilization. Until this issue was addressed, it would have been inappropriate to promote the emergency room to the community. Promotion, prior to the correction of this issue, would have been an inefficient use of resources.

CONCLUSION

Product integrity analysis provides the hospital manager with an orientation towards assessing the extent to which the hospital product meets the needs and demands of the customer. Product integrity analysis will pinpoint the specific factors affecting utilization. Only then can a realistic marketing program be developed. The fact that a product has integrity will not automatically cause an increase in utilization. However, in order to increase utilization of a product, it must first have integrity.

CHAPTER 18

Price—A Primer on the 2nd "P" for Hospital Marketers

Edward L. Leven

INTRODUCTION

The 4 "Ps" of marketing—product, place, promotion and price—are well known to health care marketing personnel. Since 1981, actions by both federal and state legislatures and agencies have resulted in a move toward more price competition. While concerns about spiraling health care costs have been longstanding, this legislative "revolution" has thrust health care providers into a new and untested marketplace where competition based on price is becoming more important.

Much has already been written about this new competitive environment. The focus of this article is on the interplay between the marketing and finance departments within a hospital setting in terms of how they can work together to successfully price hospital services. As part of contract development, the marketer must determine a pricing strategy, yet oftentimes marketers do not have specific training in financial analysis. Financial managers have the data and technical skills necessary, but may not be able to effectively communicate information to marketers. Furthermore, relationships between finance and marketing in the hospital, which have tradi-

Reprinted from William J. Winston, ed., *Innovations in Hospital Marketing*, pp. 33–41, © 1984 by The Haworth Press, Inc.

tionally been poor in many cases, are likely to be exacerbated by issues of who will control the contracting process.

This article proposes to give health care marketers some strategies and skills so that they are better equipped to work with finance to get the information they need to properly do their job.

OVERVIEW OF PRICE

Price is part of the overall offering made to the health care consumer. The actual "product" that hospitals produce is undergoing change through the unbundling of services and changes in medical practice. "Place" has been modified through the growth of ambulatory care such as medical group practices, surgicenters, and free standing emergicenters. "Promotion" has already been widely introduced to health care institutions, and while there are still some hospital administrators and physicians who do not see the value of marketing, it is clear that promotion in the health care field is here to stay.

In the future hospitals will have to compete along real dimensions and will no longer be able to be all things to all people. As hospitals move toward specialization and regionalization, they will compete in terms of the specific services they offer (e.g., one hospital may become the regional center for cardiovascular surgery), the target markets they choose to serve, and in terms of price.

There are three basic pricing theories. Usually the price that is set is a result of a combination of all three approaches. The theories are:

>*Cost-Plus Pricing*—the institution adds a mark-up to the cost of the good or service.
>*Demand Based Pricing*—the price is determined by what people are willing to pay, which may have no relation to what it actually costs to produce the product (e.g., pet rocks).
>*Competitive Based Pricing*—the price is determined by what the competition is charging.

Until recently, the cost-based reimbursement used by Medicare shielded the health care industry from the marketplace for over 15 years. The market was distorted further by the cost shifting that took place whereby charge paying patients ended up subsidizing government program patients because of the increasingly restrictive determination of costs by the Medicare program.

The essential task now is a more accurate pricing methodology, one that meets the following criteria:

1. Pricing that reflects a marketplace environment
2. Pricing that incorporates elements of the three pricing theories
3. Pricing that recognizes the tradeoffs among costs (both fixed and variable), volume, and price.

THE TRUE MARKETING BATTLEGROUND

Jane Bryant Quinn entitled her April 9, 1984, editorial in *Newsweek* "A New War On Health Costs." Her choice of words underscores the new determination by government, business, and private insurers to curb health care costs. The key changes that these groups, especially business, are pursuing include

1. Making individuals more responsible for the cost of their health care, through increased deductible and coinsurance amounts, and increases in the portion that the employee must pay for his health insurance premium.
2. Pre-admission certification programs
3. Second opinion programs for surgery
4. Increased education programs directed toward encouraging employees to take more responsibility for their health and toward making employees better health plan consumers
5. Health promotion programs in the workplace
6. Non-payment for the extra days in the hospital when the patient is admitted during the weekend
7. Increased emphasis on plan design, with financial incentives for employees to cut back on overutilized areas. In fact, at 1st Nationwide Savings and Loan in San Francisco, California, the plan design approach has coupled cutback in payments for hospital care with 100% payment for visits to licensed holistic health practitioners as well as for radical life style changes. As

Rich Hanson, Employee Benefits Manager, points out, it is less expensive to get an executive to protect his heart through an exercise program than it is to pay for surgery or disability after he has had a heart attack.

The intent of all the above trends is to make the individual more cognizant of the cost of health care and ultimately to be a better consumer of expensive health care resources.

The impact of more sophisticated individual consumers will be enhanced considerably by larger entities acting on their behalf. Businesses, insurance companies, government (at federal, state and local levels) — all can be expected to be more aggressive in their negotiations with hospitals. As other elements of the infrastructure (sewers, roads, school systems) need additional infusions of funds, the pressures will be enormous on government health programs to retrench even further. Similarly, with benefits equalling 32% of salary expenditures nationally, businesses can no longer afford to give additional benefits away. Increases in the cost of health insurance with no appreciable improvements in coverage place financial pressures on business to hold back on salary increases or the introduction of new benefits. Private insurers will no doubt have to respond to increased pressure from business to modify insurance plans.

Clearly, the price of health care will be the overriding concern of business, government and private insurers, and price will be the major marketing battleground for the foreseeable future.

CURRENT TRENDS IN PRICING

Hospital pricing is going through an evolution, and can be thought of as encompassing 4 levels:

Level 1:   Percent discount over full charges — this represents the simplest method of pricing in the competitive marketplace, and because of its simplicity is being widely used by many Health Maintenance Organization (HMOs), Preferred Provider Organizations (PPOs) and private insurers.

Level 2:   Standard per diem—this is the approach used by the Medi-Cal program in California. A standard amount is negotiated with the hospital, and this per diem is paid to the institution no matter what services are actually used by the patient.

Level 3:   Negotiated rates by service—obviously different patients use differing amounts of hospital services, and the cost incurred by a pediatric patient will be different than those incurred by a med/surg patient. With most contracts currently being negotiated on the basis of discounted charges or standard per diem, Level 3 represents the major wave in contract pricing.

Level 4:   Diagnosis-Related Group (DRG) Based Pricing— Currently being implemented by Medicare, the DRG approach is based on 467 groups. The patient's DRG classification is a function of the primary diagnosis, secondary diagnosis, primary procedure, age, and discharge status.

Hospitals are moving in the direction of product-line costing, and the "product" in most cases will be a DRG, or group of DRGs. However there are instances, a small rural hospital for example, where the "product" may not be as differentiated as a single DRG.

Although still a subject of debate within the hospital field, the DRG approach will be the method most likely adopted by other payors since it is the best definition of a specific hospital product that we have at present.

With respect to DRGs, there are really three figures to keep in mind:

1. The true cost of producing the product (or as we used to say, the cost of providing services to the patient)
2. the DRG standard payment for the product, in other words what the Medicare program will pay for the product, regardless of the cost
3. the marketing price of a product, which depending on the mar-

keting goals of the organization, may be higher or lower than the true cost and/or the DRG standard payment.

TOWARD A SIMPLE PRICING METHODOLOGY

If we integrate the three theories of pricing and the 4 levels of pricing we can see that in the process of negotiating prices, the following steps should be taken by the hospital to price a service or product:

1. Determine the Cost of Providing a Particular Service or DRG

Historically, hospitals determined their costs by department, since this was the method used by medicare for their cost reports. Currently, hospitals that do not have sophisticated cost accounting systems in place have to estimate the cost by using revenue figures and backing into cost. By going through the medical record and the patient account, the average revenue (as well as the highest and lowest charge) per DRG can be determined. Then by using the ratio of charges to costs (another figure developed for use in Medicare cost reports), an average cost figure can be estimated.

A preferable method is, of course, to have a true cost accounting system to track costs per product line. Various consulting firms are now developing marketing cost accounting systems for hospitals. A true cost accounting system can get very complicated, as the hospital has to figure out how much laboratory, x-ray etc. a particular patient type uses.

Another related area is the need for hospitals to improve their systems of allocation for indirect costs. The widely used step-down method of cost allocation used in the Medicare cost report was designed for reimbursement purposes and is not necessarily the best system of cost allocation for pricing purposes. The choice of allocation method as well as the statistics used for allocation are undergoing change as hospitals seek to develop more accurate ways of allocating indirect costs, such as laundry, to product lines. This is important because within a particular category of surgical procedures, different DRGs may consume very different amounts of laundry, and thus should be costed differently.

2. Break Down Costs into Fixed and Variable Components

Fixed costs are those costs that are necessary to provide the service, but do not vary with the volume of services provided. Fixed costs may be committed, such as rent, or discretionary, such as continuing education programs for staff. Variable costs are those costs that vary with volume. Variable costs can be pure, such as medical supplies which vary directly with volume, or step variable costs (sometimes called "semifixed" costs) such as the cost of RNs which are fixed over a certain volume of patients, but then must be "stepped up" if the increase in patients requires another RN.

Although marketers need not be involved in the details of analyzing the fixed and variable cost components, they should be knowledgeable about these important concepts for the following reasons:

a. In setting a price, marketing will often seek to cover the variable costs and make some contribution to fixed costs (known as the contribution margin approach). Marketing will argue that if there are empty beds, then it is better to provide the service, covering the variable costs and making some contribution to fixed costs, than to not have any revenue at all.

b. Finance, on the other hand, will seek to cover the full cost, both fixed and variable, of providing a service. The argument here is that all payors must pay based on the full financial requirements of the institution. If every contract signed with a third party payor is priced at less than full cost, then the institution will not survive financially over the long run.

Obviously, there are other financial and non-financial considerations that need to be taken into account, such as the existing occupancy level of the hospital, before a pricing decision can be made. Nevertheless, the analysis of fixed and variable costs is an important tool in determining whether the hospital should or should not enter into a specific contract to provide services.

3. Conduct a Demand Analysis

Volume has an impact on costs, since increased volume serves to spread the distribution of fixed costs and to allow for a lower unit cost. Volume estimates can be done by the marketer by using census tract, demographic, competitive and historical trend data. Generally speaking it is more difficult to predict volume, and thus revenue, than it is to predict costs. Therefore it would be good to make several predictions of volume, from a conservative to an optimistic estimate.

4. Conduct a Profit Analysis

Using fixed and variable cost analysis, a break-even model permits marketers to quickly project the amount of profit at various levels of prices, volumes and costs. When coupled with a demand analysis, the break-even model becomes a decision-making aid in pricing.

5. Use Data on Competitive Pricing and Price Sensitivity

Although the hospital may start out with equal mark-ups by service, the negotiation process may reveal differing price sensitivities of different payors. As private insurers, HMOs, PPOs, and government negotiate with hospitals, they will use information on pricing strategies of the competition as well as their own demand preferences to respond to the hospital's schedule of prices. In this way, a market rate for each service is established, and the hospital will end up modifying its margins since the market will bear different margins.

In the past, hospital charges were a function of costs, volume and payor mix. Essentially charges served as a "plug figure," after the expense budget and contractual allowances were determined. Now price sensitivity and competitive pricing must be taken into account and the hospital must test how much the market is willing to pay for their services. The hospital determines how much prices can rise and then solves for expenses. Thus, price sensitivity information is used to estimate revenues, and from there the hospital determines how much it can afford to increase expenses.

6. Do a Detailed Financial Analysis of All of the Extra or Hidden Costs of the Contract

The following considerations need to be taken into account, and most likely the finance department will have to conduct the analysis.

a. *Analyze the impact of the contract on the budget.* The finance department needs to examine the impact of the proposed contract on patient days. Will they increase or not? If the hospital doesn't sign the contract, will it lose patient days?

b. *Are there any additional capital improvements associated with the contract* (will we have to add another surgery suite)?

c. *How will payment be made for services provided under the contract? Will accounts receivable be reduced?*

d. *Are there any extra services that need to be provided?* (e.g., will the hospital have to pay for transportation of a transferring patient)?

e. *Will there be any special procedures in patient handling? Any unusual admitting or billing procedures* (e.g., will the hospital have to bill several different agencies)?

f. *Will there be additional criteria for utilization review?*

Many of these hidden costs will result in added operational expense. Subscribers/beneficiaries of these new health insurance packages are sometimes not as sophisticated as their employer or insurance groups would like you to believe. Patients are likely to arrive at the hospital not really understanding how their insurance plan works, which will increase admitting time and costs.

Despite a desire on the part of hospital administrators for more rigorous analysis of contracts, the bottom line on pricing for contracting is a subjective judgment. Decision-making by the hospital as well as the private insurer or government agency combines both financial and non-financial elements, and the final price will be established through the process of negotiation. There is still a lot of uncertainty in the market, and more sophisticated methods of pricing will develop as the key players gain more experience and gather more information.

DEVELOPMENT OF A SOLID WORKING RELATIONSHIP BETWEEN MARKETING AND FINANCE

No matter where the responsibility for contracts lies within the organization, it is recommended that finance be involved early on in the negotiations. This allows for greater latitude in negotiating and makes sure that negotiations aren't jeopardized at the very end. Legal counsel and operations need to be involved early on as well.

Finance and marketing should also be clear about how aggressively the hospital should be going after contracts. Strategic planning, with strong input from finance and marketing, is necessary to establish which target markets will be profitable or desirable for the hospital to pursue. Although most hospitals are responding to the many HMOs and PPOs that need to rapidly line up their provider network, in the future hospitals will need to proactively seek out the contracts that tie in best with the overall strategy and mission of the institution.

CURRENT TRENDS AND CONCLUSION

The current trend in pricing is towards specialty contracting that is volume related. As hospitals go through a period of deregulation and increasing marketplace competition, many of the most successful hospitals will either become a regional specialty center for a particular type of service or product line or will become highly efficient producers of general medical care. Pricing in the future will be based on volume related specialty contracting, and on DRGs or some type of case mix adjusted payment per case.

In the initial stages of contracting, pricing will largely be determined by discounted charges or a per diem rate. Both hospitals and insurers need to gain experience in this new ballgame. One hospital, for example, lowered its outpatient surgery charges when doctors complained they were too high. Volume did increase, but the hospital began to realize that many of the physicians were taking their inpatients and doing them on an outpatient basis. Since the hospital had lowered their charges, some of the physicians increased their own charges for outpatient surgery. The hospital is now re-evaluating its pricing decisions in light of the impact on its inpatient surgeries.

Forecasting volume in general can be difficult with new types of health care delivery systems. It is important to distinguish between developing new market volume versus retaining existing markets when evaluating contracts with HMOs and PPOs. HMOs have more authority to direct their patients to the facility than does a PPO and may be able to guarantee a certain volume whereas a new PPO will not.

Despite the flaws in contracting that need to be worked out, pricing methods for contracting of hospital services will continue to become more sophisticated. The methodology presented in this paper can provide health care marketers with a checklist for evaluating pricing strategies, and with a basis for developing more sophisticated methods of their own.

REFERENCES

Cleverly, William D. "Cost/Volume Analysis in the Hospital Industry," *Health Care Management Review*, Summer, 1979, page 29–36.

Nagy, Joseph E. "Hospitals Must Identify Fixed and Variable Costs," *Healthcare Financial Management*, March, 1982, page 50–54.

Quinn, Jane Bryant. "A New War on Healthcare Costs," *Newsweek*, April 9, 1984.

Suver, James D. and Neumann, Bruce R. *Management Accounting for Health Care Organizations*, Hospital Financial Management Association, Oak Brook, Illinois, 1981.

CHAPTER 19

Promotion—How to Promote and Advertise a New or Existing Clinic

Joan Hammer

Promotion and advertising have been mute subjects in the medical profession until recently. However, increased competition is causing many physicians to take a serious look at how they can use modern marketing techniques to increase the flow of patients to their clinics or practices.

The techniques being used are far more conservative than Madison Avenue-style advertising gimmickry, yet they go beyond long-standing traditions of maintaining a low professional profile.

The incentive to advertise one's services and professional credentials is strong. As the nation's supply of physicians continues to grow, there will be increased competition for patients. The competitive atmosphere is heightened by the Federal Trade Commission's insistence that physicians be free to advertise.

Promotion and advertising are an integral part of the total marketing plan. They add that extra "pizzazz" necessary to get a new venture off the ground. They also create more public awareness than any amount of news releases or similar-type publicity can accomplish. You need a good mix of both.

Reprinted from William J. Winston, ed., *Marketing the Group Practice: Practical Methods for the Health Care Practitioner*, pp. 61–67, © 1983 by The Haworth Press, Inc.

Before we get into some actual guidelines and examples of these exciting marketing tools, let's make certain you have already applied some basic marketing rules.

In simple terms, marketing is the fulfillment of mutual needs after careful determination that there are needs to be met.

A marketing approach to business necessitates finding out what the consumer wants in terms of product, price, and place and then planning to meet those consumer needs. It's matching what the clinic or service can do with what the consumer wants and needs. The best way to find out what the consumer wants is to ask him, and that entails market research—a critical component in the total marketing plan.

You could describe it as "getting information"—which would include your market research—and "giving information." Now that you have information based on empirical evidence rather than your own best guess, you can proceed with a marketing plan and on with the promotion and advertising. There are exceptions to this standard marketing procedure which I will explain later.

For optimum results in marketing a new clinic, the services of a qualified marketing consultant are highly recommended. If you can locate someone with health care experience, it's even better. Seldom can you find a marketing specialist who can both execute a marketing plan and initiate and implement promotional concepts and creative advertising. A good public relations person may be able to provide you with adequate promotion and advertising capabilities. And, qualified market research is a specialty unto itself and carries on a separate aspect of the job altogether. You need to determine where you are in your marketing program and make your selections accordingly.

PROMOTING A NEW CLINIC

It's wise to bring the marketing consultant into the picture right after determining the need for a service. You will appreciate the professional input pertaining to site selection, name, signage, decor, and even equipment purchasing.

After all of the above have been carefully selected, you are now ready to promote your new clinic or service. Hopefully, the signage for your clinic has been given careful consideration and can be applied to the logo design of your letterhead, envelopes, business cards, and subsequent brochures and advertising.

A marketing consultant would make certain the signage was developed with this in mind. A good name, and well-designed logo, are extremely important and will definitely relate to the success of the promotion and the subsequent success of your business. Try to blend and coordinate the colors of your stationery, and even your business forms, with the colors you've chosen for your overall decor or patient waiting room.

For example, if your offices are in taupe tones, your paper materials can run in taupe tones and your logo could be a bright royal blue. If you're considering an urgent-care facility, you may want to stick to colors indicating this type of health care (royal blue and bright green; or red, white, and blue, etc.). Always use a good quality paper stock with at least 25% rag content.

If you're planning a children's clinic, you could contract with a cartoonist to design your logo; use cartoons of children on your letterhead, envelopes, etc.; and then carry the same theme through on your walls and collateral material.

Try to locate a medium-priced printing firm and look for quality work samples in making your final decision. If you shop around, you can locate a company that does work at affordable prices. Determine the quantity you want and order a sufficient amount for approximately two years. It's usually not cost effective to order a five-year supply or more, as you may want to change something and can easily correct the original art work and do a reprint.

There are several ways to initiate promotional/advertising campaigns. You can begin with an announcement to a selected mailing list. Try to have one designed with a little flair so it doesn't resemble a wedding or graduation announcement. Your marketing consultant will be able to select a good graphic artist. Don't have a "friend" do it to save money. Use professional ancillary help for best results.

If you're amenable to advertising and willing to take a risk, run newspaper advertising simultaneously with your announcements. Keep the ad simple and well designed. Use pertinent, concise copy that explains exactly what your service offers. If it is well designed, the ad should not detract from your professionalism or offend the medical community. It's almost like patient education with some extra "punch."

If your budget can afford it, radio spots are an excellent source of communicating your message, as is television. Again, your marketing consultant will be able to write the spots, place them, and work with the television crew in producing commercials if necessary. Your local radio and TV stations will also lend their expertise, and the end product should be both effective and professional.

Your market will dictate where, when, and how you want to advertise.

You can also hold an "Open House." If you do this, try to provide educational demonstrations and displays if open to the public, to give it more appeal and a "hands-on" feeling.

You will need a good brochure describing your service, preferably with photographs. You can also use your brochure as a promotional mailing piece instead of an announcement if your budget is agreeable. If you mail a brochure, it's a good idea to write a promotional letter to go along with it, followed by a personal phone call. It's most productive if this call can be made by a physician. The personal touch is always good for business. The promotional letter should be brief and to the point, but written in a conversational tone like you're talking to a friend, so you project a friendly and inviting image of your services. The following is an example of a promotional letter soliciting referrals in a professional manner.

September 15, 1982

Dear Colleague:

I am pleased to announce the opening of The Breast Clinic of Yakima and acquaint you with our services.

As you know, breast problems and procedures, malignant or benign, often create serious emotional concerns for patients and their families. Our clinic offers a new concept in the treatment of breast disease, focusing on individualized attention and care.

The education of breast disease will be a major part of our pro-

*gram, with special emphasis on video presentations to help allevi-
ate anxiety and fear and create a better understanding of this sensitive subject.*

*I will personally be managing each case, from initial consulta-
tion through diagnosis and recommendation of treatment. The expertise of qualified oncologists, radiation therapists, and diagnostic radiationists are within close proximity of the clinic and will be
used as determined by individual patient needs.*

*I would appreciate your referrals and feel this new service will
benefit both you and your patients. I look to a referring physician as
an associate and welcome advice and counsel. You will not be losing a patient, but ultimately enhance your own physician/patient
relationship.*

*You are invited to visit our new facility for a "red carpet" tour
or call me personally if you have any questions regarding our service.*

Yours very truly,

While all this is happening, you'll need to send out news releases
to local papers and TV/radio news editors announcing the opening
date of your clinic, what your service offers, where it's located, etc.
You can mention your Open House in the news release if it's directed toward the public.

If your clinic is large and houses many specialties, you may want
to consider a monthly newsletter to mail with your billings or make
available to patients in the waiting room. Use a nice simple title like
"Medical Notes," and a good typeface for design. The "shells"
for your newsletter can be run off at a "quick" printer all at one
time on bright colorful paper. Then, once a month, you can type a
master of your message and either xerox your copies or "quick"
print them again in a color that will add additional zest and life to
the overall project.

PROMOTING AN EXISTING CLINIC

Much of the previous advice could be applied to an existing clinic or service if you're looking for general guidelines to increase your public awareness. You can also target a specific market and become "specialists" in that area.

I'm thinking of marketing to industry and business. If you have the time and a sufficient number of physicians in your facility, you could market yourselves as "the clinic to call" for industrial medicine needs. Optimally, of course, you could hire a physician specializing in occupational medicine. However, the service can be successfully handled with a generalized staff, depending on time and interest.

The purpose of this type of marketing effort would be to: provide business and industry in your area with services that would subsequently reduce their medical costs; provide on-site calls to business and industry for specific programs or when necessary; serve as consultants and support to the company medical personnel; and provide business and industry with expedient, professional service to meet their industrial medicine needs.

Once again you need a well-designed promotional brochure and envelope. When I refer to a promotional envelope, I'm talking about using a good design element and color on the front of the envelope to attract attention. This could be your logo, if it's unusual or unique. Otherwise, create a slogan that will entice your reader to open the letter. Or, you can always put together a well-designed self-mailer. You miss the opportunity to send your promotional letter this way, which I feel is important. Your budget will be the determining factor.

The brochure would describe the services of your new program, such as

1. Trauma Treatment—The clinic could be available to provide care for all trauma calls resulting from industrial accidents within proposed areas (with the exception of major accidents, which should be treated in a hospital ER room).
2. Plant Vaccinations—The clinic could make available medical

personnel to administer flu or other vaccines to employees at their work site at appropriate times of the year.

3. After-Hours Care—The clinic could provide on-call physicians to take care of after-hours calls. The treatment would take place at local hospitals.
4. Return-to-Work Evaluations—The clinic could provide exams of employees who have been off work for long periods of time due to injuries on the job to determine if employees can assume normal work duties.
5. Disability Assessment—The clinic could provide employers with evaluations of disability for workmen's compensation, long-term disability, etc.
6. Specialized Programs—The clinic could offer specialized programs designed for specific problems within companies regarding alcohol and drug abuse, stress management, etc.

The above program could be promoted with a brochure, promotional letter, personal phone calls preferably from a physician, and personal visits to the presidents of the firms from a staff member.

During the mailings, the clinic could add to the promotion by sponsoring free colorectal cancer tests. A clinic physician could make presentations at predetermined times at company lunchrooms, auditoriums, etc., discussing the warning signs of colon cancer, early treatment saving lives, high recovery rate if treated early, etc., and pass out free hemocult slides provided by the clinic. You can coordinate this type of program with your local cancer society and utilize their films for additional education and information. Inexpensive flyers could be passed out to company employees prior to each program. This type of promotion would probably qualify for free public service announcements for additional advertising.

I mentioned earlier that there are some exceptions to following all of the "standard marketing rules." You don't always have to apply *all* of the marketing rules to implement a good promotional/advertising campaign. And, there are even times when you "know" there's a definite need for a service and you make the decision to fill it on an educated guess. It's not the norm for a new business, however, so be careful.

There are numerous ways to build a stronger image, create additional public awareness, and successfully promote your service. A few ideas to consider are: Does the service have a well-designed patient information brochure? Have announcements been placed in appropriate medical journals or newspapers? Has paid advertising been considered? Is there something unique about the service that could be utilized in developing a public awareness program? Programs could include special counseling for alcohol and drug abusers; nutritional advice; service after working hours and weekends; seminars regarding subjects of interest to particular groups (asthma, cancer, sports medicine); an informative newsletter containing health promotional or wellness news or specially designed programs to meet the needs of local industry. Do you regularly distribute news releases announcing new services or updating old ones? Are patients informed when it's time for particular tests, such as pap smear or cancer? Have classes for patients — birthing, wellness, nutrition — been considered?

There are no shortcuts to learning how to market, and each business or service has a unique set of objectives and goals. However, this basic understanding of marketing principles will give you an idea of how promotion and advertising can be applied ethically and professionally.

CHAPTER 20

Place — Renovated Hospital for the Elderly

Ellen F. Goldman
Cosmo P. Morabito

After five years of searching for use for an old hospital building, the South Hills Health System (acute care, skilled nursing, home care, counseling and primary care) extended its provision of services beyond reimbursable medical care by venturing into a health-related field and opening a non-profit self-pay personal care home. The "home" provided numerous advantages since it utilized vacant space, tapped a new market, provided a feeder to other system services, and met the community's need for a supervised living arrangement for its elderly.

In 1977, acute care services were suspended at the Homestead Hospitals in Homestead, Pennsylvania. This facility had served area health care needs since 1924, providing emergency, obstetrical, pediatric, psychiatric, intensive and general medical-surgical care. The hospital building, constructed in 1959, was plagued with electrical, heating, fire safety and room size constraints too costly to repair.

Rebuilding on the site to correct these problems and bring the facility into code compliance was unfeasible. The hospital campus was located in a densely developed, inner city area, boxed in by

Reprinted from William J. Winston, ed., *Innovations in Hospital Marketing*, pp. 63–73, © 1984 by The Haworth Press, Inc.

other campus services including a skilled care nursing home and an outpatient mental health/mental retardation center. Additionally, the inner city population was declining, moving to the suburbs, and competition for patients among three local hospitals was intensifying.

The Hospital Board began searching for a suburban site on which to build a new facility. After several years of discussion and negotiation with another hospital, both were consolidated into a larger "System." A new hospital was built in a growing, suburban location, seven miles from Homestead, and the two inner city facilities were closed. As part of the consolidation agreement, the System promised to maintain emergency room services at the Homestead Hospital site. The intention was to make the Homestead campus a long-term care center, adding to the skilled nursing facility already there by turning the hospital building into a 90-bed intermediate care facility. By the time the corporation consolidated, the Homestead locale had changed somewhat, necessitating a new assessment of alternative uses of the hospital building.

MARKETPLACE

Analysis of Homestead demographics in 1981 indicated a higher than average proportion of elderly (18%) in the area. A majority of local residents (67%) were in low and middle income groups and there was a substantial number (13%) of single elderly households. The area in general had a large Slovak population, most of whom had lived locally for generations. The local economy was mostly heavy industry: steel, machinery, and metal manufacturers. The major employer, U.S. Steel, was beginning to pare back its workforce, necessitating an outflux of younger residents who could not obtain employment in the mills. Often, this meant leaving elderly relatives, reluctant to vacate their lifelong "homesteads," with no one to care for them. Being extreme, the area had a bimodel population distribution—young children in low income families and elderly residents with and without local family. Certainly, these were the only two groups which appeared to be growing (indicated by an increasing birth rate and a large number of middle-aged at the "border" of elderly). Industry trends were expected to worsen over the next few years.

ALTERNATIVES

As mentioned earlier, the initial intent was to utilize the building to provide intermediate long-term care — both for those skilled nursing patients no longer needing the intensive skilled care of the adjacent facility, and for those area residents in need of routine nursing home care. As this option was assessed, it became readily apparent that many of the same physical plant problems negating hospital use applied to intermediate care. Additionally, state reimbursement for intermediate services was below the projected cost, making the provision of intermediate care to this high Medicaid population financially infeasible.

Other institutional options were rejected for various reasons: additional skilled nursing care, because the demand was questionable; mixes of skilled and intermediate beds, because of the financial gap between costs and reimbursement; use as a County home, due to physical plant limitations affecting capital cost effectiveness.

Having exhausted all institutional medical care options, nonmedical institutional care which would not require heavy operational costs or extensive physical plant renovations appeared worthy of consideration. This amounted to housing options, which can be viewed along a continuum of levels of care required to support the resident: independent, semi-independent and personal care. Independent housing includes individuals living in their own home or apartment without any on-site social or health-related services. Semi-independent housing includes services such as congregate meals and regularly planned social activities. Personal care includes the services of congregate living plus personal assistance and supervision.

With help from the County government and the local HUD office, the housing alternatives were investigated. The area had several Federally-subsidized housing units, both apartments and congregate living arrangements. Although there was a need for additional facilities, the hospital building's usable floors could not yield enough units to meet qualifying criteria. Public officials urged the investigation of personal care, which seemed a good alternative for the building and which could fill a gap in the services available for the local elderly.

PERSONAL CARE – DEFINITION

Commonly known as boarding home or domiciliary care, personal care is a relatively new term used to describe any premise in which food, shelter and personal supervision are provided for a period exceeding 24 consecutive hours. Individual residents of personal care homes are usually not capable of sustaining all levels of self care, but are ambulatory and not in need of the nursing and other medical care provided in a nursing home. Personal care residents are relatively alert, oriented and mobile – they can use a walker or wheelchair without requiring much assistance.

A personal care home is appropriate under several circumstances: when chronically ill individuals can no longer shop, cook and clean for themselves; use of home appliances without supervision is dangerous; bathing and other activities may result in damaging falls; reminders are needed for good dietary habits and medication schedules; home maintenance becomes burdensome. In short, personal care facilities meet the needs of those individuals who could not live independently in apartments, congregate arrangements, their own homes or those homes of family not present on a daily basis.

Business Research

To better understand the "product" of personal care, several sources were tapped to answer questions such as: who wants the service and why, what price will they pay, how are personal care homes explored and decided on. A private non-profit organization, dedicated to improving housing conditions in the area, was consulted for background information, perceptions and technical expertise. Based on their recent research, it was obvious that the key decision-maker in personal care home placements is the family of the elderly person. This was reinforced by the hospital social work department, whose referral manual, referral logs and opinions provided invaluable information. Finally, three surveys were undertaken by the Planning/Marketing Department to determine actual demand. These included inquiries of: (1) referral sources (social and health service agencies) asked for data on recent personal home referrals, opinions regarding placement factors and our proposed entry into the personal care home market; (2) caretakers of former homecare patients questioned about their interest in family members being personal care residents, ability to pay for services and service preferences. Former patients were questioned where interest was high; and, (3) personal care home operators in the area surveyed to determine current demand, pricing and service features. All of the research was designed and evaluated by the Planning/ Marketing Department. Surveys of caretakers and personal care home operators were executed by trained volunteers, the latter survey via role-playing of interested families.

As indicated earlier, the family of the elderly person usually initiates the move to a personal care home. This decision is based on a combination of the following: recognition that the individual can no longer manage his own home, rising burden of home maintenance, family's difficulty in supervising the elderly individual, and the desire to provide the individual with enhanced social interaction, security and health maintenance. While recognition of the resident's declining capabilities may intensify over time, market research indicated that personal care home placements are made in a crisis-oriented situation—near the end of a hospital stay, for example, thus rendering "available slots" an important determinant of purchasing habits, and waiting lists at existing homes a poor indicator of demand.

Three different target audiences, each with varying psychologies and perceptions, began to emerge. The first audience, the potential residents themselves, are typically elderly females, widowed and over 75 years old. Conversation with the users themselves indicated preferences for double occupancy rooms, certain ethnic populations (e.g., a roommate who spoke Polish), and the ability to maintain church attendance.

Family members, the second audience, generally reacted negatively to shared rooms and attached much significance to programmed activities. Ability to pay higher prices appeared to be overstated by families as compared to actual income levels of the potential residents. Families also equated service features with price in personal care home selection. It should be noted that psychological factors play a large part in personal care home placement for both families and potential residents. The elderly individual is dealing with the facts of their limited physical state, decreased ability to take care of themselves and the potential of "never going home again." Families must cope with feelings of guilt and inadequacy in finding a "solution" outside of the home and must come to terms with their commitments of time to spend with the relative and/or financial support.

The gatekeeper audience was most concerned about traditional indicators of institutions — certifications and licensure requirements (in Pennsylvania, the Department of Welfare licenses personal care homes). This group was most enthusiastic about our entry into the personal care home market, given our reputation as a quality health care provider. Caution was expressed, however, that the service not be high priced as well, as referral agents identified price as the barrier to placing clients.

Service attributes, then, varied by target audience. Room arrangement and activities discrepancies were, to some extent, settled by what we could reasonably provide at what appeared to be the going price. Single rooms were not financially feasible and few of the other twenty or so small (2–6 residents) homes in the area had them. Demand was present at all price levels and sensitive, but not wholly dependent on price. Access was important, as residents and caretakers alike preferred locations close to current homes — this narrowed the potential draw area. An atmosphere of professionalism and caring was important to all parties. Here, the often negative publicity concerning "boarding homes" may have reduced the interest in personal care, causing perhaps a latent demand for the service. Quality perceptions obviously varied between the potential audiences; however, all agreed on the importance of a homelike atmosphere. Residents are really concerned about being left alone (the desire for roommates), families about relieving their guilt (an active environment), and referral agents about their professional reputation (meeting tangible staffing and building standards). The common thread among these various needs and perceptions is safety and security — of living quarters, decisions and recommendations, respectively. Thus, the product being sold can be succinctly described as "peace of mind," but with different implications of indicators to each audience.

Demand for personal care home services was quantified using the preceding information along with demographic data. The population base was adjusted for those over 65, living outside institutions, and in need of personal care. Income levels were then applied using local information regarding the percentage of income used for housing, utilities and food. Finally, this demand calculation was adjusted to reflect those interested in the location (based on the surveys of caretakers) and a proposed market share. A second demand projection methodology focused on more of a market-based calculation, using the gap between referral agency personal care home referrals and available and projected supply. It was difficult to access current residents of personal care homes or their families to evaluate satisfaction levels, but opinions of the local housing authorities did not indicate movement after home placement, most likely due to the excess demand.

Demand projections indicated a range of demanded personal care slots, depending on the conditions of price level, market share and competition. The most conservative estimate projected two floors, or about 52 residents. The housing organization provided an opinion on the demand county-wide, adjusted to the location, which more than reinforced our projections. Demand over time was projected to increase, with the continued aging of the population, decreased housing alternatives, transfer of patients from nursing home facilities, and increasing costs of home maintenance. Average length of stay in personal care homes being two years, referral information from the System's hospital indicated that it alone could generate a constant supply of residents.

Facility

Since our research showed that most area personal care homes were small and since the personal care concept was new to the Health System, it was decided to limit initial services to one floor of the old hospital building. Allowing for a congregate dining area, kitchen, laundry, central bathing, T.V. lounge, and staff offices, the floor could yield room for 32 residents, 16 in double rooms.

The Personal Care Home was designed with the majority of existing hospital rooms left intact, thereby minimizing the cost of demolition and new construction. Remodeling included construction of a private entrance and patio, two bathing areas, kitchen, dining area, storage space and laundry rooms, and installation of new ceilings, lighting, carpeting and plumbing. The rectangular nature of the building was of particular concern. To minimize the negative institutional image and environment, warm colors and lively designs were used in decorating rugs, walls and sides of the long corridor. Total capital requirements, including renovation, equipment, furniture and working capital, were approximately $360,000.

Pricing

Since personal care is not medical care, no insurance coverage (private, state or federal) is available. Alternatively, housing subsidy criteria require the meeting of square footage requirements, among other criteria of the facility, and are limited to low-income recipients. Even when meeting both facility and individual qualifying criteria, housing funds do not cover the expenses of the personal care aides—those who provide supervision and assistance with daily activities. Thus, personal care homes fall in the gap between health care and housing funding streams.

The Personal Care Home fees, therefore, are paid by residents or their caretakers, indicating prices be set competitively. Surveys of existing homes indicated a $100 range in room rates, and as mentioned previously, demand was price sensitive. Prices for the SHHS facility were set slightly above the local median to balance the competitive edge of having an on-site emergency room with being new in the personal care home market.

Organizational Structure

In order to price competitively, and realize the demand for personal care, the home was developed as a separate corporation under the South Hills Health System (SHHS being in the implementation of a corporate restructuring, this became part of the long-term care corporation). The separate entity was necessary in order to meet the level of operational costs necessary for competitive pricing, e.g., minimum overhead, independent support services like dietary and maintenance, and flexible job descriptions. Wages and benefits, for example, were scaled to personal care home operations, with a "home" concept of shared job responsibilities (aides bathe residents, cook meals, do laundry and supervise activities) as opposed to a very structured hospital operation that is neither necessary nor financially feasible. The personal care home was developed as a separate, tax-exempt organization under the parent South Hills Health System. Its Board of Directors consists of four individuals, two of whom are on the Parent Board, two who are other interested local citizens.

Promotion

After much brainstorming, the personal care home name, The Homestead, was chosen, reflecting both its location (Homestead Center, Homestead, Pennsylvania) and the idea of using the word "home" to soften the institutional image. Additionally, it was felt that using "homestead" would appeal to the elderly population who spent most of their lives in the local area.

A grand opening of both The Homestead and the remodeled Emergency and Family Medicine Center on the first floor was executed as a community celebration. Concurrent newspaper ads were placed and brochures mailed to referral agents. Becoming known was not a problem, since the local community and the health care delivery system alike were interested in what was done with the old hospital. Promotional evaluation has indicated that most inquiries to The Homestead came from newspaper ads and from within our own System.

Summary

To date, the Personal Care Home has more than met even the most optimistic projections — it filled to capacity within four months of opening and has been well received by the local community. Half of the residents have used the on-site emergency and family medicine services and six are receiving home care treatments. Most importantly, the Personal Care Home has provided area residents with an alternative to struggling to live by themselves or being prematurely and unnecessarily institutionalized. A few residents have transferred from other area homes in order to be back in their community and/or closer to family members.

Most of our market research conclusions were verified. Demand projections were met and price levels are appropriate. Residents are predominantly female and widowed. Referral agents are positive about the calibre of the service; families are particularly satisfied with the on-site emergency room. The rectangular design has not proven to be a handicap—residents have created their own conversational circles and seating arrangements in various areas of the long hallway.

Much to our surprise, the residents are healthier than expected. This has several implications of importance. First, more in the way of organized, external activities (trips) is expected. Second, the residents are playing a more active role in personal care selection. Finally, the psychological experience of moving into the home is more stressful—residents are often selling their own homes to enter the home rather than having already done this to move in with a child.

Coming into the facility is not an easy transition. Valuables may accompany the residents, but more are left behind. The process of getting adjusted can be compared to that experienced in going away to college, in that the individual has to learn to live with new people in a new environment while coping with their own feelings of insecurity. Living in The Homestead is a "starting over," turning the page in a book . . . making new friends, Tuesday afternoon sing-a-longs, someone else doing the cooking and laundry, and reminders to take medication. It is also, in the words of the Resident Manager, "getting their life back again."

IMPLICATIONS

Personal care homes may be a service whose time has come. As hospitals are forced to make decisions regarding the use of old facilities, personal care may prove, as in this case, a viable service option to meeting the needs of the growing elderly population, particularly those who do not have the financial means to enter complete retirement communities. Personal care homes also retain a community setting for those who can no longer live by themselves or with family, providing a flexible level of care that allows the individual to retain their dignity, need for activity, freedom and responsibility to make choices. To the extent this is done successfully, premature institutionalization can be avoided.

The personal care home market provides the hospital a health-related diversification at a relatively small capital cost. These may both be important features in selling hospital boards on new ventures. Additionally, the development of a personal care home is a step into the world of less regulated, self-pay services. As such, it requires more "housing" than "health care" skills. The need for flexibility in personal care home development and provision cannot be stressed enough, as strict application of hospital job structures, overhead and intensity of hands-on service will only result in unnecessary costs and an unprofitable new venture. Similarly, personal care should be viewed as an option for small empty buildings, rather than empty hospital floors. Personal care is a home first; assistance with living second. Unless a portion of the hospital can be completely separated, accessed independently, and is in a desirable location to live in, personal care should not be viewed as a potential conversion for unused hospital beds.

The marketing implications of this service are numerous. First, as non-reimburseable service, personal care allows the use and application of practically all the marketing methodology, psychographics, segmentation, product design, and in particular, pricing theory. Personal care homes on a large scale are new products, filling a niche in the market for less institutionalized options for the elderly, and providing a ready market for ambulatory services. Furthermore, the gap between independent housing and nursing homes is filled by personal care, bringing the health care system and the housing industry together to extend the horizontal spectrum of living environments and, most importantly, to provide another option for our growing elderly population and those they rely on for basic needs.

CHAPTER 21

A Case Study of Pricing Health Care Services: Southland HMO

Robert E. Sweeney
Stanley P. Franklin

INTRODUCTION

This chapter illustrates how management in one type of service industry, the health maintenance organization (HMO), has attempted to formalize pricing. This effort is complicated by both the intangibility of the service delivered and the relatively greater influence in service industries of non-cost price factors such as accessibility, psychology, and delays.

The presentation describes a simple computerized approach that allows the marketing manager to formally estimate the effect of incremental changes in rates on the firm's projected patterns of enrollment growth and net revenues. The changes in turn reflect underlying variations in the mix of pricing influences including psychological and other factors.

Enrollment projections are crucial to the firm's financial planning and staffing. In the past, most HMO enrollment and revenue projections of this kind were notoriously unreliable. The approach described here makes it possible for HMOs to fine-tune their pricing policies. It also provides a formal and easily understood mechanism by which management can evaluate and reach consensus on alternative scenarios for enrollment growth, staff recruitment, and capacity expansion.

Why is pricing so important? Of course, there is a clear correlation between price and profit or loss. Moreover, the published price becomes one of the measurable ways in which a potential customer can evaluate the benefits of enrollment. But pricing has significant strategic implications that go beyond the economics of revenues and expenses. Among the strategic consequences are the following:

The Creation of a Corporate Consensus. Disagreements about price frequently indicate strategic differences about the mission and objectives of the firm. The marketing department may favor "lowball pricing" to drive membership growth, with the rates to be raised at a later date. Finance could argue strongly for full recovery cost so that quoted prices would have to reflect allocated fixed expenses and an acceptable rate of return. Operations management may envision selective pricing as a means of rationing access to or utilization of various services. In a mature for-profit business, these tradeoffs are normally explicit and are adjudicated directly in executive committee or board meetings. In nonprofit organizations, lacking a formal management tradition, these differences may not be explicit or even recognized by management at all. Yet, the implicit competition of motivations surrounding pricing policy can breed frustration, internal conflict, and other morale or management problems.

Positioning. Does the firm intend to be a price competitor? Or, does it plan to differentiate along services offered, the level of quality, or the selection of target markets—thereby pricing above the competition? Does the firm have a dominant market share (price-setter position) or is it fighting for part of a fragmented market (price-taker position)? How should the benefit plan be structured, limited, and promoted to support positioning objectives? With respect to all these considerations and more, pricing frequently expresses the corporate direction (or lack of one).

Staffing Characteristics. Depending upon its pricing policy, a firm may want to hire or promote either aggressive, entrepreneurial personnel or less aggressive but perhaps more diplomatic maintenance managers. Clearly, this choice in emphasis will have profound consequences for the culture and performance of the organization. Rapid-growth firms must recruit and reward the ambitious, often idiosyncratic individual whose imagination, energy, and leadership skills can propel the firm to above-average results. Mature firms, on the other hand, usually seek market consolidation and will want to have consensus-building administrators. In the 1970s and early 1980s, a few stand-alone HMOs, such as Maxicare, made judicious choices in this regard, but many others fell by the way-side. Pricing policy for rapid-growth HMOs suggested the inevitability or desirability of direct combat with powerful entrenched competitors. However, the typical HMO marketing and general management personnel were often more academically or administratively inclined.

Pricing has implications for advertising policy, customer service levels, financial strategy, legal and regulatory relationships, and many more strategic issues. There should be no doubt that pricing policy formation is a serious strategic endeavor requiring the active participation of all senior management and the full attention of the board of directors.

PRICING HEALTH CARE SERVICES: THE HEALTH MAINTENANCE ORGANIZATION

The Issue of Pricing

Pricing for products has traditionally involved the consideration of a variety of factors such as cost of production, competition, stage of market development, nature of the product relationship to other products in the line and other more or less quantifiable factors (see *Price Waterhouse Business Review*, 1984). The transition from a manufacturing-oriented economy to one that is service-oriented has compelled management to consider a variety of less measurable influences. MacStravic (1977), for example, identifies waiting time, appointment delays, geographical accessibility, customer service features, diagnostic discomfort, and treatment pain as non-cost "price" components that strongly determine the purchasing behavior of service consumers. These components tend to be significantly more powerful where the commodity delivered is an intangible with somewhat diffused benefits and amorphous or continually changing features of delivery. Yet, management has few guidelines for incorporating these influences and is often completely unaware of their significance. (A prime example of this lack of exposure to non-cost pricing influences is the broad-ranging health industries. Because of the nature of regulation and cost-reimbursement, until very recently these industries were simply able to pass costs on to the public with little need to consider demand influences on price.) The absence of a deep marketing tradition in health care and other service industries also contributes to the uncertainty about how to properly price the firm's offerings.

This chapter presents a detailed explanation of how Southland HMO attempted to include political, psychological, and accessibility factors in pricing. The presentation draws upon both published information and evidence and the personal experience of the senior author in health care management.* The goal is to demonstrate how service firms are groping in theoretical virgin territory for tools and procedures to improve and control their marketing management functions.

The use of computer techniques to support pricing policy formation is a revolutionary development for the prepaid health care industry. The authors have developed a generic computer model specifically designed to shorten the time-consuming manual methods currently employed. The technical aspects of the model and how it can be used are explained in Appendix A to this chapter.

HMO: PROMISE UNFULFILLED

Nearly fifteen years after the federal government decided to invest in subsidizing competition in the health delivery sector, the results of that effort have become apparent. There are several HMO success stories, such as Harvard Community Health Plan in Boston and Maxicare in southern California. But for every success, there have been a dozen failures or walking wounded. The absence of managerial experience and financial staying power has made the industry susceptible to shakeout and concentration. In the 1980s, major insurance companies, such as the Prudential and John Han-

---

*The senior author, Bob Sweeney, was Marketing Director of Southland HMO from 1979 to 1981. Southland is a pseudonym for a real staff model HMO in Shelby County, Tennessee. In 1982, it was sold to a major insurance company. An earlier case study on Southland HMO as a market development case, also authored by Sweeney, was published in L. Robinson and P. Cooper, *Health Care Marketing Management: A Case Approach* (Aspen Systems, 1982).

cock, purchased vulnerable HMOs or independently developed their own health plans. Their performance record has been mixed. Investor firms offering management contracts, such as Healthamerica of Nashville, created networks of HMOs, thereby assembling large subscriber pools over which to average their fixed costs. Many of these entrepreneurial firms, including Healthamerica have foundered, merged or been bought out in the mid-1980s. The two advantages which these firms bring to the marketplace are their managerial competency and money. They are better able to absorb front-end or expansion-related capital deficits while their management climbs the learning curve to profitability. However, even the presumably more experienced managements in the insurance and investments industries have struggled with the complexities of controlling costs while trying to rapidly grow.

Smaller independent HMOs do not have the luxury of waiting for slow growth to finally pay off. They must have rapid growth to cover their start-up subsidies or loans and their field costs. Even when successfully achieved, rapid growth may bring its own dangerous side effects. Sweeney and Rakowski (1984) have analyzed the logistical tradeoffs in terms of cost, service levels, and staffing loads as embryonic HMOs strive for growth. These internal pressures may lead to physician resentment due to perceived heavy workload, customer dissatisfaction with perceived excessive treatment backlogs, or financial collapse if the HMO's enrollment rate outruns the capacity of its MIS system to track claims. In their brilliant paper on HMO strategic considerations, Hirsch and Roberts (1976) describe another potential danger during the young HMOs struggle to maturity: the morbidity filter. If an HMOs operational efficiency declines or enrollment fails to meet forecasted levels, the total cost per subscriber will rise or be higher than projected. As a result, premiums eventually must be raised. Subscribers or potential subscribers who are chronically ill may be indifferent to marginal premium increases because they can recognize treatment returns for a far greater dollar value than their payments. On the other hand, healthy subscribers will be much more likely to disenroll if premiums are perceived to be inflationary. Similarly, healthy potential subscribers will be deterred from enrolling by high premiums. The ever more expensive HMO becomes a filter, drawing in high utilizers and expelling its healthy membership. Average morbidity rises, demands for care increase, and the HMO must either hire even more expensive staff or risk consumer dissatisfaction with all its unpleasant effects on the firm's market image.

The Role of Pricing Policy

A corollary to this discussion of the side effects of growth is that a poorly conceived pricing policy can precipitate these conditions even in an otherwise healthy HMO. If premiums underprice the true cost of services, in the long run the plan will not be able to recover its fixed costs and may even fail to meet operational expenses. If premiums are higher than need be, the HMO may unwillingly become a morbidity filter.

A viable pricing policy would set the HMO's premium rates so as at a minimum to cover the firm's long-run total costs. The specific price per individual or family benefit package might be set each year taking into account several factors: forecasted enrollment, current capitation* or cost per member, estimated average family size in the current and forecasted subscriber population, competition, and the previously mentioned non-cost influences. The firm may also have a "loading" policy to attract or discourage a specific subscriber mix. Unfortunately, no HMOs have reliable forecasting techniques: many underestimate capitation (usually due to failure to properly estimate future incurred but unreported claims); most cannot predict average family size in advance; and few employ a consistent price-loading policy. In fact, the entire area of forecasting market behavior is devastatingly weak throughout the HMO industry. Even the federal government's training manual for HMO marketing managers observes that "errant forecasting procedures are responsible for significant consumption of precious resources throughout the HMO development cycle" (Office of Health Maintenance Organizations, 1980).

---

*Capitation is a term commonly encountered in the prepaid health industry. The term is used informally to mean average cost per member of an insured group. Strictly speaking, the term refers to the "per member" dollar amount that an HMO pays to some provider or insurer in exchange respectively for health care services or insurance for some defined period of time. This amount is fixed for the period agreed upon and does not vary with the rate or expense of utilization by the member.

How could a better pricing strategy help to improve HMO financial performance and market growth? There is no question but that other factors are equal in importance to the price function. However, price is probably the most easily quantified variable, and there are formal, if controversial, regulatory guidelines within which pricing policy must be established. This chapter builds on an earlier publication which proposed the use of a systematic pricing policy to strengthen HMO marketing strategy (Sweeney, 1980). Sweeney illustrated a manual pricing model which he employed to set initial premium rates for Southland HMO when it became operational in 1981. This case study considers a computerized version of the model.

Pricing Model Structure:
General Description

In the model developed for Southland, price and enrollment response levels are mutually interactive. Management begins with some best guess initial price or premium for HMO service, then modifies this price as other non-cost factors point to likely trends in enrollment response (i.e., pricing behavior). Enrollment response is a function of three primary independent variables:

1. out-of-pocket additional expense or savings to the enrollee*
2. size of the corporate employment pool
3. employer cooperation.

Therefore, the pricing policy assumes an initial enrollment response (i.e., consumer behavior) that considers cost, exposure to information, and peer group pressure. Subsequent enrollment behavior will vary with changes in these cost *and* non-cost influences on price. For example, if peer group pressure discourages enrollment, cost considerations alone may have to be set aside and the price offered might be lowered. It should be mentioned here that HMOs usually draw those who do not already have established physician relation-

---

*Under commercial insurance, it is common for the employer to pay all or a significant part of an employee's group insurance. Therefore, the employee (i.e., the subscriber) is sensitive to the change in his own contribution level as opposed to the absolute price of the insurance coverage.

ships. Lack of a family doctor may be a function of youth, the absence of a recent medical condition requiring treatment, economic status, a local physician shortage, or having been relocated to a new or unfamiliar community. Therefore, absence of a physician relationship is an informal a priori assumption about the HMO prospect. It is, therefore, not a factor considered in predicting HMO enrollment response to marketing efforts.

The model's enrollment assumptions are deliberately conservative. The maximum possible percentage enrollment from any one employer in the model is arbitrarily constrained to less than nine percent per year. This upper limit conforms to industry experience over the past decade. An enrollment forecast is developed in the following sequence of steps:

1. Selection of target market group employers
2. Calculation of the potential number of single, dual (couple only), and family enrollments for each target employer
3. Manipulation of the contract yield for each employer to determine the total number of potential members: number of family contracts times average family size plus number of dual contracts times two plus number of single contracts equals total members
4. Placement of each employer on a monthly enrollment timetable showing enrollment growth over the desired interval — typically a year.

Enrollment: Assumptions and Estimates

In developing company-specific enrollment estimates, the following factors are considered: premium differential, employee contribution, size, and anticipated employer cooperation.

Premium differential. This factor, the difference in total premium charges between the HMO and its group insurance competitor(s), is a strong predictor for HMO acceptability. In other words, the model introduces a psychological factor into pricing policy which is not, strictly speaking, a cost factor. Potential members react to the perceived price differential between two competitive offerings independently from their evaluations of actual value added. The premium differential is prominent in the decision to include or exclude specific employer groups from the primary target market in the first place.

Employee contribution. The change, if any, in employee contribution is the major acceptability predictor. What amount of money, more or less, will the employee pay or save out-of-pocket with HMO membership? This factor is used to weigh the employer group's attractiveness with respect to single, two-person, and family premiums. This is the actual out-of-pocket cost factor.

Size. Smaller groups are much easier to enroll than larger groups. Usually, a marketing representative will be able to speak face to face with all or most members of smaller groups. A face-to-face sale is more likely to succeed than an impersonal approach. The larger the group, a smaller percentage of members that can be encountered in this way. Moreover, in smaller groups, there are fewer institutional obstacles and more chance that one or a few individuals can deliver the group through careful personal solicitation. Smaller groups also require far less time and fewer calls to close and frequently are paying relatively more expensive charges for a given level of coverage from their group insurance carriers. Small groups tend to pay more per capita for insurance than larger groups for several reasons. First, there are economies of scale for administrative costs such as claims processing as the size of a group grows. Second, the demographics of larger groups, such as average family size, tend to be more stable since the addition or termination of small numbers of employees has less effect on the overall characteristics of a larger population; this factor makes the larger group more "predictable" for actuarial forecasts such as levels of morbidity and accidental injury. More accuracy in these estimates means that rates can be set with greater expectation of costs being covered. Third, there is less "adverse selection" in larger groups. For example, the appearance of catastrophic (i.e., expensive) illness is averaged in with greater numbers of relatively healthy subscribers in the large group, thereby somewhat insulating the insurer against unexpected severe losses. In effect, the small group pays a risk premium related to its size. All these factors make smaller groups easier to enroll. An informal survey of operational HMOs would strongly support this conclusion. In short, price is a function of the degree of impersonality of the method of product introduction.

Anticipated Employer Cooperation. A specific weighting value — independent of the premium differential, size, and employee contribution values — reflects an employer's cooperativeness in offering the HMO product. In other words, political acceptance or endorsement by the group will influence price. When the cooperation value is added to the employee contribution and size values, the total obtained value is then placed on an enrollment percent scale (where nine percent is highest and zero percent lowest). The scale is discussed and displayed below. This transposition enables the HMO to estimate the number of single, two-person, and family contracts which each employer will yield.

The enrollment matrix is constructed as follows:

1. *Calculate employee contribution score.* A grid is used to score the target employer's single, dual (if any), and family premiums. The scoring is a measure of whether an employee of that company would make additional out-of-pocket payments or savings after joining the HMO (see Table 21.1).

TABLE 21.1. Out-of-Pocket Expenses and Savings in an HMO

	Single	Two-Party	Family	Employee Contribution Score
Additional	> $11	> $11	> $20	0
Out-of-	$9 − 11	$9 − 11	$16 − 20	2
Pocket	$6 − 8	$6 − 8	$11 − 15	4
Expense	$3 − 5	$3 − 5	$6 − 10	8
	$0 − 2	**$0 − 2**	**$0 − 5**	**12**
Out-of-	$1 − 2	$1 − 2	$1 − 5	16
Pocket	$3 − 5	$3 − 5	$6 − 10	20
Savings	$6 − 8	$6 − 8	$11 − 15	24
	> $8	**> $8**	**> $15**	**28**

Note: Dollar differential amounts are rounded to nearest whole dollar for scoring. Therefore, a dollar differential of $4.37 between the HMO single premium and the competitor's single premium would be rounded to $4 for placement in this grid.

2. *Calculate* the score for size. The size score is determined as follows:

Number of Group Eligibles	Size Score
> 10,000	0
> 5000, but < 10,000	2
> 1000, but < 5,000	4
> 500, but < 1,000	6
> 100, but < 500	8
< 100	10

3. *Calculate the employer cooperation score.* The cooperativeness of the group for enrollment purposes is weighed into the forecasting process by scoring a group as follows:

	Cooperation Score*
Represented on HMO Board of Directors	6
Letter of Intent or Firm Verbal Offer	5
Employer Savings > $5/Contract	4
Employer Savings < $5/Contract	3
Access, On Site/On Company Time	2
Group Insurance Rate and Coverage Information Available	1
Less Cooperation Than the Above or Unknown	0

*The Cooperation Score values are not summed to obtain the Cooperation Score entered in the subsequent enrollment calculations. The highest value applicable for a given company wins out.

4. *Sum the three preceding scores and apply the result to the HMO enrollment scale.* A separate employee contribution score is obtained for the single, dual (if any), and family premiums, respectively, in each target group. The size score and employer cooperation score will be added to each of these values to obtain the respec-

tive total scores. For example, the Southern Comfort Company (a pseudonym for a real insured employee group in Shelby County, Tennessee) in Southland's service area had 3,129 employees in 1981; had a single premium under its current commercial group insurance of $50, of which the company paid $47; and had a family premium of $122, of which the company paid $105. The corresponding rates for the HMO were $45 and $110. Also, the company allowed on-site/on-time calls. The single and family premium "scores" for this firm were calculated as follows:

Single Score	Family Score
1. Employee saves $3 (50−47) by joining HMO; so employee contribution score is 20.	1. Employee saves $12 (122−110) by joining HMO; so employee contribution score is 24.
2. Size score is 4 (3500 > 1000, but < 5000).	2. Size score is 4 (3500 > 1000, but < 5000).
3. Employer saves $2 (47−45); so cooperation score is 3.	3. No employer savings, but company allows on-site/on-time calls; so cooperation score is 2.
4. Total score = 20 + 4 + 3 = 27	4. Total score = 24 + 4 + 2 = 30

The total scores were then transposed to an enrollment percent scale as follows:

Total Score	% Penetration Forecast
41−45	9
36−40	8
31−35	7
26−30	6
21−25	5
16−20	4
11−15	3
6−10	2
1-5	1
0	0

So, the Southern Comfort Company was expected to yield a six percent penetration of its single contract pool and a six percent penetration of its family contract pool. The 3,129 employees of the firm broke down as follows: 1,788 single contracts and 1,341 family contracts. Previously, the HMO had conducted a geographic analysis to determine how many potential subscribers lived more than one-half hour driving time from the HMO's health center. Beyond this distance, the influence of poor accessibility swamps all other factors in the consumer's "pricing response." In this case, 10.6% of the eligible insured pool were found to live beyond the geographical bounds of the service area. Therefore, the numbers for Southern Comfort were stepped down by 10.6% each to account for out-of-service-area residency. The resulting numbers of *eligibles* (1,598 and 1,199, respectively) were then used as the base for forecasting enrollment:

$$1598 \times .06 = 96 \text{ contracts}$$
$$1199 \times .06 = 72 \text{ contracts}$$

The total forecasted enrollment for the Southern Comfort Company was therefore 96 single members + 72 family contracts × 3.26* people per family = 235 members = 331. All targeted employers are assigned an enrollment estimate for each occasion when the HMO expects to enroll their employees through a given number of years of operations. The beauty of this model is its flexibility in permitting the premium or price quoted to be jiggled so as to obtain the most lucrative enrollment response to price as a function of cost as well as non-cost influences. Actual enrollment results are used to further modify the model's predictive assumptions.

An accurate prediction of reenrollment patterns for an HMO service/market area with no previous HMO activity would be extremely difficult to provide. However, for modeling purposes, the HMO would typically reduce the first-year single, two-person and family *enrollment rates* by 50% to forecast net enrollment for targeted employer groups in the second and third year and so on. For example, the Southern Comfort Company had a first-year single

---

*The average family size in Shelby County in 1979 was estimated by Blue Shield/Blue Cross of Memphis as 3.26 persons per family.

penetration rate of 6.0% and family penetration rate of 6.0%. For the second year, assume 3.0% single and family penetration rates, respectively. In the third year, the same assumptions would yield 1.5% single and family penetration rates. This assumed pattern of penetration would be quite conservative. That is because while those employees most attracted to the HMO might be expected to enroll in early years, there is also the prospect that a good service reputation and education to the HMO concept could attract more enrollers.

Data obtained from demographic and market surveys (Federal Qualification Application, 1981) yielded the following calculations of average contract size, average family size, and contract mix in the service area where the model was first tested in 1981:

	Two-Tier Premium	Three-Tier Premium
1. Average Family Size	3.26	3.34
2. Contract Mix:		
Single Contract	38%	23%
2-person Contract	0	30%
Family Contract	62%	47%

3. Average Contract Size: $(.23 \times 1) + (.30 \times 2) + (.47 \times 3.34)$
   $= 2.4$

The terms "two-tier" and "three-tier" refer to whether the market is analyzed as composed of just single and family contracts (hence, two-tier) or singles, couples, and family (three-tier). Obviously, in a three-tier analysis of the same population, the removal of two-person families (couples) into their own separate category will cause the average family size for remaining family contracts to increase. In 1979 in Shelby County, the average family size including couples was 3.26; when couples were counted separately, it was 3.34.

The projected distribution of enrollment contracts in the first two years projected enrollment was actually very close to the community average contract size (2.36 projected versus 2.4 for the real community). The mean local figures could, therefore, have been used as raw inputs in computing HMO premiums and enrollment projections. However, there were compelling reasons for doing otherwise, primarily the effect of federal pricing regulations (see Appendix B to this chapter).

The question remains as to how the anchor price, the single premium, is initially established. When this model was first employed manually, the senior author followed the general rule that the single premium should be set equal to the higher of two amounts: (1) the expected monthly cost of treating a single adult (set at $45 here); or (2) the employer contribution to the group's current commercial insurance rate, minus 50 cents as an incentive.

The floor (lowest possible) price was always $45.00.* In other words, if the employer's contribution exceeded the average cost of treatment, the HMO would not "leave money on the table" unnecessarily. A higher HMO rate in this case would not affect the ultimate consumer (the employee) who doesn't pay the employer's contribution in any case.

The initial starting point is arbitrary since it really only weighs in the cost influence on price. Consumer reaction to the other non-cost factors determines where the final premium value rests.

Once the single premium is set, the family rate is automatically determined according to the community rating formula described earlier. In established HMOs, groups of less than 100 eligibles may be pooled to form one large group for rating purposes. All these small groups have the same rates; the purpose in doing so is to reduce the HMO's exposure to great variances in family size, both initially and as the targeted company hires or terminates personnel. Cost exposure will be lower with a standard set of rates.

---

*The cost of delivering care to a single adult, which is what all single contract holders are, will always exceed the capitation, the cost of delivering care to the "mean" member (part adult, part child). In Memphis, capitation in 1981 was estimated at $35; the cost of treating an adult, at $45.

Enrollment and Pricing Methodology:
A Summary

The HMO marketing management begins by making some assumptions about enrollment as a function of price, accessibility, and market receptivity. The methodology illustrated here employs the following assumptions:

1. perceived differences in price (i.e., premium differentials) influence the customer's disposition to enroll (price)
2. actual changes in out-of-pocket expense are the primary determinant of enrollment behavior (price)
3. the absolute size of a potential target group defines and limits the degree and means of access by the HMO to the ultimate consumer (access)
4. the level of cooperation, resistance, or indifference demonstrated by the employer group management (the real gatekeeper to the market) strongly influences consumer perceptions and receptivity to any HMO marketing campaign (market receptivity).

A cumulative enrollment prediction is then built. Separate scores are assigned for price, access, and market receptivity, then these values are summed. This sum is applied to an enrollment percentage scale to determine predicted enrollment for that group. Separate scores are calculated for single, family, and, where applicable, two-party (couples) contracts. The enrollment percentage scale reflects and embodies past industry experience in light of variations in the combined effects of price, access, and market receptivity on enrollment behavior.

Of course, the enrollment methodology assumes a given price. A line HMO marketing manager would use the enrollment model to test market response to various pricing alternatives in the "neighborhood of acceptability" for his benefit package. He can then select whatever variable he wishes to maximize: enrollment, revenue, or profit. The pricing model becomes an experimental lab in which the general validity of group-specific sales strategies and objectives can be evaluated.

The computerized version of the model, described in Appendix

A, improved on the manual version by generating a printout of premiums and corresponding net revenues as the single premium was varied by small increments across a desired range. This procedure would be unacceptably tedious and expensive in terms of staff time if done by hand for a large number of accounts. However, in a computer model, such time delays are eliminated and the implications of pricing changes are subject to immediate evaluation. Within the constraint of covering his average cost over all insureds, the manager can develop group-specific or industry-specific pricing policies that still meet the regulatory community rating requirements or other stipulations.

REFERENCES

Atlas, Robert. *Federal Guidelines for Establishing Prepaid Rates for Federally Qualified Health Maintenance Organizations under a Community Rating System*, Office of Health Maintenance Organizations, Dept. of Health and Human Services, Washington, D.C., 1979.

Federal Qualification Application, Volume I, Southland HMO, Memphis, Tennessee, 1981.

MacStravic, Robin E. "Price of Services," *Marketing Health Care*, Aspen Systems Corporation, 1977, Chapter 12.

Office of Health Maintenance Organizations. "A Pricing Strategy for Your Business," *Price Waterhouse Business Review*, 1981-1.

Office of Health Maintenance Organizations. "Health Maintenance Organization Seminars: Marketing," Public Health Service, Dept. of Health and Human Services, Washington, D.C., 1980, p. 98.

Roberts, Edward B. and Hirsch, Gary B. "Strategic Modelling for Health Care Managers," *Health Care Management Review*, Winter 1976.

Sweeney, Robert E. "Health Care Market Analysis Through Systematic Pricing," *Proceedings*, Second International Conference on Systems Science in Health Care, Montreal 1980.

Sweeney, Robert E. and Rakowski, James P. "Logistical Considerations in the Prepaid Health Industry," *Health Marketing Quarterly*, Vol. 2, Nos. 2/3, Winter 1984/Spring 1985.

Appendix A to Chapter 21

The computer implementation of the model requires as inputs the following: the employer cooperation score, number of employees, percentage of singles, average family size, and current commercial insurance prices. It prints this information before printing the subsequent pricing run (see Figure 21.1).

In the sample run shown here, a moderate-sized company (500 employees) is modeled. The company offers minimal cooperation and pays for none of the health care costs of its employees. The amount of unit variation in the premium assumed can be chosen by

```
TRIAL RUN        12/11/80

INITIAL COOPERATION SCORE -   2
NUMBER OF EMPLOYEES -  500
PERCENTAGE OF SINGLES -   38
PERCENTAGE OF FAMILIES -   62
AVERAGE FAMILY SIZE -   3.26
CURRENT SINGLES PRICE -   55
COMPANY'S SHARE OF SINGLE PRICE -   0
CURRENT FAMILY PRICE -   110
COMPANY'S SHARE OF FAMILY PRICE -   0
```

SINGLE PRICE	FAMILY PRICE	ENROLLMENT SINGLE	FAMILY	TOTAL	TOTAL REVENUE	PROFIT
67.00	94.49	4 +	81 =	85	2597.88	74.20
66.00	95.10	4 +	71 =	75	2314.47	84.88
65.00	95.71	4 +	71 =	75	2323.97	94.38
64.00	96.33	4 +	71 =	75	2333.47	103.88
63.00	96.94	6 +	71 =	76	2462.67	147.58
62.00	97.55	6 +	71 =	76	2470.27	155.18
61.00	98.16	6 +	71 =	76	2477.87	162.78
60.00	98.78	8 +	71 =	78	2599.47	198.88
59.00	99.39	8 +	71 =	78	2605.17	204.58
58.00	100.00	8 +	61 =	68	2300.86	194.35
57.00	100.62	8 +	61 =	68	2304.66	198.15
56.00	101.23	8 +	61 =	68	2308.46	201.95
55.00	101.84	8 +	61 =	68	2312.26	205.75
54.00	102.45	10 +	61 =	70	2418.66	226.65
53.00	103.07	10 +	61 =	70	2420.56	228.55
52.00	103.68	11 +	61 =	72	2521.26	243.75
51.00	104.29	11 +	61 =	72	2521.26	243.75
50.00	104.91	11 +	51 =	62	2196.05	212.63
49.00	105.52	13 +	51 =	64	2287.25	218.33
48.00	106.13	13 +	51 =	64	2283.45	214.53
47.00	106.75	13 +	51 =	64	2279.65	210.73
46.00	107.36	15 +	51 =	66	2363.25	208.83
45.00	107.97	15 +	51 =	66	2357.55	203.13

FIGURE 21.1. Sample Run

the user. In the sample run it is set at $2. The initial single premium is arbitrarily set for this example at $12.50 more than the cost to a single employee under commercial coverage, rounded to the nearest dollar or, in this case, to $67. The program then computes the family price according to the rate formula given in the text. The program next predicts the single, family, and total enrollment, and calculates the corresponding total revenue and profit. Next, the single premium is decremented by $2 and the procedure repeated. This iteration continues until the single premium is decremented down to the cost of treating a single adult, $45, where the process stops.

Inspection of the figure shows that maximal enrollment is achieved on the first line where the single premium heavily subsidizes the family rate. Maximum total revenue occurs at a single premium of $59 but maximum profit at $52. The last two columns of the sample run graphically illustrate the nonlinear effect of the step functions in the model on revenue and profit. The implication is that unless assisted by sophisticated forecasting techniques management will simply be guessing or gambling in setting price. Of course, the non-cost pricing factors can also be varied with this model to show the response of enrollment to their changing influence. The entire sample run, including booting the computer, loading the program, data entry, calculations and printing, requires no more than ten minutes. The contrast with a comparable manual implementation is vivid. This pricing model was implemented in Microsoft BASIC on a Radio Shack Model II desk-top computer with 64K of memory. The program uses under two-hundred lines of code including internal documentation. For technical reasons, some of the step functions in the model were implemented on a case basis while others were approximated analytically.

To use this model in another setting, the structure is first adjusted to local conditions. One would then expect a competent programmer to produce, test, and document a program implementing the model within a week or two. Any business computer, micro, mini, or mainframe, could be used. Any high level language such as COBOL, FORTRAN, or Pascal could be used.

Alternatively, it should be possible to implement the model using an electronic spreadsheet package such as VisiCalc or Lotus 1–2–3.

Programming time might be considerably less. Some flexibility in the incremental range would have to be sacrificed.

Figure 21.2 is a list of variables used in the pricing program.

List of Variables
ACS = Average Contract Size in Company Population
AFS = Average Family Size in Company Population
C   = Cost (= SE*SC + FE*AFS*FC)
CAP = Capitation Rate
CP% = Cooperation Score
E   = Total Enrollment Predicted at a Given Single Price X
EF   = Employee Contribution Score - Family
ES   = Employee Contribution Score - Single
FC   = Family Capitation Rate
FE   = Number of Families Enrolled at a Given Single Price X
FY   = Percentage of Families in Company Population
I   = Interval at Which X is Decremented
NO% = Number of Employees of the Company
P   = Profit Predicted at a Given Single Price X
PF   = Percentage of Penetration Forecast for Families
PS   = Percentage of Penetration Forecast for Singles
R   = Total Revenue Predicted for a Given X
SC   = Single Capitation Rate (Single Adult Cost)
SE   = Number of Singles Enrolled at a Given Single Price X
SG   = Percentage of Singles in Company Population
SZ% = Size Score
X   = Price of a Single Contract
XO   = Current Single Price
XE   = Employer's Share of Current Single Price
Z   = Price of a Family Contract
ZO   = Current Family Price
ZE   = Employer's Share of Current Family Price

FIGURE 21.2. List of Variables Used in a Pricing Program

Appendix B to Chapter 21

Federal pricing rules at the time this case was prepared allowed rates to be set according to one of three alternative standards:

1. uniform rates for all accounts
2. rates which generate equal revenue per contract in all accounts
3. rates which generate equal revenue per member in all accounts

Most HMOs used some version of the first alternative. However, this choice was more by default and lack of familiarity with other options. Moreover, rates obtained in this way would be completely dependent upon the prices and loading factors employed by competitors, not by the HMO's financial and marketing staff. Therefore, Southland HMO rejected the first alternative.

They also rejected the second alternative, in this case because an "equal revenue per contract" standard would give no assurance of fairly allocating costs to each of the HMO's target groups. That is because substantial variance in average contract size within major companies would financially punish groups with smaller families.

To quote Robert Atlas, author of the *Federal Guidelines for Establishing Prepaid Rates for Federally Qualified Health Maintenance Organizations under a Community Rating System*, "you can most fully apportion costs to groups based on their average contract size by setting rates according to the equal revenue per member standard" (Atlas, 1979). The pricing system was, therefore, based upon the third alternative — the "equal revenue per member" standard, adjusted for group-specific demographic variance. The rate formulae were:

1. (percent Single) × (Single Premium) + (percent Family) × (Ratio of Family-to-Single Premium) × (Single Premium) = Average Contract Size × Capitation per Member,* or
2. (percent Single) × (Single Premium) + (percent Dual) × (Dual Premium)** + (percent Family) × (Ratio of Family-to-Single Pre-

---

*Capitation per Member for this article was set at $35.00.
**Dual Premium = 2 × Single Premium, if used.

mium × (Single Premium) = Average contract size × Capitation per member

Once the single premium is set, the equations are solved for one unknown (Ratio of Family-to-Single Premium). This value is then multiplied by the single premium to get the family rate. These results are then used in the HMO enrollment matrix to calculate company specific membership growth.

CHAPTER 22

County Health Department: Prenatal Program: A Marketing Case Study and Analysis

Constance W. Mahoney

INTRODUCTION

County Health Department (CHD)* is recognized nationally as a leader in protecting the health and well-being of the entire community and providing public health services to meet the needs of a large indigent population. The department recently received a state grant to provide outreach and education on the importance of prenatal care. Dr. Carl Kraft, Director and Health Officer of CHD, recognized that in most of the state the primary prenatal problem is the lack of available medical services. However, that is not the problem in his region where prenatal medical care for the indigent is more readily available. However, the prenatal problem in the County is nevertheless one of great magnitude. In 1981, approximately one-half of the state's high risk prenatal population lived in the County. Table 22.1 summarizes data relevant to the prenatal problem in the County.

In spite of the availability of nationally recognized, high quality prenatal care that is free or low-cost to indigent patients, in 1981 over 3,000 County women, including 40% of health department prenatal patients, received no prenatal care in the first trimester. Dr.

---

*County Health Department is a major public health agency in a large southern metropolitan area. Surnames and places referred to in this case are pseudonyms.

Kraft believes that it is the responsibility of the Public Health Department to encourage pregnant women to seek early and regular prenatal care. According to the Administrator, Personal Health Services, CHD, "The problem is either that they don't know that the services exist, which is difficult to comprehend, or that they just don't care." According to the Manager of the Reproductive Health Section in the Personal Health Services Bureau, "They (pregnant women) are just not motivated; perhaps a marketing study can help us figure out how to reach these women, motivate them, and educate them to use our prenatal services."

TABLE 22.1. A Listing of Prenatal Care Data, by Race — 1980

Type of Birth	Total		White		NW	
	No.	%	No.	%	No.	%
Resident births	14211	100.0	6334	45.0	7875	55.0
Women with < 9 prenatal visits among resident births	4689	33.0	747	11.8	3937	50.0
Low weight births among resident births	1463	10.3	361	5.7	1103	14.0
Births to women < 19 among resident births	1892	13.3	402	6.3	1490	18.9
Low weight births among women < 19	278	14.7	43	10.7	235	15.8
Women beginning prenatal care after first trimester among resident births	3112	21.9	595	9.4	2520	32.0
Low weight births among women beginning prenatal care after first trimester	311	10.0	42	7.0	328	13.0

Source: State Plan for Prenatal Service, State Department of Public Health FY 82–83. Selected data by region.

ORIGIN AND ORGANIZATION OF CHD

History and Services

Public health service in the area dates back to the yellow-fever epidemic in the mid-19th century and efforts to provide public sanitation for a disease-ridden community. Shortly after the turn of the century, the Public Health Department began its tradition of providing personal health care by hiring two nurse midwives to deliver babies in the homes of the indigent. In 1930, efforts to curb the excessively high infant mortality rate — 132 per 1,000 live births — led to an increase in the number of nurse midwives and the beginning of the present prenatal care system for indigents. This system, which is a cooperative program coordinating services of the Public Health Department, the City Hospital, and the Department of OB-GYN at the University Center for the Health Sciences (CHS), provides prenatal care and delivery for over 6,000 women annually. In 1941, the first neighborhood clinic was opened; there are now six neighborhood primary health care centers and 12 satellite clinics providing preventive and primary care for 200,000 patient visits annually. Since 1963, as part of outpatient services, chronic disease management has been provided by nurses under protocols developed by the Department of Community medicine, CHS. The Public Health Department oversees the Commodity Supplemental Food Program (CSFP), a U.S. Department of Agriculture directed program to provide surplus food to income-eligible participants, and the federally funded Women and Infant Care (WIC) Program. Under WIC, pregnant and nursing women and infants at high medical risk are given "prescriptions" in the form of vouchers which can be used to purchase certain foods, such as milk and orange juice, to supplement their diet. Present services also include dental care for children, family planning, infectious disease control, and a full range of environmental health services for the 780,000 citizens of the County.

Organizational Structure and Financing

Until 1941, the Public Health Department was under the auspices of city government. At that time it became a dual authority agency, reporting to and receiving funding equally from both city and county governing bodies. A board of health (four city and four county appointees) acts in an advisory capacity. Final sign-off authority, however, rests with the county; consequently the 602 CHD employees are county employees and follow county personnel policies and procedures and other county rules and regulations where appropriate. The present health department budget is over thirteen million dollars; funding comes from a combination of federal and state grants (one-third of revenue), local funding (one-sixth each from city and county) and from third-party sources (one-third from fees, permits, and reimbursements from Medicare and Medicaid) (see Table 22.2). The CHD operates on a fee-for-service charge basis for all personal health services. A $5.00 minimum payment for all non-Medicaid and non-Medicare patients is collected upon arrival for each visit; the charge for pregnancy testing is $3.00. The balance of the cost-based charge per encounter, depending on the service rendered, is either collected from the patient at the time of the visit, charged to Medicaid or Medicare, or written off under provisions of the Hill-Burton Act. According to the CHD Administrator of Administrative Services, 85% of those who receive personal health services at the health department pay "something," though service is not denied to those who cannot pay anything.

Relationship with the State Department of Public Health

In 1982, the CHD was designated a regional office, State Department of Public Health. Dr. Kraft serves as Director. Thirty-five to forty employees are staffed to this regional office, a wing of the large, modern CHD facilities located in the medical center complex in the downtown metropolitan area. No separate organizational chart exists for the regional office because state employees function, report to, and are paid by the state office. However, as an officially designated regional office, CHD receives a small amount of funding from the state to cover local administrative and clerical salaries and operating expenses for the office. Services and administration of CHD and the regional office overlap and complement one another, thereby providing additional flexibility and resources for public health protection and service delivery in the County.

TABLE 22.2. Financial Statement, Fiscal Year Ending June 30

REVENUE	1980	1981
Federal and State	$3,179,902.00	$4,295,836.00
Local	4,581,914.00	5,547,914.00
Fees, Permits and Other	1,637,059.00	1,058,373.00
Total Revenue	9,398,875.00	10,902,123.00

SECTION EXPENDITURES

LOCAL SECTIONS

Administration	860,214.00	1,008,520.00
Infectious Diseases	295,655.00	318,974.00
Dental	334,687.00	393,027.00
Insect Vector Control	583,825.00	736,289.00
Clinical Services	1,142,692.00	1,392,359.00
Nursing	1,029,352.00	921.665.00
Rabies Control	113,136.00	138,209.00
Clinical Tuberculosis	91,555.00	99,202.00
Vital Records	129,597.00	123,853.00
Stockroom	177,727.00	189,937.00
Sanitation	855,268.00	933,066.00
Local Laboratory	178,834.00	264,379.00
Disease Detection	216,829.00	167,922.00
Maintenance and Operations	269,375.00	392,375.00
Local Rodent Control	121,413.00	133,905.00
Pollution Control	260,413.00	297,460.00
Nutrition Services	95,906.00	91,139.00
Injury Control	42,081.00	47,774.00
Jail Inmate Care	113,876.00	141,046.00

GRANT SECTIONS

Childhood Lead Poisoning	123,450.00	100,293.00
E.P.S.D.&T. Outreach Program		212,615.00
School Health Education	193,733.00	60,940.00
Family Planning	971,285.00	1,088,978.00
Air Pollution	129,214.00	188,245.00
Funds for Needy Children		26,796.00
Comprehensive Rat Control	209,193.00	168,694.00
State V. D. Grant	244,349.00	386,436.00
S.D.& T. Medicaid	191,024.00	216,760.00
Immunization Program	54,534.00	54,150.00
W.I.C. Program	1,069.00	149,125.00
Refugee Assistance Program		23,627.00
Lead Abatement Grant	49,237.00	41,988.00
Child Care Food Program	97,778.00	114,919.00
Supplemental Food Program	221,574.00	277,516.00

Mission

According to Dr. Kraft, the mission of the CHD is to protect the health of all people in the county and to deal with problems that affect the health of the entire community. Traditionally this had to do with environmental concerns: safe water supply, proper sanitation, and controlling the spread of communicable disease. In recent years, the CHD has assumed increasing responsibility for providing ambulatory care to the large indigent population, estimated at 300,000, 38% of the total city-county population.

Recent Changes and Reorganization

Dr. Kraft, who came to CHD three years ago from a health department in Alabama, holds an MD from the University of Tennessee and an MPH from the University of North Carolina. Dr. Kraft has reduced the number of positions in the department by 120 and has initiated combining the vast number of categorical programs and services into three bureaus: environmental services; personal health service, which includes the management of the primary health centers and satellite clinics; and administrative services. Administrators of both environmental services and personal health service were recruited by Dr. Kraft and have strong backgrounds in public health; the administrator of administrative services has fifteen years of service with CHD.

Planning, Marketing, and Public Relations

There is no separate department to address issues of planning, marketing, or public relations at CHD. There is a public information officer who reports to the coordinator of the newly formed health promotion program in the personal health service bureau. The goal of the wellness program is to promote good health for employees and to promote wellness throughout the community. The health information specialist is responsible for preparing a bi-monthly in-house newspaper and the annual report and, upon request, providing technical assistance to managers and supervisors who handle public relations and promotion for their own programs. There is no one person designated for marketing or for long-range planning. Dr. Kraft has remarked that public health departments have been remiss in marketing to the public. Furthermore, he is concerned about long-range planning and how the CHD can best meet the needs of the growing County indigent population and avoid costly duplication of services and unnecessary expense to the public taxpayer.

BACKGROUND: PRENATAL PROGRAM

Prenatal care has long been a part of preventive services provided by CHD and is available at all six full-time primary care clinics and five of the twelve part-time satellites. Following a special study on the extent and causes of mental retardation which was chaired by the wife of the governor, the state legislature authorized funding for a state-wide coordinated plan to reduce mental retardation (and infant mortality) by improving the availability of prenatal care services — especially for adolescents, non-whites, and low-income women. As part of this plan, in the summer of 1982, state funds were made available to the County Health Department for a special outreach and education project to increase utilization of already existing services. In most of the nine public health districts in the state, funds were allocated to increase the availability of services. However in the County, a system of quality prenatal care service delivery is already available; nevertheless, as indicated by the data in Table 22.1, there is a serious problem of prenatal care utilization by several segments of the population in the County. Special funding is, therefore, designated for outreach and education. The original grant was written by the maternal and child health state employee assigned to the local regional office who is now coordinating the health promotion program for CHD.

The prenatal project got underway in November 1982 with the appointment of an RN as coordinator of prenatal services in the reproductive health section of the personal health services bureau. She was formerly the supervisor of a Primary Health Clinic that was one of the best utilized of the CHD neighborhood clinics. Since November, a staff of five nurses, one nutritionist, and five clerical personnel have been hired. A continuation grant for increased funding primarily for community education has already been submitted. Table 22.3 shows the budget request for financial year 1982-1983. The final approved budget for 1982-1983 was $40,000 less than the $193,960 requested.

TABLE 22.3. County Health Department's Prenatal Program Budget, Financial Year 1982-1983

Personnel	
Salaries	$128,620
Benefits	30,860
Total Personnel	**$159,480**
OTHER	
Travel	$12,300
Printing and duplication	1,200
Communication	950
Maintenance	350
Supplies and materials	12,820
Rentals and insurance	680
Laboratory services	2,080
Grants and subsidies	2,400
Equipment	1,700
Total Other	**34,480**
Total Program	**$193,960**

Note. Approved budget was $40,000 less than the $193,960 requested.

The Prenatal Care System

Entry into the coordinated prenatal system for indigents in the County begins with scheduling an appointment at the OBGYN Clinic in the City Hospital. The OBGYN Clinic is one of twenty-one specialty clinics which provide care to 400-500 indigent patients daily. Scheduling the first prenatal visit currently involves a three-to-four-week wait from the time the request is made until the pregnant woman is seen at the clinic. Thirty-eight new patients are booked from 8 to 10 am, Monday through Friday (see Table 22.4);

TABLE 22.4

CLINIC SCHEDULE

	MONDAY	TUESDAY	WEDNESDAY	THURSDAY	FRIDAY
8:00 am	24 New	24 New	24 New	24 New	
9:00 am	14 New	14 New	14 New	14 New	20 New
9:30 am	45 Returns	45 Returns	45 Returns	45 Returns	DIABETICS & HIGH RISKS*
10:30 am	15 Returns	15 Returns	15 Returns	15 Returns	
1:00 pm	30 High Risk*		30 High Risk*		30 Returns
2:00 pm	24 Postpartum**	24 Postpartum**	24 Postpartums**		21 Returns 24 Postpartums**

*High risk patients are to be seen by Senior residents and staff.
Patients with any of the following are considered high risk patients:

pre-eclampsia
chronic HBP
cardiac disease
anemia (Hct < 25%)
respiratory disease (asthma, pneumonia, TB, etc.)
Rh disease
sickle cell disease (SS, SC, S Thal.)
Diabetes: Class A to R

urinary tract infection
incompetent cervix (before and after Rx)
Hx of one or more previous low-birthweight infants
suspected IUGR
premature labor or treatment
third trimester bleeding
Age of < 35 years during first half of pregnancy
previous baby with chromosomal anomalies or neural tube
    defects

**Postpartums are to be seen at north end of clinic by Junior residents in pm.

347

on the average, 25 women show up for their first appointment on schedule. During the first visit, the pregnant woman receives a physical examination and medical history assessment by a house staff physician (a resident physician still in training), completes the required lab tests, and undergoes a final review by a faculty physician. Prenatal education classes are provided for all women during their first visit. Adolescents and others at medical risk also receive ultrasound testing. Nutritional counseling and screening for eligibility for special programs to supplement the diet of the pregnant woman are provided for everyone during the first visit. For women at high risk and, therefore, eligible for WIC, a two-week wait follows to allow for processing WIC vouchers which can be used to "purchase" food recommended by the nurse. For women who are eligible for CSFP, there is a three-to-four-week wait, again for paper processing, and then a visit to another site to receive the surplus food commodities.

The first prenatal visit to the Clinic begins with waiting and paper processing: signing-in at the registration desk, checking the clinic credit identification card, and validating the receipt of payment — all before being seen by a nurse or a physician. The initial visit usually takes over two hours. At the end of that visit, a follow-up appointment is scheduled, at the Clinic for those women judged by the physicians to be a high medical risk and at CHD or a satellite for the women considered not at high risk, according to medical standards. The OBGYN Clinic is located in the remodeled basement of the City Hospital. The hospital is old and crowded; however, the OB-GYN rooms are clean and appear to be freshly painted, and attractive posters decorate the walls. The Clinic is on major bus lines and is located in the downtown medical complex which include several hospitals, CHD, and CHS.

City Hospital is the institution designated by city and county governments to provide both inpatient and outpatient care to indigents. In addition to outpatient visits to the Clinic, City Hospital reports over 74,000 visits for emergency room services for 1981. Outpatient care is not provided free to indigent patients. Following public (taxpayer) demands to reduce hospital losses and a recent change in hospital administration, the hospital is now under management contract with a for-profit management organization, a subsidiary of a large, nonprofit local hospital system. New policies, effective March 1983, established a revised fee-for-service fee schedule which, in most instances, increases the amount of out-of-pocket charges to indigents who use the Clinic. When a woman calls to schedule her first visit, if she inquires about the cost, she is informed that the charge for the visit, not counting lab work, could be as high as $42.00. Each women is advised that before being seen at the Clinic, she must first obtain a clinic card. Obtaining a clinic card means making a separate trip to the clinic business office between 8 am and 10 am at least two days before her scheduled appointment. If that is not possible, she must come one to two hours early, bring $42.00 and face the fact that, if the card is not processed before the time of her scheduled prenatal visit, she will not be seen and must reschedule another appointment after her card has been approved.

Clinic card classification is based on the ability to pay. Patients receive a card designated Medicaid (no pay), Medicare (no pay), or a card marked with two numbers from 00 to 99 indicating the percent of payment expected (see Table 22.5). The first digit refers to the percent of payment per visit for registration; the second digit controls the amount to be charged for all ancillary services – lab tests, x-rays, etc. All patients (except Medicaid and Medicare recipients) pay a minimum $5.00 registration fee per visit; the top registration fee is $42.00. Payment for all charges as indicated by the percentage numbers on the clinic card is to be paid and receipted before signing in at the prenatal clinic.

Over 6,000 County pregnant women delivered at City Hospital during 1981; over 95% had records already on file at the time of delivery which means that they had entered the system through the initial visit process. Approximately 3,600 women obtained prenatal care at the Clinic; an additional 2,400, following the initial visit to the Clinic, received prenatal care at CHD.

Regular follow-up appointments are scheduled at the Clinic from 10 am to noon, Monday through Friday. High risk appointments are scheduled from 1 pm to 3 pm on Monday, Wednesday, and Friday. Later afternoon appointments are reserved for the postpartum checkup six weeks after delivery. For women judged not at medical risk, additional prenatal visits are scheduled at one of six full-time

TABLE 22.5
City of Memphis Hospital
Credit Rating Chart

SIZE OF FARM FAMILY UNIT

PAT. RESP.	1	2	3	4	5	6
0%	Less than $3,591	Less than $4,761	Less than $5,931	Less than $7,101	Less than $8,271	Less than $9,441
10%	$3,591 to $3,988	$4,761 to $5,238	$5,931 to $6,588	$7,101 to $7,888	$8,271 to $9,188	$9,441 to $10,468
20%	$3,989 to $4,387	$5,239 to $5,817	$6,589 to $7,287	$7,889 to $8,677	$9,189 to $10,107	$10,469 to $11,537
30%	$4,388 to $4,786	$5,818 to $6,396	$7,288 to $7,906	$8,678 to $9,466	$10,108 to $11,026	$11,538 to $12,586
40%	$4,787 to $5,185	$6,397 to $6,825	$7,907 to $8,565	$9,467 to $10,255	$11,027 to $11,995	$12,587 to $13,635
50%	$5,186 to $5,584	$6,876 to $7,404	$8,566 to $9,220	$10,256 to $11,044	$11,996 to $12,864	$13,636 to $14,684
60%	$5,585 to $5,983	$7,405 to $7,933	$9,225 to $9,883	$11,045 to $11,833	$12,865 to $13,783	$14,685 to $15,733
70%	$5,984 to $6,382	$7,934 to $8,462	$9,884 to $10,542	$11,834 to $12,622	$13,784 to $14,702	$15,734 to $16,782
80%	$6,383 to $6,781	$8,463 to $8,991	$10,543 to $11,201	$12,623 to $13,411	$14,703 to $15,621	$16,783 to $17,831
90%	$6,782 to $7,180	$8,992 to $9,520	$11,202 to $11,860	$13,412 to $14,200	$15,622 to $16,580	$17,832 to $18,880
100%	More than $7,180	More than $9,520	More than $11,860	More than $14,200	More than $16,580	More than $18,880

NOTE: FOR FARM FAMILY UNITS WITH MORE THAN 6 MEMBERS ADD $1,170 FOR EACH ADDITIONAL FAMILY MEMBER.

SIZE OF NON-FARM FAMILY UNIT

PAT. RESP.	1	2	3	4	5	6
0%	Less than $4,211	Less than $5,591	Less than $6,971	Less than $8,351	Less than $9,731	Less than $11,111
10%	$4,211 to $4,677	$5,591 to $6,210	$6,971 to $7,743	$8,351 to $9,277	$9,731 to $10,810	$11,111 to $12,393
20%	$4,678 to $5,185	$6,211 to $6,831	$7,744 to $8,517	$9,278 to $10,205	$10,811 to $11,891	$12,394 to $13,577
30%	$5,186 to $5,613	$6,832 to $7,452	$8,518 to $9,291	$10,206 to $11,133	$11,892 to $12,972	$13,578 to $14,811
40%	$5,614 to $6,081	$7,453 to $8,073	$9,292 to $10,065	$11,134 to $12,061	$12,973 to $14,053	$14,812 to $16,095
50%	$6,082 to $6,599	$8,074 to $8,694	$10,066 to $10,839	$12,062 to $12,989	$14,054 to $15,134	$16,046 to $17,279
60%	$6,550 to $7,017	$8,695 to $9,315	$10,840 to $11,613	$12,990 to $13,917	$15,135 to $16,215	$17,280 to $18,513
70%	$7,018 to $7,485	$9,316 to $9,936	$11,614 to $12,387	$13,918 to $14,845	$16,216 to $17,296	$18,514 to $19,747
80%	$7,486 to $7,953	$9,937 to $9,938	$12,388 to $12,389	$14,846 to $14,887	$17,297 to $17,298	$19,748 to $19,749
90%	$7,954 to $8,420	$9,939 to $11,180	$12,350 to $13,980	$14,888 to $16,700	$17,299 to $19,860	$19,750 to $22,220
100%	More than $8,420	More than $11,180	More than $13,980	More than $16,700	More than $19,860	More than $22,220

NOTE: FOR NON-FARM FAMILY UNITS WITH MORE THAN 6 MEMBERS ADD $1,380 FOR EACH ADDITIONAL FAMILY MEMBER.

Effective Date: March 9, 1981

350

CHD primary health clinics Monday through Friday 8 am to 4:30 pm, or on a part-time basis at any of five neighborhood satellite centers. Appointment clerks try to group prenatal appointments at both the clinics and satellites so that women can attend the regularly scheduled prenatal care and childbirth classes taught by the nurses hired for the prenatal project.

All public health department sites are at least close to public transportation and are located in low-income neighborhoods. Waiting time for a prenatal visit with a public health nurse is usually less than 30 minutes, comparable to waiting time at the Clinic, although there is less time spent in processing papers. A follow-up visit rarely lasts longer than one hour. All pregnant women, except those classified as indigent under Hill-Burton criteria and Medicaid patients, are expected to pay a $5.00 registration fee per visit. All women undergo financial screening and are classified according to ability to pay during their first follow-up visit to CHD. Those who are considered able to pay are presented with a bill for charges in addition to the $5.00 registration fee. However, this balance due is not stressed and no collection efforts are undertaken. The philosophy of the nurses and staff at the public health department sites appears to be: "Be sure the woman receives prenatal care; don't worry so much about payment."

CURRENT STATUS: PRENATAL PROJECT

The objectives for the CHD prenatal program are specified in the prenatal program grant application submitted to the state:

1. to increase the number of pregnant women initiating prenatal care in the first trimester by 5%
2. to increase the total number of patient visits for prenatal care to CHD and OBGYN clinic by 5%
3. to achieve a 0.5% reduction in the number of low-weight births in the County
4. to provide activities which contribute to quality assurance.

Strategy for implementation of these objectives include four areas of emphasis. The emphasis on outreach and education focuses on the provision of prenatal classes in poor neighborhoods, in churches, in community centers, etc. Five nurses have been hired to implement this component of the project.

A second focus for implementation emphasizes promotion. Included in this phase of the project are public service announcements for radio and TV, bus cards, billboards, flyers (see Figure 22.1), and posters provided by the State Department of Public Health. The promotional activities concentrate on providing general information rather than triggering specific action.

The third emphasis, follow-up of patients who have missed prenatal appointments, is meant to increase the rate of compliance. This strategy involves keeping and checking records on all pregnant women for all visits to both CHD and the Clinic. A missed appointment, at either the Clinic or a CHD site, is followed with a phone call from a prenatal project clerk who then schedules a new appointment. Prenatal nurses make home visits to pregnant women who are not reached by the follow-up phone call process.

The fourth emphasis, reducing the number of babies born with low-birth weights, stresses nutritional counseling and the placement of eligible women on supplementary food programs. During the first prenatal visit at the Clinic, each woman sees a nutritionist and is screened for enrollment in either WIC or CSFP. Paperwork processing to expedite placing the women in these programs which provide foods to supplement their diets is facilitated by a full-time nutritionist hired specifically for the prenatal project. For women at high risk who receive their follow-up prenatal care at the Clinic, a visit to the nutritionist is part of every visit. Women not at high risk who receive follow-up care at CHD receive nutritional counseling from the prenatal care nurses hired for this project. A final focus of the project involves quality assurance, training activities, and record review to document the quality of prenatal care provided by CHD.

A summary of prenatal program activities as of April 1, 1983, follows:

Promotion and Outreach

- One set of PSAs hand delivered to 3 TV stations
- One set of PSAs hand delivered to 10 radio stations
- Over 30,000 informational flyers distributed in public housing projects, neighborhood stores, churches, and drug stores
- Five billboard signs placed in low-income and black neighborhoods
- 100 posters placed in clinics, stores, etc.

Education

- Three programs in 3 schools (four one-hour sessions for 25–50 adolescents per school)
- Weekly half-hour prenatal care classes in every clinic and satellite (5 – 6 women per site)
- Three classes on prenatal and infant care at one site.

Follow-Up

- One clerk works full-time at the Clinic; 120 phone contacts.

Training

- Staff training sessions for prenatal program nurses are held every other month.

Nutrition

- One full-time nutritionist screens each new patient during the initial visit at the Clinic and provides follow-up counseling for women at high risk.

Administration

- Data collection and analysis is ongoing using birth certificate records. For example, a breakdown by census track of teenage pregnancies in the County should be collected and analyzed.

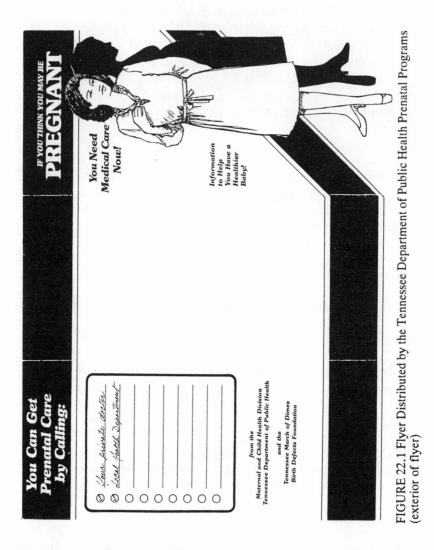

FIGURE 22.1 Flyer Distributed by the Tennessee Department of Public Health Prenatal Programs (exterior of flyer)

354

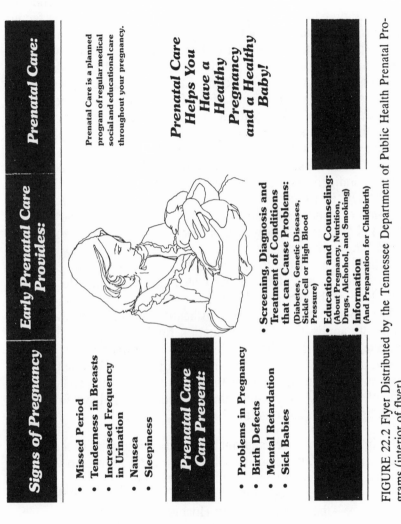

Signs of Pregnancy

- Missed Period
- Tenderness in Breasts
- Increased Frequency in Urination
- Nausea
- Sleepiness

Prenatal Care Can Prevent:

- Problems in Pregnancy
- Birth Defects
- Mental Retardation
- Sick Babies

Early Prenatal Care Provides:

- **Screening, Diagnosis and Treatment of Conditions that can Cause Problems:** (Diabetes, Genetic Diseases, Sickle Cell or High Blood Pressure)
- **Education and Counseling:** (About Pregnancy, Nutrition, Drugs, Alchohol, and Smoking)
- **Information** (And Preparation for Childbirth)

Prenatal Care:

Prenatal Care is a planned program of regular medical social and educational care throughout your pregnancy.

Prenatal Care Helps You Have a Healthy Pregnancy and a Healthy Baby!

FIGURE 22.2 Flyer Distributed by the Tennessee Department of Public Health Prenatal Programs (interior of flyer)

355

CONCERNS AND PLANS FOR THE FUTURE

The Coordinator of the program recently expressed concern about the prenatal program because of the many constraints facing the staff. She noted that they are expected to reach goals and implement a program to increase utilization of prenatal services when, in fact, entry into the system providing services and more than one-half of all prenatal visits for County indigents take place in a setting which is not under the control of the CHD. The Coordinator talked about the need to make people aware that prenatal care at both CHD and at the Clinic is indeed quality care. "If they (the general public) just knew that it was top quality, then they would come," she commented. In her assessment of the quality of prenatal services available for indigent women in the county, she concurs with the opinions of Dr. Kraft and Dr. George Reynolds, Professor and Chief, Division of Ambulatory and Community Medicine, Department of OBGYN at CHS. Dr. Reynolds reports, "The system is excellent; it is a nationally recognized model of coordinated quality prenatal care and it is available to all indigents in the city and the county." Doctors and nurses alike ponder why indigent women do not take advantage of the wonderful system.

The Coordinator is interested in health education for all adolescents; the application for continuation funding supports this interest. She is concerned about problems of illegitimacy, teenage pregnancy, and low-weight births. The Coordinator and her staff nurses work diligently to implement the prenatal program objectives, in spite of the many constraints inherent in the prenatal system of care for indigents. These constraints include:

1. time, place, price, and quality of the initial visit at the Clinic
2. time, place, price, and quality of prenatal follow-up visits for all high-risk indigent patients at the Clinic
3. time, place, price, and quality of the outcome of the pregnancy — the delivery at City Hospital.

Plans for financial year 1984 include adding three more public health nurses to the prenatal project staff to provide education in the junior and senior high schools. The educational goals focus not only on classes for pregnant teens, but also, in response to requests from some school officials, on classes for all adolescents. Two more clerical positions are also requested: one clerk to help with WIC and CSFP paperwork, and another to assist with data collection and analysis. The proposed advertising and promotion budget has been cut from the $4,000 requested in the original project grant to $1,250. This change was more because, so far, most promotional materials — the flyers, posters, and billboards — have been provided free by the State Department of Public Health; the only local promotional expenditure for outreach has been $1,250 for bus cards. Additional promotion has used free public service announcements on radio and TV. Videotapes proposed for the public school classes are being produced without any cost to the program by using public service community cable video equipment and by relying on staff nurses to write the scripts.

CASE ANALYSIS

County Health Department (CHD) recently received a grant from the State Department of Public Health to improve the outcome of pregnancies, especially among non-whites, adolescents, and low-income women in the County. The purpose of the grant is outreach and education to promote increased utilization of prenatal services available to indigent pregnant women.

This case discusses the system of prenatal care available to indigent pregnant women in the County and the efforts of CHD to implement the objectives of the state grant. Because the health department management shares the service delivery philosophy traditionally held among health care providers, they naturally believe that if a quality health service is provided, then patients, clients, or customers will automatically want and utilize that service. Unfortunately, in the County, pregnant women are not utilizing prenatal services to the extent recommended by medical experts and desired by health professionals. Table 22.1 presents data describing the prenatal problem in the county. Health Department management are concerned about how to increase the number of prenatal visits to segments of the population that traditionally underutilize preventive health services (Rosenstock, 1969, p. 173). There is frustration over increasing utilization of services that are not under the control of CHD. The challenge facing CHD is how to market, outreach, and educate those segments of the population that are not presently using the system for early and regular prenatal care, in spite of constraints and barriers inherent in that system.

CHD: Organizational Analysis

Background

CHD has a long history of providing not only environmental services but also personal health services for the 780,000 citizens of the County. Prenatal care is but one of many preventive and primary services provided at five full-time neighborhood primary health centers and 12 part-time satellite clinics.

Organizational Structure

Since 1941, the health department has been under the dual authority of both county and city governments. There is an eight-person board of health which acts in an advisory capacity. Power and authority reside in the two mayors' offices and with the health committee of the county commission. Although the final authority resides in county government, the health department, which functions as a division of county government, pretty much sets its own policy on health matters. The success and reputation of the health department seems to depend on carefully managing relationships with both city and county governing bodies and with key figures in the large, complex, medical-health care system in the city and the county.

In October 1982, CHD was designated a County Regional Office (RO), State Department of Public Health. Dr. Carl Kraft, Jr., serves as director of the RO as well as director and health officer of CHD. Both organizations share facilities, key leadership personnel, and a commitment to protecting the health of County citizens. Thirty-five persons are employed in the RO, including the coordinator of the new health promotion program in the personal health services bureau of CHD. The former health information officer in charge of public relations is now assigned to the health promotion project, in addition to her duties of editing and publishing a bi-monthly in-house newspaper and preparing the annual report. The coordination of CHD and the RO adds strength and flexibility to both organizations and increases the prestige and power of public health within the community.

Leadership

Since Dr. Kraft joined the health department as director in 1980, he has earned a good reputation with the medical and political communities and with the media. He is well respected within the organization. Dr. Kraft points with pride to the fact that CHD is regarded by the State Department of Public Health as a model program and is a trend setter for public health agencies across the state.

Staffing

Since Dr. Kraft's arrival, considerable internal reorganization has occurred. The former large number of categorical programs has been consolidated into three bureaus: environmental services and personal health services, each administered by a health professional recruited by Dr. Kraft, and administrative services, headed by a man with 15 years in the organization. Top-level management meet regularly to formulate policy and plan program operations. The total number of CHD employees has been reduced from 730 to the current level of 600; this reduction has occurred mostly by attrition. CHD has recently upgraded nurses salaries to be competitive in the community, thereby reducing nursing turnover.

Funding

The current CHD budget tops 13 million dollars: one-third of the revenue comes from state and federal grants covering categorical programs such as rat control, communicable disease, and family planning; another one-third comes from fees, permits, and third-party payments; the final one-third comes from city and county funds (one-half from each governing body) for general operating expenses. Personnel is the largest expense category. Budgets are developed internally and submitted to both city and county governments for approval. Because each government matches funds with the other, a cut from one means a cut from the other. Funding, therefore, is a precarious and political process for CHD. The RO budget is small, covering only administration of the local office. RO personnel and all program activities are funded directly from the state office in the capitol.

Environmental and Market Analysis

The job of CHD is formidable. It is charged with responsibility for the health status of the entire community. The reality is that the health department has limited resources and limited impact within the overall health care delivery system. Health and medical care service delivery involves both a fee-for-service system for those who can pay a private physician and a totally different system of clinics and emergency rooms for the indigent population. CHD is the largest provider of outpatient services in the city and county and the major provider of preventive and primary health care to the 300,000 indigent population.

Prenatal Care

For indigent pregnant women in the County, prenatal care is available through a system which coordinates services of CHD, the OBGYN Clinic of the City Hospital, and the Department of OB-GYN at CHS. The relationship of prenatal care initiated early during pregnancy (first trimester) and regular care throughout the duration of that pregnancy and the outcome of pregnancy — the delivery of a healthy baby — is well established (Governor's Task Force, 1981, p. 9). Prenatal care lowers the infant mortality rate, reduces the number of babies born with low-birth weight, and lowers the rate of mental retardation and many other handicapping conditions (Governor's Task Force, 1981, p. 9). In the County the problem of prenatal care is not with the availability of services but with underutilization of the existing system of prenatal care by the pregnant indigent population, particularly non-whites and adolescents. According to the *State Plan for Prenatal Service* (Tennessee Department of Public Health, 1982) in 1980, 3,000 pregnant women in the County did not receive care during their first trimester of pregnancy. That figure includes 40% of the pregnant women receiving prenatal care at CHD, following their initial visit to the Clinic.

Market Characteristics

The staff of the CHD prenatal program has used county birth certificate data to analyze the market for prenatal care. They have identified pregnant women by census track, age, race, marital status, and education. The breakdown of teenage pregnancies by census is being analyzed by CHD staff. Also identified are variables related to use of health services: hospital of delivery, date (trimester) prenatal care was initiated, and birth weight (an indicator of utilization of prenatal services).

Although these data and analysis present an excellent demographic picture of the prenatal market in the County, they tell nothing about the social-psychological factors relating to those who use the indigent prenatal care system. Nothing is known about why those in the target market groups—adolescents, non-whites, and low-income women—do or do not choose to seek prenatal care in the first trimester, why they keep or break appointments, with whom they consult about when to seek care, what benefits they expect from receiving medical care, and what barriers they anticipate from the available system.

A review of the literature sheds some light on the characteristics of the medically indigent population and the demand for medical services. A 1981 report by a committee of the American Medical Association, the Committee on Maternal, Adolescent, and Child Health, and the Council on Scientific Affairs notes that barriers to prenatal care may be both situational (economic) and attitudinal, including fear of loss of privacy, fear of parental reaction, and fear of unfriendly physicians and nurses (Committee on Maternal, Adolescent, and Child Health, 1982, p. 1159).

Studies of preventive care indicate that low-income persons seek preventive and diagnostic services less frequently than those with higher incomes, even when services are free or at low cost (Rosenstock, 1969, p. 178). Health beliefs affect receptiveness to preventive care. A model to explain the behavior of persons seeking preventive care includes the following variables: (1) perceived susceptibility, (2) perceived seriousness, (3) perceived benefits of taking action, (4) perceived barriers to taking action, and (5) cues or triggers to action (Rosenstock, 1969, pp. 175-78).

Other studies report that low-income persons have less knowledge of health and disease than those with higher incomes, are less oriented toward planning for the future, have little trust in the efficacy of the medical system, and have greater feelings of powerlessness — characteristics which inhibit the rational use of preventive services prescribed by the middle-class medical system (Mechanic, 1969, p. 207). The extensive use by indigents of a lay referral system rather than a professional referral system to validate symptoms and make decisions to seek medical care has also been documented (Rosenstock, 1969, p. 187). Knowledge of the utilization of preventive services, health beliefs, and the use of lay referral systems by low-income persons all influences how we understand the attitudes and behaviors of the medically indigent pregnant women in the County, also, they affect how we go about the development of a promotional and educational program to meet this constituency's needs, at the same time, meeting the needs of CHD to provide quality prenatal care early and continuously throughout pregnancy.

Goals and Strategy

As decreed by public law, the purpose of CHD is to protect the health of all citizens of the county. That mandate is carried out through environmental protection activities and certain disease prevention and immunization activities. Because personal health care services are available through the fee-for-service sector only for those who can pay, the CHD makes preventive and primary personal health services, including prenatal care, available to everyone in the county, through neighborhood clinics and satellites located in areas especially accessible to the indigent population.

With the new prenatal grant, emphasis is placed on increasing utilization of existing medical services by pregnant women, especially blacks, adolescents, and low-income women. The objectives of the state grant address four areas:

1. increasing the number of visits by pregnant women who seek care during the first trimester
2. increasing the number of prenatal visits to the Clinic and CHD
3. reducing the number of low-weight births in the County

4. increasing activities leading to quality assurance in prenatal care.

To implement these objectives, CHD has created within the personal health services bureau a new department of reproductive health to house the prenatal program and the family planning program. A nurse who supervised one of the neighborhood clinics was appointed prenatal program coordinator in November 1982. A staff of five nurses, one nutritionist, and five clerical persons has since been hired. A continuation grant has been submitted and various outreach and educational activities have been undertaken. Strategy to implement program objectives includes these activities:

1. informing, identifying, and enrolling women in prenatal and nutritional services in the first trimester
2. encouraging women, after their first visit, to keep appointments for the remaining number of prenatal visits recommended by the physicians
3. increasing the emphasis on community and patient education
4. assuring quality in prenatal care through staff training, record keeping, evaluation, and coordination with other institutions in the (indigent) prenatal care system.

Strengths and Weaknesses

CHD has many strengths which increase the likelihood of success in reaching goals of the prenatal project. However, there are inhibiting weaknesses inherent in the prenatal care delivery system and within the CHD organization. These problems are challenges not only for the prenatal program coordinator, but also for top management at CHD who recognize the serious health, social, and economic consequences of inadequate prenatal care and face responsibility for the health and well-being of the entire community.

A major strength of CHD is the good reputation of the organization and its employees. Dr. Kraft is well respected within the political and medical community and, therefore, is able to interact effectively with key persons in other institutions to affect the health care delivery system, especially as that system provides care for indigents. A good example is the supportive relationship with Dr.

George Reynolds, past president of the American College of Obstetricians and Gynecologists and professor and chief, Division of Ambulatory and Community Medicine, Department of OBGYN, CHS. CHD, Dr. Kraft and the health department staff also enjoy a good reputation with the black community and indigent population.

A weakness which affects CHD's effectiveness in dealing with other institutions to impact community-wide health status is lack of planning resources within the health department organization. Without planning and/or marketing capability, Dr. Kraft lacks market information needed to make effective and efficient long-range plans to protect the health of local citizens and control health-related social problems, such as teenage pregnancy and illegitimacy. Lack of planning/marketing expertise of staff is particularly problematic when, faced with shrinking resources, health agencies are asked to contain costs, be more accountable, and justify expenditure of public funds. It is no longer acceptable for a health care organization just to provide quality care; the public now demands that community health care needs be met cost-effectively. Even though there is little competition for the medically indigent market, competition does exist for funds to provide services. Planning/marketing expertise is needed at CHD to assure continuation of effective and efficient health care service delivery in today's competitive market.

A major weakness of the prenatal program centers around confusion and frustration over priority of program objectives and how those objectives should be implemented. Public health personnel are trained and have gained experience in providing service, including education, to those who seek care. It is only natural, therefore, that the present prenatal project be thought of by staff as a program to provide service—a program to provide prenatal care to indigent women. Consequently, confusion and frustration have arisen over how to improve quality and service of prenatal care because so much of the prenatal care system operates outside CHD's control. The problem is perceived by staff as how to implement grant objectives when there is very limited control of service delivery.

It appears that most of the program resources have been allocated to education, rather than to outreach, as the primary strategy to reach project goals. Education activities are directed toward increasing awareness among women and girls of the importance of seeking medical care when pregnant. The value of prenatal education cannot be disputed; however, as a strategy to increase utilization of the prenatal care system for indigent women in the County, such generalized education may or may not be effective. Although education is a proven tool in the long run to change attitudes (Mechanic, 1969, p. 192), unfortunately health education has a poor track record in changing health-related behavior on a short-term basis (Venkatesen, 1979, pp. 239-45). What is needed is an effective strategy to bring about almost immediate action on the part of the girl or woman as soon as she discovers that she is pregnant. To initiate prenatal care in the first trimester—given that there is a three-to-four-week wait from the time an appointment is requested until the patient is seen at the Clinic—requires immediate action.

The present outreach strategy is naive because it is not focused on any specific target market and does not trigger action; it just informs people about the importance of prenatal care. The present strategy is, therefore, not cost-effective and not likely to be successful in increasing utilization of Clinic and CHD prenatal services. The staff is working hard and trying a bit of everything to reach the market, hoping that something will work to get the pregnant women to enter the system early and then increase compliance. However, the staff lacks marketing experience, expertise, and access to marketing resources. It, therefore, cannot be expected to develop strategy and materials that will be effective in reaching the prenatal market—especially when that market is traditionally resistant to preventive services and faces many barriers related to the delivery system.

Another strategy employed in this program, one that is characteristic of a service or product philosophy, is the "stick" approach—a person who misses a follow-up prenatal appointment is contacted, after the fact, to schedule another appointment. A "carrot" approach focusing on perceived benefits of keeping scheduled appointments could surely be more effective and less punitive to the patient.

In order for this project to be successful in reaching the objectives outlined in the grant, a marketing strategy which emphasizes the needs of the potential patient rather than just the needs of the health care delivery system must be developed. Getting pregnant women to enter the prenatal care system and to keep returning to that system every month is a marketing issue. Caring for those women once they have been enrolled is a service delivery concern. This grant addresses the marketing issue—increasing utilization of prenatal services at CHD and at the Clinic; consequently, a marketing strategy must be implemented. With the "shotgun" approach—hit-or-miss strategy based on good intentions, education on the importance of receiving prenatal care, follow-up activities after the fact, and concern for the quality of care delivered are not likely to be effective in increasing utilization of services. The problem for CHD is that no one on the staff recognizes that this grant addresses a marketing problem because no one on the staff understands marketing principles. No one realizes that in order for the health department to reach its objectives, it must learn the needs and wants of the pregnant women whom it wishes to outreach. After those needs and wants are identified, a strategy can be implemented to address those concerns, and, at the same time, reach the objectives of the prenatal program, thus bringing about a marketing exchange satisfactory to both parties involved.

A cursory analysis of the marketing mix factors—those factors that affect the marketability of a product or service to a target group—indicates that there may be weaknesses in the delivery system and that these weaknesses represent barriers to indigent women who need prenatal care. Strengths, such as the quality of prenatal care provided by the system and the quality of the educational activities provided for those already in the system, are less obvious and may not be valued or even recognized by those whom the health department hopes to reach.

Product

The prenatal care system for indigent women begins at the OB-GYN Clinic, City Hospital. This system is praised by Dr. Reynolds and Dr. Kraft as an outstanding, nationally recognized example of high quality coordinated medical care; nevertheless, it may be perceived by the indigent pregnant woman as degrading, impersonal, and of low value. The literature documents that indigents place a low value on health care, particularly preventive care, and that previous experiences with physicians often predispose them to avoid seeking medical services (Rosenstock, 1969, p. 185). The number of persons a pregnant woman encounters during her initial visit at the Clinic makes for a very different experience from the ongoing relationship a "paying" pregnant woman encounters with her physician in private practice. After the initial visit, for those who are judged by the Clinic staff as not being at high medical risk, follow-up care is provided at health department neighborhood primary health care centers and satellite clinics. High-risk women continue to receive their follow-up care at the Clinic. The very fact that the health department centers and satellites are located in low-income neighborhoods and serve fewer people per site makes the CHD care less impersonal than the Clinic where 400-500 persons are processed daily through the 21 separate clinic programs at City Hospital downtown. Of the 6,000 County women who receive their initial examination at the Clinic, only 2,400 were referred to CHD for follow-up. Clearly the bulk of prenatal care service delivery is outside the scope of CHD. The prenatal project needs to recognize and accept the fact that prenatal care provided by the system may not be valued by those it is meant to serve—those whom the health department seeks to enroll in the system. Staff must than decide not how to change the system but how to get pregnant women to use the system as it is. The problem for the staff is that, because they are health professionals trained to deliver health care, they know how to change and improve the system; however, because they have not been trained in marketing, they do not know what methods to use to get pregnant women to use the system, given its constraints and barriers.

Place

The Clinic and CHD neighborhood primary health centers and satellite clinics are located in low-income areas and are on or near major public transportation lines. The Clinic prenatal facilities, which have recently been remodeled, are, nevertheless, crowded, barren, and impersonal. The public health department sites are somewhat less crowded, less dreary, and less personal. The places where prenatal care is provided may be perceived as a barrier by potential patients.

Price

Although many people believe that medical care is provided free to indigents, this is not true at the Clinic and CHD, except for those covered by Medicaid. At the Clinic, everyone (except Medicaid recipients) must pay a $5.00 or $42.00 registration fee, per visit, plus a percentage of ancillary charges. If the family income reaches a certain level, the registration fee is $42.00 per visit. Guidelines are based on family income; a pregnant adolescent living at home is charged according to the total income of all adult members of her parent's household. A single working woman, earning minimum wage, would have to pay $42.00 for her initial visit, plus 77% of all ancillary charges; if she were high risk, she would have to pay a $42.00 registration fee per visit — a total of over $350.00 for prenatal care; delivery charges are added on top of prenatal visit charges. A pregnant woman under 18 must bring a parent with her to arrange for payment before her first visit.

Patients must undergo a lengthy credit interview and pay the registration fee before being seen by the nurse or physician. If a woman indicates that she will not be able to make payment, financial counseling is scheduled. Arrangements are then made to send a bill for services; thus no one is denied care at the Clinic because of lack of funds. Delinquent accounts are turned over to a collection agency. Clinic patients are reinterviewed, reclassified, and receive a new clinic identification card every three to six months.

A pregnant woman who receives her follow-up care at CHD, unless she is a Medicaid patient, is also expected to pay a registration fee per visit — $5.00. The patient receives a bill for the remainder of charges after she completes her visit with the nurse or physician; no follow-up action is taken if she is not able to pay the balance. No one is denied care. Table 22.6 compares costs to patients at the Clinic and CHD.

Price also includes waiting time. At the Clinic, waiting time involves waiting approximately one month from the date of scheduling the first appointment until the first visit. Waiting time also involves a separate trip to the Clinic prior to the first appointment for the financial assessment. Time is also spent waiting for the appointment and the initial appointment itself may last over two hours. Waiting time at CHD sites is usually less than 30 minutes.

Other cost factors include charges (or obligations incurred) for babysitting, taxi or bus fare, and money for parking if a car is driven to the Clinic. The price of prenatal care is definitely not free to the pregnant woman in the County. In fact, for many, the price may be prohibitive to seeking care at an early date and prohibitive to seeking regular care. It is most unlikely that the prenatal program staff can do anything about the price factor except to acknowledge that price may indeed be a barrier to increasing utilization of services.

TABLE 22.6. Comparison of Costs to Patient for Prenatal Visits*

	OBGYN Clinic	MSCHD
Credit interview	long; requires a separate visit; separate department; repeated 3-6 months	short
Fee per visit	$5 + % ancillary charges *or* $42 + % of ancillary charges must be paid before appointment	$5 must be paid before appointment
Payment schedule/balance of charge	expected after each visit; may be billed if special arangements are made	bill presented after each visit; payment collected, if possible
Follow-up	letters; collection agency; garnishment of wages	no follow-up

*Does not apply to Medicaid patients

Promotion

Promotion is the one variable of the marketing mix over which CHD has direct control. The fact that an entire project has been funded for outreach and education gives recognition to the important role of promotion in the delivery of health care services in the County. Because personnel involved in the prenatal program lack marketing experience and expertise, promotion activities are weak. Staff apparently believe that if services are made available and if women are informed that prenatal care is available and important, then the women should naturally take advantage of those services and seek prenatal care. This philosophy indicates little awareness of the market exchange as the basis for meeting needs. People seek services in response to perceived needs that they believe can be met by those services, not because they have been informed that those services are important. A variety of promotional activities have been undertaken by the prenatal program staff: billboard signs have been erected; bus cards, flyers, and posters have been distributed; and public service announcements have been developed. These activities are not based on a marketing plan developed specifically to meet the needs of targeted groups, but rather appear to represent a global approach. There is no process to measure effectiveness of materials used. The promotional materials create general awareness; they do not trigger action. In fact, most materials are not specific to the County market. In light of the fact that the literature reports that preventive services are generally not valued by the poor and that the process of deciding to seek preventive care depends on perceptions of benefits and barriers and specific cues to action, the present promotional activities may not be effective.

There is no data relating to the perceptions of the present users of prenatal services in the County. However, there is much data available regarding the demographics of the market: age, address, marital status, race, date of first prenatal visit, number of visits, hospital of delivery, birth weight, and sex of the infant. The need for social-psychological data is critical to the success of the program. Prenatal care can be effectively marketed only if the perceived benefits are known and promoted and the perceived barriers are addressed in the promotional process. The lack of marketing/planning resources within CHD hurts the prenatal program. Unfortunately, it seems to be health department policy that each program is responsible for its own promotion, without benefit of marketing support staff as a program resource. Apparently the public information officer who has some expertise and experience in public relations (not to be equated with marketing expertise) has had little involvement with the prenatal project. This may be a natural consequence of having each program be responsible for its own promotion.

Evaluation of Alternative Strategies

Decision makers at CHD face three choices:

1. To continue the prenatal program as it is
2. To attempt to change the existing prenatal delivery system
3. To review the objectives of the grant with the idea of determining exactly what needs to be done to reach the markets specified, then develop appropriate marketing strategy for each target market group.

First Alternative: To Continue the Program as It Is

The first course of action is the path of least resistance for those already involved in the prenatal program. The problem is that the present course of action is causing frustration because it is not clearly focused on the objectives and will not likely reach desired results. The need for information on the importance of prenatal care is obvious because of the existence of the problem in the County; the efforts of the staff to provide education are commendable. However, in spite of the diligent efforts of the nurse educators in bringing the message of prenatal care's value to the public, education as a primary focus for this program will not bring women into the prenatal system within the first trimester nor will it get them to keep their appointments. The nutritional activities of the current program are effective because they enroll women in food programs and thereby increase the likelihood of the birth of a baby with normal birth weight. Nutritional activities should be continued; in fact enrollment in a food program may be a benefit valued by indigent pregnant women. This thesis should be tested and evaluated as a benefit for promotional activities. Follow-up activity to increase compliance for patient visits is probably neither effective nor efficient. At present, the follow-up process does not include follow-up on the initial visit appointment and, therefore, has no effect on getting women into the system within their first trimester of pregnancy. Furthermore, the present follow-up process may be received negatively by the patients. A system to promote keeping appointments could be developed in its place and still meet the objective of increasing compliance. Staff training and data collection are necessary administrative functions to address quality assurance and should be continued. However, the focus of staff training should shift from education on childbirth to marketing and outreach—the area of immediate concern in reaching program objectives. Present promotional activities are little more than shots in the dark. Although efforts are concentrated in low-income areas, they do not address specific market groups nor do they address needs as perceived by those groups. Without an understanding of the factors that these groups perceive to be benefits of receiving prenatal care through the existing system and the barriers that they associate with the system, promotional activities will be ineffective—merely busy work for the staff. The budget for promotional activities is entirely too small for the magnitude of the problem and the emphasis on outreach in the grant objectives. Essentially, this project is a marketing project, yet little money is allocated for outreach. Furthermore, there is no system to evaluate the effectiveness of any or all of the strategies currently being implemented.

Second Alternative: To Change the System

The second alternative might be preferred by the staff because it has the potential to improve the quality of the prenatal care delivery system by eliminating some of the obvious barriers to utilization of services. However, changing the system and removing any or even all of the barriers does not guarantee that pregnant women would enter the system during their first trimester nor that they would keep appointments for subsequent visits. Moreover, any significant change in the system involving other institutions is definitely outside the purview of the prenatal program staff and could be dangerous to the good relationships that exist at top levels of administration. The staff needs to accept the delivery system as it exists and recognize that their responsibility is to increase utilization, in spite of the problems in the system. This project calls for marketing (outreach) and for education, not for service delivery improvement.

Third Alternative: Marketing

The third alternative is the recommended course of action for CHD, in spite of the fact that, at first glance, this action may appear to the staff as a step backward. It is absolutely vital for the leadership associated with the prenatal program to come to grips with what this program is trying to accomplish — and what is beyond its (direct) control. Reviewing objectives is a necessary first step in program management before any other action can be undertaken. In analyzing objectives, it becomes obvious that Objective #1 (to increase the number of visits by pregnant women seeking care during the first trimester) and Objective #2 (to increase the total number of patient visits for prenatal care to CHD and the Clinic) address marketing concerns, not delivery of care. Objective #3 (to achieve a reduction in the number of low-weight births) appears under control with the placement of a nutritionist at Gailor to enroll all eligible women in supplementary food programs during the first prenatal visit. Objective #3 will be accomplished automatically with the accomplishment of Objectives #1 and #2. Objective #4 (to increase activities leading to quality assurance) is concerned with administration, data collection, and staff training and should reinforce strategy for Objectives #1 and #2. In order to meet the objectives of the prenatal program grant, strategy must focus on marketing activities. Strategy must be developed in two directions:

1. To develop outreach activities and materials designed specifically for each target market so as to promote perceived benefits, play down anticipated barriers and trigger action. This strategy needs to be implemented as soon as possible and requires immediate action by program decision-makers.
2. To develop educational activities designed to change health beliefs and attitudes of target markets and key persons in the lay referral system. This strategy is a long-term activity which

will bring eventual change in the attitudes and behaviors of pregnant women but will not, realistically, increase utilization of the health care system by those who are now pregnant and needing care during the first trimester.

The first step in developing strategy to reach program objectives should involve a careful analysis of the needs of the market, not only the demographic characteristics but also psychosocial characteristics which describe the perceived needs of target groups. Promotional activities should address two distinct and separate issues: (1) getting pregnant women into the system early in their pregnancy, and (2) increasing compliance with subsequent visits. Decisions must be made about allocating resources — personnel, dollars, and time relevant to implementing long-term educational strategy and more immediate outreach strategy. Resources are presently allocated in favor of long-term educational activities with a disproportionately small amount of total resources designated for outreach strategy necessary to reach immediate program objectives. Reallocation of resources may be difficult for the staff because of their preference for delivery of care and education and their lack of knowledge about marketing techniques. It is, therefore, most important that marketing expertise be provided to work with the present staff.

The addition of a person with marketing and planning expertise to the CHD staff would greatly strengthen not only this project but also the capabilities of the entire health department. However, an alternative action for this particular program would be to contract a consultant for the following activities: (1) to survey target market needs and perceptions, (2) to prepare a marketing plan, (3) to develop appropriate promotional materials and strategy for distribution, and (4) to train staff in marketing know-how and specific outreach skills necessary to reach program objectives.

Recommendations

1. Review objectives; recognize that the prenatal grant addresses marketing, not service delivery; allocate resources more equitably between promotional or outreach activities and education activities.

2. Obtain marketing expertise to work with the prenatal program staff; include training for staff on the value of a marketing philosophy as a responsibility of the marketing expert assigned to the prenatal program.
3. Survey target market groups (adolescents, non-whites, and low-income women) to find out their perceptions of benefits and barriers related to prenatal care available in the County; consider personal barriers and system barriers; investigate the influence of the lay-referral process locally. Care must be exercised in surveying the market so as not to alienate patients — a personal interview or a focus group discussion may be a more appropriate survey instrument than a written questionnaire.
4. Develop a marketing plan for promotional activities to trigger adolescents, non-whites, and low-income women to enter the prenatal care system during their first trimester of pregnancy; test promotional materials before market distribution.
5. Change the present appointment follow-up procedure to encourage compliance. Initiate these actions:
   a. The OBGYN Clinic appointment clerk should record the name and address and phone number when a new patient calls for an appointment.
   b. Approximately two weeks before the initial appointment, the CHD clerk at the Clinic should send a packet, in a plain envelope, to each new patient. The packet should include (1) a "welcome to the program" letter, (2) instructions for the first visit, and (3) a personalized booklet on prenatal care.
   c. At the close of the first appointment, the clerk should record the date and place of the next appointment in the patient's prenatal booklet.
   d. The clerk should send a reminder letter one week before the next visit; the patient should be encouraged to bring her prenatal care packet.
   e. Missed appointments should be followed with a reminder letter and a new appointment date.
   f. Compliance records should be kept to evaluate the efficacy of the new system.

6. Review the position of marketing and planning within the CHD and the RO; consider long-term benefits to be gained by adding planning/marketing expertise to the organization with a full-time staff position.

REFERENCES

Committee on Maternal, Adolescent, and Child Health, "Medical Care for Indigent and Culturally Displaced Obsterical Patients and Their Newborn", *JAMA* 245 (March 20, 1981).

Governor's Task Force, State of Tennessee, *Tomorrow's Children: A Special Study Report on Mental Retardation Prevention* (Nashville: 1981).

Mechanic, David, "Illness and Cure", in Rosenstock, *op cit*.

Rosenstock, Irwin M., "Prevention of Illness and Maintenance of Health", in *Poverty and Health: A Sociological Analysis*, eds. John Kosa, Aaron Antonovsky, and Irving Kenneth Zola (Cambridge: Harvard University Press, 1969).

Tennessee Department of Public Health, *State Plan for Prenatal Service*, FY 82 – 83 (Nashville: 1982).

Venkatesan, M., "Marketing Management: Health Care in General, Preventive Care in Particular", in *Health Care Marketing: Issues and Trends*, ed. Philip D. Cooper (Germantown, Maryland: Aspen Systems Corporation, 1979).

CHAPTER 23

Marketing Mix Case Study: Family Service Agency of San Francisco

Rosanna M. G. Pribilovics
Ira Okun

INTRODUCTION

Marketing has become one of the most important tools of managing today's social and human service agencies. Marketing allows the human service administrator to communicate effectively internally and externally with the different publics with whom the agency serves and interacts. It can be a valuable tool for making human service agencies more effective. This article describes the variety of successful marketing strategies which have been used to market one of the oldest and most established human service agencies in California, the Family Service Agency of San Francisco (FSA/SF).

Brief History

In 1889, San Francisco was an untamed and intemperate city. It was characterized by a high incidence of child abuse and neglect, poverty, and very limited amounts of social service assistance for

Reprinted from William J. Winston, ed., *Marketing for Human and Social Service Agencies,* pp. 75–87, © 1985 by The Haworth Press, Inc.

the local citizenry. In response to the need for coordinated provision of social services and proliferating charitable agencies, the predecessor to FSA/SF, Associated Charities, was formed. This organization and its successors were involved in such activities as the 1906 earthquake relief, great flu epidemic of 1918, development of foster homes and adoption programs, and the relief efforts related to the Depression. In 1938 the Family Service Agency of San Francisco was formed, became incorporated and joined the Family Service Association of America. It also became a member of the Community Chest which now is known as United Way. In 1944 it merged with the Children's Agency of SF to form the Family and Children's Agency of San Francisco. The agency changed its name for the last time and became known again as the Family Service Agency of San Francisco in 1958.

The agency has been located in San Francisco for ninety four years. Kitty Felton, the first director of FSA/SF, commissioned Bernard Maybeck, the famous California architect, to specifically design a building for the agency on Gough Street in 1928. The building was built by a grant from the Prescott Estate and is characterized by an aesthetic and functional urban but Spanish Colonial style. It has been declared a historical landmark in San Francisco (see Figure 23.1).

Through the years FSA/SF continues to meet its mission of providing services to families and children under stress, promoting the general welfare of the total community, advocating for the elimination of conditions that cause family life to deteriorate, preventing unnecessary institutionalization of family members, preventing dependency on public welfare systems, and aiding families to promote the physical, mental, and emotional development of their children.

The agency has continued to expand its service base. Today, it provides such services as child abuse prevention, case management for the developmental disabled, family counseling, aftercare for chronic mentally ill, geriatric care, child care, comprehensive care for pregnant teens and teen parents, counseling for Japanese and Chinese populations, advocacy for nursing home residents, foster grandparent program, senior companions, parental stress line, group counseling, respite care for high risk parents, family violence programs, and others. These services have been developed to meet

FIGURE 23.1

the current health needs of the county of San Francisco, without regard to financial constraints. An affirmative action policy exists for all sectors of the agency's clientele. FSA/SF consists of twenty-five programs organized into three major departments.* The agency has a budget which exceeds five million dollars per year and employs approximately two hundred people. Funding is derived from a variety of sources including United Way, private foundations, public agencies, fees, and individual donations.

MARKETING STRATEGIES AS APPLIED TO THE MARKETING MIX

An excellent way of presenting the wide variety of marketing strategies that FSA/SF has utilized through the years is to group them into the components of the marketing mix. These components include the Product, Place, Price, Promotion and People. The strategies are applicable to multiple types of non-profit social and human service organizations. They are systematically organized for easy reference.

Product

A quality human service organization must have an attractive service which offers value to the client. These values have to satisfy the unique health needs of the client. A product/service portfolio must be established which outlines the service mix which most effectively serves these health needs of the population.

Family Service Agency of San Francisco offers a variety of services in its portfolio to meet selective health needs of the community and to diversify and remain financially viable. The bottom line is to serve humanity and in order to do so, FSA/SF has had to approach this need by effectively managing the organization. FSA/SF has used the concept of opportunity management which emphasizes (1) the development of organizational mission, goals and objectives, (2) market opportunity identification, (3) strategic planning

---

*See Organizational Chart Figure 23.2.

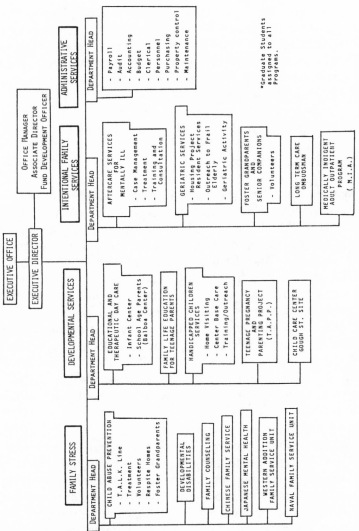

FAMILY SERVICE AGENCY OF SAN FRANCISCO - 1984

FIGURE 23.2. Family Service Agency of San Francisco Organizational Chart (1984)

for taking advantage of these market opportunities, and (4) effective implementation.

For example, the Teen Pregnancy and Parenting Project (TAPP) at the FSA/SF followed this systems approach to its development and implementation. The original director, Kitty Felton, was involved in trying to get better services for pregnant teens and teen parents. For ten years, she began a successful campaign to close a foundling hospital with the highest infant mortality rate in the city. This activity satisfied the organizational's mission of providing services to high risk families and the organizational goal of meeting the needs of teen parents. There is a growing incidence of teen pregnancies and teen parents during the past few years. FSA/SF had the foresight to identify this health need, or market opportunity, many years ago. The passage of federal legislation and monies in 1976, presented a funding option to implement the market opportunity. Using FSA/SF's historical precedence and existing small teen parent infant program, coordination was established between social work, education and the health community. FSA/SF became the fiscal agent and spokesperson of the teen parent service community. The market opportunity now changed to require the offering of comprehensive services such as medical, nutrition, education, day care and career planning. This allows the teen parent to become economically independent, lowers the risk of children being born with abnormalities, and potentially reduces the likelihood of child abuse. In collaboration with the San Francisco School district and thirty other human service agencies, a methodology for providing these services was developed.

Under the direction of the current Executive Director, Ira Okun, a strategic plan was developed through the years for providing this wide scope of services to this group. This plan included identifying the problem, soliciting funding sources, establishing staffing requirements, lobbying for effective legislation, educating the community as to the existence of the problem, networking with other human service agencies for the provision of comprehensive services and the prevention of duplication, and obtaining input from community groups, coalitions, advisory committees, users of the services and other relevant sources.

FSA/SF has effectively implemented this program through the

networking of multiple private and public human service organizations such as SF Unified School District, SF Dept. of Social Services, Florence Crittendon, Children's Home Society, Legal Services for Children, SF Public Health Dept., etc. All of these organizations are components of TAPP. Their complementary resources are collaborated to meet the needs of the pregnant teen and teen parents. The program has been successful in serving over 500 clients with excellent independently documented results and generating millions of dollars in cash and in-kind programs.

This program is a good example of a marketing strategy which emphasizes the importance of linking the historical and current mission of the human service organization. It also exemplifies how the agency does not operate in a vacuum. The agency provides services by obtaining input from the community for opportunity identification. This means identifying a social need, planning for satisfying this need, and implementing programs designed with input from other human service organizations.

The reputation and longevity of the agency is a key attraction to clients. Being one of the oldest agencies of its type in California and known for quality services provides for a strong base of referrals.

The foundation of longevity for this successful agency has been the ability to create and implement the service mix. This success reflects a marketing sensitivity to understanding the people it serves, their needs, and an ability to network with other human service organizations to provide these services. The networking aspect is vital for preventing duplication, containing costs, and being able to adequately allocate scarce human service resources.

Place

A key aspect of developing a marketing strategy is related to access to the service, location, availability, waiting times, etc. FSA/SF has consistently attempted to market their services through a strategy of lowering the barriers for client access. FSA/SF has never had a lack of clientele. There are waiting lists for several programs. However, client access to the services is important whether the agency is trying to attract new clients or not. FSA/SF considers access to be an important consideration in planning for the delivery of services.

It is reflected by having various sites depending on the need of the clientele, such as the Chinese Counseling Program. This program is a service which is physically located in the Chinatown section of San Francisco. The residents will not come for services at the main agency. Therefore, the service must be provided where it will be needed and utilized. The closer a service is to the source the greater the likelihood of being used by its target population. Other examples include FSA/SF's Family Stress Programs based at the Naval Station at Treasure Island and the Army Base at Presidio of San Francisco.

Another example of the place component is improved access to public transportation. For example, the agency is physically located between two main bus lines, within walking distance to BART, and in close proximity to a major freeway. One service actually possesses funding for bus passes for clients. Another one provides a van for transportation to and from the agency.

The hours of operation are a key ingredient for the place component. For example, FSA/SF operates an average of approximately twelve hours/day. This allows for evening counseling appointments and group meetings. The agency permits other organizations to use their facilities for optimum utilization. Another example is the twenty-four hour parental crisis line, the TALK Line, which provides telephone counseling to high risk and abusive parents. The Child Care Center operates from 7am to 6pm. Working, low-income parents from the local community drop their kids off before going to work and are able to pick them up after a normal work day is completed.

The flexibility of how services are provided is a characteristic of the place component. Some services are provided entirely in the home. For example, the Developmental Disabilities Unit and the Home Education Program For Handicapped Infants delivers its services in the home. If necessary, other services such as counseling can be provided in the home, senior public housing, nursing homes, and board and care homes depending on the need of the case and funding source.

FSA/SF has a good screening methodology to make sure the client is linked to the needed service. Assistance is given to triage clients to the most appropriate FSA/SF and other community services. Examples would be referring battered women to a shelter, clients to Dept. of Social Service for entitlements, and children to St. Luke's Hospital's Speech and Learning Center for evaluations. An effective agency will keep up-to-date with information about current community services. This is especially important in large metropolitan areas where human service turnover is high.

In the counseling department, an intake worker is available during working hours for drop-ins or telephone counseling. An individual or family in crisis can obtain assistance immediately on this basis. In addition, for continuing clients receiving service, efficient appointment systems is vital for long-term relationships.

The way in which services are provided in term of access makes a difference in the success of the service. This ensures that the client is able to use the service more effectively.

Price

The pricing component of the marketing mix is an important factor for human service organizations. FSA/SF's policy to pricing is that no client will be turned away due to their inability to pay. The agency does not rely solely on fee-for-service. Instead, revenues are derived mainly from private and public contracts.

FSA/SF/s success is based on its pricing abilities. The key form of pricing for FSA/SF is the charge to funding sources based on the efficiency of operations. A large part of FSA's funding is derived from government sources. An RFP will be issued by a government agency and interested human service agencies will competitively bid for the program. FSA/SF has been able to submit strong bids because a broad base of funding has been developed, thereby controlling indirect costs. Fore example, in 1978 the agency's indirect costs were 18% of total costs as compared to 15.5% in 1984. The use of professionally trained and supervised volunteers also assists in lowering costs. Because of today's competitive market for financial resources, FSA/SF will selectively take risks in bidding for contracts at a rate lower than the actual costs of operating the program. At a later date, the full value of the programs can be recouped as refunding occurs for successful operating programs. In addition, United Way of Bay Area is an important funding source. Its flexible dollars allow FSA/SF to bid for programs which are weakly funded by other sources. Therefore, the client receives the service they need without concern for their ability to pay.

There are two methods used in determining fees for FSA/SF services. FSA/SF funded services such as the Parental Crisis Line, Mothers' Group and Single Parent Support Group have no direct charge to the client. A sliding fee scale developed for FSA/SF's Counseling Services has an hourly charge based on the client's income and family size. In this case, the scale ranges from no charge to forty-five dollars. The second method depends on public funding requirements, i.e., the Universal Method of Determining Ability To Pay (UMDAP). It is a formal scale used by community mental health system and is based on monthly income and number of dependents. Those programs funded by Community Mental Health, such as the Japanese Mental Health Program, Aftercare, and Geriatric Program, are required to use this fixed fee schedule. Another public funding system is the California State Department of Education Fee Schedule, i.e., Child Care Center. Fee-for-service does restrict the clientele an agency can serve in terms of income constraints.

From a marketing perspective, it is important to be competitive through exploring a wide range of funding sources, operating as efficiently as possible, communicating these different pricing methods effectively to clients, and to establish a strong network of support from financial and political resources. In today's competitive marketplace, an agency cannot depend on any one funding source. Funding and pricing analysis is an on-going component of marketing.

Promotion

Promotional strategies relate to the methods of communicating with the different publics with whom an agency serves or interacts. Promotion typically includes such areas as public relations, personal selling, sales promotion and publicity. These strategies usually encompass soft-sell, hard-sell or educational approaches. Most human service agencies utilize soft-sell and educational methods for promotion. This is especially true when a large proportion of agencies are not in need of more clients. When this is the case marketing becomes an effective communication tool to enhance relationships with staff, boards, other human services in the community, governmental agencies, and clients. Many human service agencies dependent on fees and insurance compete heavily for clients and orchestrate their promotion to obtaining clients. Most promotion for agencies which do not need more clients, as exemplified by FSA/ SF, is related to (1) improving and sustaining the image of the agency in the community; (2) attracting Board and advisory members; (3) developing strong relationships with current and future funding sources; (4) creating an effective internal communication link with staff; and (5) reinforcing the referral network with other community human service resources.

FSA/SF utilizes public relations for informing the community about their programs and services. This is accomplished through the use of brochures, flyers, newsletters, annual reports, speeches and other strategies initiated by management staff.

Brochures/Flyers: The agency maintains a regularly up-dated group of brochures developed for specific purposes. These include a low-cost mass distribution brochure about the entire agency; an additional detailed brochure describing the entire agency for use with professionals; individual program brochures to target specific publics such as the elderly, teen parents, and Chinese population; and program announcements/flyers for distribution.

Newsletters/Annual Report: Three newsletters describing specific services and/or fund raising activities are distributed to thousands of current and potential donors. These donors can include individuals, select corporations, foundations, board members, and staff. An annual report highlighting the prior year's activities and outlining future agency goals is also distributed to the donor base.

Speeches: The management staff make speeches to community and business groups for advocating issues, educating on available services, and for fund raising activities. Individual program staff will occasionally give presentations on specific programs and current social issues.

Meetings: The executive director or delegates are active members in many community organizations and associations. These include such organizations as: Teen Parent Coalition, SF United Way Executives, Mental Health Contractors of SF, Mental Health Advisory Board, Mayor's Sexual Trauma Advisory Committee, Elderly Abuse Prevention Consortium, Developmental Disabilities Council and many other key community groups. The executive director is expected to participate in activities that are in the best interests of the clients we serve or the fiscal needs of the agency.

Fairs and Special Events: Whenever financially feasible, the agency sets up information tables and booths at community events. These include such activities as: SF County Fair, Independent Living Exposition, Children's Network Conference, and various United Way campaign events.

Working with Board: The Board of Directors plays a vital role in marketing the agency in terms of image-making, networking, fund raising, and public relations activities. FSA/SF employs a fund development officer who works closely with the board on these activities in conjunction with the executive director. The fund development officer acts in the capacity of educating and training the board of directors for fund raising needs and their role and responsibility in fund raising and public relations. An example of a fund raising event in association with the Board of Directors is Operation Home Run. This event is a baseball game between media personalities and politicians. Tickets are sold to the general public and proceeds are designated for the child abuse prevention programs at FSA/SF. Besides actual funds, the event strengthens support and publicity for the entire agency.

Public Service Announcements/Advertisements: Close ties are maintained with local media for educating the public about select services through public service announcements. Advertisements are placed in newspapers to educate select target groups about services. Posters are placed in public transportation, child care centers, laundromats, supermarkets, and other high-visibility avenues. Stuffers are also placed in utility bills for diaper services for select programs. Telemarketing is utilized, for example, in relation to the annual fund raiser, Operation Home Run, for contributions. Telemarketing has the potential to be a key marketing strategy for human services agencies in being able to communicate with a large group of people quickly and at relatively low cost.

People

The most important strategy for marketing an agency is the effective utilization of the agency's human resources. This is evident by the important roles that the board, administrators, staff, and volunteers play in marketing FSA/SF. The Executive Director of FSA/SF, Ira Okun, is the main planner and coordinator of marketing activities for the agency. Through his leadership during the last seven years, FSA/SF has expanded significantly in terms of programs offered and financial base. If a human service agency is to be effective in its marketing activities a strong executive director is essential. The Executive Director at FSA/SF administers the agency through his management team which consist of a controller, department heads, project directors, associate director and developmental officer.

The backbone of delivering quality services to the public is the staff of FSA/SF. The staff consists of such professionals or direct service personnel as family counselors, social workers, psychiatrists, psychologists, child care workers, volunteers, and various administrators. Every staff member is a marketing representative of the agency. It is important for each staff member to be educated and believe in the mission and goals of the agency and their individual programs. In-house training and effective newsletters are important strategies in enhancing the marketing role of each staff member. For example, FSA/SF is currently developing an internal newsletter to meet these needs.

A major human resource for most agencies are volunteers. These volunteers are involved at FSA/SF in telephone counseling for the TALK Line, tutoring in math and reading in the Chinese program, advocating for seniors in nursing homes through the Nursing Home Ombudsman Program, being an adjunct parent for children in hospitals, respite care homes, and child care centers, and offering to be companions to the home-bound frail elderly. All of these volunteers are formally trained by the agency for their assignments. There are as many volunteers as paid staff at the agency. There is also an internship program for graduate students from local universities. These interns provide monitored services in a clinical setting. The volunteers and interns provide a cost-effective, quality mode of delivery. They become marketing representatives for the agency in their interactions with clients, staff, and other community resources.

FSA/SF has strong ties with the community through the use of specialized advisory groups. These groups allow for community input and a base for agency networking. Some of these groups include: Navy Family Service Center Advisory Group, Elderly Abuse Prevention Task Force, Nursing Home Ombudsman Advisory Group, and Board and Care Advocacy Group. The members of the groups include representatives from the general public, organizations, and professionals in their specialized field.

CONCLUSION

FSA/SF is a fine example of a human service agency which has been effective in sustaining and expanding its base despite tumultuous economic times. Marketing has played a vital role in this success with attention being given to the five Ps of the marketing mix: Product, Place, Price, Promotion and People. There are some valuable lessons to be learned by human service administrators in terms of effective marketing. Since the majority of human service administrators and clinicians are not trained in marketing, it is important to begin to integrate this tool into their management repertoire. Marketing is a much broader and useful management tool and rarely recognized as such by the majority of social and human service providers. As financial pressures become more acute in the human service marketplace, it is important to adapt and strategically plan for the future. Managers need to be active rather than reactive to changing environmental conditions. Comprehensive marketing methods can assist human service agencies in taking advantage of opportunities. However, marketing must be integrated along with financial, economic, and human resource management techniques for effective strategic planning. Effective strategic market planning has to take into consideration these components of the marketing mix. As an agency increases in their professionalism, the more sophisticated strategic market planning must become.

Part VII

Strategy and Tactics

CHAPTER 24

Introduction to Market Strategy
and Tactic Development

Robert L. Berl

Strategy has been defined in a multiplicity of ways. For our purpose, strategy is the determination of the organization's objectives and goals and the policies and plans for the accomplishment of these goals. This process includes deciding on the allocation of resources and the appropriate organizational structure necessary to achieve the firm's objectives.

> Briefly, strategy deals with two broad questions: (a) what the company wants to be, and (b) how it hopes to get there, i.e., the purpose of the corporation and the course that should be taken to achieve the designated purpose. The purpose is broken into three parts: mission, objectives, and goals. Mission is the chief executive's conception of the organization's *raison d'être*, what it should work toward in light of the long-range opportunity. Objective is a qualitative statement about the direction the company intends to pursue in a given field in order to increase market share and obtain a reasonable return on investment. Goal is the specific achievement desired, usually in quantitative terms, with reference to stated time. An example of a goal is to seek 20 percent market share during the next two years. (Jain, 1981, p. 20)

WHAT IS A TACTIC?

Tactics are the operational ways in which a strategy is implemented. While strategies are somewhat general, tactics are more specific and outline the courses of actions which are to be taken. Figure 24.1 indicates the relationships between corporate objectives, strategies and tactics, and examples of each.

The use of correct tactics is extremely important. Many a fine strategy has failed due to a poor use of tactics. In turn, questionable strategies have been known to succeed through the use of excellent tactics. Tactics are neither good nor bad. The situation that the manager is facing will dictate the appropriate tactics to be employed. However, there are no perfect tactics. Many tactics may work, some better than others.

> Many administrators mistakenly use the same tactics repeatedly, regardless of the circumstances. They develop such habits because the favored tactics have worked for them previously. Success reinforces the habit of using a tactic. But success can be lulling. There comes a time when the tactic will not work, and that is usually a most critical time.
>
> The classic example of administrative inability to vary tactics is the forceful, hard-hitting executive who uses strong, authoritarian tactics to climb through the ranks. Such an executive will discover that at the top such tactics are not effective in dealing with others of equal ability. The manager who is unable to make the necessary tactical adjustments fails. (Stanton & Buskirk, 1983, p. 33)

TYPES OF STRATEGIES

The following series of strategies has been suggested as appropriate for health organizations:

1. A rational problem-solving strategy assumes a smooth flow between fact-gathering, developing plans or solutions to a problem, and implementation. This classic approach depends

on a reasoned response to reasoned plans. Its greatest draw-
back is a long history of ineffectiveness. It doesn't work by
itself because it is too logical.

2. The community development strategy suggests that the organization mobilize efforts of many persons around a given problem or opportunity. They are helped to plan and implement
their own objectives. This strategy is used by neighborhood
associations that depend upon the concern of their members to
get things done.

3. The negotiation strategy assumes that each organization has
something of value to exchange and that the home care agency
is capable of bargaining without being put in the position of
being a beggar.

4. The joint investor strategy involves bringing together a group
of target organizations to pool their interests and resources to
accomplish a particular objective. This also might be called
the coalition strategy (Kaiser, 1978).

Organizations must determine which type of demand it desires to
stimulate: primary or selective demand. Primary demand strategies
are designed to increase the level of demand for a product class,
while selective demand strategies stimulate the demand for a particular product or service within a product class. Advertisements for
"full-service" banking are attempting to increase primary demand,
while an ad for a specific bank within the community is striving to
stimulate selective demand. Table 24.1 shows primary and selective demand strategies and the various tactics wich can be used to
implement the strategies.

Primary demand can be effected by increasing a customer's willingness to buy, raising the ability to buy, and stimulating the rate of
purchase. Selective demand strategies call for retaining current customers and acquiring new ones. Customer retention can be reinforced by maintaining client satisfaction, making buying easier, and
reducing the attractiveness of alternative choices. Organizations can
acquire new customers by going head-to-head with the competition
and developing superior offerings or going after a market segment
that has not been exploited by the competition.

FIGURE 24.1. Relationship Between Corporate Goals, Objectives, Strategies, and Tactics

	Example
Formulate corporate objectives	Increase market share from 8% to 20% in two years
↓	
Formulate marketing strategies	Intensify market efforts in domestic markets so as to increase sales volume by $3 million next year
↓	
Formulate division strategies	Division: Salesforce A. Enter new geographic markets and sell to new types of customers B. Cover existing geographic markets more aggressively
↓	
Develop division tactics	1. Stress missionary selling in sales training and supervision 2. Conduct more sales contests 3. Stress commission features in compensation plan 4. More frequent field supervision

Source: *Management of the Sales Force* (p. 40). By William J. Stanton and Richard H. Buskirk. Homewood, IL: Richard D. Irwin. Copyright 1983.

SIMPLE VERSUS COMPLEX STRATEGIES

Strategies can be rather simple in nature or very complex. The following is an example of the former:

Case 1

A community recreation center serving families sought to use its health and gymnastic facilities throughout the day instead of mainly at noon, late afternoon, and evening hours when men and boys "took over the place." It encouraged women to use the 8 a.m.-to-noon opening, and at first there was some limited interest and activity. Within a year the agency decided that its strategy was only in its interests rather than in those of its women members. With the use of an advisory group, it developed a new approach. A structured preschool program was set up for the children of the mothers, and for the latter, a two-part plan of organized fitness and family life education classes was established. Thus, in half a day, mothers could enjoy both physical and mental activities and have their children cared for at no extra expense. (Rubright & MacDonald, 1981, p. 143-44)

TABLE 24.1. Marketing Strategies/Tactics for Stimulating Demand

Primary-Demand Strategies	Tactics for Implementing Strategies
1. Increase number of users by	
• Increase willingness to buy	1. Advertise benefits of product form or class
	2. Develop product-line extension
• Increasing ability to buy	1. Reduce price
	2. Provide financing
	3. Provide broader distribution
2. Increase rate of purchase (through different uses, greater consumption rates, faster replacement)	1. Promote alternative uses
	2. Design new benefits for exiting customers
	3. Reduce price
	4. Repackage in different sizes
	5. Promote use of related products
Selective-Demand Strategies	
1. Retention of customers by	
• Maintaining satisfaction	1. Advertise quality
	2. Advertise familiarity
	3. Redesign product
	4. Provide special services
• Simplifying the buying process	1. Provide superior delivery
	2. Offer bundles of products
	3. Use sole-source selling
	4. Provide price protection
	5. Use system selling
• Reducing attractive of or opportunities for switching	1. Develop brand extension
	2. Offer multiple brands
	3. Facilitate system expandability
	4. Reduce price
2. Acquisition of customers by	
• Head-to-head positioning	1. Develop superior features on determinant attributes
	2. Reduce prices
	3. Advertise more
	4. Use broader distribution
• Differentiated positioning	1. Design and promote unique benefits
	2. Use unique distribution channels, package, service, pricing

Source. Adapted from *Marketing Management: Strategies and Progress* (pp.137-144). By Joseph P. Guiltinan and Gordon W. Paul. New York: McGraw-Hill Book Company. Copyright 1982.

The recreational center involved mothers in the planning process and thus developed programs and services to attract women in the morning hours.

An example of a more complex strategic situation is as follows:

Case 2

A health systems agency undertook a study to establish a new treatment program in drug abuse to replace an agency that had lost federal funding and had been dismantled. Normally, the agency might have conducted a special study, prepared a report and recommendations, transmitted it to the appropriate funding sources and authorities, and then awaited their response and implementation. The HSA's operational philosophy was that it would become involved in studies only if it also had responsibility for execution of recommendations.

The planning organization established these steps:

• **Involvement** of key funding and service agencies in the study operation
• **Precommitment** to some kind of action on the problem
• **Cultivation** of those likely to oppose or be lukewarm to creation of a new drug treatment program
• **Participation** of several key agencies in the study's staff work
• **Preparation** of a report that was nontechnical, graphic, and easily understood
• **Staging** of the study's recommendations so as to attract as much public support as possible
• **Pledging** of financial support from a few key resources as the recommendations and appropriate actions began to emerge

Obviously, the HSA used several strategies to ensure productive results. It acquired respect because its work was not conducted in a vacuum. It provided an exchange of benefits with several of the actors it had involved. Its chance of success was assured when it distributed responsibility and credit where it was needed and due. (Rubright & MacDonald, 1981, p. 144)

The chief executive officer of an organization is the one responsible for basis strategy. It is the role of the marketing team to provide the CEO with advice. The more reliable the advice, the more influence the marketing function will have on setting policies and strategies.

Case Study of Strategies and Tactics: Cureville Hospital

Strategic and tactical development will be examined in terms of the following example:

Cureville Hospital is located in a large metropolitan area in the northeast. Its original location was in the core area of the city. In recent years, it has opened several suburban satellite facilities. This growth necessitated the expansion of the hospital's laboratory. The laboratory is one of the best equipped facilities in the area. Not only can it perform all standard analyses, but it can also handle a host of more sophisticated tests. Most of the other lab facilities in the area lack Cureville's technical expertise. At the present time, the lab is being utilized at approximately 60% of capacity. The hospital administrator wants the lab used at or near full capacity. He has instructed the assistant administrator, whose area of responsibility covers the laboratory facility, to develop a marketing strategy which will achieve this objective.

To prepare a marketing strategy the assistant administrator must have a complete understanding of the market. In this case, the laboratory market is the grouping of all institutions and individuals who have an actual or potential need for laboratory analyses. In reality, this market is made up of different types of customers. The assistant administrator has identified the following potential market segments: other hospitals, other independent laboratories, and medical practitioners (see Figure 24.2).

The assistant administrator realizes that there are five possible market coverage patterns: product specialization, market specialization, product/market concentration, selective specialization and full coverage. With product specialization a firm deals in only one product such as the marketing of sophisticated laboratory tests. Market specialization centers around a single market segment such as independent laboratories. Product/market concentration combines both of the above concepts. As an example, the marketing of sophisticated laboratory tests to only independent laboratories. The marketing in more than one product market segment with no relation to each other is selective specialization. If the hospital marketed standard laboratory tests to medical practitioners and sophisticated laboratory tests to other hospitals, it would be using a selective specialization approach. Full coverage deals with marketing a full range of products to all market segments (Abell 1979, p. 8).

After researching these alternatives, the assistant administrator decided to concentrate on a product specialization—marketing sophisticated laboratory tests to the other hospitals and independent laboratories. It was felt that sufficient additional volume could be generated from these sources without having to concentrate on the individual medical practitioners. Marketing to the individual medical practitioners would require additional personnel (a new business solicitor plus an additional pick-up/delivery person) and equipment (additional pick-up van).

The next step is to determine the hospital's positioning strategy. Competitive positioning is establishing a unique position in the consumer's mind as compared to competitors serving the same market. This can only be accomplished through a thorough understanding of the attributes used by the target market to evaluate competitive laboratories. Additional research indicated that three major attributes were important in decision making: the quality and dependability of the analyses, the turnaround time, and price. Cureville Hospital felt that it had a distinct advantage over its competition. Research had established that all three market segments viewed the hospital's laboratory work as not only professional, but also equal to or superior to the other laboratory facilities. The assistant administrator felt he could develop delivery systems to provide efficient and speedy turnaround service. In addition, they had a pricing advantage as their current internal volume covered their fixed costs and they only had to be concerned with their variable costs.

Next, the assistant administrator developed the hospital's marketing mix strategies.

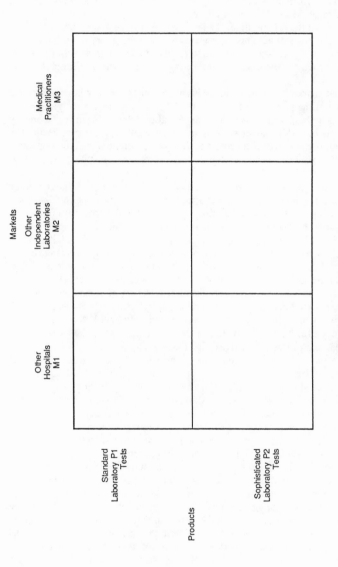

FIGURE 24.2. Market Segments

Source. From *Strategic Market Planning: Problems and Analytical Approaches* (pp. 389-407) by Derek Abell and John Hammond. Englewood Cliffs, NJ: Prentice-Hall, Inc. Copyright 1979. Adapted by permission.

Product

It was felt that the hospital should concentrate on maintaining its quality image. This would be accomplished by continuing to update its laboratory equipment and retaining and hiring high quality personnel. Additional research would be conducted to ensure that the hospital's wage structure for laboratory personnel was equal to or superior to the competition.

Place

The hospital's strategy was to develop efficient and speedy pick-up and delivery services. Currently, the hospital employs an individual who picks up and delivers the laboratory work from the satellite hospital facilities. The morning and afternoon runs take approximately two hours each. During the remaining portions of the day, the employee is used to perform various odd jobs around the hospital. It was decided to utilize this employee on a full-time basis to pick-up and deliver from, not only the Cureville Hospitals, but also from the other hospitals and laboratories in the area.

Price

Because the hospital's current volume of internal business more than covered the fixed costs associated with operating the lab facility, the price offered to customers could be at least 15% to 25% below the few competitors which had the capacity to run the same type of sophisticated tests. Since the competitors were operating close to capacity, it was felt that, even though the industry was an oligopoly, there would be a minimum of competitors who could or would meet their reduced prices.

Promotion

The assistant administrator has determined that there are seven local hospitals and five independent laboratories which are the prime potential customers. He plans on sending the laboratory directors a letter outlining Cureville Hospital's sophisticated laboratory services. The letter will then be followed up with a telephone call to arrange for an appointment with the laboratory directors. During their face-to-face meeting, the assistant administrator will actively solicit their business. Care should be taken as to control the volume of additional laboratory business to ensure that the laboratory is not overloaded. It has been estimated that the laboratory business from only a third of the prospects (four hospitals and/or indepedent laboratories) will provide Cureville Hospital's laboratory with the additional volume necessary to achieve the objective.

The following chapter demonstrates the role of strategic market planning and tactical development in achieving marketing objectives.

SUMMARY

Strategies outline an organization's goals, objectives, and plans. Tactics are the means by which the firm intends to accomplish their goals, objectives, and plans. Tactics are neither good nor bad, nor are there any perfect tactics. In a given situation, one tactic may prove to be appropriate, while under a different set of circumstances, the same tactic may turn out to be a complete failure.

Organizations can use strategies to stimulate primary demand for a product class or selective demand for a specific brand within a product class: the demand for emergency health care clinics versus the demand for the Acme Emergency Health Care Clinic. In addition, strategies can be simple or complex. Complex strategies use a combination of approaches.

REFERENCES

Abell, Derek F. Strategic Market Planning (Englewood Cliffs, NJ: Prentice-Hall, Inc., 1979).

Jain, Subhash C. Marketing Planning and Strategy (Cincinnati, Ohio: South-Western Publishing Co., 1981).

Kaiser, Leland. Annual Implementation Plan (Denver, Colorado: University of Colorado Medical Center, PACT Health Planning Center, 1978).

Rubright, Robvert and MacDonald, Don. Marketing Health and Human Services (Baltimore, Maryland: an Aspen Publication, 1981).

Stanton, William J. and Buskirk, Richard H. Management of the Sales Force. 6th ed. (Homewood, Illinois: Richard D. Irwin, 1983).

CHAPTER 25

Developing Marketing Strategies and Tactics

William J. Winston

STRATEGY FORMULATION PROCESS

After identifying segments and targets to whom to direct the marketing activities, the action phase begins in the planning process. As the reader can tell no actual marketing activities have taken place to communicate to the organization's publics. This is a very important concept to understand in marketing. No action is taken before all of the prior steps have been completed as background. One of the major reasons for programs failing is the common error of jumping the gun and initiating strategies and tactics before solidly completing the prior marketing planning functions.

To better understand the step we are about to undertake, a schematic diagram of the strategy development process is demonstrated below.

This schematic diagram demonstrates the interrelationship of the systematic approach that is necessary for strategic marketing planning. Marketing strategies and tactics will be developed as an outcome of the prior steps in the planning process. In other words, the strategies and tactics must:

Reprinted from William J. Winston, *How to Write a Marketing Plan for Health Care Organizations*, pp. 52–62, © 1985 by The Haworth Press, Inc.

1. be consistent with the original marketing mission;
2. attempt to satisfy specific goals and objectives;
3. be directed to select target groups which are based on the audit analysis; and
4. be in sync with the positioning niche which the organization desires to possess in the marketplace.

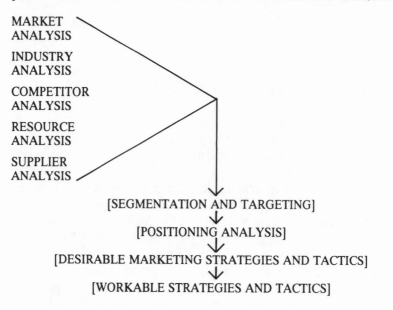

[MARKETING MISSIONS, GOALS, AND OBJECTIVES]

↓

[MARKETING AUDIT: ECONOMIC/DEMOGRAPHIC/TECHNICAL/ETC.,]

MARKET
ANALYSIS

INDUSTRY
ANALYSIS

COMPETITOR
ANALYSIS

RESOURCE
ANALYSIS

SUPPLIER
ANALYSIS

[SEGMENTATION AND TARGETING]

↓

[POSITIONING ANALYSIS]

↓

[DESIRABLE MARKETING STRATEGIES AND TACTICS]

↓

[WORKABLE STRATEGIES AND TACTICS]

WHAT ARE MARKETING STRATEGIES AND TACTICS?

Marketing strategies outline a broad plan of action to best use the organization's health resources to achieve a marketing goal and objective. In addition, marketing strategies are the specific actions taken by the organization to communicate with the select primary target groups. *Marketing tactics* are specific plans of action which further define specific marketing strategies. In other words, objectives further describe goals just as tactics will be provided but a basic example would be the following for marketing a hospital's wellness program to the target of commuters:

Marketing Strategy: to developing an advertising campaign for the hospital

Marketing Tactic: to run an ad for the wellness clinic at the hospital on the local radio station.

In this example the marketing strategy briefly describes the action to be taken in marketing the hospital's wellness clinic. The marketing tactic describes the strategy in greater detail with specific information. There can even be *marketing sub-tactics* which can describe the marketing tactic. For the example above, more information about the radio ad may be available. Therefore, a sub-tactic could be created such as: to advertise on the radio station with three one-minute ads; during the morning commute period; and spread out one per hour during the three hour commute program. In addition, for every marketing strategy there are typically multiple marketing tactics developed. *As a guideline for a typical marketing plan should be the presence of three to four marketing strategies for each target group and two to three marketing tactics for each marketing strategy.*

FRAMEWORK FOR DEVELOPING THE MOST COMMON FIVE MARKETING STRATEGIES

In today's competitive environment health organizations are exploring some very common, broad marketing strategies. These are *market penetration, vertical integration, horizontal integration, new service development,* and *diversification*. It is important to briefly differentiate these basic strategies because of their implementation by the majority of health organizations. These strategies are differentiated according to their application to the typical community hospital.

Market penetration: This is the action of obtaining more patients for the present hospital and its current services. It is a typical strategy implemented to sustain or increase the hospital's market share of its current target groups. Currently many hospitals just want to communicate more effectively to the service area they have always served and to attract more of this existing group to use their hospital over another hospital.

Market expansion: This is the action of attracting patients from new target groups and marketplaces. The difference with this strategy is to market to entirely new segments for an increase in the utilization of existing services. For example, many hospitals are attempting to attract segments of the community to use the hospital that live in areas geographically located outside of their usual service area.

Vertical integration: This strategy is related to attracting more patients by adding to the supply side of existing services. In other words, vertical integration implies, for example, taking over similar hospitals in the community by takeover, merger, or a sharing process. The hospital is still in the hospital business and it is still providing similar services to what is used to offer except for an increase in the amount of these services. The proprietary hospital chains are a great example of vertical integration through the years as these firms have added similar hospitals through purchase, construction, or management contracts.

Horizontal integration: This action differentiates from horizontal integration by the addition of new services to the hospital's offering. The hospital is still in the hospital business — it has not added any new entire hospitals to its organizational structure — but it has attempted to increase the number of patients by attracting them to utilize entirely new services not previously offered. This is reflective of hospitals expanding into wellness programs, same-day surgery centers, urgent care centers, pharmacies, and laboratories during recent years.

Diversification: This action is usually mistaken for either vertical or horizontal integration. The marketing definition of diversification implies adding programs or purchasing other organizations that offer services which your organization never offered. These services are typically out of the usual scope of the hospital's business line. For example, hospitals are currently diversifying out of the hospital industry into real estate, consulting, investment banking, and in some cases, retail activities. This diversification is occurring as liquidity, profit margins, and return on investments shrink due to reimbursement constraints.

One or more of these broad marketing strategies is at the base of most hospital marketing campaigns in this country.

DEVELOPING MARKETING STRATEGIES BASED ON THE SERVICE LIFE CYCLE

Regardless of service type, geography, or marketplace, certain broad strategies seem to be appropriate based only on the *stage of the service in its life cycle*. As mentioned in the first chapter, every health organization "lives a life similar to human beings, meaning Introduction, Growth, Maturity, and Decline Phases." It is important for the administrator or marketer to identify the strength of its current service activity base and place it in its appropriate life cycle phase. Of course, there can be instances where an organization is on the borderline between two phases or experiencing characteristics of two different phases. However, typically the health organization settles into a distinct life cycle phase. This distinction allows for the development of individualized marketing strategies related to the select life cycle phase. The following characteristics and strategies are broadly applied to each phase. It is hoped that some of these basic characteristics can be helpful in developing unique strategies for the services.

Introduction phase: In the introduction phase the health organization's service is new to the marketplace. The common characteristics for services in this life cycle are

1. There is a consumer group unaware about the service offered;
2. A limited number of varieties of the basic service are usually offered by the organization;
3. Emphasis is placed on market penetration and encouragement for consumers to "trial use" the service;
4. Concentration on the most interested and promising target group is initiated;
5. A positioning statement of quality service is the main framework;
6. Service probably faces future competition and it is preferable

to build brand preference and loyalty by the most promising target groups;

7. A monitoring system is established to track customer usage patterns and perceptions; and

8. Pricing and promotion can be directed in different ways for achieving the desired market penetration. These different pricing and promotion strategies can be grouped into:

Rapid-skimming: setting a high price and having high levels of promotion to rapidly enter the market for those who can pay the high price. The promotion tends to justify the high price and relates the price to a quality service.

Slow-skimming: having a high price but low promotion. This is directed to keeping marketing expenditures low, enlarging the profit margin, not facing stiff future competition, having a consumer group aware of the service, and directing our attention to those targets which can afford the high price. Rapid-skimming strategies desire to penetrate the market quickly and hang on to their share of the market for a long time through service loyalty and referrals. The slow-skimming strategy is differentiated by no future competition and an emphasis on penetrating the market and building service loyalty over a long time frame. For example, open-heart procedures were good examples of rapid-skimming when many hospitals got on the bandwagon and charged extremely high charges for these sophisticated techniques and promoted their availability at the facility extensively. In comparison, plastic surgery techniques in the 1960s and early 1970s were very high priced but promoted sparingly (slow-skimming). These services were directed at a select high income group and the organizations and providers of these services were willing to build service loyalty very slowly.

Rapid penetration: strategies in the introduction phase are related to charging a low price with high promotion. This mix of pricing and promotion encourages rapid acceptance by a wider number of segments in the marketplace. The strategy attempts to go after a large share of the market quickly. The market for these services is generally large and is aware of the services rendered. The consumers are price sensitive and there is usually strong competition for similar services currently or in the near future. For example, hospitals expanded their outpatient departments during this last decade. These services attempted to position themselves into the minds of the consumer as being lower-priced than traditional inpatient services and were heavily promoted to the many segments in the community.

Slow penetration: implies a low pricing policy with low amounts of promotion. This strategy encourages rapid acceptance of the service by the marketplace, keeps marketing costs low, markets to a large number of segments, has a service which is very price sensitive for consumers, possesses little or no competition, and has a consumer base which is not motivated very much by promotion programs. An example of this type of service which utilizes a slow penetration strategy is public health programs. Typically, public health programs, especially educational services, have been terribly marketed through the years. However they have used this type of strategy by possessing a very low price (free in many cases); having little money to promote to the general public; desiring rapid penetration by a large marketplace of all income levels; and having almost no competition for similar services.

The second major phase of a service's life cycle is the *growth phase*. In this phase services are characterized by

1. Experiencing its fastest sales or utilization trend;
2. Selecting the most profitable delivery mode;
3. A drop in price if competition materializes;
4. A constant planning for targets to add for future utilization;
5. Making sure services are available for consumers when they desire them;
6. Developing alternatives or options of the original service for maximum utilization;
7. Beginning to design a potential successor service;
8. Reinvesting some cash flow from the service to maximize efficiency of service delivery; and
9. Promotion and pricing strategies are dependent upon market conditions. Typically this phase is characterized by a strong word of mouth or referral process. The service is constantly being improved and we are adding other services to substitute or compliment the main service. New competitors are also

present in order to cash in on your main service's success. Demand is still increasing at an increasing rate while the price for the service remains the same or begins to fall. The marketer usually decides the right time during this phase to lower prices to attract the next layer of price sensitive consumers. We tend to start searching for new segments or new delivery modes in the marketplace in order to keep this exponential growth continuing. At this point in time consumers are well aware of the service so promotion shifts toward service acceptance and actual purchase instead of education about the need for the service. In many ways the health organization must face the trade-off between emphasizing the strategies for obtaining a higher market share versus earning a higher profit margin. Examples of services which have experienced these characteristics during growth periods have been: family counseling, hospice centers, home care programs, and preferred provider organizations. In other words, every service will experience a growth phase with various degrees of these characteristics. However, the majority of services are usually faced with strategies related to (1) attempting to continue the growth phase; (2) positioning the service in the minds of the consumer against strong competition; (3) using pricing and promotion more effectively; and (4) developing alternative services to complement or potentially substitute the original service.

The third phase every service typically experiences is the *maturity phase*. *Most health and human services in the United States are currently in the mature phase of their life cycle.* Therefore, this phase may be the most important to many hospital, clinic, public health, and long-term care administrators. During this phase demand starts to slow down and the health organization may be characterized by being in this phase longer than any other. For example, most older community hospitals are definitely mature services and have been for a considerable amount of time. So, most marketing strategies deal with the mature phase in our health industry.

There are usually considered three main sub-phases of maturity for the health service: *continued growth maturity*, *stagnant maturity*, and *decaying maturity*. Continued growth maturity is a sub-phase in which the services start to experience increasing demand but at a decreasing rate. In other words, the market is still expanding but the marginal increases are smaller and market saturation is materializing. Stagnant maturity is a second sub-phase in which demand levels off due to definite market saturation. Most growth during this sub-phase is occurring due to replacement and population growth rather than pure attraction to the main service. The decay maturity sub-phase experiences a definite gradual decline in demand as consumers begin to move toward other competitor services. This sub-phase possesses very apparent intense competition and a marketplace which is overcrowded. The three main strategies used for services or products which are in one of the maturity sub-phases are: *modification of the service's marketplace, modification of the service*; and *modification of the marketing mix*.

Modifying the service's marketplace involves finding new consumers, markets, target groups, and stimulating greater utilization by current clients for the existing service. Repositioning the service in the minds of new segments which haven't been addressed before can be very successful strategy. For example, an HMO could have been mainly attracting the middle-income, union members and their families. There are many additional segments such as younger, poorer, and older groups which have not been served.

Modifying the actual service involves changing "real" characteristics of the service. This can be a physical and quality-related change. A new feature to the service can be added. In addition, the strategy is aimed at improving the style of the service (in other words, changing the positioning of the aesthetic appeal of the service rather than the functional attractions). A great example of services implementing this type of change are group practices of various types of medical providers. Tremendous competition has materialized for the typical community physician group practice in urban areas. This has led, for example, to groups opening their offices on weekends and even reinstituting home visits by the medical provider!

Modifying the market-mix implies changing the four Ps of marketing: pricing, place, product, and promotion. *These four Ps do not operate independently*. They must be *orchestrated* together for a successful marketing strategy. Therefore, for example, our same group practice in the prior paragraph could decide to develop a sliding fee schedule for office visits (*price*); expand their office hours in the evening (*place*); add on some new specialties to the practice (*product*); and begin to distribute higher quality and more informative brochures about the changes in the other marketing mix components to the community.

In summary, the maturity phase is characterized by

1. Keeping constant changes in existing services to a minimum;
2. Concentrating on select market segments;
3. Expanding the life cycle through service redesign for new potential segments in the marketplace;
4. Increasing client follow-up or complimentary services; and
5. Arranging for promotion to restimulate demand for the service.

The final phase of the life cycle for a service is the *decline phase*. In this phase the demand for the service is rapidly or slowly declining due to technological changes, new substitutes in the marketplace, or changes in client tastes for the service. Typically, health services in this phase can hang on for a considerable amount of time or be discontinued quickly. In many cases, services can last forever if the service is a main part of the organization's mission and philosophy. For example, many clinics directed toward lower income clients and associated with religiously affiliated hospitals are definitely in the decline phase. Some of these clinics have been in decline for many years but the service represents the backbone mission of the religiously oriented hospital in service poor patients. Unfortunately, economic changes in Medicaid and Medicare reimbursement are beginning to force some of these clinics to be discontinued. The strategies typically used in this phase are: a decision to drop the service and reallocate resources to more cost-effective investments, reduce expenses as much as possible, concentrate current resources in the strongest segments, or develop compliment services which receive higher reimbursement in order to counter the decline aspects of the main service. During very recent years the old-fashioned in-patient revenue base is beginning to experience a decline phase in many community hospitals around the country.

However, these services will still represent the main focus of the community hospital. Alternative services are being emphasized in order to counter any revenue decline.

Most of these life cycle strategies are broad and should not be taken as definitive rules. In addition, the length of any one phase can vary dramatically for different services. However, since health administrators and marketers must preserve revenue generator services, knowing the characteristics of strategies related to the life cycle can be helpful. One common point is the fact that most services maximize their cash flow to the organization at the end of the growth phase and during maturity. Therefore, strategies related to extending the growth and maturity phases may justify priority. The strategies related to this important cash flow period are related to: redesigning the actual service for new segments; adding complements to the main service, such as follow-up care; refining the components of the marketing mix so they are orchestrated; implementing a cost control mechanism into the marketing function; and beginning developing future substitute services.

SPECIFIC EXAMPLES OF MARKETING STRATEGIES

The foundation of strategies must be directed to concentrating on what must be done, where it must be done, and when it must be done to communicate with select targets and satisfy specific goals and objectives. Strategies can be developed in many different ways. One additional method is to develop strategies as applied to the components of the marketing mix. It is important to always fall back on the marketing mix for developing marketing strategies. The following lists examples of actual marketing strategies and tactics for a typical hospital, as applied to each component of the marketing mix.

The assumed marketing goal will be: *to increase in-patient utilization*.

The assumed marketing objective related to this goal will be: *to increase patient utilization by 10% before December*.

The target groups will be: *general public or physicians*.

Price Strategies

1. Establish quantity discounts to encourage larger unit purchases of the services.

Tactics: (a) Give percentage discounts for families who use the OB units of the hospital for their second, third, etc. child. (b) For patients using outpatient pharmacy services, offer discounts to extended users.

2. Expand the use of credit for patients with large deductibles or co-payments.

Tactics: (1) Expand the use of credit cards for patients. (b) Offer hospital-backed loans for patients with catastrophic illnesses.

Place Strategies

1. Develop a stronger relationship with attending physicians through construction.

Tactics: (a) Build a professional medical building nearby to link physicians to the hospital. (b) Offer the office space as a part-time second office to remote physicians.

2. Provide additional outlets for provision of services.

Tactics: (a) Expand the use of emergency room as a potential admitter for inpatients. (b) Expand the hours the outpatient clinic is opened.

Product Strategies

1. Distinguish the hospital's services from that of its competitors as viewed by your clients.

Tactics: (a) Attract top medical providers in the community to become affiliated with the hospital. (b) Develop an internal marketing program to make sure the hospital's staff believes and communicates the high quality of the services provided by the hospital.

2. Add new staff members who will become admitters.

Tactics: (a) Assist physicians in relocating to existing officers attached to the hospital. (b) Assist junior members of a group to establish their own private practices in the community.

Promotion Strategies

1. Address advertising and promotion to key patients and best prospects.

Tactics: (a) Have established medical staff give formal speeches at local business association meetings. (b) Send brochures to employee benefit directors about the outpatient services available at the hospital.

2. Work with the city to improve hospital publicity.

Tactics: (a) Construct additional signs to enhance hospital visibility on key access roads. (b) Join the chamber of commerce so the hospital is listed for local businesses and general public.

These strategies and tactics are just examples of how a marketer or administrator can apply them to the components of the marketing mix. One of the most important strategies that many organizations overlook is first developing an internal strategy base before marketing externally. The following section briefly describes the importance and examples of internal marketing strategies.

INTERNAL MARKETING STRATEGIES

Internal Marketing is the development of an organizational environment in which marketing becomes an integral part of our everyday managerial or clinical activities. In other words, a hospital, nursing home, or department must create a marketing orientation and philosophy for the entire organization and its employees. Marketing in health care organizations unfortunately begins by jumping the gun and initiating marketing strategies and tactics before most providers and staff understand their marketing roles within the organization. It is imperative to never market to the external community before internal marketing is completed.

All staff members in the health organization are using marketing with every interaction. Before initiating an internal marketing program it is important to relate to the patient as a client. Even with extensive insurance coverage most of the patients are involved in an exchange process with the health organization. The clients exchange money, time, inconvenience, and stress when obtaining typical health services. By relating to the patient as an exchange "client," it allows for a better acceptance of our role in marketing with every interaction.

Most internal marketing is related to (1) understanding that employees represent the health organization in marketing; (2) communicating effectively with our clients, providers, community representatives, or other employees; (3) providing for marketing oriented atmospherics; and (4) creating a long-run philosophy for the entire organization.

All employees represent the organization for which they work. This is important because most of the clients develop their perceptions of the organization related to how they are treated while using the service. For example, their perceptions of the quality of care are typically determined by the way in which they interact with the employees of the health organization. If employees understand the importance of effective interaction, it can carry over to a referral being made by a satisfied client, employee, or provider. The major success of marketing health services is a satisfied client and receiving a referral. The quality of the interaction between an employee or provider and the client can be the key ingredient for this referral.

Some key suggestions in improving communication include

1. Being careful to avoid highly technical jargon with a patient;
2. Listening carefully to the client;
3. Maintaining eye contact for establishing interest and trust;
4. Restating your ideas for clarity, especially when giving instructions to patients; and
5. Not being afraid to use appropriate body language and facial expressions when emphasizing certain points.

Other areas for effective internal marketing include: using the telephone effectively by greeting the caller, speaking distinctly, and not putting people on hold for long periods; being careful not to put people off by using typical sayings such as, "It's just routine," "This won't hurt," or "It's hospital policy"; remembering to smile; greeting people who look lost in our hospital complexes; introducing yourself; avoiding endearing names such as calling people "honey," "dear," or "darling"; trying to exceed people's expectations in giving information; complimenting a client when the opportunity arises; and presenting a professional image in terms of dress and physical presence.

The atmospherics, or physical environment, of the health organization also relate to internal marketing. Atmospherics include the physical layout, accessibility, waiting time for service, colors and furnishings, neatness of treatment area, smells or noises, and the efficiency of our treatment and triage systems. These environmental factors have an influence on the client's perception of the service being provided.

Nurses, medical providers, support staff, counselors, technicians, billing clerks, admission personnel, dieticians, and volunteers are some examples of the variety of people who come into contact with our clients. these people can better understand how they represent the organization through an effective internal marketing program. Making sure the organization is internally marketing-oriented can become the strategies which will lay the framework for successful external marketing endeavors.

An organization which is internally marketing-oriented provides a strong base from which to develop external marketing strategies. It also allows for more cost-effective marketing.

SUMMARY: DEVELOPING MARKETING STRATEGIES AND TACTICS

Most people associate marketing with public relations and advertising. These activities are included, finally, in the creative phase of marketing — strategy development.

This phase must include an entrepreneurial spirit by the marketer and health organization. All of the prior steps in the planning process have finally led up to our "taking some action to communicate with the selected target groups." As the reader can tell, all of the prior steps have laid a base for strategy development. For example, the marketing missions, goals, and objectives direct us to specific purposes and outcomes we hope to achieve with the strategies that are implemented. The audit identified opportunities and assisted in selecting target groups to better direct to whom we are marketing.

The positioning phase provided key niches in the marketplace the organization desires to possess and perceptions in the minds of the target groups that require nurturing.

The reader should have grasped an understanding of (1) the strategy formulation process; (2) a framework for five very common market strategies being used today; (3) how to develop strategies for specific phases of the life cycle; (4) differentiation between market strategies and tactics; and (5) applications of strategy and tactic development to the components of the marketing mix.

This is the action phase of the strategic marketing plan. The success or failure of the plan will materialize from the measurement of the effectiveness of these strategies and tactics achieving the marketing missions, goals, and objectives established in the beginning planning steps. The next chapter discusses this evaluation or control process in addition to the important aspects of organizational design for marketing and the marketing budget process.

CASE EXAMPLE:
MARKETING STRATEGIES AND TACTICS
FOR TODAY'S MODERN COMMUNITY HOSPITAL
WITHIN THE COMPLEX MEDICAL MARKETPLACE

The hospital industry is in a state of flux. There is a new look to hospital practice in most metropolitan and suburban areas of the country. The entrepreneurial spirit is quite evident, and occasionally flamboyant in many of these areas. With occupancy rates on the decline for traditional inpatients and cost-cutting policies being initiated by government and private insurers, a marketing-oriented management style has emerged. This has become very important as hospital occupancy, for instance, has declined from a national average of 76% in 1980 to approximately 71% in 1984. Payments for inpatient care by third-party payors is under attack so hospitals are seeking new ventures to be developed. There is a whole new approach to health care as doctors and administrators begin to view themselves as highly trained businesspeople. The risk inherent in this change is that the contract between the health profession and society will be lost sight of as these changes progress. Just five years ago the idea that non-profit hospitals might actually think about and participate in competition with other hospitals would have been called a fantasy by many professionals, and a nightmare by others. Today, it is no longer the question of whether a hospital should compete, but it is a question of how to compete.

The question of how to compete is reflected in marketing strategy and tactic development within the marketing planning process. Many of the changes in existing services and development of new services are part of the strategy formulation process. In response to the changing marketplace, hospitals around the country have developed some creative and entrepreneurial strategies. Some of these include

- Development of 365-day-a-year walk-in clinics;
- Acceptance of credit cards for payment;
- Expanded hours of most clinics;
- Additional services such as podiatrists, optometrists, chiropractors, and even acupuncturists;
- Advertising by mail, billboard, flyers, on transit, radio, TV, and newspapers;
- Development of same-day surgery centers;
- Development of home care programs;
- Reduced staff for inpatient services or staff shifted to ambulatory centers;
- Established dietary consultation for other hospitals and nursing homes;
- Created "Meals on Wheels programs" for the elderly and handicapped;
- Contracting out the hospital's janitorial services to medical offices;
- Created urgent care centers, emergicenters, convenience care centers, etc.;
- Offers of bundle packages for physical exams, ob-gyn services, laboratory testing, etc.;
- Experimenting with cut-rate package offerings of hospital services or even complements such as gourmet meals and upper-income private rooms;
- Actually advertising prices for hospital services and even some comparative prices with other hospitals;

- Created sport care programs, wellness programs, etc.;
- Started risk reduction programs for executives and businesses for alcohol, drugs, stress, etc.;
- Created separate foundations as part of the hospital for fund raising or for-profit functions;
- Mass purchasing and shared services;
- Established consulting divisions for management consulting, employee benefit analysis for businesses, etc.;
- Transferred inpatient into outpatient services—i.e., brain scanning, health screening, laboratory testing, surgery, rehabilitation, etc.;
- Contracted with, or formed, PPOs, IPAs, HMOs, etc.

All of these strategies are quite creative for traditional hospitals. Of course, many investor-owned facilities have been experimenting with some of these ventures for some time. Hospitals in the non-profit sector are getting a rude awakening to the realities of marketplace capitalism. The impacts of these changes, especially upon loss leader services being offered and access for the poor and elderly, are just now beginning to be examined. Installing competition does promote entrepreneurial activity. Marketing strategy development is becoming one of the most important, and sought after, tools of marketers, planners, administrators, and board members.

Besides market strategies, it is important to remember that most public relations activities fall into the classification of market tactics. Tactics can vary dramatically in their scope but most of them are related to specific mechanisms for communicating with select target groups. For example, the following promotional tools, or tactics, are typically used in today's modern hospital: * brochures * news releases * internal newsletters * external newsletters * public service announcements * factsheets * traveling displays * videotape presentations * educational forums * direct mail flyers * educational classes * social events * special business letters * seminars * symposiums * handbooks * manuals * bulletin boards * films * hotlines * information racks * speaker's bureaus * inserts * open houses * tours * news conferences * posters * public address systems * annual reports * billboards * contests * signs, etc.

Part VIII

Organization, Budgeting, and Control Systems

CHAPTER 26

Introduction to Organization, Budget, and Control

Robert L. Berl

It is the responsibility of marketing managers to effectively plan and control so as to optimize profitability. There are four types of marketing controls which should be employed: (1) annual evaluation and control procedures, (2) financial controls, (3) efficiency controls, and (4) strategic controls. Annual control procedures are the responsibility of top and middle management and are used to determine whether the planned results are being achieved. Financial controls are used by top management to determine the factors that affect the company's return on net worth. Operating managers use efficiency controls to identify whether specific areas of the firm are at peak efficiency. Strategic controls are the province of top management and the marketing auditor and are used to determine if the company is pursuing its best opportunities regarding markets, products, channels of distribution, price, and promotion.

Figure 26.1 shows the marketing control process. Marketing management is responsible for setting goals and objectives, allocating resources and effort, developing the marketing plan, and organizing for implementation. The plan is then executed and evaluated to ensure that the organization's goals are being accomplished.

ANNUAL CONTROL PROCEDURES

The marketing plan provides quantitative guides for management in terms of such factors as sales volume, market share, profit mar-

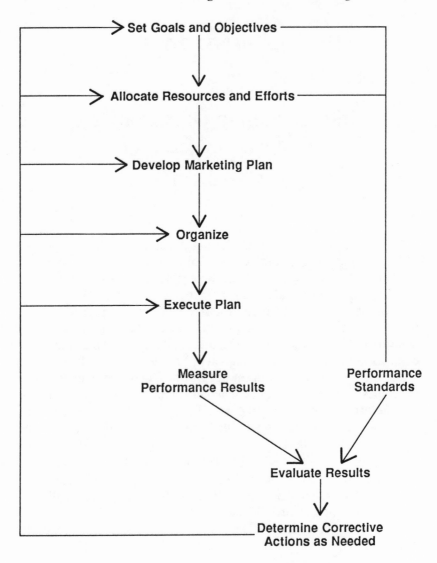

FIGURE 26.1. Control Process

Source. Adapted from *Sales Management: Decision Making for Improved Profitability* (p. 363). By Dan H. Robertson and Danny N. Bellenger. New York: McMillan Publishing Co., Inc. Copyright 1980.

gins, and sales expenses. These quantitative guides act as standards of performance for the marketing department. An offshoot of the marketing plan is the budget which permits management to track performance relative to both revenues and expenses. A detailed discussion of the marketing budget can be found later in the chapter.

Control of the annual plan is conducted in multiple areas: sales analysis, market share analysis, and marketing cost analysis.

Sales Analysis

Sales analysis is performed on two levels: (1) the overall difference between planned results and actual results, and (2) the difference between planned results and actual results by product, territory, and the like. The relative contribution of different factors is compared to the sales plan. For example, a hospital's gift shop planned on selling 1,000 boxes of candy during the first quarter of the year at $5.00 per box for a total of $5,000. At the end of the quarter, it was determined that 700 boxes of candy were sold at an average price of $4.50. This produced total sales of $3,150. The sales performance variance was 300 boxes of candy or 30% of planned sales ($1,850). It is important to determine how much of the underperformance was due to the price and how much to the decline in sales volume. This can be determined in the following manner:

Variance Due to Price Decline			
($5.00 - $4.50)(700)	=	$ 350	18.9%
Variance Due to Volume Decline			
($5.00)(1,000 - 700)	=	$ 1,500	81.1%
		$ 1,850	100.0%

The vast majority of the sales variance (81%) was due to the failure to achieve the targeted sales volume. The hospital should investigate to determine why the expected sales did not materialize.

Management should also look at specific products, territories, and the like that failed to achieve planned sales. Suppose a hospital has three locations in the city and operates a gift shop in each location. The anticipated gift-shop sales were $120,000, $99,000, and

$87,000 respectively for a total of $306,000. The actual sales volume was $100,000, $103,000, and $109,000 for a total of $312,000. The first gift shop experienced a 17% shortfall in planned sales, the second shop was above expected sales by 4%, and the third location achieved a 25% increase in sales. Marketing management should attempt to determine the cause of the shortfall in the first location. Are the gift shop's personnel loafing, is the merchandise displayed properly, are they opening and closing at the proper times, or is some other factor at fault?

If the hospital management looked only at total gift shop revenues, they would have been pleased with a $6,000, or 2% increase. This illustrates the so-called iceberg principle: a lot of valuable information is hidden in summary data. Icebergs show only about 10% of their mass above the surface of the water. The remaining 90% is hidden below the water's surface. The same is true when evaluating sales and cost performance data. It is vital to analyze sales and cost figures on a micro basis to reveal important product or territory variances.

Market Share Analysis

Periodically a company should review its market share position. Is the company gaining or losing ground relative to its competition? Market share measures can be determined in a number of ways. First, a company can use an overall market share measure which evaluates the firm's sales as a percentage of the total industry served. This is the most commonly used measure of market share. Market share can also be expressed as a percentage of the served market rather than the total market. A hospital located in the northern suburb of a city might well use a served market measure. Their market share would be calculated using the percentage of people living in the northern suburb who used the hospital and not the population of the entire city. Market share can also be calculated by comparing the firm's sales to its leading competitor or its top three competitors. An increase in the company's relative market share means that it is gaining on its leading competitor(s).

Marketing Cost Analysis

Expenses can be allocated to the various cost categories using either a full-cost approach or a contribution-margin approach. Under a full-cost approach, all costs are allocated. This method requires that difficult-to-allocate costs be split on some basis. There is an assumption that these cost categories are, to some degree, beneficial to whatever group to which they are allocated. As an example, the hospital administrator's salary is allocated to each of the hospital's major departments. The contribution-margin approach concentrates on variable costs rather than on total costs. Under this method, the departments would be held responsible for only those costs that they can control. Table 26.1 contrasts these two approaches. Under the full-cost approach, the product "A" division of the company had a net profit of $90,000. Using the contribution-margin approach, the division is only held responsible for those expenses it controls and the resulting contribution-margin is $150,000.

TABLE 26.1. Full-Cost Approach vs. Contribution-Margin Approach: Acme Company Product "A" Division Profit-and-Loss Statement

	Full-Cost Approach		Contribution Margin Approach
Sales	$ 1,000,000	Sales	$ 1,000,000
Cost of Goods Sold	800,000	Cost of Goods Sold	800,000
Gross Margin	200,000	Gross Margin	200,000
Other Expenses		Direct Expenses	
Sales	50,000	Sales	35,000
Administration	60,000	Administration	15,000
		Contribution Margin	150,000
		Indirect Expenses	60,000
Net Profit	**$90,000**	**Net Profit**	**$90,000**

The full-cost approach often leads to conflicts within the company, as it makes some customers, products, or allocated groups appear less profitable. Departments argue that they have no control over the magnitude of many of the costs and that they should be evaluated based on those costs they can control. In addition to showing operating mangers how they are doing, the contribution-margin approach is especially useful for evaluating alternatives. Since, in the long run, all products, customers, and departments must pay for both fixed and variable costs, top managers find the full-cost approach more useful.

Costs can be classified as natural accounts or functional accounts. Natural accounts are those cost categories to which various expenses are charged in the normal accounting process. These accounts would include such categories as salaries, wages, supplies, raw materials, and the like. Functional accounts show the purpose for which the expenditures were made, such as advertising, personal selling, and so forth. Table 26.2 shows both natural and functional costs. This table assumes that the company's only functional accounts are advertising and personal selling. In reality, a firm would have many more functional accounts.

The functional accounts can be analyzed by products, geographic territories, customers, or some other classification. The following analysis depicts this type of examination:

Functional Accounts		Product Groups	
		Product A	Product B
Advertising	$ 76,000	$ 35,000	$ 41,000
Personal Selling	211,000	121,000	90,000
Total	$287,000	$156,000	$131,000

A key ratio to follow is the marketing-expenses-to-sales ratio. This aggregate ratio might have several component parts, such as the sales-force-to-sales ratio, the advertising-to-sales ratio, public-relations-to-sales ratio, fund-raising-to-sales ratio, marketing-research-to-sales ratio, and sales-administration-to-sales ratio. Management needs to track these ratios over time. Small fluctuations can be ignored, while unusually large deviations are a cause for concern and should be investigated.

TABLE 26.2. Natural vs. Functional Accounts

Profit and Loss Statement			
Sales	$ 500,000		
Cost of Goods Sold	250,000		
Gross Profit	250,000		
		Functional Accounts	
		Advertising	Personal Selling
Expenses (Natural Accounts)			
Rent	140,000	$ -	$ 140,000
Salaries	90,000	30,000	60,000
Supplies	10,000	4,000	6,000
Advertising	40,000	40,000	—
Freight	5,000	1,000	4,000
Insurance	2,000	1,000	1,000
Total	$287,000	$76,000	$211,000
Net Profit (Loss)	$ (37,000)		

FINANCIAL CONTROLS

Management uses financial analysis to identify the factors which effect the company's rate of return on net worth. Figure 26.2 provides a profit-and-loss statement, balance sheet, and the factors which determine the return on equity. Return on net worth is the product of two ratios: return on assets and financial leverage. A company can increase its return on equity by increasing either or both of these ratios. Return on assets is a product of two ratios: profit margin and asset turnover. For a nonprofit institution, man-

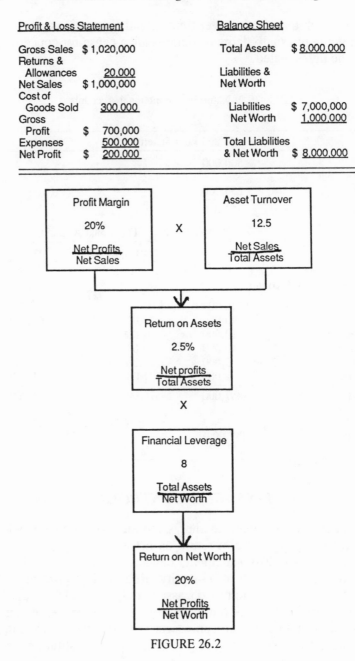

FIGURE 26.2

agement might use "contribution margin" or "contribution to funded reserves" instead of "profit margin." For evaluating overall performance, it doesn't matter so much what we call the variables as long as we realize that financial resources must be accounted for and used efficiently. In our example, provided in Figure 26.2, the return on assets appears to be quite low. Management should review the composition of its assets (e.g., cash, accounts receivable, inventory, and plant and equipment) to see if it could reduce its assets and thereby improve its return on assets and net worth. They should also examine selling and administrative expenses to see if these costs could be reduced. If assets could be reduced by $1,000,000 and expenses decreased by $100,000, the return on assets would be increased to 4.3% and return on net worth would rise to 34.4%.

BUDGETING

What Is a Budget?

A budget represents the organization's objectives expressed in financial terms. It is a plan of anticipated revenues, expenses, and financial position. The budget is a management tool and is used for both planning and control purposes.

The marketing budget encompasses those revenues and expenses which are under the control of the marketing department. The budgeting procedure is quite a detailed and complex process. In addition, it is quite time consuming. It follows that the more complex and detailed the budgeting process, the more management time is required for its preparation. At some point, an organization must decide how important the additional information is which will be generated. The benefits which will accrue from this additional information should be greater than the costs associated with the additional work entailed in creating the more detailed budget. In reality, there are multiple budgets which make up the firm's overall budget. One source identifies 19 different budgets and discusses them at length (Doris, 1975, p. 106). These budgets are as follows:

1. Sales Budget
2. Cost-of-Sales Budget
3. Inventory Increase or Decrease Budget
4. Production Budget
5. Direct Materials Budget
6. Direct Labor Budget
7. Machine-Hour Budget
8. Direct, Indirect Labor Budget
9. Utility Budget
10. Indirect Supplies Budget
11. General Factory Overhead Budget
12. Selling Expense Budget
13. Advertising Expense Budget
14. Administrative Expense Budget
15. Other Operating Income and Expense Budget
16. Nonoperating Income and Expense Budget
17. Profit-and-Loss Budget
18. Capital Expenditure Budget
19. Cash Budget

The marketing budget would be made up of the sales budget, cost-of-sales budget, selling expense budget, and advertising budget. Table 26.3 shows what a marketing budget might be like for a company selling several products. Table 26.4 delineates the more detailed items which might be found in the selling expense budget.

Budgeting provides numerous benefits to an organization. Certainly, budgeting provides a control mechanism for expenses and revenues. In addition, the budget acts as a coordinating device. For example, production must be coordinated with sales. It makes no sense for production to produce materially more or less than what will be sold. Similar discussions can be developed for finance, personnel, and the like. The budget provides the firm with a tangible standard of performance. In turn, the budget becomes a tool for evaluating performance.

Not all firms operate using a budget. Unless the sales forecast is fairly accurate, it is quite difficult to create a reliable budget. Other organizations feel that the budgeting process takes more time than it is worth. Some firms think that budgets can be inflexible and may

TABLE 26.3. Marketing Budget

	Product A	Product B
Sales	$1,000,000	$725,000
Less: Returns and Allowances	(25,000)	(15,000)
Gross Margin	$975,000	$710,000
Less: Cost of Goods Sold	(350,000)	(350,000)
Gross Margin	$625,000	$360,000
Less: Selling and Administrative Expenses		
Office Supplies	(10,000)	(6,000)
Postage	(2,000)	(1,000)
Wages	(200,000)	(150,000)
Research	(100,000)	(80,000)
Legal Expense	(25,000)	(20,000)
Telephone	(60,000)	(50,000)
Equipment	(10,000)	(7,000)
Utilities	(8,000)	(5,000)
Selling Expenses	(15,000)	(10,000)
Advertising Expenses	(10,000)	(7,000)
Sales Promotion Expenses	(9,000)	(6,000)
Contribution Margin	$176,000	$18,000

TABLE 26.4. Selling Expense Budget

Expense	Cost
Office Supplies	$ 3,000
Postage	5,000
Salary	50,000
Commission	150,000
Travel	8,000
Lodging	12,000
Automobile	23,000
Entertainment	9,000
Insurance	3,000
Telephone	8,000
Recruiting	10,000
Training	17,000
Total Selling Expense	$298,000

prevent the organization from taking advantage of market opportunities that have not been anticipated. Inflexibility can also lead to waste.

> Another criticism leveled against budgets is that they lead to waste, because the various departments feel it is necessary to spend budgeted funds regardless of need. The criticism of waste is essentially a reflection of weakness caused by inflexibility in budgeting. Frequently administrative officers plead with their departments to spend all the funds in a certain budget before the end of the period, so the surplus will not revert to a general fund and the amount will not be reduced in the next budget.
>
> . . . Waste in budgeting can also occur when funds are allotted to one budget and then allowed to be transferred to others at the whim of a department head. Executives often find it easier to get funds for one budget than for another. Therefore, they ask for more than is needed in the easy-to-get areas and then later they transfer the surplus to other areas. (Stanton & Buskirk, 1978, pp. 473-74)

Most of the firms that utilize budgets operate on an annual budget basis. Some companies also divide the annual budget into quarterly segments. When deciding how long the budget period should be, a firm is trading off closeness of management control with flexibility and the costs of compiling the budgets. The shorter the budget periods, the more the flexibility and the greater the budgeting costs. In addition, short planning periods tend to produce budgets which are more accurate.

The Budget-Making Process

The first step in creating a budget is developing a sales forecast. Each administrative unit of the sales department must then determine how much money it will need to operate for the coming period.

This is usually accomplished by the tedious task of (1) surveying each of the activities the unit must perform, (2) determining just how many individuals will be required to accomplish the job, and (3) figuring what materials and supplies will be required for them to do it properly. (Stanton & Buskirk, 1978, p. 469)

Once the sales department's budget has been compiled, it is forwarded to the organization's chief financial officer, who disseminates the information to other departments. These departments then prepare their own budgets. These individual departmental budgets are sent to the chief financial executive who compiles the departmental budgets into an overall organizational budget. Figure 26.3 outlines the budget-making process.

Budgeting Approaches

There are two basic methods used to allocate funds to the organizational divisions: line-item budgeting and zero-based budgeting.

Line-Item Budgeting

Line-item budgeting is the traditional method of apportioning corporate funds. Monies are allocated in considerable detail to each identifiable cost center. Under a line-item budget, the sales department might have a selling expense budget as illustrated in Table 26.4. Each item is forecasted and accounted for in considerable detail.

Zero-Based Budgeting

Zero-based budgeting was developed to overcome a problem inherent in traditional budgeting procedures. It is not uncommon for an organization to budget by adjusting the previous period's budgeted amounts. Many times this practice perpetuates activities after their reasons for existence have diminished or passed.

Under zero-based budgeting each period starts from zero. The funds allocated in the previous period have no bearing on what, if anything, will be allotted in the upcoming period. Managers must justify each dollar requested. While this approach ensures that all

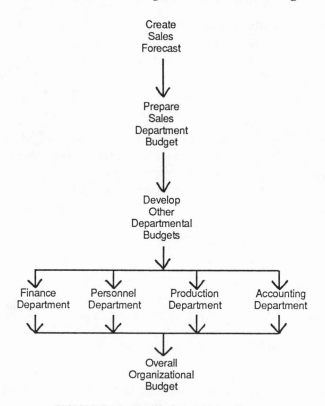

FIGURE 26.3. The Budget-Making Process

the budgeted amounts are necessary, it is extremely time consuming. The question must be raised as to whether the additional managerial time is worth the resulting streamlined budget?

Budget Evaluation

Figure 26.4 is provided to explain the analytical framework associated with the budget evaluation process. A company has a practical capacity at which it can operate. A firm's practical capacity is its ideal capacity less unavoidable interruptions. Forecasted sales will be some percentage of the organization's practical capacity. In Figure 26.4, forecasted sales are 90,000 units, which is 86% of the

FIGURE 26.4. Summary Framework for Analyzing Utilization of Capacity

Time of Computation and Use	(1) Practical Capacity	(2) Master Budget Sales Forecast Capacity
When the master budget is being prepared.	105,000 Units	90,000 Units

Expected Idle Capacity Variance

(1)-(2) = 15,000 units, a measure of the total current expected idle capacity

	(2) Master Budget Sales Forecast Capacity	(3) Scheduled Production	(4) Units Produced and Sold
	90,000	82,000	80,000
At the end of the period, when results are being evaluated.	Sales Forecast Opportunity Variance		Schedule Variance

(2)-(3) = 8,000 units, a measure of the failure of the sales force to get orders equal to the current sales forecast in the master budget

(3)-(4) = 2,000 units, a measure of the failure of the production departments to adhere to production schedules

Total Volume Variance

(2)-(4) = 10,000 units, the difference between master budgeted sales and actual sales

---

Source. From *Accounting for Management Control: An Introduction* (p. 248) by Charles T. Horegren. Englewood Cliffs, NJ: Prentice-Hall, Inc. Copyright 1965.

105,000 unit practical capacity. A firm's scheduled production may not coincide with the sales forecast. This could be true for several reasons. The sales force may not be able to sell at the forecasted level, or there can be lags between the sale and production of the sold units. Scheduled production is 82,000 units, which is 91% of forecasted sales. Eighty thousand (80,000) units were actually produced and sold. The difference between the sales forecast and scheduled production represents the sales forecast opportunity variance. In this case, the sales forecast opportunity variance is 8,000 units and is a measure of the failure of the sales force to get orders equal to projected sales. The difference between scheduled production and actual sales/production is the schedule variance. Figure 26.4 shows a 2,000 unit schedule variance. Schedule variance is a measure of the failure of the production department to meet its scheduled production. The total volume variance is the combination of the sales forecast opportunity variance and the schedule variance, 10,000 units.

Variances can also be expressed in dollars. Assuming a selling price of $15 less variable costs per unit of $12, the unit contribution margin is $3. Fixed costs are $150,000. Table 26.5 expresses the variances in dollars. Table 26.6 depicts the comparison of the budgeted income statement with the actual results.

This discussion and the examples provided in Figure 26.4 and Tables 26.5 and 26.6 have been simplified in two respects. First, most firms have multiple products. With more than one product, this type of analysis is conducted on a product-by-product basis. Second, a uniform contribution margin was assumed. It is not unusual that volume increases are obtained through reducing unit prices. In this case, the dollar measure of the opportunity variance has to be adjusted.

Internal Departmental Conflicts and Budget Trade-offs

Departmental relationships are often characterized by misunderstandings and differing corporate perspectives. Often, there are differences of opinions as to what courses of action are in the best interest of the firm. Some interdepartmental conflicts result from trade-offs between departmental well-being and company well-be-

TABLE 26.5. Dollar Variances*

Master Budget Sales Forecast	Scheduled Production	Actual Production
(90M Units × $3) $270,000	(82M Units × $3) $246,000	(80M Units × $3) $240,000
8M Units @ $3 = $24,000 Sales Forecast Opportunity Variance		2M Units @ $3 = $6,000 Schedule Variance
	10M Units @ $3 $30,000 Total Volume Variance	

*Assumption: Contribution Margin = $3.00

Source. From *Accounting for Management Control: An Introduction* (p. 248) by Charles T. Horegren. Englewood Cliffs, NJ: Prentice-Hall, Inc. Copyright 1965.

ing. Unfortunately, some interdepartmental conflicts are produced by departmental stereotypes and prejudices.

In the typical organization each department has an effect on customer satisfaction through its activities and decisions. Under the marketing concept, it is desirable to coordinate those activities and decisions because customer satisfaction depends on the totality of customer-impinging stimuli, not simply the stimuli managed by the marketing department.

The marketing department is willing to accept this responsibility and use its influence. A marketing vice-president has two tasks: to coordinate the marketing activities of the company, and to deal with the vice-presidents of finance, operations, and so on, on a regular basis so that they develop a deeper appreciation of the benefits of a customer orientation. But there is little agreement on how much influence and authority market-

TABLE 26.6. Budget vs. Actual Income

	Budget 90,000 Units	Actual 80,000 Units	Variance
Sales (@ $15)	$1,350,000	$1,200,000	
Variable Costs (@ $12)	$1,080,000	$960,000	
Contribution Margin (@ $3)	$270,000	$240,000	$30,000
Fixed Costs	$150,000	$150,000	—
Net Income	$120,000	$90,000	$30,000

Departmental Analysis

Sales Department

Sales department failed to obtain enough orders: (90,000 units budgeted – 82,000 units scheduled for production) × $3 = Salesforce Opportunity Variance $24,000

Production Department

Production departments failed to meet production schedule: (82,000 units scheduled – 80,000 units produced and sold) × $3 = Schedule Variance $6,000

Total Volume Variance

Total Volume Variance (Explains difference in net income) $30,000

*Assumptions: Selling Price = $15.00
              Variable Costs = $12.00
              Contribution Margin = $3.00
              Fixed Costs = $150,000

Source. From *Accounting for Management Control: An Introduction* (p. 248) by Charles T. Horegren. Englewood Cliffs, NJ: Prentice-Hall, Inc. Copyright 1965.

ing should have over the other departments to bring about co-ordinated marketing.

Other departments may resist bending their efforts to the will of the marketing department. Just as marketing stresses the customer's point of view, other departments stress the importance of their tasks. (Kotler, 1984, p. 729)

It is human nature for department heads to define company problems and objectives in terms of their point of view. Table 26.7 summarizes the main point-of-view differences between the marketing department and other departments within the organization.

For example, the finance department is concerned with control considerations: strict rationales for spending, hard and fast budgets, and pricing to cover costs. Marketing, on the other hand, is concerned with intuitive arguments for spending, flexible budgets to meet changing needs, and pricing to further market development.

These interdepartmental conflicting interests must be harmonized before the budget is "put to bed." The process of harmonizing these differing points of view requires a series of trade-offs on the part of all concerned. Normally neither department gets everything they want. These trade-offs constrict marketing in many areas: price setting, product features, service benefits, and so on.

The medical area has historically operated as a cost-free endeavor. This has led to the perspective that any health or medical condition can be overcome by a sufficient application of money, equipment, medicine, and physician power. The HMO concept implicitly challenges this method of operation by introducing a number of cost-service trade-offs.

> HMOs succeed to the extent to which they put their physician providers at risk . . . (generally) patients are only reimbursed for care approved by an HMO physician. Therefore, they are "locked in" to the plan's medical staff. Second, the physicians are compensated in such a way that risk is reintroduced as a factor in medical decisionmaking. There are three general ways of compensating HMO physicians, depending on the type of HMO. (See Table 26.8.)

> The impact of these compensation schemes, in decreasing order of effectiveness, is to make the physician economically liable. If the HMO fails or loses money, he personally is at risk. (Sweeney & Rakowski, 1985, p. 6-7)

TABLE 26.7.

SUMMARY OF ORGANIZATIONAL CONFLICTS BETWEEN MARKETING AND OTHER DEPARTMENTS		
Department	Their Emphasis	Marketing's Emphasis
R&D	Basic research	Applied research
	Intrinsic quality	Perceived quality
	Functional features	Sales features
Engineering	Long design lead time	Short design lead time
	Few models	Many models
	Standard components	Custom components
Purchasing	Narrow product line	Broad product line
	Standard parts	Nonstandard parts
	Price of material	Quality of material
	Economical lot sizes	Large lot sizes to avoid stockouts
	Purchasing at infrequent intervals	Immediate purchasing for customer needs
Manufacturing	Long production lead time	Short production lead time
	Long runs with few models	Short runs with many models
	No model changes	Frequent model changes
	Standard orders	Custom orders
	Ease of fabrication	Aesthetic appearance
	Average quality control	Tight quality control
Finance	Strict rationales for spending	Intuitive arguments for spending
	Hard and fast budgets	Flexible budgets to meet changing needs
	Pricing to cover costs	Pricing to further market development
Accounting	Standard transactions	Special terms and discounts
	Few reports	Many reports
Credit	Full financial disclosures by customers	Minimum credit examination of customers
	Low credit risks	Medium credit risks
	Tough credit terms	Easy credit terms
	Tough collection procedures	Easy collection procedures

TABLE 26.8. HMO Compensation Methods

Model	Organizational Description	Compensation Method
Staff model HMO	Physicians are full-time employees of HMO	Straight salary, perhaps with bonuses for coming in under budget.
Group model HMO	Physicians work for a group which is contracted by HMO for services. Group must do 50% of business with HMO if the plan is qualified.	Group receives a capitation fee (fixed amount per member) in advance each month. Revenues shared out to member physicians. Group must absorb losses above capitation, but keeps savings.
Individual Practice Association (IPA)	Physicians keep individual practices and offices, but agree to treat HMO patients.	The HMO is a claims paying agent for the IPA physicians. Physicians get usual customary or reasonable fees or an agreed amount, but 10-15% of fees are held back until year-end. Then losses are taken out of hold-back; savings are shared.

In the area of cost-service and trade-offs, HMOs have proven to be quality health care providers. A survey, conducted by Johns Hopkins University of 26 operational HMOs competing with fee-for-service insurance over a 20-year period, has demonstrated conclusively that HMOs are equal or superior to fee-for-service in quality of care (Cunningham & Williamson, 1980, pp. 4-25).

. . . if an HMO physician skimped on care to save plan funds, it would be a false economy. Improperly treated patients would only return at a later date with more severe and more costly conditions. In short, the balancing forces of cost-consciousness and quality care impel the HMO physician to a delicate cost-service balance. (Sweeney & Rakowski, 1985, p. 7)

EFFICIENCY CONTROLS

If an analysis found that the company were earning poor profits in regard to a specific product, territory, or market, a question would be raised as to whether there might be a more efficient way to manage the salesforce, advertising, and sales promotion efforts. Table 26.9 lists some of the primary analyses that should be conducted. In addition, a similar examination of distribution efficiency, public relations, and fund-raising activities should be undertaken.

STRATEGIC CONTROLS

Periodically, companies need to examine their overall marketing performance. Because of the ever-changing external environment, there is a likelihood of rapid obsolescence of marketing policies, objectives, strategies, and programs. For companies to stay abreast of change, a marketing audit is used. A marketing audit critically examines marketing's environment, objectives, strategies, organization, systems, productivity, and functions. Appendix A to this chapter outlines the comprehensive questions addressed by the marketing audit.

SUMMARY

The organization expresses its objectives for the period in financial terms with the budget. In addition, it is both a planning tool and an evaluation mechanism. Most firms operate with an annual budget. Many of these organizations also break their budget down into quarterly increments. While shorter budget periods require more

TABLE 26.9. Efficiency Analyses

Sales Force Efficiency	Advertising Efficiency	Sales Promotion Efficiency
Average number of sales calls per salesperson per day	Advertising cost per 1,000 buyers reached overall, for each: media category, and media vehicle	Percentage of sales sold on program Display costs per sales dollar
Average sales call per customer contact	Percentage of audience who noted, saw/associated and read most for each media vehicle	Percentage of coupons redeemed
Average dollar sales per call	Consumer opinions on the ad content and effectiveness	Number of inquiries resulting from a demonstration
Average cost per sales call	Before-after measures of attitude toward the product	Sales promotion costs as a percentage of total sales
Entertainment cost per sales call		
Travel cost per sales call	Number of inquiries stimulated by the ad	
Percentage of orders per 100 sales calls		
Number of new customers per period	Cost per inquiry	
Number of lost customers per period	Advertising costs as a percentage of total sales	
Sales force cost as a percentage of total sales		

management time in the preparation process, they are more flexible and tend to be more accurate.

The budgeting process starts with the development of the sales forecast. After the marketing department has prepared its budget, the firm's financial officer disseminates this information to the other departments. They, in turn, prepare their budgets. The chief financial officer then combines all of the departmental estimates to develop the overall corporate budget.

Most organizations use a line-item approach to budgeting. Under this approach, funds are allocated to individual line items such as telephone, travel, and staff salaries. Zero-based budgeting is an alternative approach. With this method, each period starts from zero and previous periods' budgets or actual expenditures have no bearing on what will be allocated in the forthcoming period.

Deviations from budget are analyzed to determine what problems are being encountered. Major budget variances can result for many reasons: sales could fall short of expectations or production could fail to meet its budgeted production schedule.

The budgeting process entails numerous trade-offs. These trade-offs result from interdepartmental conflicts. There can be differences of opinions as to what is in the best interest of the firm, differences between departmental well-being and company well-being, and departmental stereotypes and prejudices.

It is the obligation of marketing managers to effectively plan their activities and then evaluate the results to see if planned outcomes have been achieved. This evaluation process should take place using several different control procedures: (1) annual controls, (2) financial controls, and (4) strategic controls.

Annual control procedures use analyses of sales, market share, and marketing costs. These analyses are conducted on both a macro and micro level. Financial controls identify the factors which affect the company's rate of return on net worth. Efficiency controls are used to determine if there are more efficient ways to manage various departments, such as the sales force, advertising, public relations, and fund raising. Strategic controls are utilized to examine the company's overall performance. Marketing exists in a very fluid environment which is likely to cause an obsolescence in strategies and procedures. A comprehensive marketing audit should be used to evaluate the firm's current position.

REFERENCES

Cunningham, Frances C. and Williamson, John W., M.D., "How Does the Quality of Health Care in HMOs Compare to that in Other Settings?", *The Group Health Journal* (Winter 1980); 4-25.

Doris, Lillian (ed.), *Corporate Treasurer's and Controller's Encyclopedia* (rev.) New York: Prentice-Hall, Inc., 1975.

Horngren, Charles T., *Accounting for Management Control: An Introduction.* Englewood Cliffs, NJ: Prentice-Hall, Inc., 1965, p. 248.

Kotler, Philip, *Marketing Management: Analysis, Planning, and Control* (5th ed.). Englewood Cliffs, NJ: Prentice-Hall, Inc., 1984.

Ibid., p. 731.

Stanton, William J. and Buskirk, Richard H., Management of the Sales Force (5th ed.). Homewood, IL: Richard D. Irwin, Inc., 1978.

Sweeney, Robert E. and Rakowski, James P., "Logistical Considerations in the Prepaid Health Industry: An Exploratory Analysis", *Health Marketing Quarterly* (Vol. 2, Nos. 2/3, Winter 1984/Spring 1985), pp. 6-7.

Appendix A to Chapter 26
Marketing Audit Questions*

Marketing Commitment: Corporate Culture

1. Does the chief executive believe in marketing planning and is formal planning ingrained with all top managers?
2. Are plans prepared with the participation of functional managers or dictated by the president?
3. Do you have a coordinated marketing program or an isolated sales department?
4. Are you using the computer as a marketing tool and do your managers understand its capabilities?
5. Do you implement a marketing plan, measure performance, and adjust for deviation?
6. Are all marketing functions under the direction of one executive who reports to the chief executive officer?

Products/Services: The Reason for Existence

1. Is the product/service free from deadwood? Do you have a well-defined, continuous program to weed out unprofitable products and add new ones?
2. What is the life-cycle stage?
3. How will user demands or trends affect you?
4. Are you a leader in new product innovation?
5. Do you have a systematic liaison with the research/development group?
6. Are inexpensive methods used to estimate new product potentials before considerable amounts are spent on R&D and marketing introduction?
7. Are new products introduced with forecasts and budgets?
8. Have you investigated possible advantages resulting from new materials or technology?
9. Do you have different quality levels for different markets?

---

*Reprinted from *Marketing News*, published by the American Marketing Association. In Hal W. Goetsch, "Marketing Audit Questions," *Marketing News*, Section 2 (March 18, 1983): 14. Adapted with permission.

10. Are packages/brochures effective salesmen for the products/ services they present?
11. Do you present product services in the most appealing colors (formats) for markets being served?
12. Are there features or benefits to exploit?
13. Has the safety of the product/service been brought to a satisfactory level?
14. Is the level of customer service adequate?
15. How are quality and reliability viewed by customers?

Customer: User Profiles

1. Who is the current and potential customer?
2. Are customers younger or older, on average, than those of competitors?
3. Are there geographic aspects of use: regional, rural, urban?
4. Why do people buy the product/service; what motivates their preference?
5. Who makes buying decisions; when, where?
6. What is the frequency and quantity of use?

Markets: Where Products/Services Are Sold

1. How is the market shaped; where is the center of gravity?
2. Have you identified and measured major segments?
3. Are you overlooking small but profitable segments of the market in trying to satisfy the tastes of the majority?
4. Are the markets for the products/services expanding or declining?
5. Should different segments be developed; gaps in penetration?
6. Do segments require marketing differentiation?

Sales History: Previous Results

1. How do sales break down within the product/service?
2. Do you know where sales are coming from; segments and customer classification?
3. Are there abnormal cycles or seasonalities and, if so, how do you plan for them?
4. Do sales match previous forecasts?

5. Which territories/markets do not yield potential?
6. Are growth and profit trends reflected?

Competitors: Their Influence

1. Who are the principal competitors, how are they positioned and where do they seem to be headed?
2. What are their market shares?
3. What features of competitors' products/services stand out?
4. What are their strengths and weaknesses?
5. Is the market easily entered or dominated?

Pricing: Profitability Planning

1. What are the objectives of current pricing policy: acquiring, defending, or expanding?
2. Are price limitations inherent in the marketplace?
3. Are price policies set to produce volume or profit?
4. How does pricing compare with competition in similar levels of quality?
5. Do you understand how your prices are set?
6. Is the price list understandable and current?
7. Does cost information show profitability of each item?
8. What is the history of price deals, discounts, and promotions?
9. Are middlemen making money from the line?
10. Can the product/service support advertising or promotion programs?
11. Will size or manufacturing process require more volume?
12. Are there cost problems to overcome?
13. Are profitability and marketing cost known by the customers?

Marketing Channels: Selling Paths

1. Does the system offer the best access to all target markets?
2. Do product/service characteristics require special channels?
3. Have you analyzed each market with a view toward setting up the most profitable type of presentation: direct versus reps, master distributors or dealers, etc.?
4. What are the trends in distribution methods?

5. Do you provide cost-effective marketing support, selling aids, and sales tools?

Sales Administration: Selling Efficiency

1. Have you analyzed communications and designed paperwork or computer programs to provide meaningful management information?
2. Are customers getting coverage in proportion to their potential?
3. Are sales costs properly planned and controlled?
4. Does the compensation plan provide optimum incentive and security at reasonable cost?
5. Is performance measured against potential?
6. Are selling expenses proportionate to results and potentials within markets or territories?
7. Are there deficiencies in recruitment, selection, training, motivation, supervision, performance, promotion, or compensation?
8. Do you provide effective selling aids and sales tools?

Delivery and Inventory: Physical Performance

1. Are adequate inventories kept in the right mix?
2. Is inventory turnover acceptable?
3. Do orders receive efficient, timely processing?
4. Are shipping schedules and promises kept?
5. Is the product/service delivered in good condition?
6. Are forecasts for production planning acceptable?
7. How does performance compare with competition?
8. Are warehouses and distribution points properly located?

Advertising: Media Program

1. Are media objectives and strategies linked to the marketing plan?
2. What are the objectives of the ad program?
3. How is media effectiveness measured?
4. Is advertising integrated with promotion and sales activity?
5. Is the ad agency's effectiveness periodically evaluated?

6. Do you dictate copy theme and content to the agency?
7. Are you spending realistically, in relation to budget?
8. Do you use trade publications effectively?
9. How do you choose the ad agency?

Promotion: Sales Inducement

1. Does the promotion support a marketing objective?
2. Was it carefully budgeted?
3. Is it integrated with advertising and selling activity?
4. How is it measured for results?
5. What was the reason for its success or failure?
6. Are slogans, trademarks, logos, and brands being used effectively?
7. Is point-of-sale material cost-effective?
8. Do you have satisfactory displays of products/services?
9. Are you effectively using coupons, tie-ins, incentives, sampling stuffers, combination offers?
10. How do you evaluate trade shows for effectiveness?

Public Relations: Prestige Building

1. Do you have a clear idea of the type of company you want people to think you are?
2. Do you have a consistent communications program?
3. What kinds of ideas and impressions have you created about your company?
4. Do you really know what your image is on a factual basis, or are you relying on customers' letters, salesmen's reports, and publicity in the press?
5. Does your company name, brand, and logo add to or conflict with the image you want?
6. Are you getting a share of favorable, unpaid publicity in editorials of the media?

CHAPTER 27

Organization, Budgeting, and Control Systems

William J. Winston

CONTROL SYSTEMS

A control system is required to measure the performance and effectiveness of the marketing plan in achieving the plan's marketing goals and objectives. A control system is the step necessary to assure the plan is adjusted if necessary. Actual outcomes of the plan are measured against the original projected outcomes. Since every marketing plan will require some adjustment and refinement, it is important to remember that the marketing plan is not fixed. It has to be a flexible process which can be updated and altered when it is required. In addition, the planning process is never-ending so the control process must also be implemented periodically.

Control systems need to be an essential ingredient of the planning process. The feedback system:

1. Pinpoints problems and deviations;
2. Provides a mechanism for adjustment; and
3. Accumulates data for future planning.

The control or feedback system reflects the health organization's performance in obtaining its marketing objectives through the im-

Reprinted from William J. Winston, *How to Write a Marketing Plan for Health Care Organizations*, pp. 95–107, © 1985 by The Haworth Press, Inc.

plementation of the strategic marketing plan. Since the goals and objectives are the comparison base it is important to make these goals and objectives as specific and measurable as possible. Some of these outcomes can be patient revenue, costs, profits, number of patients, utilization of services, changes in goodwill and image in the community, levels of quality of care, consumer preferences, etc. The control process is integrated into the planning process by the following flow:

PLANNING PROCESS ————→ PLAN IMPLEMENTATION
PLAN RESULTS ———→EVALUATION OF RESULTS VERSUS
GOALS AND OBJECTIVES ————————→DECISIONS ON
ALTERATIONS IN PLAN ————→PLANNING PROCESS.

The information flow is a key ingredient to a quality control system. The decision of which managers will receive what kinds and amounts of information in what time frames is the framework of a quality control process. A new planning cycle is initiated when these decisions and alterations have been completed. The base of a quality control system is the process of continuous reports back to managers reflecting the plan's performance level versus its goals and objectives.

The ingredients of a control system are

1. Marketing goals and objectives;
2. Actual results of plan;
3. Projected results of plan;
4. Variance between actual and perceived outcomes; and
5. Decisions about changes in plan.

Performance should be evaluated on a monthly or on a bi-monthly basis. The plan should be evaluated frequently for alterations and identification of deviations. This evaluation process can be one of the most important steps in the entire planning process. It is the plan's only feedback system to boards, executives, and managers about the success of the strategic marketing plan. Therefore, an effective control system is required to measure performance, provide for effective action to correct deviations from expected standards, and communicate to management. Performance must be measured and analyzed as early as possible after implementation. When deviations are detected, their cause should be uncovered. Some questions which need to be asked when evaluating a plan's performance include the following:

1. Is utilization increasing at the expected rate?
2. Are referrals increasing?
3. Are the marketing goals and objectives realistic?
4. Is the marketing mix of pricing, place, product, and promotion correct?
5. Is additional marketing audit information needed?
6. Is enough money being spent on implementing the strategies?
7. Should we switch some of the primary and secondary targets?
8. Are marketing expenditures at levels planned?
9. Are the positioning strategies being imprinted in the minds of our consumers?
10. Should we evaluate (control) the outcomes of the plan more frequently?
11. Is our internal staff playing their roles in marketing the organization?
12. Should we switch some resources from one strategy to another which is being more effective?

Remember that the plan has not actually been implemented yet when the control system is being developed. This is the reason a control step is included in our strategic marketing plan. When the time comes for evaluating the performance of the plan, the marketer will be ready to implement the system.

MARKETING BUDGET

A projected marketing budget is an integral part of the marketing plan. The marketing budget reflects a projected total cost of developing, planning, and implementing the marketing program. The budget should include all direct and indirect expenses you expect to spend for successful completion of the strategic marketing plan. It needs to reflect, for example, a three-month development and planning process and a nine-month implementation process.

The typical types of expenses for a marketing program include the following:

I. *Marketing administration salaries and benefits*

A. Marketing Director
B. Public Relations Director
C. Marketing Research Assistant
D. Fund Raiser
E. Director of Planning
F. Administrative Assistant/Secretarial
G. Advertising Firm Fees
H. Public Relations Firm
I. Mail Order House

II. *Rent and utilities*

A. Office Space
B. Storage Space for Brochures and Supplies
C. Telephone, Lights, etc.

III. *Office supplies*

A. Paper
B. Equipment
C. Word Processors

IV. *Travel*

A. Meeting Registration Fees
B. Conventions
C. Meals
D. Hotels, Airfares, Car Rental

V. *Promotional expenses*

A. Shows, Tours, Films, Open-Houses, Printing, Lectures, Seminars, Workshops, Posters, Mailers, Postage, Newsletters, Mail Order Houses, Brochures, Typesetting, Cocktail/Dinners, Signs, Newspaper Ads, Media Coverage, etc.

Marketing activities incur a considerable amount of expenses. For example, a decision might be made to mail out a brochure. The expenses involved include: designing the brochure, typesetting the brochure, printing the brochure, paper for brochure, stuffing by mail order houses, postage, envelopes, purchase of labels, labeling of envelopes, etc. As you can tell, each marketing activity has considerable costs which are not typically considered. Marketing can be very expensive when marketing research, advertising, and public relations firms are utilized. The projected budget needs to include as many expected and realistic expenditures as possible. One mistake is not to call for advice when developing an estimate. For example, very few people really know what its costs to rent time on a radio station or rent a billboard. Call the appropriate resources for accurate estimates.

A guideline for a total budget for marketing activities including marketing research, planning, fund development, and public relations can be about 1-3% of an organization's total annual budget. Most hospitals, for example, still spend less than 2% on these functions. In today's competitive marketplace, health organizations need to allocate a share closer to the high end of the scale for effectiveness. One of the key reasons for failure in marketing programs is the lack of financial support for the marketing function.

ORGANIZATIONAL DESIGN FOR MARKETING IN HEALTH ORGANIZATIONS

As part of the strategic marketing plan a design of the organizational chart for the marketing function is included. There are many different forms of organization charts for marketing in health care organizations. This is especially true when some organizations' full-time directors of marketing, part-time directors, and others share the marketing function among all of their administrators. *Two important common ingredients in the organizational chart is the necessity of having the director of marketing report directly to the executive director and the functions of planning, public relations, fund raising, and marketing research report directly to the director of marketing.*

As an example, a proposed organizational chart for marketing in a large community hospital might look like the following.

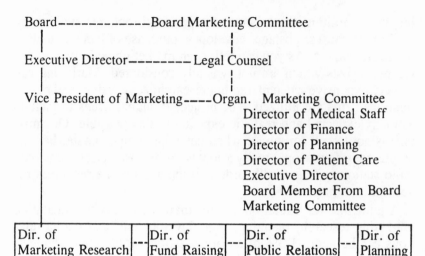

THE MARKETING FUNCTION

The marketing director's role needs to include:

1. Setting up the marketing plan;
2. Directing the execution of the marketing plan; and
3. Evaluating and controlling the marketing plan.

The marketing director's position requires the ability and knowledge to do the following:

1. Know what the markets are;
2. Know where the markets are;
3. Know how to provide a quality health service;
4. Know how to provide the right service at the right time to the right target group at the right price;
5. Know how to be selective in targeting;
6. Possess an effective communications system including all four components of the marketing mix;
7. Continually strive to improve the service;
8. Continually strive to increase the marketshare;
9. Develop a strong relationship with internal staff and peers for marketing support; and

10. Develop a strong relationship with the board and executive director.

KEY TASKS OF THE DIRECTOR OF MARKETING

There are many different roles in which the marketing director must represent and perform. Most of these duties are typically found in informal job descriptions. They include being a(n):

1. *Educator*: The director of marketing will be continually educating its publics and staff about the importance, functions, and applications of marketing.

2. *Researcher*: In order to understand the consumers he/she serves, the director of marketing needs to research consumer behavior, audit information, and competitor data.

3. *Planner*: By being in charge of the strategic planning process the marketer will need to be familiar with the different planning methodologies that are current in the field.

4. *Coordinator*: Coordinating and mobilizing marketing programs and resource allocation are a main function of the marketer.

5. *Liaison*: The marketing director is a liaison with the community. The director represents the organization with all of the health service's publics. He/she also is the main lobbyist with special interest groups and legislative bodies.

6. *Media spokesperson*: Many times the director represents the organization with the press and media, especially if a director of public relations or communications director does not exist.

7. *Marketing manager*: The director is in charge of multiple people and disciplines including research, planning, fund raising, board relations, etc. This requires excellent management abilities.

8. *Politician*: The marketing function requires tremendous internal political ability when dealing with power positions and territorial domains within the organization. The marketer is also the main lobbyist for the organization by interacting with government agencies and special interest groups.

9. *Forecaster*: The marketer makes forecast of potential demand, utilization trends, resource requirements, and environmental changes.

10. *Communicator/promoter*: The marketer is a promoter for the

organization. Charisma, personal energy, and ambition are important qualifications for the position. Excellent communication skills as well as technical marketing abilities are also important.

11. *Advisor/consultant*: Advising the executive director and board about potential changes or resource allocation decisions are part of the job. Giving advice is a key component of the position for members of the medical staff, regular management staff, etc.

12. *Change master*: The health environment is constantly changing. The marketing director must be able to identify these changes, recommend actions related to these changes, and be able to evaluate the potential impact on the organization of these changes. The marketer must anticipate, evaluate, and manage change.

The marketing function in the organization is not a vogue or a passing fad. The competition and reimbursement trends in the health field are real. Only those who have strong marketing talent on their management team will be able to survive in the coming years.

TRENDS IN SELECTION OF MARKETING DIRECTORS

It has been estimated by the American Marketing Association that over half of the hospitals in the United States will have a director of marketing by the late 1980s. This is a far cry from the less than 10% in 1980. Hospitals, HMOs, nursing homes, proprietary chains, home care agencies, same-day surgery centers, and other types of delivery mechanisms are seeking out professional assistance in marketing. Unfortunately, the early 1980s witnessed a trend for health organizations to attempt to make marketers out of planners, public relations directors, advertisers, community relations directors, and fund raisers. In fact, in most surveys three out of every four marketing directors possess no marketing background and they have been in their positions less than three years. In addition, the high expectations of what marketing will achieve and this lack of professional training in marketing has created a very high turnover rate of less than three years tenure in these positions.

The marketing directors in hospitals, for example, are coming from many different occupational and educational backgrounds. In fact, a very small percentage of today's marketing directors have had any service, industrial, or consumer goods experience. Either these professionals know the health industry well and are expected to learn marketing or they have strong marketing backgrounds with very little knowledge of the health industry. The directors are being derived from health insurance firms, industrial corporations, government agencies, health associations, consulting firms, consumer goods industries, HMOs, pharmaceutical and supply firms, and other sources. This trend is very typical in health care as there is a time lag between the demand for select backgrounds and the supply of qualified and trained personnel. Unfortunately, health administration education usually lags behind the needs of the marketplace. Speaking of education, it appears that most marketing directors have a graduate degree in health care administration, marketing, management, planning, social sciences, or physical sciences. This will shift toward a greater emphasis in health marketing and planning as the scope of the study advances as a specialty area in health administration education.

Health care marketing directors across the country are also still not equivalent in their functional areas to their counterparts in other industries. For example, most marketing directors in health care still are not organizationally settled with public relations, fund raising, community relations, marketing research, lobbying, and patient liaison activities reporting to this position. In many instances, the marketing function is on the same organizational level as these other areas. Probably the greatest area of activity for marketing directors still lies in planning, public relations, and promotion. One important area, physician and staff relations, appears to be negligible in most hospitals. In addition, the level of vice-presidency is not yet widespread for the marketing position. The titles of director, assistant administrator, planner, community relations director, and others prevail.

All of these characteristics of the state of the art of health marketing indicate that health marketing is becoming more accepted, understood, and utilized in health organizations. However, the learning process is slow while the demand for the service is high. It will be a decade before qualified marketing directors will be available for organizations seeking to fill well-defined marketing director positions. Organizations still have a considerable amount of learning to do about the need and overall application of marketing, while marketers require greater amounts of specific education in health care marketing and planning. When I was involved in developing one of the first graduate courses for practitioners in health care marketing over ten years ago I never envisioned such a spiraling interest in the scope of study and application. It is an exciting discipline which will continue to mature into an advanced management tool for health and human service administrators.

SUMMARY:
ORGANIZATIONAL, BUDGETING, AND CONTROL SYSTEMS

As the final steps in the marketing plan, a thorough control system needs to be established to measure the effectiveness of the marketing plan. In other words, the control system answers the question, "How well did we meet the goals and objectives that were laid out in the beginning of the marketing plan?" This control system allows for the identification of any problems or deviations, and lays the groundwork for adjustments in the plan. No prior step in the plan should be considered fixed. Fine tuning of the plan is usually required for successful programs.

In addition, the marketing function in terms of organizational structure requires attention. Exactly who is going to be responsible for implementing and monitoring the marketing plan?

Of course, no marketing plan would be implemented without an accurate forecast of what it is going to cost. The budget process may be one of the most important areas to address when attempting to have administration or the board agree upon the implementation of the marketing plan.

The reader should have derived an understanding of: (1) the purpose, the importance, and basic framework for a control system in the plan; (2) the role and tasks of a marketing director; and (3) the systematic process for creating a marketing budget.

CASE EXAMPLE:
JOB DESCRIPTION OF VICE-PRESIDENT
OF MARKETING FOR A COMMUNITY HOSPITAL

The following provides a detailed example of the job description for the Vice-President of Marketing for a typical community hospital. Of course the size of the hospital and budget constraints will expand or contract the human resources related to this description. This description is based on a composite from various marketing directors around the country.

Position title: Vice-President of Marketing, Stratmore Hospital

Reports to: Chief Executive Officer

Other positions on same line of authority:
Vice-President of Finance
Vice-President of Patient Care

Supervises:
Director of Public Relations
Director of Planning
Director of Fund Raising
Director of Patient/Community Relations
Director of New Service Planning (including Marketing Research)

Basic function:
Responsible for planning, directing, controlling, and coordinating the overall marketing activities of the hospital in order to meet or exceed organizational goals within approved constraints established by the Board of Directors.

Adjunct reporting areas:
Directs the marketing subcommittee of the Board of Directors.
Directs the Organizational Marketing Committee
Works closely with general counsel and medical staff to insure hospital's marketing activities are conducted in accordance with regulations, and ethical and medical standards.

Works closely with Vice-President of Finance and Vice-President of Patient Services.

Works closely with operating managers of departments and service centers to insure effective coordination between day-to-day operations and marketing goals, objectives, strategies, and tactics.

Major responsibilities:

I. Coordinates all marketing, public relations, planning, fund raising, and community relations functions for the hospital.

II. Develops for approval by the CEO and Board of Directors short- and long-term marketing goals and objectives.

III. Develops for approval by the board and CEO a short- and long-term marketing plan for the hospital.

IV. Coordinates the overall strategic plan for the organization including planning for financial, organizational, human resource, and marketing goals and objectives.

V. Coordinates decisions related to service design, access to care, service pricing, and promotional activities (four P's of marketing mix).

VI. Directs the development of strategies and tactics for achievement of goals related to:

    expansion
    community outreach
    new service development
    service mix composition
    media selection
    pricing policies
    reimbursement contingencies
    promotional scheduling
    image and positioning of services, etc.

VII. Directs the execution of approved marketing and strategic plans.

VIII. Reviews and controls hospital performance relation:

    revenue performance against plan
    competitive position in the marketplace
    market share by service type and target group
    utilization rates
    image and community perception rates

IX. Coordinates the collection of marketing research and audit information for identifying target groups and trend analysis.

X. Keeps abreast of all key economic and market environmental changes affecting the hospital and the industry.

XI. Maintains a strong network with other marketing directors, local and national marketing associations, legislative and regulatory agencies, competitors, consumer and special interest groups, general community leaders, health and medical associations and unions, medical providers affiliated with the hospital, and the advisory and board members.

XII. Represents the hospital at appropriate industry, trade, and community functions.

XIII. Coordinates the development of new services based on market analysis and within local regulatory constraints.

XIV. Directs and coordinates all fund raising activities related to the Director of Fund Development, Board of Directors, advisory groups, and volunteers.

XV. Coordinates internal training for staff, board members, and medical providers on their roles in marketing their services and the hospital.

XVI. Maintains strong relations with key members of the medical staff who play an administrative or political role related to potential effectiveness of marketing activities.

XVII. Insures the hospital's strategic plan and marketing plan is in tune with industry trends and market opportunities.

XVIII. Coordinates all contracting and negotiation for the formulation of new delivery modes, i.e., preferred provider organization, health maintenance organization, mergers, etc.

XIX. Directs all administrative planning and marketing committees.

XX. Directs all advertising campaigns with appropriate marketing resources such as advertising agencies, consultants, planning firms, marketing research organizations, etc.

Part IX

Public Relations and Fund Raising

CHAPTER 28

Introduction to Public Relations and Fund Raising

Robert L. Berl

Public relations involves those promotional activities designed to create and maintain favorable relations between the company and its publics such as clients, employees, stockholders, government and regulatory officials, and the community. These activities are very important to health care organizations and social service agencies. Many of these institutions, particularly those in the nonprofit sector with extremely limited advertising budgets, must place significant dependence on public relations.

THE RELATIONSHIP BETWEEN PUBLIC RELATIONS AND MARKETING

Like advertising, sales promotion, and personal selling, public relations is a communication tool. However, the following differences between public relations and marketing are evident:

1. Public relations is primarily a communication tool, whereas marketing also includes need assessment, product development, pricing, and distribution.
2. Public relations seeks to influence attitudes, whereas marketing tries to elicit specific behaviors, such as purchase, joining, voting and so on.

3. Public relations does not define the goals of the organization, whereas marketing is intimately involved in defining the business' mission, customers, and services (Kotler, 1982, p. 382).

Table 28.1 compares marketing and the firm's public relations function.

THE PUBLIC RELATIONS MIX

The organization's public relations mix includes institutional advertising, publicity, face-to-face communications, and other image creation techniques. Figure 28.1 depicts this process.

Institutional Advertising

Institutional advertising deals with the image of an organization or an industry rather than a specific product. It tries to develop goodwill. For example, many of the oil companies used institutional advertising during the oil boycott of the early 1970s when they were being criticized for making too much profit. The ads concentrated on informing the public of their quest for new oil sources.

Publicity

Publicity differs from the marketing communications tool of advertising in the following ways:

1. Publicity is not paid for by the firm.
2. Publicity has no identified sponsor.
3. The firm does not control the content of the coverage, although it may have initiated the media interest and supplied the information included.
4. The firm cannot schedule repetitions of the publicity material.
5. Publicity is presented as news by the media rather than as a persuasive ad, and, therefore, may have more credibility than advertising that ordinarily is set apart from broadcast programs or editorial content in print media (Schoell & Ivy, 1982, p. 496).

TABLE 28.1. Sizing Up Marketing versus Public Relations

Marketing	Public Relations
A planned system of achieving objectives	A tool, vehicle, channel to communicate messages favoring the sender
Very directive in method	Most often generalized in method
Internal management of time, effort, and investment	Often reactive to public statements, events, occurrences; sometimes dictated by whim instead of by management planning
Target oriented	Public oriented
Strategy oriented	Dependent on will, as well as mood, of media persons
Selective in use and investment in tools	Reliance upon traditional promotional publications and publicity; not too selective in tool preparation
Focused on knowing client or patient desires	Focused on knowledge of management predilections, directives, likes, and dislikes
Focused on exchanges of values	Focused on hopes, threats, incomplete actions, and decisions
Accent on controlled promotional channels	Accent on partially controlled promotional channels
Based on a marketing plan or system	Based on a possible publicity plan, budget, or orders from management
Heavy stress on projects, programs	Heavy stress on publications, publicity
Judged by project completion, thoroughness, interrelationships with internal and outside groups	Judged on ability to produce publications, change agency image, amass newspaper clippings, and draw grateful thanks from patients/clients
Often reports directly to highest administrative officer	Often reports directly to an associate executive director

Source. From *Marketing Health and Human Services* (p. 227) by Robert Rubright and Dan MacDonald. Rockville, MD: Aspen Publishers, Inc. Copyright 1981. Reprinted with permission.

FIGURE 28.1. Public Relations Mix

Source. From *Marketing: A Managerial Approach* (p. 287) by William H. Cunningham and Isabella C. M. Cunningham. Cincinnati, OH: South-Western Publishing Co. Copyright 1981. Adapted by permission.

The following example will illustrate some of the differences between publicity and advertising. A local hospital sends the newspaper a two-paragraph press release and picture on the promotion of one of its executive personnel. The newspaper will decide whether to use the information at all, and, if used, whether the picture will be shown and how much of the copy will be used. What is likely to occur is that the promotion will be reported using the picture and a couple of lines of copy.

Face-to-Face Communications

Face-to-face communications includes such public relations tools as speeches, audiovisual presentations, and inviting members of the community to tour the firm's facilities. Some college recruiters now use audiovisual aids to illustrate life at their institutions.

THE PUBLIC RELATIONS PROCESS

The following five steps are associated with the public relations process: (1) identifying the organization's relevant publics; (2) measuring images and attitudes of relevant publics toward the organization; (3) establishing image and attitude goals for the key publics; (4) developing cost-effective public relations strategies; and (5) implementing actions and evaluating results (Kotler, 1982, p. 382).

An organization's publics include its clients, employees, and the community. It is essential that the organization maintain the goodwill of these publics. A loss of goodwill could result in clients going to other service providers, employees resigning, and the community becoming disinterested, at best, or quite hostile, at worse. This turn of events would affect fund raising negatively.

Since there are many publics with which an organization interacts but only limited corporate resources, it is important for the firm to determine which of the various publics are most important to the long-term survival of the organization. The major public relations efforts should be directed at these primary publics.

After the primary publics have been selected, the organization should determine how these publics view the company and their attitudes on those issues which impact the firm. This process might well require the use of marketing research.

Once it is known what image and attitudes are held by the relevant publics, image and/or attitude goals should be established. For example, a hospital might find that its potential patients view the hospital's personnel as professionally competent but rather aloof and unfriendly. One of its public relation goals might well be to improve the public's impression of the friendliness and concern for patients on the part of the hospital staff.

Since an organization has finite resources, it must develop public relation strategies that can be accomplished within this financial constraint. In developing cost-effective strategies, it is important that the organization understand why an image and attitudes are held by its publics.

Finally, the appropriate public relations strategies should be implemented and the ensuing results should be evaluated. For example, Clean Tennessee, an anti-litter campaign for the state of Tennessee, distributed three sets of public service announcements with three spots of three different lengths to all of the state's radio stations. One hundred and fifty-one stations (21%) responded with documentation of 23,109 spots valued at $297,279 of air time. It cost approximately $2,000 to produce the radio spots. The administrators of the Clean Tennessee program concluded that the radio public service announcement program was quite successful and very cost-effective (Clean Tennessee Program, 1983–1984).

PUBLIC RELATIONS TOOLS

The major public relations tools are (1) corporate publications, (2) speech and audiovisual materials, (3) corporate identification materials, (4) news, (5) special events, and (6) telephone information services. Table 28.2 provides examples of these tools. Usually, the public relations personnel in a health care organization or human service institution perform such functions as

- planning for, gathering raw material for, writing, editing, and proofing news releases and publications, promotional and information publications, reports, and other aids
- contacting communications media regularly with story ideas, tips, background items, explanations, rebuttals
- issuing instructional publications for employees and prospective employees, clients, potential donors, government and regulatory agencies, community groups
- developing audiovisual, film, and videotape projects
- conceiving, arranging for, writing, and placing institutional advertisements and public service announcements
- collecting and sampling comments and complaints

- working with graphic designers, typesetters, photographers, and printers
- helping plan and conduct special events
- "caring for and feeding" the board public relations or communications committee
- spreading goodwill in all quarters
- maintaining the archives and clipping file (Rubright & MacDonald, 1981, pp. 225-6).

FUND RAISING

Many nonprofit health care organizations and social service agencies must attract funds in order to survive. The marketing techniques, discussed in previous chapters, are applicable to this vital function. First, organizations must analyze their donor markets to determine which sources are the most important and what appeals will be most effective. Fund-raising objectives and strategies should be established. Specific tactics should be employed and the organization's fund-raising effectiveness must be evaluated.

Analyzing Donor Markets

An organization can receive funding from a number of financial sources. There are four primary donor markets: individuals, foundations, corporations, and government.

Historically, individuals are the major source of funding and account for approximately 83% of all charitable giving (Kotler, 1982, p. 425). Why do individuals give to charity? People give because they expect something in return: for example, a sense of well-being, a feeling of pride, or a tax deduction. Even the so-called altruistic giver expects the organization to use his funds effectively, to acknowledge the gift in some appropriate manner, and so on. It is very important that an organization understand the giving motives of its individual donors. The following individual giving motives have been suggested:

TABLE 28.2. Public Relation Tools

Public Relation Tools	Example(s)	Discussion
Corporate publications	Annual reports, Employee newsletter, and posters & flyers	Must be concerned with the publication's purpose, cost and aesthetic appeal
Speeches and audio-visual materials	Films, slides, and audio cassettes	Used in conjunction with corporate public relations speakers
Corporate identification materials	Logos, stationery, brochures, signs, business forms, calling cards, buildings, uniforms, and vehicles	Used to create and reinforce a corporate identity
News	News releases	Major task is to find or create favorable news about the organization
Special events	Anniversary celebrations, art exhibits, auctions, bingo games, book sales, cake sales, dances, dinners, fashion shows, rummage sales, and tours	Can create events that attract the attention of the public
Telephone information service	Telephone information	Telephone number through which the public can receive information about the organization

— Need for Self-Esteem: An individual builds his/her self-esteem by feeling good about giving
— Need to be Recognized by Others: An attempt to enhance his/her prestige in the eyes of others
— Fear of Contracting Disease: Insurance against the future
— The Habit Giver: Giving because "everyone else" is doing it
— The Nuisance Giver: Gives to get rid of the solicitor
— Required to Give: Required to give at work
— People-to-People Givers: These individuals have a real "feeling" for other people
— Concern for Humanity: We are all "God's Children." (Kotler, 1982, p. 427)

It has been suggested that an examination of mass donor markets will reveal three distinct groups:

Responsible Donors:	1/3 of Donors	They give without being solicited.
Responsive Donors:	1/3 of Donors	They give when they are asked.
Compulsive Donors:	1/3 of Donors	They give because of pressure. (Seymour, 1966)

Givers should be segmented according to the size of their potential gift. While a major portion of the fund-raising resources and activities should be concentrated on the "large giver," it is a wise idea to involve all potential givers.

Foundations also provide a source for charitable funding. There are four types of foundations: family foundations, general foundations, corporate foundations, and community trusts. The Johnson Foundation (general) was established to provide funds in the health field. With over 26,000 foundations, it is important for an organization to know which foundations might be a source of potential funds. There are a number of sources which might provide this information.*

---

*For more information on foundations, refer to *The Foundation Grants Index*, *The Foundation Directory*, *The Foundation News*, and *Fund Raising Management*.

478 *Cases and Select Readings in Health Care Marketing*

The most common criteria used by foundations to evaluate various "giving opportunities" are (1) the importance and quality of the project, (2) the organization's need for the funds, (3) the organization's ability to use the funds effectively, (4) the importance of satisfying the people who have submitted the proposal, and (5) the benefit that the foundation will receive from supporting the proposal.

Proposals should include, at a minimum, a cover letter, the proposal, a budget, and the personnel involved. Proposal writing is both difficult and demanding of precise formats. Various guides are available to assist proposal writers (see DeBakey & DeBakey, 1978; White, 1975; Jacquette & Jacquette, 1973).

Corporations have been quite supportive of health, social services, civic, cultural, and higher education. At present, corporate giving amounts to roughly one percent of business pretax income. With a legal maximum giving level of five percent of pretax income, corporations have the potential of providing considerable additional charitable funding. Corporations tend to be responsive to projects that will increase community goodwill. In addition, corporations can provide support in many forms: (1) money, (2) securities, (3) goods (e.g., furniture), (4) services, and (5) space (e.g., use of some corporate facility).

Health care organizations and social service agencies should carefully identify good corporate prospects. The best prospects for corporate fund raising have the following characteristics: (1) locally based (2) kindred activities, (3) declared area of support, (4) large givers, (5) personal contacts available, and (6) the corporation has the capability of providing for the specific needs of the nonprofit organization (Kotler, 1982, p. 432).

Various government agencies provide grants to support the arts, health care, education and social services. Government sources require a good deal of red tape, however, they are willing to fund projects which contribute to the public interest.

Fund-Raising Goals and Strategy

Fund-raising goals are essential to the organization. Fund-raising goals permit the organization to budget for the fund-raising endeavor and, subsequently, measure fund-raising effectiveness. After establishing its fund-raising goals, an organization must determine what strategy it will use in reaching potential donors. For example, the American Cancer Society must decide whether to use a "fear" or "hope" appeal or some other emotional motive to reach its donor publics. In addition, the strategy assists in the allocation of scarce resources to different donor groups and geographical locations.

Fund-Raising Tactics

Various donor groups can be reached using different tactics. Four potential donor groups are the small gift market; members and their friends markets, the affluent citizens market, and the wealthy donor market. The tactics used in the small gift market are low-cost methods of fund raising. At the other extreme, the wealthy donor market calls for considerable personal attention. Table 28.3 outlines the various fund-raising methods which might be used to reach each of these markets.

All of these fund-raising tactics are organized as parts of a campaign. A campaign "is an organized and time-sequenced set of activities and events for raising a given sum of money within a particular time period." (Kotler, 1982, p. 442). Nonprofit organizations often conduct an annual campaign to generate operating funds for the coming year. In addition, periodically, capital campaigns are run. A capital campaign raises funds for long-term expansion purposes.

Evaluating Fund-Raising Effectiveness

The effectiveness of a particular fund-raising endeavor can be evaluated in several ways. Some common ways to evaluate fundraising activities are as a percentage of the goal that was attained, the composition of the gifts, the market share acquired, and using an expense/contribution ratio.

If the nonprofit organization establishes an annual goal, the amount collected is compared against the goal. For example, if a home for unwed mothers has a goal of $250,000 for the year, fund raising in the amount of $225,000 would represent 90% of the annual goal.

The composition of gifts should be examined by looking at the

TABLE 28.3. Fund-Raising Methods

Mass Anonymous Small Gift Market

Charity cans in stores	Raffles
Direct mail	Rummage sales
Door-to-door solicitation	Sporting events
Street and sidewalk solicitation	Tours
TV and radio marathons	Walkathons, readathons, bikeathons,
Thrift shops	danceathons, jogathons, swimathons
Plate passing	Yearbooks

Members and Their Friends Market

Anniversary celebrations	Dances
Art shows	Dinners, suppers, lunches, breakfasts
Auctions	Fairs
Benefits (theatre, movies, sports events)	Fashion shows
Bingo games	Parties in unusual places
Book sales	Phonothons (also called telethons)
Cake sales	

Affluent Citizens Market

Convocations	Parlor meetings
Dinners (invitational and/or testimonial)	Telephone calls from high-status
Letters from high-status individuals	individuals

Wealthy Donors Market

Bequests	Testimonial dinner for wealthy
Celebrity grooming	individuals
Committee visit to person's home,	Wealthy person invited to another's
office	home or club
Memorials	

Source. From *Marketing for Nonprofit Organizations* (p. 439) (2nd ed.). By Philip Kotler. Englewood Cliffs, N.J.: Prentice-Hall, Inc. Copyright 1982.

number of donors and the average size of the gifts received (see Table 28.4). In general, the organization hopes to increase the number of donors and the average gift size each year.

The analysis indicates problems with a reduction in the number of affluent citizens donating and a reduction in the average gift size for the small gift market and the affluent citizens market. The organization was successful in increasing the number of donors and the average gift size in the wealthy donors market.

TABLE 28.4. Composition of Gifts

Donor Market	Number of Donors			Average Gift Size		
	1983	1984	% Dif.	1983	1984	% Dif.
Small Gift Market	3,110	3,200	+2.9%	$21	$20	−4.8%
Members & Their Friends Market	555	612	+10.3%	$50	$55	+10.0%
Affluent Citizens Market	400	375	−6.3%	$252	$247	−2.0%
Wealthy Donors Market	50	53	−6.0%	$5,312	$5,700	+7.3%

	Total Gift		
	1983*	1984*	% Inc.
Small Gifts	$ 63,310	$ 64,000	+1.1%
Members & Friends	27,750	33,660	+21.3%
Affluent Citizens	100,000	104,975	+5%
Wealthy Donors	265,600	302,100	13.7%
Total	**$456,660**	**$504,735**	**+10.5%**

*Annual Gift = Number of Donors × Average Gift Size

Comparisons can also be made between an organization's fund-raising efforts and that of comparable organizations. For example, a major nonprofit hospital compared its results to the results of four comparable hospitals and found it led the group in total donors but was lagging as to the size of the average gift.

Evaluations can be made as to the amount of money spent to raise collected funds. Normal expense-to-contribution ratios run 10 to 20%. Some years ago, the American Kidney Fund spent $740,000 to raise just over $779,000. Needless to say, this expense-to-contribution ratio of 95% created a scandal (Kotler, 1982, p. 445). This is a key measure of the efficiency of the organization's fund-raising ability.

SUMMARY

Public relations use various promotional activities to create and maintain good relations between the organization and its publics. The public relations mix includes institutional advertising, publicity, face-to-face communications, and other promotional activities.

Organizations reach their publics through a five-step process: (1) identifying the organizations' relevant publics, (2) measuring images and attitudes of the relevant publics toward the organization; (3) establishing image and attitude goals for the key publics; (4) developing cost-effective public relations strategies; and (5) implementing actions and evaluating results. The following public relation tools are utilized in implementing the process: corporate publications, speeches and audiovisual materials, corporate identification materials, news releases, special events and telephone information services.

Many nonprofit organizations must engage in fund raising from individuals, foundations, corporations, and government to attract sufficient operating funds. This is accomplished by the organization conducting an analysis of donor markets to determine which are the most likely sources, establishing fund-raising goals and strategy, implementing appropriate fund-raising tactics, and evaluating the organization's fund-raising effectiveness.

REFERENCES

Clean Tennessee Program 1983-1984 Annual Report. Memphis, TN: Memphis State University.

Cunningham, William H. and Cunningham, Isabella C.M. *Marketing: A Managerial Approach*. Cincinnati, OH: South-Western Publishing Co., 1981, p. 287.

DeBakey, Lois and DeBakey, Selma. "The Art of Persuasion: Logic and Language in Proposal Writing", *Grants Magazine*, March 1978, pp. 43-60.

Jacquette, F. Lee and Jacquette, Barbara J. *What Makes a Good Proposal*. New York: Foundation Center, 1973.

Kotler, Philip. *Marketing for Nonprofit Organizations* (2nd ed.). Englewood Cliffs, NJ: Prentice-Hall, Inc., 1982.

Rubright, Robert and MacDonald, Dan. *Marketing Health and Human Services*. Rockville, MD: Aspen Systems Corporation, 1981.

Schoell, William F. and Ivy, Thomas T. *Marketing: Contemporary Concepts and Practices*. Boston, MA: Allyn and Bacon, Inc., 1982.

Seymour, Harold J. *Designs for Fund Raising*. New York: McGraw-Hill Book Company, 1966.

White, Virginia P. *Grants: How to Find Out About Them and What to Do Next*. New York: Plenum Press, 1975.

CHAPTER 29

The Making of a Logo:
Scott and White Develops a New Look

Donald W. Nelson

INTRODUCTION

In 1891, the Gulf, Colorado and Santa Fe Railroad headquarters in Galveston, Texas, decided to move its hospital to the central Texas town of Temple, a major division center for the rapidly expanding rail line. In central Texas, the hospital would be easily accessible for all railroad workers.

A year later, Dr. A.C. Scott, a 27-year-old surgeon, joined the new hospital and three years later became associated with Dr. Raleigh R. White, whose score on an examination was so impressive that Dr. Scott hired him on the spot.

Although Dr. Scott remained Chief of Surgery at the Santa Fe Hospital until his death in 1940, he also had time to develop a private practice. Along the way he and Dr. White started two hospitals; one now called Kings Daughters in Temple, and the other now internationally known as Scott and White Hospital and Clinic.

Scott and White grew rapidly during the early years of the 20th century and in 1963 moved from 28 scattered downtown buildings to a new building which is the center of its present complex.

From the beginning, the practice started by Doctors Scott and White consistently strived to provide "personalized, comprehensive, high quality health care enhanced by medical education and clinical research" for its patients. While this endeavor has remained

Reprinted from William J. Winston, ed., *Innovations in Hospital Marketing*, pp. 91–96, © 1984 by The Haworth Press, Inc.

as part of Scott and White's mission statement for the past 80 years, many changes have taken place in the Scott and White organization, and today it is housed in an 883,000 square foot building. "Scott and White" now includes the Scott and White Memorial Hospital and Scott, Sherwood and Brindley Foundation, the Scott and White Clinic, and its part of the Texas A&M University College of Medicine Temple Campus (Figure 29.1). It also operates two satellite clinics with a third scheduled to open in May.

In addition, a fleet of cars circulate throughout central Texas picking up lab tests from hospitals and physicians for examination at the central lab in Temple. Scott and White operates an alcohol and drug dependence treatment program, an executive health plan, a health promotion program, a home care agency and its own health maintenance organization. In 1983 it purchased the Santa Fe Hospital in Temple and operates it as the Scott and White Santa Fe Center. There are 200 physicians on the group practice staff, representing nearly all medical specialties.

During this period of growth, the people of central Texas have come to rely upon this major medical center as a source of excellence in medical practice, education, and research. Patients come from throughout the Southwest, the nation and the world for consultation, diagnosis, and treatment.

However, Texas was developing during this period, too. In 1970, Texas, the second largest State in land area, had only 11,199,000 people. By 1980 this population had grown by 31.9% to 14,776,000, making it the third most populous State, and the growth continues as people move to the Sunbelt. With this increasing population of "new Texans" and with the continuing growth and expansion of medical services and educational opportunities available at Scott and White, a major identity crisis confronted the multifaceted institution.

MARKETING ISSUE

The problem facing Scott and White was how to readily identify its several medical components (400-bed hospital, internationally-known clinic with several satellites and its teaching hospital connection) for the new people coming to its service area.

Creating a symbol to represent the many functions performed at

FIGURE 29.1. Scott and White Memorial Hospital and Scott, Sherwood and Brindley Foundation and Scott and White Clinic, Temple, Texas

Scott and White was no simple task. And the decision to create such a symbol was not made lightly. A preliminary study of Scott and White's many roles led to the conclusion that no single phrase could adequately describe the complex organization without losing one or more of the dimensions of Scott and White. "Hospital," "Clinic," "research center," "education center," — any one of them eliminated the other functions.

METHODOLOGY

The first step was to define the name of the institutions. The executive committee of the Hospital's Board of Trustees and the Clinic Board, all physicians, had begun to hold a monthly "communications" meeting to help solve common problems and reduce the conflict of separate decisions that could be contrary to each other.

Donald W. Nelson, newly appointed Director of Public Affairs, explained to the joint boards the problems he faced with using the name Scott and White Memorial Hospital and Scott, Sherwood and Brindley Foundation and Scott and White Clinic, particularly in electronic media. The people who were new to the area did not identify "Scott and White" as a medical institution. Some thought it was a law firm, others an advertising agency. Clearly something had to be done if Scott and White's communications and marketing programs were to utilize the synergism created by the three entities.

"What is a Scott and White?" was the subject of several meetings. Should "medical center," "medical institutions" or even an address like "Medical Park," "Science Station," etc., be added to help with the identification?

After several serious debates, the decision was made to refer to the whole medical complex as "Scott and White" — with no descriptive tag line. And it was that decision which made it necessary to create a symbol that would position it as a medical organization, no matter what specific division was involved.

The symbol — logo — had to say visually what could not be said in words. The integrity of the original Scott and White partnership and its subsequent broadening had to be maintained.

At this time Scott and White was using six different logos which meant fragmentation of impact as people came in contact with the organization.

Nelson, as Director of Public Affairs, began a methodical search for communications specialists — advertising, marketing and public relations professionals who would work with Scott and White to develop a powerful unifying symbol to tell our story. After reviewing several marketing firms, Nelson and the hospital and clinic boards selected the William Lacy Company in Austin, Texas (now re-named Fellers, Lacy & Gaddis Marketing Consultants) to develop the overall graphics plan for Scott and White.

The joint boards had asked that the firm develop the new graphics program, complete through the preparation of a graphics manual. Cost estimates were prepared for this program with several alternative programs considered.

At this point a special committee was selected to work with Nelson, two from the hospital executive committee and two from the clinic board. Dr. Jesse Ibarra, an endocrinologist, and Dr. Dennis J. Lynch, a plastic surgeon, were selected to represent the clinic. Dr. Robert E. Myers, a pediatrician, and Dr. Ronald Walsh, pulmonary medicine, were chosen from the hospital. This committee of five had the responsibility of meeting with the agency people to explain to them what Scott and White represents and to work through the various elements of a new graphics program. This program would be presented to the joint boards for approval. After this approval, the recommendations would be reviewed by the Staff Executive Committee comprised of all Scott and White department chairmen. Implementation would then begin.

The Lacy Company had designed several logos for various companies and had experience in working for a medical organization.

Account Executive, Gay Robirds, now vice-president of Fellers, Lacy & Gaddis, in describing the complexities and challenges involved in the design of the logo, outlined the selection process her design and marketing people used in creating the symbol for Scott and White.

"We started with Scott and White's Mission Statement which states that its purpose is personalized high quality, comprehensive health care enhanced by medical education and clinical research," Robirds explained. The design group searched for universal images that symbolized medicine, education and research based on initial conferences with the Liaison Committee.

The internationally recognized cross was examined as a possibility. It was discarded for several reasons—first, because of its various religious connotations and the fact that it is widely used by the American Red Cross.

The eternal flame, symbolizing knowledge, was tapped as a possibility because of Scott and White's reputation as an innovative diagnostic and research facility and because of its medical education programs. That, however, eliminated the hospital and clinic group practice.

A third symbol, the staff of Aesculapius, was also considered. This symbol has one serpent and is used by such physician organizations as the American and Texas Medical Associations. A fourth image, the caduceus—the winged staff with two serpents which is the symbol of the U.S. Army Medical Corps and is considered by some to be the symbol of the medical profession as a whole—was researched and greeted with enthusiasm by the Lacy group and the Scott and White committee.

There is significant disagreement within the medical profession itself as to which of these latter two symbols really represents the profession and which mainly represents the physician alone. However, the broad use of the two serpent symbol by the military has caused this symbol to be nearly universally recognized by the general public as the equivalent of "medicine."

THE DESIGN

A senior art director was then assigned to develop a graphic treatment that incorporated an identifying medical symbol and the name Scott and White in one meaningful symbol. After reviewing hundreds of typefaces, a classic logotype was chosen—the ITC Garamond typeface. This particular style was selected for its elegance and classical appearance. It is a type style that continues to look modern and yet has very successfully stood the test of time in the design world. In fact, it is a type style that Scott and White used several years ago and then abandoned.

Next on the design board was the question of a symbol. The first uses of a symbol as an identifying mark date back to ancient Greece. Pottery excavated from Greece include items marked with identifying symbols.

In one sense the symbol is an expression of the individuality of the organization. At the same time the symbol identifies or distinguishes the organization from others in the same field. In colonial America, shops were often identified with a symbol, either a representation of what was available inside like a boot or a tankard of ale, or as a distinguishing symbol like "At the Mark of the Fox" and the like.

Scott and White needed a representative mark or symbol, one that said "medical." The symbol had to identify Scott and White as medical while the logotype (words) said "Scott and White."

In addition to it "saying" medical, it had to be technically adaptable to the various applications: stationery, name tags, posters, business cards, signs, etc. It had to be able to be used in a large format, in a very small format, in black and white as well as in color.

The task force and the agency felt that the Scott and White initials would be suitable since so many people also referred to the institutions by these letters.

The artist took the two letters and the ampersand and began to modify them. The top of the "W" was extended both to balance the somewhat flowery ampersand and to become a stylized medical symbol. Together, the task force and the artist moved, enlarged, reduced and altered the letters until a satisfactory symbol and unique logo type resulted. Both the agency staff and the task force spent many hours of research and discussion before the final design was put together for the two boards to review. By kerning the letters of the two words Scott and White and by adapting the initials to include a stylized caduceus, a unique graphics design emerged (Figure 29.2).

Before any presentation was made, however, the logo was put to one final test—a formal market survey. Several versions of the logo were reproduced on special survey cards and presented to a randomly selected number of people by a national research firm. These people were asked what type of organization the logo represented. When a remarkably high percentage of unaided responses said a

SCOTT & WHITE

PMS 327 (green) and PMS 404 (gray) are used in the new Scott and White logo.

FIGURE 29.2

medical organization, Scott and White had the final proof that the new logo did exactly what it was supposed to do — tell people at a glance that Scott and White has a medical orientation, no matter which of its functions or facilities was using it.

The symbol and the logotype were designed so the symbol was in a blue-green color and the words in a warm grey. From a study of the therapeutic and psychological aspects of hues and colors of the spectrum, the blue-green (PMS 327) was selected because it was neither extensively "warm" or "cool." Warm colors (such as red) are thought to increase restlessness and nervous tension and evoke highly emotional responses in people. Cool colors (such as blue) are said to inhibit the healing of wounds and can be bleak if applied to too large an area. Although blue is a favorite color for many hospitals, it has a low attention value and is a color which many find hard to focus on.

The blue-green Scott and White color, therefore, is a combination of warm and cool hues. A pacific color, it should help reduce nervous and muscular tension. It is also a color without a primitive quality, both pleasing and "livable." The color should wear well and meet the test of time.

The blue-green is set off by a warm grey which adds dignity and when used together become a sophisticated and pleasing combination.

Because the colors are from the Pantone Matching System (PMS), they can be easily duplicated by printers anywhere.

The colors and the graphic program were then presented to the meeting of the joint boards and approved for use throughout Scott and White.

Work then began on the preparation of a graphics standard manual which would demonstrate to those using the logo how it should be presented. The colors and why they were selected, and type face and rules for the paper system (letterheads, envelopes, business cards, etc.) are all explained in the manual.

The manual explains that the straight line logo is preferred but that in some applications a "stacked" version could be substituted. Detailed grids are included to show placement of the symbol and logo type so it can be presented in the same manner each time it is used.

While blue-green and warm grey are specified as the "Scott and White colors," the manual explains that other colors can be used — or it can be used in black and white. If another color (other than blue-green or black) is selected, the logo should be darker than the paper it is printed on so it can be "reversed."

The manual also contains examples of the ITC Garamond type — Bold, Book and Italic — which are permissible. There are also unacceptable examples of the logo use (such as the symbol with other type than ITC Garamond, abbreviations, etc.) so the user can quickly understand the preferred style.

There is a section on administrative forms — letterheads, envelopes, bills, prescription pads, etc. — and instructions on how to put a long and a short letter on the paper correctly.

Interior and exterior signs are included as well as directional signs. There is a section on print advertising showing how the logo should be applied in the signature and a section on its use in brochures.

The book ends with a page of the logo in various sizes and with color swatches of the preferred colors for use with printers.

The logo was introduced to Scott and White's 3,200 employees with a special issue of *Rapport*, the house organ. The special issue explained the process and what the symbol meant. One of the first uses of it was as a pocket patch on a scrub shirt which was the souvenir for the Second Scott and White 10K and Fun Run. More than 500 shirts were used for the race participants.

Individual department presentations were made to the various Scott and White departments, explaining the philosophy and the design of the new graphic system. Colors, rationale, type style were all carefully explained to people who would be implementing it on the thousands of forms, signs, medical record cards, invoices, checks, etc., which would eventually use it.

Since May, the new logo has been applied to many items as they were reprinted or replaced. Scott and White actually was able to effect several economies in the process of the logo implementation. Instead of stocking separate envelopes in various sizes for both the clinic and the hospital the new Scott and White "alone" envelope served both purposes, saving storage space and enabling the purchase of larger quantities of envelopes.

The old stationery was embossed, the new one is two color (Figure 29.3). Even with a new watermarked paper, Scott and White was able to reduce stationery costs because the two color paper could be printed in-house by the hospital printing department. This not only reduced costs but enabled the printing of smaller orders since it could be available much more quickly.

A new clinic being built in Belton, Texas, will have an exterior feature stripe of the blue-green color. New pocket patches with the logo identify the new Home Care Agency personnel. Name badges with the symbol identify the senior staff and their specialties.

Although, as with most subjective programs, everyone is not thoroughly pleased with the new logo, many feel it serves to unify Scott and White and at the same time create synergism for its programs. A Texas Certificate of Registration has been received for the symbol and the logo type which will protect its use in the State.

In retrospect, the program would probably have been easier to implement if the materials (stationery, business cards, etc.) had been ready when the initial announcement was made. Because of the delay and the phase-in of new materials, the subjectivity of the subject, there were many second guesses and some "re-designing" on the part of the staff. If as much of the "package" had been ready to go, there would have been less confusion.

SCOTT & WHITE CLINIC
An Association Affiliated
With Scott and White
Memorial Hospital and
Scott, Sherwood and
Brindley Foundation

2401 South 31st St.

TEXAS A&M UNIVERSITY
COLLEGE OF MEDICINE,
TEMPLE CAMPUS

Temple, Texas 76508   817/774-2111

FIGURE 29.3

Part X

Advertising

CHAPTER 30

Introduction to Advertising

Robert L. Berl

Advertising is a "paid form of nonpersonal communication about an organization and/or its products that is transmitted to a target audience through a mass medium" (Pride & Ferrell, 1980, p. 411). It is one of the promotional mix tools (advertising, sales promotion, personal selling, and public relations) available to the marketing manager.

FACTORS INFLUENCING THE USE OF ADVERTISING

Unless the product/service characteristics and market environment are favorable, advertising may not be of value to the firm. Some of the factors that influence the use of advertising include the following:

1. *Does the product possess unique, important features?* Advertising will be helpful if the product/service has unique features which differentiate it from its competition.

2. *Are "hidden qualities" important to buyers?* For example, a certain dosage of pain killer, though not visible, is an important quality in the purchase and consumption of aspirin.

3. *Is the general demand trend for the product favorable?* If a product class is experiencing a long-term favorable demand trend, advertising can potentially be of assistance. On the other hand, if a

product is in the decline phase of the product life cycle, advertising is less likely to be beneficial.

4. *Is the market potential for the product adequate?* There must be sufficient potential sales volume to justify the expense of advertising.

5. *Is the competitive environment favorable?* If the competition is extremely strong, a much greater marketing effort is required. This would include sales promotions and personal selling, as well as advertising.

6. *Are general economic conditions favorable for the marketing of the product?* The advertising program is affected by the state of the general economy. For example, the advertising of luxury goods such as sailboats, vacation homes, and the like tends to be more effective during good economic times when disposable income is high.

7. *Is the organization financially able and willing to spend the amount of money required to launch an advertising campaign?* If a firm is unable or unprepared to spend the funds necessary to support an appropriate advertising campaign, the resulting advertising effort is less likely to be effective.

8. *Does the firm possess sufficient marketing expertise to market the product?* The successful marketing of a product requires expertise in strategic planning, research, product/service development, pricing, distribution, and promotion. If there is a weakness, in any of these areas, the firm is less likely to be able to market its product successfully (Patti, 1977).

For example, emergency medical clinics have been doing a good bit of advertising. This advertising should be relatively effective since a number of factors favor this type of organization:

Unique Product Features:	Multiple Suburban Locations
Hidden Qualities:	Competent Medical Personnel
General Demand Trend:	Stable Demand
Market Potential:	Large
Competitive Environment:	Heavy
General Economic Conditions:	Relatively Stable in Both Good and Bad Times

Firm's Financial Ability: Frequently Have a Strong Cash Flow Position

Firm's Marketing Expertise: Inconsistent

Table 30.1 provides a simple model for appraising advertising opportunities.

ADVERTISING OBJECTIVES

If advertising is to be effective, specific advertising objectives must be established. The following advertising objectives are typical of those which firms might adopt:

Table 30.1. A Simple Model for Appraising Advertising Opportunities

	For Advertising	Against Advertising
Product Factors		
1. The presence of unique, salient product qualities	_____	_____
2. The existence of "hidden qualities" in the product	_____	_____
3. The possibility of appealing to powerful buying motives through advertising	_____	_____
Market and Financial Factors		
4. The generic demand trend	_____	_____
5. Adequacy of market potential	_____	_____
6. The competitive environment	_____	_____
7. Economic conditions	_____	_____
8. Adequacy of funds for a sustained advertising program	_____	_____
9. Possibility of developing and implementing an effective marketing program	_____	_____
TOTAL	_____	_____

Evaluate each of the factors as either being favorable or unfavorable to the use of advertising to stimulate brand demand, and place a check in the appropriate column. Add the number of checks in each of the two columns to make an initial judgement about the role advertising should play in the marketing program.

Source. From *Advertising Management: Cases and Concepts* (p. 6) by Charles H. Patti and John H. Murphy. New York: John Wiley. Copyright 1978. Reprinted with permission.

To Provide Information

- New product information
- Suggested new uses
- Pricing information
- Product demonstrations
- Build corporate image

To Persuade the Target Market

- Induce immediate purchase
- Build brand preference
- Induce brand switching

To Remind the Target Market

- Maintain brand awareness
- Tell where to purchase the product

It has been suggested that consumers go through an adoption process: Awareness ——→ Interest ——→ Evaluation and Trial ——→ Decision ——→ Confirmation (Lavidge & Steiner, 1961). Various types of promotional efforts lend themselves to the stages of the adoption process.

TYPES OF ADVERTISING NEEDED

The advertising objectives determine the type of advertising which a firm might choose to use.

Product versus Pioneering Advertising

Product advertising is designed to sell a product either to the final user or to members of the channel of distribution. Institutional advertising attempts to create goodwill for the company. Some authorities consider institutional advertising a component of the public relations mix. See Part IX: Public Relations and Fund Raising for a discussion of institutional advertising.

Pioneering Advertising

Pioneering advertising is used during the introductory phase of the product life cycle. It is designed to create primary demand for the product class rather than for a specific product brand. The intent is to inform consumers of the existence of the product and its uses. Pioneering advertising does not have to mention a specific company or brand. For example, the American Banker's Association runs television ads on the advantages of doing business with a "full service" bank.

Competitive Advertising

Competitive advertising is associated with the growth and maturity phases of the product life cycle. During these phases, a company faces intense competition. Competitive advertising is intended to build selective demand. Selective demand refers to the demand for a specific brand within a given product class. Building on the previous banking example, competitive advertising would offer ads for specific banks such as the Bank of America, Citicorp, and First Tennessee Bank.

Competitive advertising may be either direct or indirect. Direct advertising is designed to get consumers to purchase the product. It is associated with the evaluation and trial stage of the adoption process previously discussed. Indirect advertising stresses product features and advantages with the intent of influencing future buying decisions. It is associated with the awareness and interest stages of the adoption process. For example, much of the advertising run by hospitals is indirect in nature. It is designed to persuade clients, when they require hospitalization, to influence their doctor so that they are admitted to the hospital doing the advertising.

Comparative advertising is a form of competitive advertising. When comparative advertising is used, comparison is made between specific competitive brands. For example, Chrysler may point out specific areas where its car is superior to comparable models of General Motors or Ford automobiles.

Reminder Advertising

Reminder advertising is intended to maintain brand awareness in the minds of the target market. It is designed to reinforce earlier promotions and is associated with the latter maturity and decline stages of the product life cycle. As the market for a product class shrinks, a company should minimize its advertising expenditures. In this regard, reminder advertising is appropriate. The old billboard showing a frosty Coca Cola bottle and the caption, "The Pause That Refreshes!" is a classic example of reminder advertising.

Cooperative Advertising

Many manufacturers feel that they can increase their market exposure by helping channel members to advertise their product. This process is accomplished by granting channel members advertising allowances. For example, a manufacturer may offer to pay 50% of the ad expense for their products to any retailer willing to run an advertisement.

ADVERTISING MEDIA

The major advertising media are newspapers, television, direct mail, radio, magazines, and outdoor. Table 30.2 lists these media, the amount expended by media, and the advantages and disadvantages of each medium.

Media selection is determined by finding the most cost-effective means to get the desired number of message exposures to the target market. The desired exposures depends on the number of exposures needed to generate the desired level of brand awareness. The effect of exposure depends on reach, frequency, and impact. Reach refers to the number of different households exposed to a particular medium at least once during some specified time frame. Frequency is the number of times during a specified time frame that an average household is exposed to the message. Impact refers to the quality of the exposure. For example, a home improvement ad has more im-

TABLE 30.2. Comparison of Advertising Media

Medium	Estimated Ad Expenses for 1983* (000,000)	Percent of Total	Advantages	Disadvantages
Newspaper	$20.1	34.3%	Timely; Flexible; Local market; Credible source	Short life; No "pass-along Poor reproduction quality; Clutter
Television	16.2	27.7%	Mass usage; Appeals to sight, sound, and motion	Expensive; Clutter; Short life
Direct Mail	11.8	20.2%	Selective; Flexible; Intense coverage; Can personalize	Costly on a per readership basis; Junk mail Image
Magazine	4.4	7.5%	Selective; Long life; Credible sources Good reproduction; Good "pass-along"	Long lead times; Inflexible
Radio	5.2	8.9%	Mass usage; Selective; Inexpensive; Short lead time	Short exposure; Audio only; Weak attention; Limited to simple messages
Outdoor	0.8	1.4%	Flexible; Geographically selective; Repeat exposure Low cost	Very short exposure; Limited to short and simple messages

*This information is from "Advertising Agencies: Strong Gains for 1984," Standard & Poors, Industry Surveys (August 9, 1984), pp. M92-M93.

pact in *Southern Living* than in *True Romance* magazine. The relationship between exposure, reach, frequency, and impact can be expressed with the following mathematical expressions:

Total Number of Exposures = Average Reach × Average Frequency

Weighted Number of Exposures = Total Number of Exposures × Average Impact

There is a dispute as to the total number of exposures needed. Many advertising authorities believe that the target market needs a large number of exposures (Lucas & Britt, 1963, p. 218). Still others believe that only a few quality exposures are needed (Krugman, 1975).

Message Decisions

Message creation, message evaluation, and message execution are the three decision areas relating to message formation. Message creation refers to the development of alternative messages that are designed to generate desired responses from the members of the target market. These messages might well employ different appeals and themes. These appeals are basically emotional or rational in nature. Emotional appeals play on such emotions as love, fear, guilt, and envy. Rational appeals include quality, price, durability, and service support. Many times, both appeals are used in the same advertisement. In addition, many health care institutions and social service agencies use moral message appeals. Moral appeals play on what people view as right or wrong. For example, the appeal for the American Heart Association is "We're fighting for your life."

Message selection and evaluation deals with selecting the best message out of the alternative messages created. It has been suggested that messages should be evaluated based on desirability, exclusiveness, and believability (Twedt, 1969). A message with a high rating in all three categories would be judged as being quite potent in its communication ability. For example, the March of Dimes had the following three messages evaluated for on interest, distinctiveness, and believability (see Table 30.3). The last message ("The March of Dimes has given you: polio vaccine, German measles vaccine, 110 birth defects' counseling centers'') was judged most effective.

TABLE 30.3. Three Messages Evaluated by the March of Dimes

	Interest	Distinc-tiveness	Believ-ability	Total
Seven hundred children are born each day with a birth defect.	70	60	80	210
Your next baby could be born with a birth defect.	58	50	70	178
The March of Dimes has given you: polio vaccine, German measles vaccine, 110 birth defects' counseling centers.	70	80	90	240

Source. From William A. Mindak and J. Malcolm Bybee, "Marketing's Application to Fund Raising," *Journal of Marketing* (July, 1971): 13-18.

How a message is delivered is equal in importance to what is being said. Both of these message components will determine the impact of the message. Messages have a particular style, tone, ordering, and format. Styles can vary from a commercial showing a slice of life, to a testimonial, or an allegory. Tone refers to whether an ad is serious, humorous, or otherwise. Ordering deals with decisions involving what conclusions the ad should draw, whether the ad should use one-sided or two-sided arguments, and the ordering of the arguments. Format refers to such elements as the ad's headline, copy, illustration, and color. More complete discussions of message decisions can be found in other books on the topic (see Wright, Winter, & Zeigler, 1982).

ADVERTISING BUDGETS

Advertising budgets are established in the following ways: percentage-of-sales method, competitive-parity method, what the firm can afford method, and the objective-and-task method.

The method most commonly used to set the advertising budget is percentage-of-sales method. With this method, a company uses last year's sales or forecasted sales as a means of establishing the advertising budget. If a firm budgets 10% of forecasted sales on advertising, the following advertising budgets would be set:

Year	Forecasted Sales	Advertising Budget
1982	$1,000,000	$100,000
1983	1,500,000	150,000
1984	900,000	90,000
1985	1,100,000	110,000

This method ensures that the firm can afford the amount spent on advertising. Provided that a company's competitors are using the same method, it facilitates stability of advertising levels within the industry and minimizes the likelihood of advertising wars between competitors. However, if a company is overspending or underspending on advertising, this situation will be perpetuated into the future. In addition, a case can be made that more advertising is needed during depressed economic conditions. Under the percentage-of-sales method, less is spent on advertising during bad times and more is spent during good times.

The competitive-parity method means that a firm meets its competitor's advertising expenditures. This method is often found in oligopolies where the industry is dominated by a few large companies. Many of the disadvantages discussed under the percentage-of-sales method also apply to the competitive-parity method.

Many companies allocate what they can afford to spend on advertising. Firms using this method tend to have the false opinion that advertising is independent of the other marketing functions. For small companies, there is a strong likelihood that an advertising budget will be insufficient.

The objective-and-task method is the best of the methods as it determines advertising budgets based on what is required to achieve some predetermined objective. Using this method, advertising objectives are established. The level of advertising, media, and the like are determined and cost estimates are calculated. If these cost estimates are more than the firm can afford, the advertising objectives must be altered. This process is repeated until the objective-and-task advertising budget is acceptable to management.

ADVERTISING AGENCIES

Many companies use independent service organization called advertising agencies. An advertising agency prepares advertisements, buys space/time, performs marketing research, conducts mail campaigns, and often provides public relations services and other functions. Firms use an advertising agency because they want the services of a specialist in the field.

Advertising agencies' major source of income is the 15% commission they earn from placing ads in the various media. For example, if an agency places a $1,000,000 ad on one of the television networks, the agency would get a $150,000 commission. Many small companies, with small advertising budgets, pay fees for the services that the advertising agency performs, since the standard commission is not sufficient to cover the agency's expenses.

MEASURING ADVERTISING EFFECTIVENESS

It is important for a firm to measure the effectiveness of its advertising efforts. Advertising effectiveness can be measured either before the ad has been placed or after it has been run.

The major before advertising measurement methods are judgmental checklist evaluations, consumer-jury tests, and recognition-and-recall tests. The judgmental method consists of the proposed ad being judgmentally evaluated by an individual or groups of individuals using a checklist with a number of specific attributes.

Consumer-jury tests use a sample of consumers to rate an advertisement. Usually, the advertisement is rated in comparison to one or more other commercials. Consumer panels can also be exposed to an advertisement among a series of advertisements and then asked to recognize or recall the particular ad in question.

Recognition-and-recall tests are also used to measure the effectiveness of advertisements after they have been run. Sales records are also used to evaluate advertisements after they have been shown. This method is particularly appropriate for advertisements designed to stimulate immediate purchase.

SUMMARY

Advertising may or may not be of value to a company. Some of the factors that influence the use of advertising are the uniqueness of product features, the general demand trend for the product, the market potential for the product, the competitive environment, the general economic conditions, the organization's financial capacity, and the degree of marketing expertise possessed by the firm. If the majority of these are favorable, the use of advertising might well be beneficial.

Specific advertising objectives should be established by the firm. Advertising objectives might cover such areas as providing information to the target audience, persuading the target market, or reminding the consumer. Depending upon the objectives established, the company might use product or institutional advertising. The advertising might be pioneering, competitive, or reminder in nature.

Advertising media such as newspapers, television, direct mail, radio, magazines, and outdoor are used to reach the target market. Advertisers are concerned with generating a desired level of ad exposures which, in turn, generate brand awareness.

In addition to media decisions, advertisers must make decisions as to the message to be delivered. The message decision areas are message creation, message evaluation, and message execution.

Prior to the beginning of the year, firms establish advertising budgets for the year. These can be set using the percentage-of-sales method, competitive-parity method, what the company can afford method, and the objective-and-task method.

Many firms retain outside advertising specialists, typically an advertising agency, to develop their advertisements. Advertising agencies specialize in preparing ads, buying space/time, performing marketing research endeavors, providing public relations services, and the like.

Since advertising is expensive, it is prudent for a company to evaluate the effectiveness of its advertising. Advertising effectiveness can be measured either before an ad had been shown or after it has been run.

REFERENCES

Krugman, Herbert E. "What Makes Advertising Effective?" *Harvard Business Review*, March-April 1975, pp. 96-103.

Lavidge, R.J. and Steiner, G.A. "A Model for Predictive Measurements of Advertising Effectiveness", *Journal of Marketing*, October 1961, p. 61.

Lucas, Darrell B. and Britt, Steuart Henderson. *Measuring Advertising Effectiveness*. New York: McGraw-Hill Book Co., 1963.

McCarthy, E. Jerome and Perreault, William D., Jr. *Basic Marketing* (8th ed.). Homewood, IL: Richard D. Irwin, Inc., 1984, p. 531.

Mindak, William A. and Bybee, H. Malcolm. "Marketing's Application to Fund Raising", *Journal of Marketing*, July 1971, pp. 13-18.

Patti, Charles H. "Evaluating the Role of Advertising", *Journal of Advertising*, Fall 1977, pp. 32-33.

Patti, Charles H. and Murphy, John H. *Advertising Management: Cases and Concepts*. Columbus, OH: Grid, Inc., 1978, p. 6.

Pride, William M. and Ferrell, O.C. *Marketing: Basic Concepts and Decisions* (2nd ed.). Boston, MA: Houghton Mifflin Co.

Standard & Poors. "Advertising Agencies: Strong Gains Seen for 1984", Industry Surveys, August 9, 1984, pp. M92-M93.

Twedt, Dik Warren. "How to Plan New Products, Improve Old Ones, and Create Better Advertising", *Journal of Marketing*, January 1969, pp. 53-57.

Wright, John S., Winter, Willis L., Jr. and Zeigler, Sherilyn K. *Advertising* (5th ed.). New York: McGraw-Hill Book Co., 1982.

CHAPTER 31

Minimizing Advertising Risks

Thomas J. Coleman

A common, yet serious problem for most advertisers is that almost any advertising action will result in at least some response. Although this may sound more like a blessing than a problem, it can be the cause of a great deal of complacency and poor strategic planning.

Over many years we have learned that those advertisers experiencing the greatest degree of long-term success are those that take as many steps as possible to *minimize the tremendous risks inherent in advertising*. The fact that one's advertising program produced some positive results is absolutely no reason to assume that it was successful. Cost efficient advertising must be based on the creation of programs that produce maximum response. We can seldom afford to feel good about an ad campaign that simply "worked." We must ask whether or not it "worked" as well as it could have. Even at its best, advertising is a significant gamble. The only way to win is to cut the risks.

Over the last year we have discussed advertising with dozens of administrators and public relations directors of hospitals and related

Reprinted from William J. Winston, ed., *Innovations in Hospital Marketing*, pp. 83–89, © 1984 by The Haworth Press, Inc.

Tolman Advertising Associates has recently published an advertising manual called *AD AID*, which is designed to assist health care organizations and small businesses. A free six-page report describing *AD AID* is available by calling toll-free 1-800-453-3232.

treatment facilities. Although notable exceptions exist, we have found that many institutions are moving in the direction of advertising with a sort of naive excitement that may all too soon turn sour. Our purpose is not to advocate health care advertising. There are undoubtedly numerous factors, both pro and con, that will ultimately influence your decisions with regard to advertising. But if you do plan to begin or continue investing dollars in advertising, we believe a few points may help make the process less expensive and more productive.

An old, but often forgotten, advertising principle states that you should buy advertising when you need it, not when it's sold to you. Unfortunately, almost everyone in the advertising field, from media salespeople to agency account executives, is in some way or another usually trying to "sell" you advertising. It's how they make their living. This is not to say that those of us in the advertising business are any less honest or sincere than any other group of professionals. (Although a 1977 Gallup poll did reveal that in a comparative raking of twenty occupational groups in terms of honesty and ethical standards, advertising practitioners ranked nineteenth, beating only automobile salespeople.) It does imply however, that seldom will an advertising salesman, agency executive, consultant or anyone else ever understand the unique qualities and strengths of your services to the extent that you do. It also implies that you, the advertiser, are ultimately responsible for the efficiency and quality of your advertising. You may be making a serious mistake to believe otherwise. Take a specific example. Let's say you have determined that you are going to use a daily metropolitan newspaper to present your message. In addition to numerous other considerations such as what days of the week to run the ad, which sections of the paper best fit your demographic needs, how frequently the ad should run, etc. you must also select the size of ad to use. This is where efficiency (or lack of it) can hit us head on. On the one hand you may have a newspaper representative who believes that anything less than a full-page just won't do you justice. On the other hand you have a limited budget complicated by a skeptical board of directors. More often than not this type of confusion results in a decision that does very little to minimize your risk. Look at Figure 31.1. It dramatically illustrates what we mean by cost effectiveness.

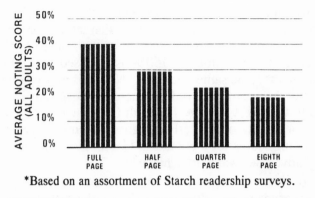

*Based on an assortment of Starch readership surveys.

FIGURE 31.1. Newspaper Ad Size/Readership Comparison*

As you can see, an average full-page ad is noted by approximately 40% of all the individuals reading that day's newspaper. An eighth-page ad delivers about 19% of the readers.

Simply put, when compared to the eighth-page ad, the full-page ad you might be considering will probably cost you about eight times more money while only delivering about twice as many readers. (Just try and apply that type of logic to any other aspect of your institution's management and you'll be out looking for a new job in a hurry.) Why then do so many companies use full-page ads? Don't they realize what they are doing? Quite frankly, in many cases businesses do not understand the realities of advertising. They want a big response so they run a big ad. How hard can it be, right? Wrong! In almost every aspect of advertising there are efficient ways of doing things and there are wasteful ways of doing things. Sometimes the waste is only very slight, but still it is waste and very often it is largely unnecessary. Continuing with our newspaper example, we don't want to imply that a full-page or half-page ad has no value over a smaller ad other than improved noting scores. Big ads do produce big impact. But large size is only one of several ways to increase the impact of an ad. Two other ways are *frequency* and *color*. And unless an advertiser can specifically identify why they need a big ad (the need to list numerous products, etc.) they will probably be better off looking in other directions.

From a theoretical perspective we can see that if an advertiser chooses to run eight one-eighth page ads in the same edition of the paper they could feel fairly confident that almost every reader would take not of at least one or more of their ads. (A combined noting score of approximately 150% as opposed to a full-page's 40% and for about the same total cost.) Now this may be considered overkill, but the use of three or four one-eighth page ads in the same paper may work very nicely. The high frequency of exposure to a single ad (or a series of similarly designed ads) produces big impact *and* big noting scores for a good deal less money. Isn't that exactly what any advertiser wants to achieve?

Now consider the use of color in newspaper advertising. Unlike most forms of magazine advertising where color may have a significant impact on the perceived quality and desirability of a product, in newspaper advertising color really serves only one basic function: to attract attention and insure page dominance. The critical question of course, is whether or not the benefits of adding color sufficiently outweigh the additional costs involved. The first and most important element in answering this question is knowing how much the newspaper intends to charge you for adding an additional color of ink to the existing black (two colors). Since with almost all publications the cost of adding an additional color to any ad is the same, regardless of size, the cost effectiveness of color is almost totally based on what this charge is. For example, a newspaper may require the same $350 to add red to your ad, whether it be a full-page or eighth-page. Figure 31.2 shows the relative relationship between increased noting scores (how many people take note of an ad) due to the addition of a second color and increased expense of the ad due to the addition of color. Because every newspaper will charge a different amount to add color, we have provided four different samples (Newspapers A,B,C, and D) for each of the four different ad sizes we used in the previous chart (full-page, half-page, quarter-page and eighth-page). To determine which sample newspaper most accurately reflects the paper you are considering, find out how much your paper charges to add one color and then divide this amount by the cost of a full-page ad. This will give you a percentage somewhere in the neighborhood of 10%. For this chart, Newspaper A is based on a 5% figure; Newspaper B on 7%; Newspaper C on 10%; and Newspaper D on 15%. Say, for example, you have

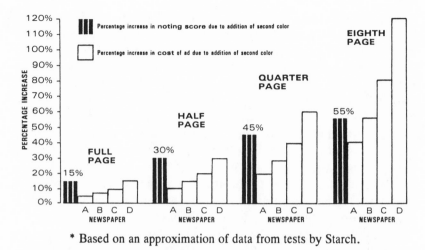

* Based on an approximation of data from tests by Starch.

FIGURE 31.2. The Effect of Color on Newspaper Ad Readership and Cost*

determined that a newspaper you are considering advertising in charges $275 to add red to the existing black. A full-page black and white ad in this paper costs about $2800. Dividing 275 by 2800 gives us 9.8%. So using the Newspaper C sample (based on 10%) we can get an idea of how much more we can expect to pay for each of the four different ad sizes relative to the average increase in noting scores the addition of color will produce. In this example, a half-page ad using two colors (black and red) in Newspaper C will give us an increase in noting scores of about 30% while costing us about 20% more money. Hence it looks reasonably attractive. It becomes easy to see which ads in which newspapers are cost effective from a color usage standpoint. Although it should be noted that numerous other factors such as being the only advertiser on a page using color (a guarantee that most newspapers will make) or how the color is used in the ad will significantly affect your noting scores, it is hopefully clear that the use of color in newspaper advertising is sometimes efficient and sometimes wasteful.

Unfortunately, too few advertisers approach these types of decisions with a commitment to efficiency. Often a business will consistently run a particular type of ad simply because that's the way they've always done it, or because that's what their competitors do, or because someone in an agency once recommended doing it that way. It is just assumed that everyone knows what they are doing. Not surprisingly, assumptions of this type can be very costly. No advertiser can afford to sit back and consistently accept recommendations at face value. Those of us in advertising are like anyone else. We only have so many hours in a day and not every recommendation we make is as thoroughly reasoned out as we might like. Those clients that question and probe and analyze most of our major suggestions will ultimately be the ones to receive the best advice. (The squeaky wheel gets the grease.) If advertising agencies were infallible clients wouldn't drop them so often. If any one form of media offered all the solutions to advertisers' problems we wouldn't find so many competing media continuing to thrive.

Another example may help strengthen this point. Let's say your hospital is opening a new Women's Health Center and that you've decided to run a one month radio schedule to supplement your newspaper announcements. You and your ad agency have reasoned that because the Center is the only one of its type in the area that it will have broad appeal and attract women from a large geographical area. Based on data from a similar Women's Center in another state you believe that the primary appeal will be to women between 25 and 49 years old who have somewhat better than average family incomes. Using all of this information in combination with available ratings and cost data your agency is recommending the use of two particular radio stations. Up to this point everything appears to be in order. Now let's throw in a small, but important catch.

A quick glance at the station ratings for Saturday and Sunday confirmed that the Center's target audience was lower on both stations for those two days. Your agency is recommending a Monday through Friday package that will run for the entire month. The cost for each spot will be a little higher ($26.00 as compared to $20.00) for this type of schedule, but there is no point wasting money by advertising on weekends. The agency's logic may be accurate in nine out of ten cases but in this instance a mistake is being made.

A closer examination shows that on station KAAA the Average Quarter Hour (AQH) audience for women 25-49 in the selected time slots (dayparts). Monday through Friday, is 1300. The Saturday and Sunday audience for the same dayparts is 1100. A little arithmetic reveals that the Monday through Friday schedule only delivers an average of about 5% more listeners per spot than the seven day schedule while increasing the average spot cost about 30%. Just the opposite could be true for the other station being considered. This is just the point. It is almost always a wise use of your time to check these types of details, either by asking the right questions of those people making the recommendations or digging through them yourself.

It is hopefully clear that cost effective advertising doesn't happen all by itself. More than anything it requires an attitude on the part of the client which demands thoroughness. It is erroneous to assume that because a recommendation has come from an advertising professional it should be considered totally correct. There are several reasons why it might not be. First, those of us in advertising agencies probably devote 80% or more of our time and energy to the "creative" side of advertising. Hour after hour might be spent coming up with just the right headline while all of fifteen minutes is set aside for media placement. It's not surprising that every year hundreds of ads win awards in local and national competitions that look or sound fantastic from a creative standpoint but, when tested for actual response, bring more embarrassment than pride.

Media salespeople have their own unique handicap. Despite their best intentions and sincere concern, most media representatives can only see a solution to your advertising problems through the eyes of their own medium. A newspaper salesman can seldom understand why a client wants to spend so much money on radio. The radio saleswoman might tend to think that television is usually an extravagant advertising expenditure. The television representative can only shake his head in condescension when you tell him you have just committed your remaining budget to billboards. At times they are all probably correct in their assessment of your strategy. At other times their built-in bias simply will not allow them to objectively evaluate your needs.

All of this is not to say that you cannot rely on the expertise of those advertising people you choose to work with. Listen to their recommendations. Consider their proposals. Take advantage of everything they have learned. But do not be intimidated into accepting everything they say. It is important to remind yourself that the commitment of almost any advertising representative to the success of your advertising is seldom as great as your own. You have a good deal more to lose if your program goes flat than they do. Attempt to arm yourself with the types of information that will allow you to more knowledgeably question and analyze the advice you are receiving. Take the necessary steps to minimize your risks. Advertising is simply too expensive and too precarious to do it any other way.

CHAPTER 32

"The Bottom Line on Advertising": Keynote Speech at a One-Day Conference Sponsored by the Hospital Council of Northern California and the Hospital Public Relations Association of Northern California

John Pinto

I have been asked to speak to you about health care advertising: its relationship to marketing and public relations; why you should do it; and what it will cost you.

Were you like most kids growing up? Did you go nuts over stories about medieval castles? Maidens in distress? Allegiances between warring lords and overlords? Struggles for survival, territory and power?

Then you're lucky. Because as a health care manager today, that was probably the best career training you could have received.

In fact, if you had paid slightly more attention to Camelot, and slightly less attention to your science fair projects, you would prob-

Reprinted from William J. Winston, ed., *Innovations in Hospital Marketing*, pp. 73–82, © 1984 by The Haworth Press, Inc.

ably have fewer doubts today about the financial future of your institution.

Here are a few similarities between the Middle Ages and Modern Medicine:

- You'll remember the birth of trade unions . . . today independent physicians are forming guilds to protect their interests.
- New allegiances called PPOs and IPAs are being formed, and there is great confusion as to who is on what side. Many physicians belong to several competing PPOs.
- The ruling class . . . large physician groups, clinics and hospitals . . . are consolidating their power base by controlling groups of patients and making pacts with neighboring kingdoms . . . kingdoms called employer health cost containment coalitions and Blue Cross.
- Small battles for control are breaking out between these competing groups; nothing deadly serious yet, but the campaigns will intensify as the stakes increase.

By analogy, hospitals are the king and castle, clinics and large groups play the role of barons, while most individual physicians in private practice are rapidly being turned into serfs . . . the smallest economic units with little control over the system.

Around our firm, we call it the "medievalization of medicine." Like most transition periods, it represents tremendous opportunities for some hospitals . . . economic disaster for others. A sub-committee of the California Legislature recently predicted that within the next few years, twenty percent of all hospitals in the state would be closing their doors.

Quality competition of just a few years ago has given way to a survival mentality. Hospital operating budgets are being close-shaved just at a time when any other kind of business would be assembling capital reserves to invest in service development and service sales.

Today, most hospitals are still being run by an "administrator." The term, itself, suggests a passive, status quo approach. Which Fortune 500 company would entrust its affairs to an "administrator?" Or to a public information officer? What's called for is entrepreneurial leadership. A concentration on product development. A willingness to risk and a demand for accountability.

As leaders, health care managers are facing tremendous pressure. By the year 1990, our industry will surpass agriculture to become the single largest business category in America. Is the new medical-industrial complex we see growing going to be in the control of "administrators?" "Community relations managers?" Not likely.

The adaptation of your institution to this change will be easier if you begin to think of yourselves as business men and business women. As Chief Executive Officers and Marketing Vice-Presidents. You and your hospitals will survive only if you begin to measure your performance by the same yardstick used in every other sector of the market economy.

Start by considering the changes we have weathered already. Are we still just selling bed space, nursing care and laboratory tests? Of course not! Our hospitals have day-surgery, alternative birthing centers, substance-abuse clinics and a dozen other profit centers. You are operating a health care delivery *system*.

Once you get clear about that, you can move beyond your reliance on syrupy public service announcements. Move beyond daily supplications to your local medical writers.

To survive in today's competitive health care market, you'll have to. Because publicity alone is a little like General Motors listing its name and a few technical details to sell cars. It takes controllable communications, and it takes budgets which may exceed in a month what your hospital's PR department spends in a year. It takes advertising.

Before discussing advertising pros and cons and how-to's, we need to be on the same wavelength. Let's start by defining "advertising." According to most dictionaries, advertising is simply "the act of calling public attention to one's product or service, especially by paid announcements." Nothing about trying to arrest the human intellect long enough to sell it something.

Definition number two: Competition. "A contest or match; contending or vying with another." Nothing about competition being evil or unethical.

Definition number three: Monopoly. "Exclusive control of a commodity or service in a given market." Nothing about monopoly being the exclusive right of phone or utility companies. In fact, hospitals and physicians might even be eligible.

Definition four: Ethical. "Pertaining to ethics or morality; conforming to right principles of conduct as generally accepted by a specific profession." I'd like to repeat that last part: " . . . principles of conduct as generally accepted by a specific profession."

This is where the controversy arises. Is advertising a generally accepted practice in health care? That all depends on what color glasses you wear.

In case you hadn't guessed, my glasses are somewhat tinted. When I look at advertising, I see nothing unethical, immoral or fattening about it. What I see is a useful tool to help people convey a message to a broad audience.

The legitimacy of advertising has been proclaimed by many professional groups. Six years ago the American Hospital Association published guidelines . . . it wasn't a matter of "should we," but rather, "how should we." And under pressure from the Supreme Court and the Federal Trade Commission in 1977, the American Medical Association reversed its anti-advertising bylaws.

Sure, there may be a few people who disagree with a health care institution's decision to advertise. So what? When does a hospital or clinic ever do something that pleases all the people all of the time?

It's really ironic. A hospital administrator who doesn't bat an eye at asking the board for permission to buy a linear accelerator will quake at spending a few thousand dollars on mass media advertising. Yet that same administrator will think nothing of spending thousands on an employee magazine or audio-visual equipment for inservice education. Aren't they paid communications?

From our experience, most boards have no problem understanding the concept of advertising . . . particularly if there are business people on the board. They know about competition — and about the benefits advertising can bring.

One of our clients . . . a progressive administrator in most respects . . . had some of the usual fears when he first considered an advertising program proposed by his community relations directors.

He decided to slide the topic into a board agenda . . . way at the bottom. And he decided to slip quickly through it with a comment like: "Oh, by the way, we're going to begin expanding our public relations program by using paid communications vehicles."

No sooner had he made the announcement, when a board member slammed his fist on the table and bellowed, "My God, it's about time this hospital started advertising!"

If you consult enough experts, you can confirm any opinion. I suppose that's what meetings like this are all about.

In the next segment of today's program, you'll hear testimony from experts who will settle forever the controversy over health care advertising. Meanwhile, at least for the next few minutes, let's assume it's ethical . . . how do you get started with an advertising program of your own?

It has to begin with a marketing concept . . . a broad plan. Advertising, like any other form of communications, is just a tool. It's there in the tool box alongside publicity and health fairs and newsletters and speakers bureaus. But unlike PR or community relations, the advertising tool is very expensive. So most administrators make a very human error.

They jump on their PR directors for a small-scale ad campaign. They want a test before committing funds to a major project. One PR director I know was called into her boss's office two months ago. And this is what her boss said: "In the next two days, I would like you to develop this hospital's 1984 advertising campaign." She asked him about budgets. He said, "Let's keep it under $10,000."

Advertising is like drug therapy. You can't get results unless you prescribe a minimum dose. Buying a $10,000 ad campaign is like being a diabetic and using insulin once a month. Don't run an inch-high ad two or three times, then condemn advertising because your census didn't quadruple. You've got to commit to a total program, with sufficient dollars to make an impact. This can range anywhere from one to ten percent of your gross revenues, depending on the size of your organization.

Marketing is a buzz word these days in the health care field. Most of you have probably been to seminars and read books about strategic market planning . . . market based strategy . . . microanalytic sales models. For the moment, I'd like to deflate all of those complex words.

Marketing is nothing more than establishing and maintaining exchange relationships. In simple terms, developing a marketing plan for your hospital is a five-step process:

- First, identify all audience segments: physicians, employees, health planners, and the dozens of categories the general public falls into: women and men, the old and the young, single and married, rich and not so rich, healthy and sick, near and far.
- Then, for each audience segment in your long list, write down the chief problems each has with you . . . what holds them back from a better relationship with your hospital? What keeps them from buying your brand of services? It's at this point that market research should be performed. It would be easy to second guess what each of our publics thinks about us. But remember I said that advertising is a very expensive tool. Market research is a kind of insurance policy you take out to help assure that you'll be using this tool to fix the right problems.
- Next, prioritize these problems. Is it more harmful that the elderly can't travel to your outpatient screening clinic, or that new physicians can't lease office space near your hospital? Each problem you have is going to cost money to fix . . . you should allocate your resources from the top of your list down, rather than skip higgly-piggly from one pet program to another.
- Next, what are your goals for each problem, and how shall achieving these goals be measured? By an increase in patient visits per day? Bed occupancy rates? Program revenues?
- Then, and only then, should you begin to develop new programs and employ new communications strategies . . . one of which may be paid advertising.

Here's an important point: The health care industry's love affair with advertising doesn't mean and end to community relations programs. Hospitals will continue to hire publicists and special events coordinators. However, those of you who remain cast in these roles will see your influence dwindle.

At any one time, our firm is conducting several executive searches for hospital marketing directors. The CEOs' primary requisite? Someone with a proven track record of results. They don't even need any experience in health care. We recently placed a brand manager from a packaged goods company. That should tell you something.

Looking at most every other kind of business selling services or products to the general public, public relations is seen as an adjunctive tool . . . to advertising. Not the other way around.

Let's go back to that tool box, and examine what advertising can and can't do.

Advertising isn't a panacea for a poor product. While it can create an awareness of your services, and make people want to try them, it can't blind them to inferiorities. Anyone who believes that also believes in the tooth fairy.

Like all mysterious new things, health care advertising is endowed with a variety of myths. Here's one: Advertising will make people flock to your hospital. Rubbish! Advertising cannot make people want to be sick! Advertising can only help those services in which people have a choice. Obstetrics. Substance abuse. And a host of outpatient services.

Myth number two: If we start advertising, we can spend less time on physician relations. Wrong! Your medical staff is still the primary audience in your marketing efforts. Without them and their cooperation, you'll have nothing to sell. Instead, involve them with your campaign. Contract with them to develop a product that research tells you is needed in your community.

Myth number three: Newspapers are more effective than TV. Or TV is more effective than radio. Or radio is more effective than anything else. All wrong. There is no single effective medium. It depends on the product being advertised, the marketplace and the media available.

While case histories are instructive — including the cases you'll be hearing today — don't fall into the trap of reproducing these verbatim. What works for one hospital won't necessarily work for you.

Many of the myths, opportunities and constraints you now labor under as health care promoters were generated centuries ago.

Some of you may have had a chance to hear Dick McDonald, America's dean of health care advertising, at the 1983 ASHPR meeting in Tennessee. Dick heads our sister firm in Milwaukee, and for those of you who didn't make it last year, I'd like to recap some of his observations about the evolution of health care advertising:

One of the first recorded forms of advertising was found in ancient Pompeii, where archeologists discovered the following message written on a wall:

> There will be a dedication or formal opening of certain baths. Those attending are promised slaughter of wild beasts, athletic games, perfumed sprinklings, and awnings to keep off the sun.

Even then, people knew what made a good ad . . . tell people what you've got and what's in it for them.

Over the centuries, the principles remained the same, but the techniques changed. Town criers in the 11th Century. Handbills in the 15th Century. Newspapers. Radio. Television.

But while everyone else in our society accepted advertising as a legitimate form of communication, something happened to retard the professionals.

It was called "quackery." Hucksters peddling magic potions and cure-all tonics appeared. "Ladies and gentlemen, boys and girls, step right up and listen to me. Never before has a product offered the promise of long life . . . vigor . . . *and* amazed approval from your wife or sweetheart. Step right up and be the first to own Dr. Scott's Electric Flesh Brush."

A poorly educated populace, who didn't have a base of knowledge to understand the complexities of medicine, was hurt.

To combat this problem, lawmakers applied typical wisdom. They passed laws banning professions from advertising. And the medical, dental, legal and accounting professions imposed similar sanctions on their members. Better to do nothing than do something that might be misunderstood.

That mind-set generally prevailed until the 1970s, when some hospitals began using paid communications to get their messages across. They realized it was silly to ignore one of the most powerful tools in communications. And they joined the rest of the 20th century.

A few entered this new era boldly. Others dipped their toes in the water. They did audacious things like inserting their annual report in the daily newspaper. But even then, most of the first hospital ads were self-serving. Telling the world how great the hospital was, and how dedicated its trustees were, and how wonderful the medical staff was. Everyone at the hospital got their egos stroked, but nothing much was sold.

Then, in 1977, the U.S. Supreme Court struck down state laws and professional codes forbidding advertising.

Since 1977, increasing competition and brutal battles for survival have accelerated the evolution. Hospital advertising has been in constant change over the past five years. It has already moved through two eras and is about to enter a third.

Dick McDonald calls the first era the "gee whiz" period. Everybody was having so much fun buying space and air time that they really didn't spend much energy on their message. Everything sounded like a news release, or a page out of a patient handbook. None of the ads offended anyone. The main thing was to make the ads pretty—and make the administrators feel good.

This is the era of hard-hitting slogans like: "We care." "We're here to serve you." "Our equipment is modern." And of course, our favorite: "Our nurses love you." But, it was a start.

During the past few years, we've seen another era evolve. McDonald calls it the "product era." Here we see hospitals beginning to focus on specific programs. The advertising is more results oriented, more attuned to the bottom line. Hospitals moved away from the strictly institutional approach, and began touting specific services.

Today, the health care profession is entering into its third evolutionary phase. It's the era of bold, gutsy selling. Advertising that gets to the heart of the matter; that talks to people in their frame of reference. That gives consumers specific reasons for using a hospital's services. Selling that asks for the order . . . and gets it!

Advertising isn't just a passing fad in the health care industry. It's going to be an increasingly vital component in everyone's game plan for growth and survival. It's an ethical, effective and appropriate new tool in your communications toolbox.

Go to any meeting of hospital PR people, meetings like this one, and you'll invariably hear grumbles about how "management doesn't understand us."

Turn to the nearest administrator in this room today and ask what he or she wants. What management understands is results . . . measurable results. Today's hospital administrators need space-age planners and strategists, not blacksmiths working with a limited selection of tools. In short, the hospital communicator of the future will have to earn a position as a top member of the management team.

Some of you in the audience might not survive the cuts. But to those of you who do, I wish you well. You are entering a new era in which health is managed as a business. In which effective communicators begin to earn every bit of position, respect and compensation they deserve.

Thank you.

CHAPTER 33

The Fundamentals of Developing
an Effective Advertisement
for Health Care Organizations

William J. Winston

INTRODUCTION

It wasn't too long ago that health professionals considered advertising unnecessary to increase or maintain business. More importantly, they were restrained by their professional organizations from using ads. But these attitudes and barriers have quickly changed and the trend toward advertising by health organizations and professionals is expanding. Unfortunately, most health administrators, planners, and marketers are not experienced or educated in developing advertisements for their organizations. Since astute marketing, advertising, and public relations techniques are no longer elective management tools for health professionals, this section is being presented as a basic reference for developing a more effective advertisement. However, it must be understood that advertising is only one tool of marketing strategies, but it will be a key option as part of marketing plans in the future.

A major marketing association has estimated that health care will be spending in excess of $500 million per year by 1990 for advertising their products and services, with hospitals, clinics, and group practices being the largest spenders. In fact, in 1984 over $50 mil-

Reprinted from William J. Winston, *How to Write a Marketing Plan for Health Care Organizations*, pp. 131–148, © 1985 by The Haworth Press, Inc.

lion was spent just on television advertising by health organizations, up from just $1 million in 1978. As an example, it is estimated that over 25% of all practicing dentists now advertising in different media channels. Some of the biggest advertisers have been proprietary chains such as Schick-Shadel, Advanced Health Systems, Comprehensive Care Corporation, and the American Dental Council.

All of this pressure to advertise has occurred due to the awareness that oversaturated marketplaces exist, especially in metropolitan health markets, and that competition is here to stay. In addition, the advent of newer forms of health delivery systems such as clinics, preferred provider organizations, independent practice associations, emergicenters, urgent care centers, and service franchises have expanded the need for communicating effectively and quickly to our target groups through advertising. The constraints placed on the reimbursement systems have supported this trend toward seeking new service development and more effective marketing strategies.

It is important to remember that advertising can be subject to scrutiny under the FTC, FCC, state laws, rate review systems, and professional association standards. All professional advertising and promotion was altered by a landmark ruling on June 27th, 1977, by the U.S. Supreme Court in the case of John R. Bates and Van O'Steen versus the state bar of Arizona. The marketer needs to carefully check with local professionals' guidelines and their legal counsel before initiating any advertising campaign. However, the legal risks involved need not deter health care organizations from engaging in proper and effective competitive advertising. From the First Amendment to the U.S. Constitution, advertising is viewed as commercial speech and a mechanism to disseminate information to consumers. However, the legal aspects of all advertising campaigns require attention in order to prevent any significant long-term reactionary problems.

ROLE OF ADVERTISING IN MARKETING

There will be greater pressure on health facilities and programs to advertise in the future. A lot of this pressure is based on the premise that, "Let's Advertise—Everyone Else is!" It is important to remember that advertising, again, is only one tool of marketing and may or may not be appropriate for the particular situation.

Advertising is not a miracle worker. It can only guide people's perceptions of the health organization until they use it for the first time. Advertising is only one part of the communications mix, which may include phone calls, brochures, admittance procedures, follow-up, etc. Advertising can really do only one thing. *It can convince a logical prospect for a service to try it one time!* It can't sell to someone who has no basic need for the service and it cannot make a satisfied client or patient. It also cannot save a bad service. The best advertising can do is cause reasonable prospects to try a service. Advertising is a simple business and process. "Keep it simple, it becomes difficult because we tend to make believe that better advertisements have to be more and more informative and complex. However, advertising goals for health organizations should be related to:

I. Creating an awareness of the service or organization;
II. Positioning the service in the minds of the consumers as to the differences between the service and its competitors;
III. Educating the public as to the need for select services and the availability of these services;
IV. Creating referrals for the main services;
V. Stimulating the usage of the services for the first time;
VI. Assisting in the creation of an environment in which the clients and patients will quickly and effectively accept the services in the marketplace; and
VII. When appropriate, improving the financial viability of the health organization.

Health organizations cannot depend on advertising to provide a successful service. The delivery of the service must come through in order for advertising to be effective. Advertising can only bring a person to use a service once. If the service is poorly delivered, treatment is inadequate, or the person is overcharged, repeat business will not be forthcoming. The success of any marketing campaign is the referral and advertising can only initiate the contact. In fact, word of mouth is credited with generating over 60% of all new clients and patients, while advertising generates 25%. In addition, all interactions and contacts between the staff and the clients should relay a consistent image or message of the organization as reflected in the advertising campaign.

Organizations also cannot expect miracle effects from an advertising campaign. It needs to be nurtured and refined over a long time frame so that constant improvement is seen rather than immediate jumps in utilization of the services. It will not occur over night.

There appears to be little evidence of false or misleading advertising by health care professionals. Actually, the majority of complaints comes from peers in the same profession rather than consumers. Most complaints lodged with the FTC were from other health professionals, and most of those ads demeaned the profession but were not considered misleading or false.

Health care advertising unquestionably is on the upswing. However, the application of the money being spent on advertising is often amateurish and ineffectual. For example, it has been estimated that over two-thirds of all medical and dental ads were created by the medical/dental professional. In fact, over 75% of ads for solo and group practices are created by the medical provider and they do not employ professionals in any capacity, including media placement specialists. The small budgets allocated to advertising account for much of this self-creativity trend. For instance, over 80% of all solo practitioners spend less than $15,000 a year and 64% are actually below this level.

Finally, it is important to remember that advertising is not for everyone. There are risks involved as in any business decision. However, effective ads can prove cost-beneficial. The early stages of feedback from those professionals and organizations who do advertise is favorable. From recent surveys, over 90% of those polled indicated that they were satisfied with the results and planned to advertise in the future. However, most of the feedback also indicated that they needed professional advice on (1) what to look for in developing an effective ad and (2) advice on media selection and placement. The next few sections outline the types of advertising strategies available and some basic tips on creating an effective advertisement for those who decide to develop their own or need to evaluate ads produced by external consultants or agencies.

TYPES OF ADVERTISEMENT AND MEDIA

There are many different forms of advertising. Some of these advertising channels include: television, radio, newspapers, journals, direct mail, yellow pages, shoppers/pennysavers, magazines, billboards, directories, transit space, posters, pens, memo pads, newspaper supplements, and others. The selection of the type of media channel depends mainly on:

1. the image the organization wants to promote;
2. the target groups it is addressing; and
3. the budgetary constraints

A mix of these different media channels should be part of an advertising campaign in order to communicate with a large number of people. However, advertising needs to be sufficiently concentrated and repetitive in order to be effective in getting people to try the service. It has been proven that a person comes into contact with an advertisement four to five times before he/she tries the service. It is preferable to fund one media sufficiently before adding a second. In other words, a recommendation would be to end up with a smaller segment of the market fully aware of the service and organization rather than a larger segment or segments only a little aware. However, the media mix selection process is one which should be done by marketing professionals just as the mix of medical treatments for a patient requires professional medical advice!

FUNDAMENTALS IN WRITING
A SUCCESSFUL ADVERTISEMENT

The following six basic steps provide a base for developing an effective advertisement:

1. *Identify the target groups and their psychographic profile:* Creating an advertisement which will cause a prospect to try the service can be relatively easy. First of all, determine what you are

trying to say as a basic message and identify the audience or target group to whom you are saying it. An underlying rule of advertising is to make sure the ad is developed to relate to the values and interests of your target groups. Developing a differentiated or concentrated approach to advertising can be more effective than an undifferentiated one. All of the auditing, segmenting, and targeting analysis comes into play for identifying primary and secondary targets. A special emphasis should be placed on the psychographic/ lifestyle analysis related to understanding the psychological, lifestyle, and behavioristic aspects of the potential consumer groups. Advertisements must relate to the consumer's values, perceptions, and interests. To make things easier always contact the newspaper, radio station, or TV channel where you are advertising to inquire whether they have completed some key demographic and psychographic profiles of their listeners or readers. For example, some local newspapers have some excellent profiles of their readership and subscribers which may assist in picking the right media channel and the most cost-beneficial target groups.

II. *Get attention:* Nobody is waiting anxiously in the community to read or hear your advertisement! In addition, most people are usually oversaturated with advertisements through print and other media channels. Your advertisement must get the attention of a consumer quickly and have a lasting effect. It has been proven that most people will spend no longer than five to ten seconds reading a print ad and fifteen seconds listening to an audio advertisement. Therefore, uniqueness through headlines, color, creative graphics, catchy slogans, or pictures must catch the attention of your reader or listener long enough for them to be interested in reading or listening to the rest of the ad. Again, this is especially important when, for example, the average American is exposed to over 3,000 television ads every year. *The New York Times* often carries 350 pages of advertisements on an average Sunday, and radio stations can offer 40 minutes in every hour to commercials.

III. *Demonstrate an advantage:* If we can get the attention of the reader or listener then the ad must answer the question, ''What will this professional service do for me?'' It is important to inform the consumer exactly how the service may impact them mentally, physically, on their state of well-being, level of self-respect, satisfaction, security, etc. The actual copy of the advertisement should be kept short but potent. In other words, explain in the ad how your service is unique and what positive outcome will be derived from trying it. There are different methods to communicate these ideas. For example, ads can use humor, present settings which approximate real life, have testimonials, present demonstrations, show solutions to problems, offer pitchmen and women, give specific reasons, and stimulate emotional ties to the service.

IV. *Prove the advantage:* After we identify the key advantage give some facts which prove the validity of the uniqueness. Facts may be necessary. For example, the ad can show the educational degrees of the professionals involved, the variety of services offered, the number of people successfully treated, or even the time required to obtain the service. Use understatement because it carries more conviction than overstatement. "Always see the ad from the eyes of the consumer."

V. *Persuade people to take advantage:* It is important to make a quick but potent impression in the minds of the consumer. Portray what the service can do for them and how easily they can obtain it. For example, discuss access, pricing, parking, types of staff, payment plans available, or insurance coverage. Plan the ad to persuade your *toughest* target group. In other words, the ad should be addressed to attract even the most difficult group. If that group is attracted then the easier target groups will follow. Persuasion must get the potential consumer to the point they are *aware of the service, understand the need for it, and are potentially ready to use it.*

VI. *Call for action:* The ad must make the consumer take action. However, the ad should ask for the consumer to act in some way. There has to be some type of "do-something" statement in the ad which makes it simple, easy, specific, and special for the consumer to try the service for the first time. In other words, we may suggest that people call, send in a coupon, mail something to us, or come by and visit us. A traditional way has been to have an open house whereby people can come and check out the service before making any commitment.

These six basic steps can be used as a checklist when designing an advertisement. Since most ads will probably be designed by external marketing firms it is important to have the copy ready before the design and layout are developed. This requires the health organization to have the basic concept organized before sending it out to the agency. Discuss the concept carefully with the designers so they can have a guideline from which to develop a layout which communicates the organization's important ideas and services. An excellent source of communication for health organizations is radio advertising. Unfortunately, radio has become the Cinderella of advertising media, representing only 6% of total advertising in the United States. When getting the right message across on radio ads, there are four important ingredients:

1. Identify the name of the service early in the ad;
2. Repeat the name often;
3. Promise the listener a benefit for trying the service early in the ad; and
4. Repeat the ad often.

You have to get people to listen to your ad. Wake them up! Then talk to them! Get them involved! It is also important to make several ads as people quickly become bored with the same ad on the radio. However, there is truly very little accurate research on exactly which type of advertisement is the most cost-effective in actually increasing sales or bringing in clients and patients.

TYPES OF ADVERTISING AGENCIES

Advertising agencies are independent firms which develop and place ads in various media channels. There are thousands of advertising agencies in the country. The agency is mainly responsible for working with a client to (1) plan an advertising campaign for the health organization; (2) select and contract for the media in which they feel will produce cost-effective results; (3) prepare the advertising copy, layout, photography, and artwork; (4) produce the final ad in the format acceptable to the media channel; and (5) handle all transactionary and placement duties related to the ad in the media channel selected.

Advertising agencies range from small creative boutiques which only write copy to full range service agencies which can provide assistance in a wide range of marketing functions including research, planning, design, media selection, and strategy development. In picking among these types of agencies it is important to balance convenience and expertise. An agency which is local may supply convenience and knowledge of the local health marketplace. The national firm may be less convenient but may have more talented support staff. Unfortunately, there is no rating service which rates the quality of the services provided by advertising agencies. Therefore, it is important to ask for a list of prior or current clients who you can contact for evaluations. Some TV and radio stations will also sometimes supply the names of firms which have been easy or difficult to work with through the years. Feeling comfortable with the people at the agencies is just as important as finding one with the highest quality staff or resources.

ADVERTISING EXPENSES

Fees range dramatically for advertising agencies. For example, most agencies have averaged about 15-20% commission on media purchases and add on hourly charges for production costs and retainer fees. There is beginning to be some very creative pricing by agencies during recent years so negotiating with agencies is strongly recommended. For example, the fees may be based on (1) a fixed retainer that is estimated on the work to be performed plus retention of all commissions received; (2) a variable monthly rate depending upon the commissions received by the agency; and (3) an hourly rate based on the exact functions of copywriting, artwork, or layout.

Advertising on TV, radio, newspaper, billboards, or other media channels may be expensive. It is important to call the different TV stations or newspapers to compare fees as it ranges significantly among channels, size of the ad, frequency of the ad, and positioning of the ad according to the time it plays or days it is published or viewed. In other words, shop around and compare. Most health organizations spend a small amount of marketing, and even less on advertising. This budget allocation will continue to grow. Of course, it will never reach the levels of consumer product companies such as Proctor & Gamble which spends more than $600,000,000 per year on advertising!

As a guideline, recent surveys by the Advertising Council indicate that service-oriented businesses spend an average of 3.5% gross sales for advertising. Health care organizations are not even above 1% of gross revenues!

CONCLUSION

Creativity, not budget size, is vital to advertisements' becoming popular and effective. In an overcrowded marketplace marketers can become afraid to take chances. Marketing productivity is declining as we have tended to look for quick financial success rather than satisfying, long-range objectives. An advertising campaign must be creative and will involve some risk, whether it is financial or the fear of poor feedback from our peers. However, health organizations must establish the climate of willingness to change and tolerate risk if you are to have innovation. In addition, pretesting is essential when creative ads are developed. People may perceive differently the message being delivered by the ad. It is important to pretest to see if the intended message is clear and understood by consumers and meets the objectives of the campaign and the organization. Pretesting must be done with people who are similar to those who will be listening or reading the advertisement in the long-run. Most health organizations are new to the concept of advertising. They are currently advertising similar to the statement by Will Rogers, "Advertising is like the rattling of a stick inside a swill-bucket." Gradually advertising will become more sophisticated and be a major new tool for health administrators and marketers.

If we can recap the basics of developing an effective advertisement, it is that any good ad must possess three ingredients:

1. Information about the service and its uniqueness;
2. A clear statement which expresses this advantage and relates to the target group; and
3. A creative and attention-getting presentation.

These three ingredients must be based on two premises; simplicity *and* believability. *The essential framework to express an advertisement that an ad must have something to say and offer value and it should be expressed straight and simple.*

ADDITIONAL RESOURCES ON ADVERTISING

When it is necessary to acquire information for the preparation of an advertising budget, program, or media placement, seek out the *Rate & Data Service Directory*. SRDS Directories, of Shokie, Illinois, provide directories for rates in newspapers, business publications, consumer magazines, transit space, etc. These directories are typically available in most business libraries.

A second key directory is the *Ayer Directory of Publications*, Philadelphia, Pennsylvania, which has been published for over 100 years. It provides an in-depth look at thousands of newspapers, magazines, trade publications, college publications, etc.

A third source is advertising trade journals. Some of the more popular journals include the following:

Advertising Age
Adweek Magazine
Art Direction Magazine
Broadcasting Magazine
Marketing Communications

There are many of these types of reference journals.

A fourth area of resources is from seminars and workshops put on by colleges and marketing associations. For example, the American Marketing Association, Chicago, Illinois, has a subdivision titled Academy of Health Care Marketing, which produces excellent resources. The AMA also produces quality references on advertising. Most cities have local chapters of this organization. Some other key organizations for advertising resources include the following:

THE ADVERTISING CHECKING BUREAU, INC., Chicago, Illinois
THE ADVERTISING COUNCIL, New York, N.Y.
ADVERTISING RESEARCH FOUNDATION, New York, N.Y.

AMERICAN ADVERTISING FOUNDATION, Washington, D.C.

ASSOCIATION OF NATIONAL ADVERTISERS, New York, N.Y.

NEWSPAPER ADVERTISING BUREAU, New York, N.Y.

RADIO ADVERTISING BUREAU, New York, N.Y.

The Directory of Associations in most business libraries can provide current addresses and names for many other organizations which can provide excellent information on advertising.

EXAMPLE OF EXCELLENT ADVERTISING

South Bergen Hospital in Hasbrouck Heights, New Jersey, adopted an advertising campaign for its 40-bed facility in 1984. The hospital's reputation had been tarnishing due to an aging facility. Holy Names Hospital, a 370-bed local facility, began managing South Bergen Hospital and began a series of physical improvements to the facility.

B&B Advertising in Bogota, New Jersey, was hired to design an advertising campaign for (1) improving the image of the hospital; (2) demonstrating the hospital's innovative management; and (3) to demonstrate that the hospital was more than capable of serving the health needs of the local community.

B&B Advertising decided to concentrate on marketing South Bergen Hospital's (1) Senior Citizen Health Program; (2) Emergency Services; and (3) Podiatric Center. The agency decided on targeting their ads to the general public in the local community as well as to local doctors and podiatrists. The goals were to attract more people to the hospital as well as more physicians who might affiliate themselves with South Bergen Hospital. The ad campaign included a six-month program of quarter page ads that were also incorporated into a full-page advertisement stressing the "The New South Bergen Hospital" The first series of quarter page ads stressed the Senior Citizen Health Program and it appeared in three local newspapers for the month of June, 1984. During the first month of appearance over 40 new patients had joined the program!

The second series of ads featured the emergency care center and this series began during the month of July, 1984. An immediate increase in usage of the emergency room occurred in response to the ad.

A similar response was initiated by the placement of the third series of ads for the podiatric center at the hospital.

Author Index

Subject Index